OXFORD
GNVQ

Intermediate
BUSINESS

Second Edition

Dan Moynihan & Brian Titley

OXFORD

OXFORD
UNIVERSITY PRESS

Great Glarendon Street, Oxford OX2 6DP

Oxford University Press is a department of the University of Oxford. It furthers the University's objective of excellence in research, scholarship, and education by publishing worldwide in

Oxford New York

Athens Auckland Bangkok Bogotá Buenos Aires Calcutta Cape Town Chennai Dar es Salaam Delhi Florence Hong Kong Istanbul Karachi Kuala Lumpur Madrid Melbourne Mexico City Mumbai Nairobi Paris São Pailo Shanghai Singapore Taipei Tokyo Toronto Warsaw

with associated companies in Berlin Ibadan

Oxford is a registered trade mark of Oxford University Press

First published 1996
Second Edition 2000

British Library Cataloguing in Publication Data

Data available

ISBN 0 19 832 832 X

Typeset by Tech Set Limited
Printed in Italy

The publishers would like to thank the following for permission to reproduce photographs:

p13: Ace Photo Agency/ Eric Pelham; p17: *bottom* Nissan Motor GB; p20: *top & bottom left* Ford Motor Services, *bottom right* Carl Witham; p20: *bottom right* Rob Judges; p22: *centre* Sanyo UK, *bottom left* Holt Studios International/ Jeff Henley, *bottom right* Telegraph Colour Library/ J Young; p27: Brian Titley; p29: Format/Mo Wilson; p35: *top* Greenpeace/Dorreboon; p39: Unilever Historical Archives; p41: Mattel Consumer Products; p64: IBM UK; p69: *top* The Science Museum, *centre* Sanyo UK, *bottom* Transport Research Laboratory; p73: *left* Parker Knoll, *centre* Ford Motor Services, *right* Robert Harding Picture Library; p75: *bottom left* Sporting Pictures UK; p84: gettyone stone/Michael Rosenfeld; p91: gettyone stone/Dan Bosler; p95: *right* Photo Reportage; p96: *bottom* gettyone stone/Bill Truslow; p97: *top* gettyone stone/Jeff Zanuba, *bottom* gettyone stone/Charles Thatcher; p98: *top* gettyone stone/Steven Peters, *bottom* gettyone stone/Frank Herboldt; p99: *top* Alan Owens, *bottom* gettyone stone/Bruce Ayres; p101: Alan Owens; p129: *left* Format/Brenda Prince; p133: *top* North Western Museum of Science & Industry; p134: *top* Telegraph Colour Library, *centre* British Steel, *bottom left* Chris Westwood, *bottom right* Philip Davies; p140: *top* Format/Brenda Prince, *centre* gettyone stone Steven Peters, *bottom* Ace Photo Agency/Malcolm Birkett; p143: The Press Association; p144: The Financial Times; p159: *left* gettyone stone/Walter Hodges, *right* Archie Miles; p165: British Telecom; p179: Cussons/Sidney Harris; p188: *left* Chris Honeywell; p194: *bottom* Robert Harding Picture Library; p195: *top left* Birmingham Post & Mail; p214: *left* J A Whitaker, *centre* Alan Owens, *right* C M Whitaker; p215: *left* Popperfoto, *right* Rex Features; p216: *bottom right* British Petroleum; p217: *right* Shell Industries; p218: *left* Nissan Motor GB, *centre* gettyone stone/Michael Rosenfeld; p219: *right* Tesco Stores; p221: *right* Powerstock; p229: *left* Corbis; p231: *bottom right* Corbis; p232: *left* Corbis, *right* Corbis; p236: Corbis; p237: Nissan Motor GB; p245: *left* Hulton Getty, *right* Robert Harding Picture Library; p250: *left* Corbis, *right* Airbus Industries; p251: Chorley Handford; p279: British Tourist Authority; p281: National Meteorological Office; p282: *bottom* Chorley Handford; p284: PA Photos; p288: P&O; p291: Environmental Picture Library/Paul Glendell; p301: gettyone stone/John Lawler; P304: *left* Pontins Holiday Club, *right* Philip Davies; p305: PA Photos; p309: Greenpeace; p319: *top left* British Steel, *centre* Ford Motor Services, *bottom right* Telegraph Colour Library, *bottom left* Environmental Picture Library/Martin Bond; p325: *left* IBM UK, *right* Nissan Motor GB; p370: *bottom* Ace Photo Agency/Peter Hince; p400: Datawatch Corporation.

All other photographs by Martin Sookias, Nicholas Read, and the OUP archives.

Illustrations by Tech Set, Gecko, and David Mostyn.

Contents

Preface   iv

Introduction for Students   1

About the Intermediate GNVQ course in business   2

Preparing and investigating data   4

Unit 1

Investigating How Businesses Work   15

1 What is business?   16

2 Inside a business   58

3 Managing human resources in business   105

4 Business communications   157

Unit 2

How Businesses Develop   201

5 Business activities   202

6 Types of business organization   261

7 The business environment   287

Unit 3

Business Finance   328

8 Business costs and revenues   329

9 Business transactions and documents   356

Index   409

Preface

This book aims to provide everything that you need in order to pass the mandatory Intermediate GNVQ Business Units. The book has been carefully written to match closely the GNVQ 2000 Business specifications.

The book can be used as a course text to support either a course with a high proportion of teacher/lecturer contact time or one with less contact time and more supported self-study. Students will find a large number of activities designed to deepen learning and also to provide evidence against the assessment criteria, as well as numerous questions to help prepare students for unit tests. All of the activities and questions have been tried and tested by experienced GNVQ teachers and students.

As well as helping students to pass their Intermediate GNVQ with a good grade, the book has been designed to provide a thorough insight into the dynamic and exciting world of business by using a wide range of case studies and real world examples. Each chapter is packed with up-to-date articles and statistics in order to assist students in carrying out research and in producing coursework using recent research and case studies.

Thanks are due to Linda Jenkins for assistance with indexing, and to Sarah and Tom for their patience and support.

Dan Moynihan

Brian Titley

Introduction
for Students

Introduction

About the Intermediate GNVQ Course in Business

Preventing and Investigating Data

About the Intermediate GNVQ Course in Business

The aim of the Intermediate GNVQ in Business course is to give you a wide knowledge of business, and at the same time to allow you to practise a range of vital skills which you will need for success in the world of business and enterprise. This combination of skills and business knowledge will provide you with a head start when entering employment or further and higher education.

How to demonstrate your business knowledge and skills

The Intermediate GNVQ in Business is very different from any other course you have taken so far. To do well in GNVQ, you will need to solve problems, carry out research, work with others, and show that you can plan what to do on your own when necessary. This has the advantage that your success does not depend on one final exam, but it does mean you need to work steadily throughout the course, and to use your own initiative.

In order to pass your Intermediate GNVQ Business course, you will need to provide **evidence** of the business knowledge and skills you have acquired. This means you must plan your work in order to build up a **portfolio** of coursework which shows you have understood each part of the course. The quality of your portfolio will determine your final grade, so it is important to:

- Plan what you intend to do in advance
- Collect and use information about business
- Check the quality of your completed work
- Keep a well organized and up-to-date portfolio

Do not expect to produce all of your evidence in the form of written coursework or reports. Some of your evidence will be in the form of records of your contribution to the work of a group of fellow students, or in the form of evidence from a workplace supervisor. Some may be presented in the form of graphs and tables, or video or audio recordings of interviews, discussions and presentations in which you have participated.

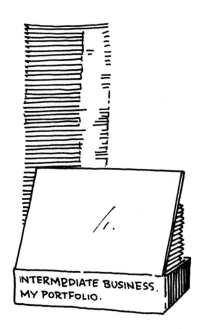

INTERMEDIATE BUSINESS.
MY PORTFOLIO.

Planning your portfolio

Each unit in your Intermediate Business course contains guidance on the kinds of work that you need to produce. Your work should build up over time to form a portfolio of your coursework. Your portfolio is very important because, along with your test results, it is your evidence of achievement in the course.

This book contains a variety of activities you can complete for your portfolio. But before you start these or other activities look carefully at the course unit specifications.

Your teacher or lecturer should be able to provide you with a copy. They will tell you what you need to do to get a **pass, merit or distinction** for your work. You will then be able to plan your work to achieve the highest grade that you can. You can do this by matching the work that you plan to do against the list of **assessment evidence** you need to produce for each grade. Then tick off each task as you do them, and always remember to list the sources of information you have used to help complete them, such as books, magazines, business reports, etc. You should write down the dates, titles and authors of the sources at the end of your written work.

Keep an index sheet detailing the contents of your portfolio and update it as you receive assessed work back from your tutor. If any work is referred because part of it needs to be attempted again, do not automatically file it away in your portfolio. You might forget about it and find at the end of your course that you have unfinished work to catch up on. Either complete the referral immediately or make a note of it on your portfolio index sheet.

Finally, your portfolio may be sent away to be assessed by an external examiner or an examiner might visit your course and see the work there. Always keep your work tidy so that it would be easy for an external examiner to check it.

Remember that if you lose your work, you lose your evidence, and you may have to do it all over again. You must store your work securely and safely. If possible, keep back-up copies of computer work on disk. Label your files and disks, and never leave your work in an unlocked file or cabinet.

To pass the Intermediate GNVQ in business you will need to complete and pass three **mandatory units** and three **optional units**. This book contains information and activities on business to help you complete the three mandatory units:

1. **Investigating how businesses work**

2. **How businesses develop**

3. **Business finance**

Presenting and Investigating Data

Presenting data

The collecting, recording, and presenting of data are useful skills for your GNVQ Intermediate Business course.

Quantitative and qualitative data

Data simply refers to the information you can collect to help you study business. **Quantitative** data refers to numbers, such as pounds worth of revenues and profits, or numbers of people employed. **Qualitative** data refers to information which cannot be written as a number. For example, a customer might be asked by a business organization to rate their services as either 'very good', 'good,' 'poor,' or 'very poor.' This is useful information about how well the organization is delivering its services to customers, but it can only be written in words and not in numbers.

All the things you can collect data on are called **variables**. For example, if you were to collect figures on the sale of chocolate bars over time, the value of sales can change. They can go up, down, or stay the same: they are variable. Similarly, the number of employees working in a business will also be variable. Numbers employed may rise or fall over time, or simply stay the same. 'Numbers employed' is a variable.

Prices, levels of output, production costs, interest rates – are all variables. There are an endless number of things – or variables – you can collect quantitative data on in business.

Methods of presenting data

This section describes various ways to present quantitative or numerical data on all aspects of business. Your portfolio of completed activities and assignments should contain evidence that you have used and understood different ways to present data.

Today, there are many computer software programs that help you to produce high-quality tables and graphs easily and quickly. You will demonstrate core skills in information technology if you use a computer to produce tables and graphs. This will include preparing data for input, editing and saving that data, and then printing it out and presenting it.

Tables

One of the easiest ways to present data is in **tables**. They are especially useful if data on a large number of different variables needs to be shown at the same time, or where numbers are needed to make calculations.

Tables are also useful for presenting information expressed in words *and* numbers. For example, Table 1 contains both words and numbers to show the number of people employed in the major industrial sectors in selected countries in 1998. Numbers in the final column for total employment can be found by adding up each row of numbers in columns 2, 3, and 4.

▼ Table 1: Employment by main sector of business activity, 1998

Selected countries	Agriculture	Industry	Services	(in thousands) Total
United Kingdom	216	6 211	17 020	23 447
France	299	5 353	14 013	19 664
Germany	515	11 400	19 721	31 635
Italy	482	5 180	8 733	14 395
Portugal	107	1 409	1 866	3 382

European Commission, 'Eurostatistics' July 1999

All tables and graphs should have clear, easy-to-understand titles.

Always show the source of your data

Charts and graphs

Charts and graphs can be a much better method of displaying numerical information in an easy-to-read way than tables. However, they must be accurately drawn and well presented.

The main ways of presenting data graphically are:

● Pie-charts

● Barcharts

● Scatter plots

● Line graphs

Pie-charts

Pie-charts are a popular method of presentation. They are simply circles divided up into segments to represent proportions.

Any circle (or pie) can be divided into 360 degrees which represents the total amount, or 100%, of your data. Each segment will, therefore, have an angle less than 360°. For example, if one segment is half the total, then the angle of it will be 180° (i.e. 0.5 × 360°). Similarly, a segment which is only 10% of the total will have an angle of 36° (i.e. 0.1 × 360°).

Using Table 1 we can draw a whole pie to represent the total number of people in employment in the UK in 1998. Each segment can then represent the proportion of all those people employed in agriculture, industry, and services. This is shown in Figure 2.

▼ Figure 1: How to draw a piechart

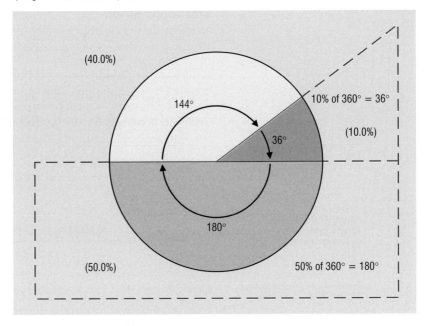

▼ Figure 2: Employment by main sectors of business activity, UK 1998

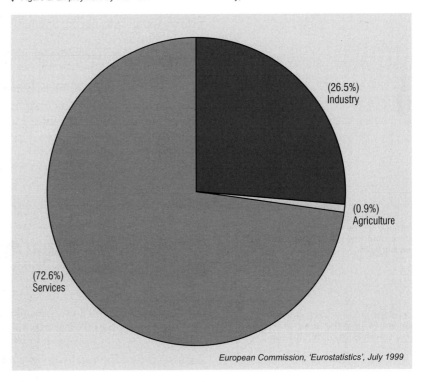

European Commission, 'Eurostatistics', July 1999

Provide a key. Use colours or shading where possible to distinguish between different components.

Key Employment in agriculture

Employment in industry

Employment in services

To calculate the angle of each segment in Figure 2 you need to use the following equation:

$$\frac{\text{Value of the individual component} \times 360°}{\text{Total}}$$

The angle, and therefore size of each segment in Figure 2 can be calculated as follows using the figures in Table 1:

For numbers employed in agriculture:

$$\frac{216\,000 \times 360°}{23\,447\,000} = 3°$$

For numbers employed in industry:

$$\frac{6\,211\,000 \times 360°}{23\,447\,000} = 96°$$

For numbers employed in services:

$$\frac{17\,020\,000 \times 360°}{23\,447\,000} = 261°$$

Pie-charts of different sizes can show different totals. For example, a pie-chart for employment in Germany could be shown as twice as large as a pie chart for employment in Italy and almost ten times the size of one for Portugal.

Bar-charts

Bar-charts are one of the easiest methods of graphical presentation. Bars are drawn along the bottom of a pair of axes to represent the value of different variables. The vertical axis, known as the '**y-axis**', gives all the possible values of your chosen variables, usually from zero upwards.

The height of each bar is proportional to the value it represents. For example, Figure 3 uses data from Table 1 to show how many people were employed in agriculture, industry, and services in Germany in 1998, with each business sector represented as a different bar.

▼ Figure 3: Employment by main sector of business activity, Germany 1998

Always label your axes with the names of the variables they show and the units they are measured in.

Keep the scale of axes simple. As far as possible, draw axes with intervals of 1, 10, 100, or 1,000, etc.

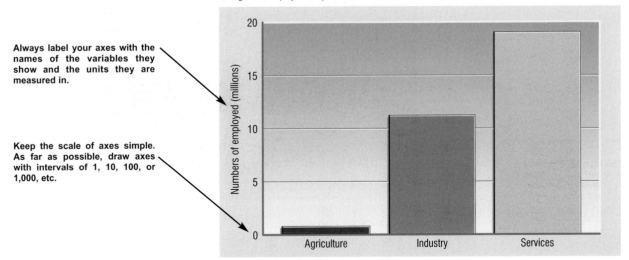

European Commission 'Eurostatistics' July 1999

Bar-charts are usually presented vertically but can also be displayed horizontally. They can present whole numbers or percentages.

Stacked bar-charts

More information can be presented in bar-charts by dividing each bar into several parts. For example, Figure 4 uses data from Table 1 on employment in different business sectors for the UK, Germany, and France.

▼ *Figure 4: Stacked bar-chart of employment by main sector of business activity, selected countries 1998*

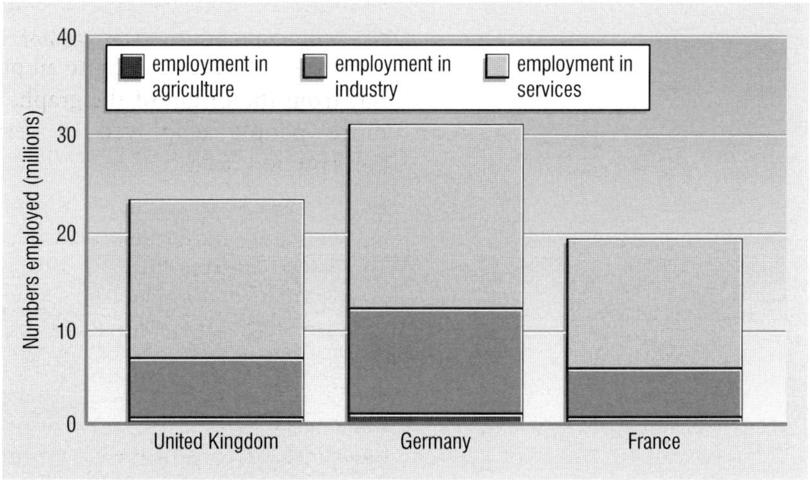

European Commission 'Eurostatistics' July 1999

Instead of using numbers employed, we can also use percentages. The total number of people employed in each country is now 100%, so that each parallel bar in Figure 5 is the same length. The graph shows more clearly how much more important services are in providing employment in the UK compared to Germany.

▼ *Figure 5: Employment by main sector of business activity, selected countries, 1998*

European Commission 'Eurostatistics' July 1999

Scatter plots

These are plots of data relating one variable to another, for example, height of person by age. However, to make sense, the two variables should be related in some way. For example, it would be silly to draw a scatter plot of the amount of rainfall in different countries by the number of people employed.

In a scatter plot the values of one variable are represented along the vertical (*y*) axis and the value of the other variable along the horizontal (*x*) axis.

In the scatter plot in Figure 6, numbers employed in industry have been plotted against numbers employed in services in 1998 for the G7 countries in Table 1. Because all points lie above a 45-degree line drawn out from the origin of the graph, it shows that all these countries have more people employed in services than in manufacturing and construction industries.

▼ *Figure 6: Scatter plot of employment by main sector of business activity, selected countries 1998*

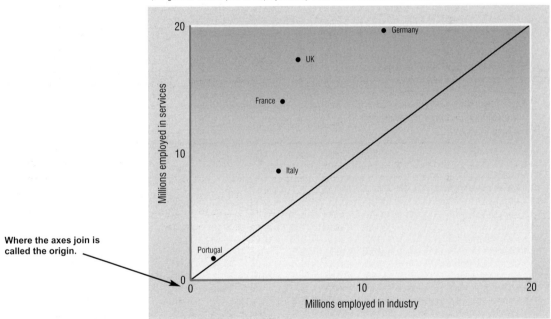

Where the axes join is called the origin.

European Commission 'Eurostatistics' July 1999

Line graphs

A mass of points scattered in a graph does not always tell us very much. Sometimes it is more useful to join up the scattered points to form a **line graph**. This can be used to show clearly how two variables are related.

Line graphs are most often used to plot data on the same variables collected over successive time periods – for example, each day, week, month, or year. These time intervals can be plotted along the horizontal axis, and more than one line can be shown on a graph. For example, Figure 7 shows how total UK employment in industry and services changed between 1971 and 1998.

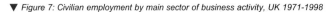
▼ Figure 7: Civilian employment by main sector of business activity, UK 1971-1998

The dependent variable in a graph, for example, sales, output, employment, costs, is normally plotted against the vertical or '*y*' axis.

The independent variable, for example, years, quarters, months, is normally plotted against the horizontal or *x* axis.

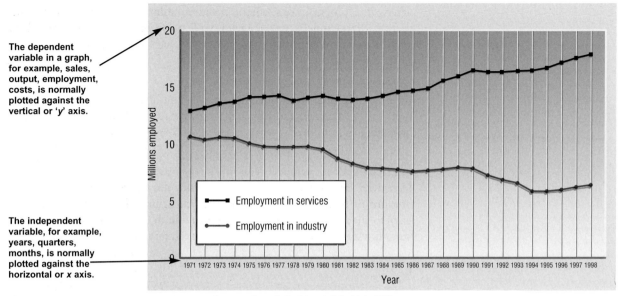

European Commission 'Eurostatistics' July 1999

Portfolio Activity

Households and their expenditure
United Kingdom

	1987	1988	1989	1990	1991	1992	1993	1994 /95	1995 /96	1996 /97	1997 /98
Average weekly household expenditure on commodities and services (£)											
Housing	30.42	35.81	38.44	44.42	50.24	47.36	44.85	46.42	48.25	49.10	51.53
Fuel and power	10.55	10.48	10.58	11.11	12.25	13.02	13.24	12.95	12.92	13.35	12.66
Food	35.79	38.28	41.67	44.81	46.13	47.66	49.96	50.43	52.88	55.15	55.92
Alcoholic drink	8.70	9.19	9.53	10.01	10.83	11.06	11.95	12.32	11.41	12.41	13.33
Tobacco	4.67	4.45	4.77	4.82	5.15	5.38	5.59	5.61	5.81	6.07	6.12
Clothing and footwear	13.32	14.52	15.25	16.03	15.80	16.39	17.40	17.13	17.15	18.27	19.96
Household goods	13.48	15.01	19.17	20.00	20.13	21.90	23.05	22.66	23.45	26.74	26.90
Household services	8.23	9.80	9.73	12.28	13.00	13.40	15.44	15.08	15.13	16.36	17.89
Personal goods and services	7.02	8.13	8.48	9.47	9.97	10.18	11.04	10.78	11.55	11.64	12.54
Motoring expenditure	23.80	25.31	30.42	33.83	34.12	35.66	36.28	36.17	36.99	41.20	46.63
Fares and other travel costs	4.60	4.88	5.35	6.19	5.58	7.20	6.95	6.64	6.17	7.45	8.12
Leisure goods	9.03	9.65	10.97	11.28	12.06	13.32	13.26	13.89	13.23	15.17	16.35
Leisure services	18.11	18.13	19.02	21.54	22.20	27.56	25.56	31.20	32.05	33.95	38.81
Micellaneous	0.88	0.78	0.93	1.37	1.59	1.75	2.10	2.30	2.37	2.21	2.02
Total	188.62	204.41	224.32	247.16	259.04	271.83	276.68	289.86	289.86	307.07	328.78

Annual Abstract of Statistics 1999

1. If possible, input the data in the two tables above into a computer spreadsheet with graphics functions.

2. Choose data from the table to present in the form of a pie-chart, barchart, and line graph (use a computer to help you if possible).

3. What business organizations might find the data of use, and why?

Investigating data

Throughout your Intermediate Business course, you will collect and record a large amount of quantitative data on many different variables, such as sales volumes, output, wage levels, employment, prices, etc.

Each item of information you collect on a variable is called an **observation**. The name refers to the fact that you have observed that information. For example, imagine you collect figures on the total number of ice creams sold at a local sweetshop each week. The number sold each week is an observation. After ten weeks you will have ten observations making up your dataset. After one year, your dataset will consist of 52 observations on ice cream sales.

However, lots and lots of numbers will not tell you very much. If a large amount of data is to be of any use to you it must be organized into an easy-to-read format, such as a graph or table. It can also be very useful to summarize your data with one or more single numbers called **summary statistics**. For example, when a large amount of data has been collected, it is very useful to work out an **average value**, such as average monthly sales, the average cost per unit of output, or the average level of spending per person. It may also be useful to show the **range** in your collection of data on a variable, by showing only the highest and lowest values.

Average values

There are three ways an average value can be calculated from a set of data: the arithmetic mean, median, and mode.

The arithmetic mean

The arithmetic mean, or **mean** for short, is the measure most people think of as an average value. It can be calculated very simply by adding together all the individual values in a set of data on one variable, and dividing that sum by the total number of observations on that dataset.

So for example, imagine that you had collected the following data on sales of ice creams at your local sweetshop over the last 10 weeks.

▼ Table 2: Number of ice cream lollies sold per week in local shop

Week	1	2	3	4	5	6	7	8	9	10
Number of ice creams	39	43	38	43	46	43	97	71	52	48

The mean of the number of ice creams sold each week in Table 2 is calculated as:

$$\frac{(39 + 43 + 38 + 43 + 46 + 43 + 97 + 71 + 52 + 48)}{10} = \frac{520}{10} = 52$$

That is, on average, 52 ice creams were sold at the shop each week over the last 10 weeks. This is rather a high figure and suggests that your dataset may not be truly representative of weekly ice cream sales. This is because the mean number of ice creams sold has been affected by the very large number sold in weeks 7 and 8. These were extraordinary weeks caused by a heatwave. The arithmetic mean is, therefore, a very useful measure, but it can be affected by extreme values.

Because the mean has been distorted, it would be wrong for the sweetshop to stock enough ice creams to meet this average level of demand each week. Instead, it would be more sensible to exclude the observations on sales during weeks 7 and 8 and recalculate the mean number of ice creams sold during the other 8 weeks. This gives a figure of 44, a much more sensible figure on which to base a decision on how many ice creams to hold in stock.

The formula for calculating the mean ($\bar{x}$) is given by:

$$\bar{x} = \Sigma \frac{(x_1 + x_2 + x_3 + \dots + x_n)}{n} = \frac{\text{Sum of observations}}{\text{number of observations}}$$

where: $\bar{x}$ is the symbol used for the mean of dataset

n is the total number of observations in a dataset

x_1, x_2, x_3, etc., are all the individual observation values in a dataset

Σ denotes the sum of all the individual observations

The median

The **median** is the value of the middle observation in a dataset. Unlike the mean, the value of the median does not depend upon the size of any other numbers. Instead the median only depends upon which number is in the middle of a group of numbers. Therefore extremely large or small 'freak' values have no effect on it.

For example, the median of 5, 10, 15, 20, 25 is 15. The median of 1, 2, 3, 4, 5, 6 is 3.5. In the first example there was an odd number of observations so finding the middle value is easy. Where there is an even number of observations, there are two middle values. You will need to add these together and divide by two to get the median value.

Arranging the weekly sales of ice creams from Table 2 in order of magnitude, we can find the median level sold each week as follows:

Weekly sales of ice cream 38   39   43   43   43   46   48   52   71   97

The middle two numbers in the dataset are 43 and 46. The median is therefore (43 + 46) ÷ 2 = 44.5

The main problem with using the median is that it ignores all other observations except those that are in the middle. For example, if the shop only held stocks to meet weekly sales of ice creams of 43, it would be totally unprepared for those periods when demand for ice creams was higher.

The mode

The **mode** is the observation value which occurs the most in a dataset. From Table 2 we can see that sales of 43 ice creams occured in three weeks out of ten. This level of sales is, therefore, called the **modal** value. The shop may use this value to indicate the number of ice creams it must stock each week, given that the chances are that weekly sales will be 43 more often than not.

The range

While it is useful to know the average of a set of data, it can also be very useful to know how the values of all the individual observations are spread around the average. That is, are individual observations widely dispersed or within a narrow range around the average?

Where observation values vary widely, the average value will not be particularly representative of the sample. For example, if a survey revealed that consumers were on average willing to pay £10 for a given product, yet over 50% of those interviewed said they were willing to pay anything up to £5 either side of the average, a firm could not be confident that setting price equal to £10 would maximize sales. If, however, the majority were willing to pay between £9.50 and £10.50 then the price of £10 would be more representative of consumers' willingness to pay.

The range is a simple measure of the spread of observation values in a dataset, calculated by subtracting the difference between the highest value and the lowest value. From Table 2 we can calculate the range in the number of ice creams sold per week by deducting 38 from 97. This gives a range in the number sold of 59.

However, because weeks 7 and 8 are not particularly representative of weekly sales in general, due to the heatwave, we could ignore them. This gives a new range of 14 between weekly sales of 38 and 52 ice creams. Like the mean, therefore, the range can be distorted by very high, or very low, values.

Now try the following activity using a computer spreadsheet to help you. Many computer software packages have functions which allow you to calculate the mean, median, mode, and/or range of a series of numbers.

Portfolio Activity

Whitford Stores is a small independent supermarket. It would like to encourage repeat sales by giving regular customers discounts on their shopping bills. However, it first needs to find out how many trips a 'regular' customer makes to their supermarket. To do this it has collected the following information from customers over a one-week period. The data simply lists the number of times each customer used the store that week to make purchases.

2	2	6	1
2	2	1	1
12	3	4	3
3	4	9	2
5	2	5	4
4	4	3	4
5	3	2	3
2	2	4	9
11	5	7	1
2	1	2	1
1	2	1	2
5	1	8	3
3	1	3	10

If possible, input the above data into a spreadsheet, then undertake the following tasks:

1. Calculate the mean number of times a person visits the supermarket each week.

2. Sort the data into order from the least number of visits to the most, and then find the median number of times a person can be expected to shop at the supermarket.

3. What is the modal number of visits per customer?

4. What is the range in the dataset?

5. Use your calculations to advise Whitford Stores on how many visits a 'regular' customer could be expected to make to the store each week. Your advice should include the advantages and disadvantages of using either the mean, median, mode, or range to summarize information about visits to the supermarket.

Investigating How Businesses Work

unit **1**

About this unit

Every business is set up to meet specific aims. Many businesses aim to make a profit. Others have important aims such as providing a service to the community. Businesses measure their success by how well they meet their aims. This unit is about how businesses organize themselves in order to achieve their aims and objectives successfully.

You will investigate the different functional areas of a business organization and how they affect each other, including production, marketing, customer service, finance, administration, and human resources. You will also look at how businesses work differently depending on how they are organized.

chapter 1	*What is business?*
chapter 2	*Inside a business*
chapter 3	*Managing human resources in business*
chapter 4	*Business communications*

chapter 1 *What is business?*

What you need to learn

Business involves productive activity to provide goods and services to satisfy the needs and wants of consumers. Business is organised in **firms**. The business activities of firms can be local, national or international.

Consumers demand **goods** and **services. Producers** supply goods and services to consumers.

All business organizations have **aims** to help them plan and set targets for what they want to achieve. Most business organizations aim to **make a profit** from their productive activity, but some will aim to **provide charitable, voluntary or public services**.

To achieve these aims businesses may also aim to:

- **survive as a business or expand**
- **maximize sales and increase market share**
- **improve the quality of a product of service**
- **provide a highly competitive service**
- **be environmentally friendly.**

Businesses must decide on practical **objectives** in order to help them achieve their aims – for example:

- **to sell more of a product than a competitor**
- **to improve an existing good or service**
- **to produce a new good or service**
- **to improve customer service levels over those of rival businesses**

You will need to find out the objectives of different businesses and which areas of the business they particularly affect.

Successful businesses must **evaluate their performance** to find out how well they are doing and what they must do to improve. They review their activities and may change or set new objectives in order to help the business meet its aims.

Section **1.1**

Investigating business

What is business?

Evidence of business activity is all around us; the food we eat, the beds we sleep on, the houses we live in, the television we watch, the schools and colleges we attend, the stores we shop at, our doctors and dentists, the cars or trains we travel in – are all examples of goods and services provided by business activity. However, business activity can also create harmful air and noise pollution.

In any society, most people are both consumers and producers. **Consumers** are people, or other businesses, who demand goods and services to satisfy their needs and wants. For example, when we eat meat and vegetables we are satisfying our need for food. When we wear clothes and live in houses we satisfy our needs for warmth and shelter. We visit cinemas and play compact discs and computer games because we want to be entertained. When a business uses up electricity to power equipment, it is satisfying a want to produce other goods and services.

Most people go out to work to earn the money they require to buy the goods and services they and their families need and want. **Producers** are people who work to supply goods and services to satisfy the needs and wants of consumers. **Production** is, therefore, the process of making goods and services, or **products**.

Inputs and outputs

Goods and services are the **outputs** of production by firms. A **firm** is simply a business organization. All businesses are organizations in which people, working together with materials, machines, and other equipment, produce a good and/or service. For example, in the production of bread, a bakery will first need premises in which to operate. It will then require flour, sugar and salt, fridges, ovens, mixers, ladles, spoons and knives, electricity, and bakers, as well as office staff and equipment, and probably some means of transport.

Workers, materials, power supplies, machines, and other equipment are the **inputs** to productive activity. Inputs are likely to have been provided by other firms, known as **suppliers**. Thus, the bakery also consumes goods and services produced by other firms as well as producing goods for other consumers.

▼ Consumers

▼ Producers

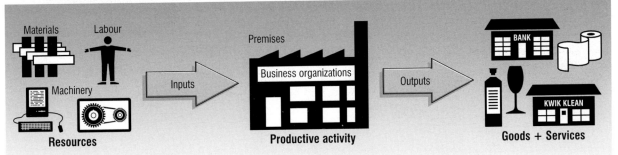
▼ Firms use INPUTS such as natural resources, industrial equipment, and labour to produce OUTPUTS (goods and services)

Materials   Labour

Machinery

Resources

Inputs →

Premises

Business organizations

Productive activity

Outputs →

BANK

KWIK KLEAN

Goods + Services

Business refers to the co-operation and organization between people and firms, their materials, buildings and machines, for the purpose of production to satisfy consumer needs and wants. There are a great many different types of business producing many millions of different goods and services for consumers in the UK and all over the world.

Production involves a chain of activity

If the aim of production is to make products to satisfy consumers' needs and wants, the process is not finished until goods and services reach the people or firms who want them.

Production involves a **chain of productive activity** linking a number of business organizations – from those that produce natural resources such as coal, wheat, and oil, to those that use these materials to make finished goods and services, and finally to those who operate warehouses and shops to sell products to the consumers who want them. Every good or service will have a chain of production linking suppliers with customers.

▼ *Figure 1.1: A chain of production for bread*

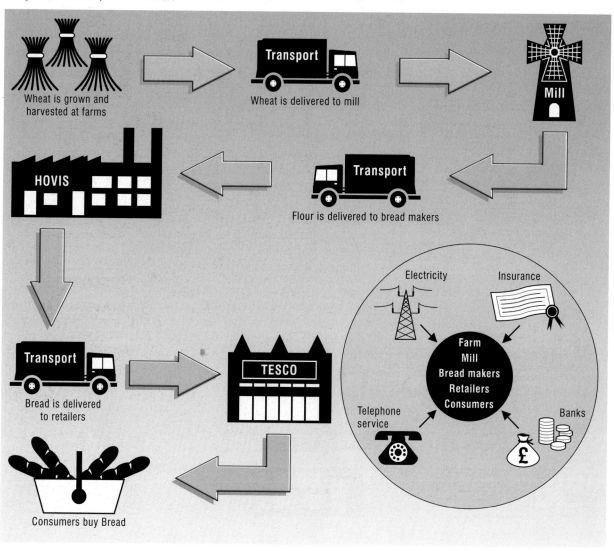

Portfolio Activity 1.1

1. Below is a jumble of pictures and descriptions explaining how audio compact discs (CDs) are produced.

   Work in pairs to match each picture to a description. Write down the descriptions to form a chain showing how CDs are produced, from their initial stage to their sale to consumers. Some descriptions can be used more than once.

Descriptions

1. Recording engineers record group in studio

2. Coal and oil are used to generate electricity for use by firms and households

3. Crude oil is refined

4. Shops sell CDs

5. Transport companies deliver goods and materials

6. Consumers buy CDs

7. Coal and oil are dug and drilled from the ground

8. Chemical firms use oil to produce plastics

9. Insurance firm provides insurance to protect firms from risk, damage or theft

10. Discs are pressed

11. Pipeline carries oil to oil refinery

12. Consumers play CDs

13. CDs are packed into CD cases

14. Banks provide finance for firms

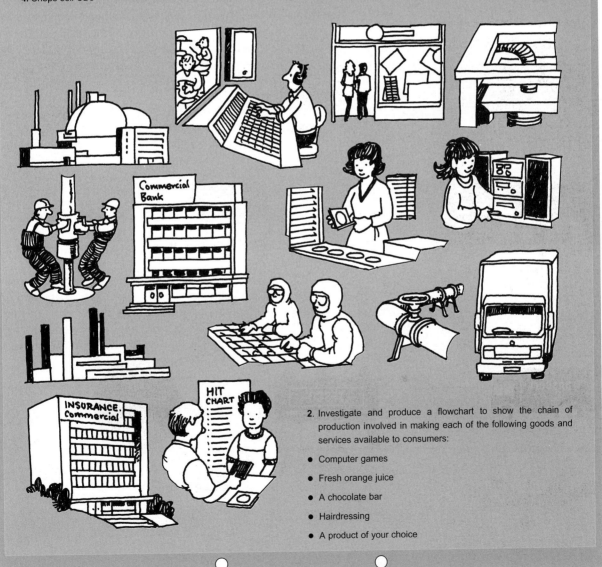

2. Investigate and produce a flowchart to show the chain of production involved in making each of the following goods and services available to consumers:

- Computer games
- Fresh orange juice
- A chocolate bar
- Hairdressing
- A product of your choice

Let us consider the chain of production involved in producing compact discs for sale to consumers. In the earliest stages, natural resources such as coal and oil need to be extracted from the ground to power electricity stations. Oil, in turn, is the raw material used to produce plastic for CDs, which are pressed and shaped by machines. Tape recorders and sound engineers are needed to record the music of a pop group for the record. The shop is the final destination of the CD before it is bought. During this process, a great many banks have probably lent money to firms to help them complete their part of the chain. Insurance companies have been involved in case of damage or theft, and transport companies have delivered raw materials and finished goods to those business organizations that require them.

Business products

Once a business has moved to its chosen location, it can set about the task of organizing production. Raw materials, labour, machinery, and other equipment can be organized to produce all manner of different items in modern industrial countries. The products (goods and services) of business activity can be classified under two main headings:

Consumer goods and services

A **consumer good** is any good that satisfies consumers' wants. **Consumer durables** are goods that last a long time, for example, cars, videos, washing machines, furniture. **Non-durable goods** (sometimes called **consumables**) are goods that are used up quickly or have a relatively short life, for example, food, drink, petrol, washing powder (see also chapter 5).

Ordinary consumers also want services such as banking, insurance, hairdressing, teaching, dry-cleaning, to satisfy their many wants. These are called **consumer services**.

Industrial goods and services

Some firms do not produce goods or services for ordinary consumers. Instead, they provide goods and services for other businesses and for central and local government. Ploughs, robots, power stations, computers, factory buildings, power stations, roads, juggernauts – these are all examples of industrial goods used by business organizations to help them produce and distribute other goods and services.

There are also many **commercial services** available to business consumers and government, such as advertising, insurance, banking, transport and communications.

▼ *Consumer durables*

▼ *Industrial products*

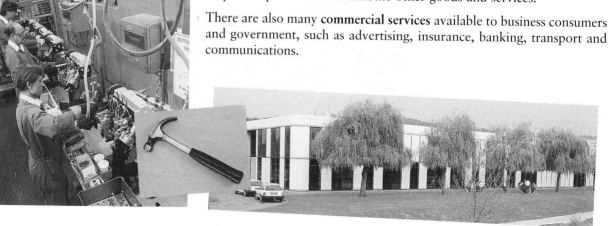

Portfolio Activity 1.2

1. Look at the 3 photographs. Which retail outlet sells:

   a non-durable consumer goods

   b durable consumer goods

   c personal services ?

2. Visit examples of the types of business organizations shown in the photographs and make a list of the industrial goods they use, and what they are used for.

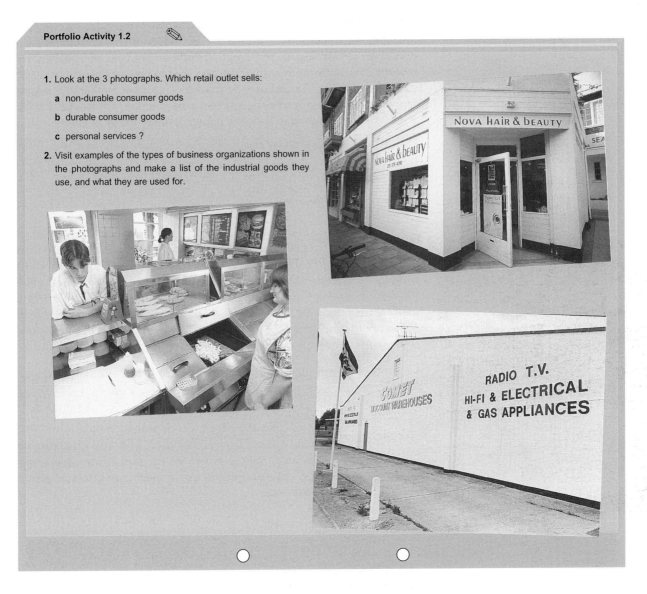

What is a market?

All goods or services produced by business organizations are sold in markets. A **market** is defined as consisting of all those people willing and able to buy goods and services and all those willing and able to supply them. For example, the market for televisions will consist of the producers of televisions and the people who buy them. Similarly, there will be a market for cars, hairdressing, video recorders, window cleaning, and all other goods and services.

For a market to exist, consumers must need or want the product that producers are willing and able to supply. If a producer makes a product nobody wants, then there is no market for that product. But if consumers want something that producers have not yet provided, then there is a clear market opportunity.

▼ *National lottery instant cards have a domestic UK market*

Types of market

Markets for most products today are made up of consumers and producers spread across very large areas. For example, the market for recorded music is international, because both consumers and producers of recorded music live and operate in many countries. Similarly, products like oil, sugar, video recorders, and insurance are sold all over the world. These goods and services have huge **international markets**.

Other markets may be in one particular country only and are called **domestic markets**. For example, the market for a local newspaper in Manchester will be confined to the immediate surrounding area. Similarly, national newspapers like the *Daily Mirror* or *The Times* are unlikely to sell very well abroad.

Sometimes the market for a product such as toothpaste is made up of many millions of individual consumers buying from just a few producers like Unilever and Procter and Gamble who together sell most brands of toothpaste. Other markets are made up of firms buying components and finished products from each other such as computer hardware components and software in order to make other products. Some markets can be very specialized – for example, the market for weapons is made up of just a small number of firms selling to governments.

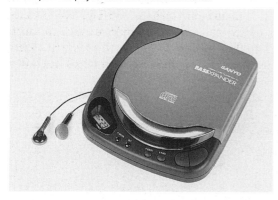

▼ *Compact disc players have an international market*

Consumer needs and wants

Everyone needs a minimum of food, drink, and clothing or shelter to protect them from the elements. However, our **needs** are few compared to our **wants**. People want cars, video recorders, designer clothes, pop concerts, foreign holidays, and much more, for the pleasure they give, not because they are necessary to maintain life and ensure survival.

Business organizations can help to create wants for their products today by **advertising** (see chapter 4). Advertisements use clever slogans and catch-phrases to try to persuade people to want particular goods and services.

▼ *Needs?*

▼ *Wants?*

Demand

Businesses do not produce goods and services just to satisfy needs or wants. Their primary aim is to make a profit (see 1.3). This means they will only be willing to provide goods and services to consumers who are willing and able to pay for them.

Consumers are said to **demand** goods and services when they are willing and able to buy them. When someone wants a good or service but cannot pay for them, they are unable to demand them. Therefore, if profit-seeking producers are to supply the products that consumers demand, consumers must be able to pay for their products at a price which exceeds their costs.

Today, most people earn money to buy the things they need and want by working in one particular occupation, such as nursing, accountancy, bricklaying, company management. Very few people attempt to satisfy their own needs and wants by their own work. That is, in a modern society, most people rely on business organizations to satisfy their needs and wants.

Consumer or customer?

From the point of view of businesses which produce goods or services, there is an important difference between a consumer and a customer. Consumers are *potential* customers for a business. For example, you may be willing and able to buy Pepsi Cola at a Sainsbury's supermarket. This makes you a **consumer** in the markets for cola drinks and supermarket retail services. Cola producers and supermarkets will be competing for your custom. However, the fact that you choose to buy Coca Cola at a Tesco store means you are neither a customer of Pepsi or Sainsburys, but a paying **customer** for Coca Cola and Tesco.

Firms can lose customers to rival firms. However, they can also lose customers if there is a general fall in demand for their product – perhaps because of a change in consumer tastes. Without enough demand for their products, firms soon run into difficulties.

Contracting markets

▼ *Typewriters*

▼ *Vinyl LPs*

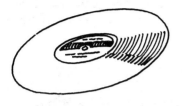

Expanding markets

▼ *Multimedia personal computers*

▼ *Mobile phones*

Contracting and expanding markets

Consumer wants are always changing because of factors such as fashion, social and cultural change, growing incomes, new legal requirements, and many more (see chapter 5). It is important that firms keep pace with changing consumer wants and develop existing or new products that people will continue to buy.

If consumer demand for a particular good or service is falling over time, the market for that product is said to be **shrinking** or **contracting**. Firms making that good or service will suffer declining sales and profits. Some may even be forced to close down.

If, on the other hand, consumer demand for a particular good or service is rising over time, the market is said to be **expanding**. Those firms already producing the good or service will experience rising sales and profits. They may have to expand production to meet demand, and it is likely that other firms will be attracted to the market too. New firms will also want to produce the same good or service because of the opportunity to earn sales revenues and profits. Some examples of contracting and expanding markets in recent years are shown in the pictures on this page.

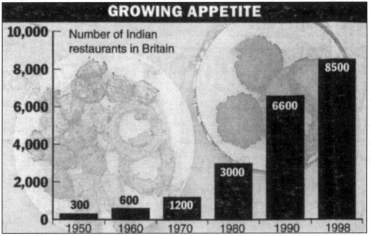

GROWING APPETITE

Number of Indian restaurants in Britain

300	600	1200	3000	6600	8500
1950	1960	1970	1980	1990	1998

Evening Standard, 19.2.1998

Getting a share of the market

Competition for consumers between rival firms is rather like fighting over slices of a cake. Most firms will want to get a bigger slice than their rivals.

The cake represents all the spending of consumers on a particular product. The size of the cake, therefore, reflects the size of the market for a good or service, measured by the total amount spent on that product by consumers in any one period of time – usually one year. The **market share** of a business is, therefore, its share of total sales.

If you decide to produce a good or service that is in competition with those provided by existing firms, your first objective will be to make sales and obtain a share of the market.

For example, suppose you want to make and sell dried flower arrangements. Imagine that consumers spent £900,000 on them last year and are expected to spend £1 million in the current year. If you make and sell £50,000-worth of dried flower arrangements this year, you will have captured 5% of the value of the market (£50,000/£1,000,000 × 100 = 5%). However, because you are a new firm supplying the market for dried flower arrangements, your market share of 5% must mean that existing firms have lost 5% of the value of total sales to you. It is unlikely you will be able to do this without making flower arrangements that are much better than existing products, selling them at a lower price, and using a lot of advertising to create consumer wants for them.

Portfolio Activity 1.5

1. From your own knowledge and further research, identify and list at least three markets that are currently expanding and three which are contracting.

2. For the goods and/or services you have identified in Task 1, list and explain possible reasons for the growth or decline in sales. Useful sources of data will include newspapers and magazines, discussions with shop sales staff and business owners/managers.

3. Propose a new or existing good or service which you would like to produce if your ran your own business. Give reasons for your choice based on your knowledge of consumer wants and needs, the growth in consumer demand for it, and the amount of competition from existing firms.

4. To find out more about the market for your product, design a short questionnaire to use on a group of people. Try to establish how much people might be willing to pay for your product, how often they are likely to buy it, what the main rival products are and who provides them, and the particular design features consumers would like to see.

5. Make a sketch of the good or service you chose in Task 3. Show and describe features it will have, including size, shape, colour, texture, weight, materials used (and a list of possible suppliers), labelling, and packaging.

6. Write up your proposal and research findings in a word-processed report, including diagrams.

7. Ask your class group to act as joint owners of your new business venture and present your proposals to them. Your research findings and written proposals should be no longer than a one-page summary. Hand out copies of this at the beginning of your presentation. The presentation itself should last no more than 10 minutes. Make good use of any diagrams or models you have constructed to illustrate your product.

Section 1.2

Business operations

The purpose of any course in business is to study and understand business operations. It is useful to look at and compare different business organizations in terms of:

- **The goods and services they provide:** Some firms provide goods and services for other firms, such as industrial machines or advertising services, while others provide goods and services for ordinary consumers, for example, chocolates and hairdressing.

- **Their size:** Business size can be measured in many different ways. For example, by how many people a firm employs, by how much revenue they earn from sales, or the total value of the buildings, machinery, and other equipment they use (i.e. the value of their capital employed). Table 1.1 lists the top five firms in the UK in 1997/98 in order of how much profit they earned. It also gives information on their main activities, capital employed, sales revenues, and number of employees.

▼ *Table 1.1: Top 5 profit makers 1998*

Organization	Main business activities	Capital employed £ billion	Turnover £ billion	Pre-tax Profit £ billion	Number of employees
HSBC Holdings	Banking	26.9	18.1	4.5	109,298
Shell Transport and Trading	Oil , gas and nuclear fuels	21.0	32.8	4.3	101,000
British Petroleum	Oil , gas and nuclear fuels	20.6	44.7	3.7	53,700
British Telecommunications	Communications	17.5	14.5	3.0	135,200
Glaxco Wellcome	Chemicals	4.0	8.3	2.9	53,808

The Times 1000, 1998

- **Their purpose for being in business:** Some organizations are in business to make profit. Others may provide a charitable or public service, for example, the Comic Relief charity and the National Health Service.

- **Where they are located:** Some firms will locate near to the source of their supplies. For example, a colliery will locate over coal deposits in the earth. Firms that import materials from overseas may locate near to ports with good access by road and rail. Other firms may choose to locate near to a supply of skilled labour, or to be close to their customers. For example, banks and building societies are usually found in large towns near to where people live and shop (see chapter 7).

- **Their links with other organizations:** Most business organizations tend to specialize in the production of one or a handful of different goods and/or services. Most will, therefore, rely on other firms to provide the other goods and services they need to carry out their business, such as power supplies, office stationery, computer equipment, lighting, transport, banking, insurance, and much more.

  Many firms also rely on other firms to be their customers. For example, producers of chocolate bars will rely on wholesalers and shops to buy their products, which they in turn sell on to their customers.

- **How they are owned:** Most business organizations are owned and managed by private individuals. These organizations are said to belong to the **private sector** of the UK and include sole traders, partnerships, limited companies and co-operatives (see chapter 6). Most business organizations in the private sector aim to make a profit for their owners (see 1.3).

  State-owned organizations are owned and controlled by the government and belong to the **public sector** of the UK. Some public sector organizations operate for profit, but most aim to provide a cost-effective public service (see chapter 6).

  Because the UK has both private and public sector organizations, it is said to have a **mixed economy**. In fact, most countries have mixed economies although some, like China, have more public sector ownership than others.

  All of these aspects of business, and more, are considered in this book. We start by looking at the purposes or aims of business organizations.

Small, medium or large?

A firm that employs less than 30 people is usually considered small. However, a firm may be relatively small in terms of how many people it employs but still earn a lot of revenue each year.

Most small organizations in the UK have only one or relatively few owners. They are **sole traders and partnerships** (see chapter 6). They tend to provide local personal services, or goods tailored to customer requirements that cannot be mass-produced.

Medium-sized organizations employ between 30-200 employees. They tend to be **private limited companies** that are able to raise money to expand their business operations by selling shares (see 1.3).

Large organizations with over 200 employees will usually be **public limited companies (plc's)** if they are UK-based (see chapter 6). However, many of the very largest organizations in the UK are foreign-owned **multinationals** operating in more than one country. They mass-produce the same products, or offer the same service to customers all over the world. Those based in the USA will usually have 'Corp' or 'Inc' after their names.

Business operations – an example

Business name: Stefan Alexander

Ownership: Private sector partnership owned by Mario and Linda D'Andrea

(Business start-up was funded from family savings. Salon is named after Mario and Linda's two children)

Products: Haircutting and styling service

Purpose: To make a profit by providing a friendly and good quality service

Size: 5 full-time employees (including Mario and Linda)

1 part-time employee

1 apprentice hairdresser

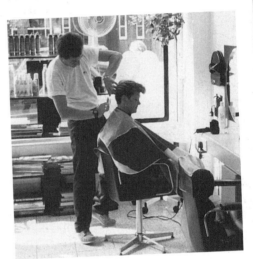

Annual revenue 1999: = £100,000 approximately

Location: Motspur Park, Surrey
Reasons for choice of location include:
Near large residential area
Premises were affordable
Only one other hairdresser close by
Owner was familiar with area
Good schools in area for Mario and Linda's children

Links with other organizations: Commercial estate agent helped to find suitable premises
Brother's building firm decorated and fitted out the premises
Shampoos and other haircare products supplied by Goldwell Ltd and Capital Hair and Beauty Trade Warehouse
Electricity from South Eastern Electricity Plc
Telephone service from British Telecom Plc
End of year accounts prepared by local self-employed accountant
Government-sponsored apprentice trainee hairdresser supplied by Pruners College
Council Tax paid to Royal Borough of Kingston-Upon-Thames
Water supplied by Thames Water
Income tax paid to Inland Revenue
Customs and Excise department collects VAT receipts

Portfolio Activity 1.6

Investigate a local business organization of your choice and, with the co-operation of the owner(s) or manager(s), produce a written record of the business operations, similar to that for 'Stefan Alexander' above.

Section 1.3   The aims of business

What is the purpose of business activity?

The main aim of most private sector business organizations is to make a **profit** by producing goods and services consumers want and are willing and able to pay a price for that is greater than the cost of producing the good or service.

However, some business organizations may have **non-profit** motives, for example, providing a **charitable** or **voluntary service** to help people, animals or the environment. In addition, there are government organizations which provide **public services.** Their services may be provided for just a small fee or even free to people who need them.

Providing charitable, voluntary or public services or making a profit are **primary business aims.** In order to better achieve these primary aims, firms may attempt to achieve certain a number of other business aims first. For example, to achieve the long run goal of making as much profit as possible, a firm may initially aim to produce a new product which will out sell similar products from rival business organizations. So the goal of achieving increasing or even maximizing sales or market share might be required before profits can be maximized.

Portfolio Activity 1.7

What do you think are the purposes of the business organizations in the articles and pictures below.

Tesco kick-starts Scooter price war

Forget the groceries. Today Tesco becomes the first UK supermarket to tempt shoppers with a shiny new 50cc motor scooter.

The scooters go on sale at more than 100 stores nationwide and carry a £1,200 price tag, some £500 cheaper than normal dealers. The move into scooter selling is part of Tesco's long running campaign to beat selective distribution. It follows its previous efforts to sell designer clothing at discounted prices in its high street stores.

A spokesman for Tesco said "we will continue to campaign to overcome the obstacles of selective distribution in the UK where brand owners control the supply of products to keep prices high".

London Evening Standard, 2.6.1999

Virgin joins circus record sales battle

The battle of the record retail giants is about to escalate as Virgin Megastore embarks on an ambitious expansion plan. The music chain has acquired the lease for a 20,000 ft shop in Piccadilly Circus on of the most sought after sites in Europe.

The new store is part of an aggressive expansion plan which will also see Virgin opening its largest shop outside London in Glasgow and another in Middlesborough.

London Evening Standard 3.6.1999

World Society for the
Protection of Animals

RSPCA

Libearty

The world campaign for bears

WHALE & DOLPHIN
CONSERVATION SOCIETY

Britsh Telecom's regular customer satisfaction surveys show that British phone users have never been happier with the service they are offered, but the company is not resting on its laurels. Constant efforts are being made to improve customer service, and the facilities offered. The research and development department is working as hard as ever to find answers to more of their customers' needs.

Taken from an advertisement for British Telecom Plc

Making a profit

Most firms hope to persuade consumers to buy their goods and services at a price greater than the cost of making them. Selling goods and services generates **revenue** for a business organization. **Profit** is what is left from revenues after all costs have been paid. A firm that is unable to cover its costs with enough sales revenues will make a **loss** and could be forced to close down if losses continue. It is important for a business to make a profit so that it can:

● Pay for wages, materials, rents and other bills, and have enough revenue left over to satisfy the business owners who have invested their money in the business

● Borrow money from banks and other lenders who will want to be sure the business is successful and can afford to repay them

● Use the money to buy new equipment and machinery when it becomes worn out or out-of-date

Business accounts 2000	
	£
Wages	60,000
Rent	10,000
Materials	120,000
Electricity	1,500
Telephone	500
Equipment hire	4,000
Total costs	196,000
Revenue	250,000
Profit	54,000

Business accounts 2000	
	£
Wages	45,000
Rent	8,000
Materials	100,000
Electricity	2,300
Telephone	1,200
Equipment hire	10,000
Total costs	166,500
Revenue	156,000
Loss	−10,500

To help a firm make a good profit from its business activities it may be necessary for it to fulfill certain other aims.

Surviving as a business or expanding

In some markets there is so much competition between rival firms to supply that good or service to consumers that the aim of all firms might be simply to survive. That is why some people say 'business is war'!

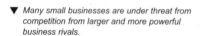

▼ Many small businesses are under threat from competition from larger and more powerful business rivals.

Staying in business requires making enough money to cover business costs (see chapter 8). Survival is often the most important aim of a new business. If it is able to then its next aim may be to expand and try to earn a profit. However, for some businesses it is getting more and more difficult to survive. For example, many small corner shops in cities find that they cannot match the low prices and variety of products in supermarkets. As a result many thousands of small shops have gone out of businesses in recent years.

Other businesses may seek to grow in size by producing and selling more of their goods and services. This will be easier to do if the consumer demand for that type of good or service is growing (see 1.1). If consumer demand isn't growing, or may even be falling, then a business may only be able to expand if it able to attract customers away from rival firms.

To increase consumer demand for its products and grow market share a business will need to make it's products more attractive than rival products, by selling at a lower price, by improving the product, and/or by increased advertising. If the business is successful and consumer demand for their product does rise, the firm will have to produce more. All this will cost money but in the long run it will help the business expand. Alternatively, business organizations will often join together to become bigger (see chapter 5).

Maximizing sales and increasing market share

If a firm is to make a profit, it will need to persuade consumers to buy its products. The total number of people willing and able to buy a given product is said to form the **market** for that product. For example, the market for cars is made up of all the people who buy cars. Similarly, the market for oranges is made up of all the people who buy oranges. In fact, every product will have a market if consumers want it.

▼ *Newspapers battle it out for market share every day*

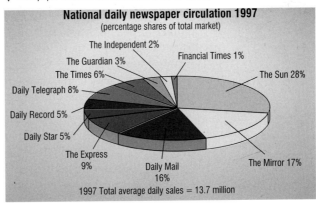

National daily newspaper circulation 1997
(percentage shares of total market)

The Independent 2%
The Guardian 3%
The Times 6%
Daily Telegraph 8%
Daily Record 5%
Daily Star 5%
The Express 9%
Daily Mail 16%
Financial Times 1%
The Sun 28%
The Mirror 17%

1997 Total average daily sales = 13.7 million

Marketing Pocket Book 1997

Most firms will compete for consumers with rival firms producing the same or similar goods or services. For example, Coca Cola competes with other cola drinks such as Pepsi, Virgin, and supermarket own brands. Firms will compete to increase their share of the total market.

The size of the market for any particular good or service can be measured by the total value of sales to consumers of that product. Firms, therefore, compete for a share of the total spending by consumers. **Increasing market share** is, therefore, an important objective for many firms.

A new firm entering a market for the first time may initially price their product very low and spend a lot of money on advertising to attract consumers to buy it. Established rival firms may respond by cutting the prices of their competing products too and increasing advertising. These business strategies can be very expensive for firms. Heavy spending on advertising raises costs and price cutting lower sales revenues, so profits will fall. However, if a business is successful, it will increase sales and may in future be able to raise its prices so that eventually it will increase profits.

Providing a highly competitive product or service

A business is unlikely to be able to increase its sales and market share if it does not have a highly competitive product. Businesses that produce goods and services which are not very good quality, are priced too high, have poor or out-of-date image, do not incorporate the latest technologies, or that take too long to respond to customer enquiries or complaints, will fail to compete with business rivals that do. For example, would you pay £5 to a window cleaner who always leaves dirt and smears on your windows if another window cleaner offers to make your windows spotless for only £3 or your money back?

Many markets for goods and services are very competitive. For example, people who shop in supermarkets want the widest possible choice of products at the lowest possible prices. This is why price cutting wars between the big supermarkets keep breaking out. Similarly, consumers of computers and other hi-tech equipment always want the latest products and designs and they expect technology to improve every few months. Only those firms that can anticipate what customers will want next and then alter their production to make it for them will survive.

Being environmentally friendly

Care for the environment is an issue that is important to a growing number of people. Many firms have changed the ways they promote and produce their products because of pressure from consumers and organisations such as Greeenpeace and Friends of the Earth – organization which campaign for greater care of the environment, including rivers and seas, forests, animals and marine life, and the air we breathe (see chapter 7).

The 'green' consumer movement involves millions of people who actively choose not to buy products from those firms whom they suspect are damaging the environment or testing product on animals. This means that those firms who can persuade the public that they do no damage to the environment or that they actually improve the environment can increase their sales and profits. It is for this reason that many business organizations now have 'green' policies and targets, and undertake regular 'green audits'. These involve looking at all the different areas of their business operations to see how environmentally friendly they are, and how they could be improved. These improvements can include:

- recycling waste

- conserving energy use, for example by turning off computers after use

- using more recycled materials and biodegradable products

- not testing chemicals and finished products such as cosmetics on animals

- only buying wood from replanted forests

- only buying products from suppliers who have a good environmental record

What some businesses are doing for the environment

The 'good'...

Body Shop: Good recycling record. Negotiates successfully with Third World communities.

Co-operative bank: Won't lend to organisations with a poor environmental record, the arms industry or Third World nations with a bad human-rights record.

Tradecraft: Ethical trading policy for coffee. Fair wages for Third World workers.

British Polythene: Successful recycling policy.

Kingfisher (owners of B&Q, Dixons, Superdrug, Woolworths, and other retailers) Superdrug will not sell goods tested on animals after 1987. B & Q helps replace trees it has cut down for wood supplies.

Grandmetropolitan (brewing, hotels and leisure): Good ethical record

Whitbread (brewing): Good local community development programme.

And the 'not so good'?

Banks (Barclays, NatWest, Lloyds TSB): Lending policies to Third World countries resulting in destruction to rainforests.

Hanson (a holding company with many different business activities): Mining in areas owned by American Indians

Nestlé (food products): Selling powdered milk to mothers in Third World countries where safe drinking water is in short supply

Exxon (oil and gas extraction): Owners of the Exxon Valdez oil tanker which spilled 11 million gallons of crude oil off Alaska.

RTZ (mining): Damage to the environment caused by their mines in the Third World

Daily Mirror 27.6.1995

▼ Showing customers that the organization cares for the environment has become an important element in customer service.

...ENVIRONMENTAL INFORMATION.....ENVIRONMENTAL INFORMATION

SAFEWAY

Safeway Stores plc
Corporate Affairs Dept.,
6 Millington Road,
Hayes,
Middlesex. UB3 4AY

EFS1

SAFEWAY ENVIRONMENTAL POLICY

1. Safeway will operate in harmony with the global environment and promote environmental protection as part of its business activities.

2. Particular attention will be paid to the following areas:-

    a) Conservation of energy

    b) Sustainable use of raw materials

    c) Environmentally responsible waste management

    d) Progressive reduction of the company's environmental impact in all its premises, activities and developments

    e) Environmentally responsible marketing

    f) Compliance with the law and best available technology in environmental protection

    g) Effective environmental audit systems

    h) Staff training and recruitment to meet the environmental objectives.

    Printed on recycled paper

Telephone 081 848 8744 Facsimile 081 756 2910 Telex 934888
Registered Number 746956. Registered in England. Registered Office: 6 Millington Road, Hayes, Middlesex, UB3 4AY

▼ People who were 'very worried' about various environmental issues, 1989 and 1996

England and Wales

	Percentages			Percentages	
	1989	1996		1989	1996
Chemicals put into rivers and seas	64	65	Loosing Green Belt land	27	28
Sewage on beaches/bathing water	59	61	Global warming	44	35
Toxic waste: disposal and import	...	60	Fouling by dogs	29	34
Radioactive waste	58	60	Effects of livestock methods	...	33
Oil spills at sea and oil on beaches	53	56	Acid rain	40	31
Traffic exhaust fumes and urban smog	33	48	Litter and rubbish	33	30
Ozone layer depletion	56	46	Over-fishing of the seas	...	30
Use of insecticides/fertilisers	46	46	Smoking in public places	...	28
Loss of plants/animals in UK	...	45	Difficulty in travelling by means other than car	...	26
Tropical forest destruction	44	44	Decay of inner cities	22	23
Loss of plants and animals abroad	...	44	Using up UK's natural resources	...	23
Traffic congestion	...	42	Vacant and derelict land/buildings	16	18
Fumes and smoke from factories	34	41	Not enough recycling	...	18
Loss of trees and hedgerows	34	40	Noise	13	15
Drinking water quality	41	39			

Social Trends 1998

Not-for-profit business aims

Providing a charitable service

A number of business organizations belong to what is called the **voluntary sector**. Charitable organizations rely on donations of money ('voluntary income') to provide help and care for people and animals in need and other deserving causes. Charities can also raise money by holding special events, such as fêtes and sponsored walks, or even by selling goods, such as T-shirts and Christmas cards.

Organizations such as Greenpeace, Libearty, Oxfam, and the British Heart Foundation do not aim to make a profit from their productive activities. All the money received by these and other charities is used to cover the cost of their operations, from day-to-day management and administration, advertising to attract donations, and ultimately – and most importantly – to provide the goods and services to those they aim to help.

Providing a voluntary service

Many organizations rely on the unpaid skills and help of volunteers. For example, your local hospital may require people to greet patients and visitors, drivers to take elderly and disabled people on excursions, or disc jockeys to run a hospital radio station. Local environmental groups may need help to clean up rivers and areas of wasteland.

Many national and international organizations are pleased to accept the help of people who can simply hand out leaflets as well as those who are able to advise on accounts, using computers, construction, veterinary care, etc. Some people also volunteer to risk their lives for others by manning lifeboats or rescuing people trapped on mountains or in caves.

Opportunities also exist for voluntary work overseas. The **Voluntary Service Overseas (VSO)** organization recruits people to work in developing countries all over the world, normally for a two-year period. People with skills in medicine, teaching, building, and farming are much in demand. VSO organizes contracts which pay living expenses or a small income to cover essentials only.

The Fundraising Group

We are a small active group looking for ways to raise funds for Oxford MIND. Meetings of the group take place the last Thursday of each month at 12.15 p.m.

If you think you can spare even two hours a month, please join us. For details of the next meeting please contact Nicky Clargo on (01865) 511702.

The MIND Shop

If you are interested in working among a friendly group of people in the MIND Shop, please call Lyn Blizzard on (01865) 510668. Donations of clothes, stamps and bric-a-brac are always appreciated.

Oxford Befriending Scheme

The Oxford Befriending Scheme is looking for volunteers who are willing to spend some regular time with someone who has become lonely as a result of long term mental health problem. Anyone can apply. Your friendship might make a difference to someone who is isolated or lonely.

For further details please contact Veronica Young on (01865) 311252.

The charitable organization

There are over 170,000 charities in Britain, all of which have **trust status**. This means a person, or group of persons, are appointed as trustees to look after their funds and other assets, such as premises and equipment.

Charities are normally exempt from the payment of tax. The Registrar of Charities therefore exercises careful control on the types of activity that can be registered as charities. This is to prevent corrupt business organizations or individuals from setting up bogus charities in order to avoid paying tax on their incomes.

▼ *Greenpeace – working to protect the environment*

A charitable trust can be set up for the following reasons:

● To help the poor in the UK and overseas, for example, Save the Children and Oxfam

● To advance education, for example, a voluntary aided school or public school

● For religious purposes, for example, to restore or maintain an old church

● To protect and conserve the environment and animals, for example, Greenpeace and the RSPCA

Although charities do not exist to make a profit, they must be organized and run just like any other business organization. They will be interested in generating as much revenue as they can from donations and other sources, to pay for the service they provide to those in need, and they must try to keep their costs as low as possible. They need good managers and workers, and must keep detailed financial records.

Charities can go bankrupt if their income is less than their costs, and they can be closed down if it is found that trustees have misused money – for example, by using it for non-charitable purposes.

Providing a public service

Unlike firms that exist to make a profit, a number of organizations provide goods and services which it is felt everyone should benefit from, regardless of their ability to pay. State education, the National Health Service, the police and fire service, the army and navy, coastguards and street lighting, are all examples of **public services**. Instead of being paid for directly by consumers, these public services are paid for by money raised by the government in taxes (see chapter 6).

▼ *Street lights and schools provide a public service*

Mission statements

Most business organizations have a **mission statement** which summarizes their main aims in business. Some examples of mission statements from well known organizations are:

Royal Brompton & Harefield NHS Trust

To be the leading national and international centre for the diagnosis, treatment and care of patients with heart and lung disease, creating and disseminating knowledge through research and education.

The Honda Motor Car Company

'We are dedicated to supplying products of the highest efficiency at a reasonable price for worldwide customer satisfaction.'

The Boots Company Plc

'Our objective is to maximize the value of the company for the benefit of its shareholders. While vigorously pursuing our commercial interests we will, at all times, seek to enhance our reputation as a well managed, ethical and socially responsible company.'

British Airways Plc

'To be the best and most successful company in the airline industry.'

Tesco plc

'Our core purpose is to create value for customers to earn their lifetime quality.'

Section **1.4**   **Business objectives**

Turning business aims into practice

Business organizations will have particular aims like making a profit, or simply trying to stay in business when times are hard. These aims may change over the life time of the business. For example, a new business may aim simply to survive for its first year. An established business might aim to expand its market share from 30% of the total market to 50% and then, after it has done this, seek to increase profits by 5% each year over the last.

Once a business has decided upon its aims it will need to choose some practical objectives and methods to achieve them. For example, in order to achieve the aim of expanding market share a business may choose the objective of beating its closest rival in terms of sales over the next twelve months. Therefore, the objectives of a business are the practical ways in which it will go about achieving its aims.

Portfolio Activity 1.8

Read the news articles below.

1. What do you think is the primary business aim of each of the business organisations and products mentioned ?

2. What are the business organisations in the articles doing in order to achieve their business

Carlsberg before its makeover

The new-look Carlsberg

THE ads claimed it was probably the best lager in the world, but the drinking public weren't convinced.

A year ago, Carlsberg was 13th in the canned lager popularity charts and the brewers were getting desperate.

But a subtle facelift — bolder colours and a boast about the alcohol content — more than doubled its sales and sent it to number one. It is still in the top five today.

The way a product looks can tip the balance between success and failure. And companies are spending millions on re-packaging them.

Four years ago, very few people were getting Tango'd — it was just another orange drink which had been around for years.

But design wizards came up with a spiky new image and Tango is now Britain's biggest-selling fizzy fruit drink in a can.

Daily Mirror, 29.10.1996

Carlsberg: Sales **UP** 160%

THE PROBLEM: Carlsberg ranked 13th in sales of standard lagers in off-licences and supermarkets last January.
THE BRIEF: "Research showed it was the 'John Major' of lagers — ordinary and dull. We had to make it modern and dynamic so that it

stood out on the shelf," says managing director, Andy Cole.
WHAT THEY DID: The can was redesigned to give it authority. The pale green colour was replaced with a striking dark green and gold. The new and higher alcohol content was

shown in red along the neck of the can.
THE RESULT: Sales increased by 160 per cent in the first six months to £35million, making it the best seller. Carlsberg is still among the top five selling lagers.
DESIGN CONSULTANTS: Lawson Marshall Cole.

Probably
THE BEST FACELIFT IN THE WORLD

BA cuts routes, capacity and jobs as profits slump by £116m

BRITISH AIRWAYS today revealed an 84 per cent slump in pre-tax profits for the three months to end-June and said it would stop flying on unprofitable routes and cut its capacity by 12 per cent over the next three years.

Pre-tax profits slumped by £116 million, from £139 million to £23 million, excluding exceptional gains of £177 million largely from the sale of BA's remaining shares in the Galileo ticketing business.

Chief executive Bob Ayling refused to say whether BA would make a profit for the year as a whole, describing the immediate future as "very difficult to call". He accused competitors, particularly on transatlantic routes, of offering "mind-boggling" deals because of overcapacity.

Daily Mail, 9.8.1999

SUNDAY MIRROR, June 13, 1999

Return food to M&S if you don't want it
STORE'S NEW BID TO WOO BACK LOST CUSTOMERS

FRESH CAULIFLOWER CHEESE

IT'S every shopper's worst nightmare. You arrive home with a load of groceries to find your children have turned vegetarian, your husband has decided he hates French wine and even Rover is turning his nose up at your choice of dog food.

But at least shoppers at Marks and Spencer won't find themselves out of pocket. As part of a drive to reverse a £500million plunge in profits, the store is extending its no-quibble refund policy on clothes to cover groceries too.

Shoppers will get their money back on any food item...and they won't have to give a reason.

The goods will be destroyed, given to charity or passed to staff.

"There is no way we could put returned goods back on the shelves," said M&S spokesman Sue Sadler. "Once they have left the shop we cannot guarantee what has happened to them.

"But this policy will reinforce our reputation for providing the best possible customer care."

On Digital steps up subscriber battle

The gloves came off in the battle for digital television subscribers as On Digital, the group owned by two ITV companies, announced a large subsidy of the equipment needed to receive the new channels.

On Digital, the 30-channel terrestrial service owned by Carlton Communications

and Granada Group, said that from Friday it would give subscribers free digital set-top boxes, worth £200. This matches an offer announced three weeks ago by British Sky Broadcasting, the satellite company. BSkyB launched 140 digital channels last year.

Financial Times 25.5.1999

To achieve their business aims organizations will try to:

- **sell more of their products than competing businesses**
- **improve their existing products and services over their rivals**
- **produce a new product or service that consumers will want**
- **improve customer service levels over those of rival businesses**

Selling more than a business rival

Particular business objectives may affect different parts of the business. For example, in aiming to sell more of a product or service than a competitor, a firm may need to develop a new marketing strategy and advertising campaign to make their good or service appear to be more attractive. This will involve extra work for people employed in the marketing and sales department of that firm. Business profits may fall at first because advertising can be very expensive and will increase business costs. The price of the products may also be reduced below the selling price of the rival firm's product to attract more consumers to buy it. However, if this strategy works, sales and profits will begin to rise but only if the production department can produce enough to meet increased demand. A firm may need to buy more machinery, hire more workers, and even move into larger premises to expand production. It may even consider moving overseas if workers and premises are much cheaper there.

A firm that is able to out sell all its rivals may eventually dominate the market supply of the product. It may become so big and powerful that it can cut prices below the production costs of rival firms and drive them out of business. If a particular product is available from only one supplier, that firm is called a **monopoly**. For example, Railtrack is the monopoly supplier of railway lines in the UK. Rail operators, such as Virgin Trains and Silverlink, have to pay Railtrack to run trains on their tracks. Railtrack may be tempted to use its monopoly power to make rail operators pay very high charges for the use of their railway lines but is prevented from doing so by the Government who employs a Rail Regulator to agree with Railtrack what are reasonable charges. Railtrack can be fined if it is found to be using its powerful market position to overcharge. The same goes for any powerful firms who try to overcharge their customers because of their dominant position over the supply of a particular good or service.

Developing an existing product or service

A Charity might redesign it's promotions to attract people to make more donations or buy their charity cards and other gifts. Similarly, a business might attempt to increase sales and profits by redesigning an existing good or service to make it more attractive to consumers than rival goods and services. This could involve expensive research to find out the improvements consumers want and then working on alternative designs that meet their wants. This work will require additional resources from the marketing and the research and development areas of the business. It is important to pick a good or service for which the market is expanding. More opportunities for business organizations exist in expanding markets. Market research can help to identify which these are (see chapter 2).

▼ *Developing existing products to keep up with changing consumer wants can give old products a new lease of life and increase their sales*

An expanding market will not make a business a success, but you will have a better chance of doing well if demand for your chosen good or service is growing.

Once a business has decided which good or service to produce, it must then decide to improve on what is already on offer, so that it can attract customers away from rival firms. Factors which will influence consumers to buy include:

- product quality
- product appearance (size, shape, colour, texture, taste, smell, labelling, incorporated technology, etc.)
- product image (often created by advertising)
- price
- where the product is sold
- delivery times
- after-sales service

Remember that rival firms are also likely to be re-designing their goods or services as materials improve, technology advances, and consumers' tastes change. Old products may even be given a new lease of life in the market simply by designing new packaging and advertisements just as Carlsberg lager was in the article in activity 1.8.

Producing a new product or service

Alternatively a business might think of an entirely new good or service that no other firm makes, for which there is a **gap in the market**.

Many of the products we take for granted today started as the innovations of private individuals. For example, Percy Shaw became a multi-millionaire after inventing 'cat's-eyes' for roads. The idea came to him after seeing his car headlights reflected in broken glass. Swedish brothers Gad and Hans Rausing made £5.2 billion from their simple invention, the TetraPak Milk Carton. Similarly, Sony filled a gap in the market for 'music on the move' by inventing the Walkman.

As long as consumers want or need the new product, a business could be a success by being the first producer in the new market. The business might even advertise heavily to create an attractive image for the product so that consumers will want it.

▼ *Businesses can improve on existing products, or produce entirely new goods or services?*

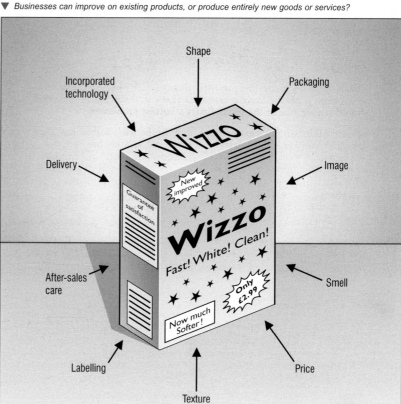

Some recent product developments

- Unpacking your shopping trolley at a supermarket checkout could soon become a thing of the past thanks to the new Supertag technology developed by the British-based computer firm ICL. Simply wheel your shopping trolley through an electronic arch and it will automatically add up your bill from barcodes printed on packaging.

- Video phones allow telephone users to see each other as they speak. Sound and pictures from a tiny camera in the video phone are converted into signals which can be sent in an instant over telephone lines to another video phone which then displays the video picture. Just don't use it in the bath!

- Microsurgery using optical fibre and laser technology is now possible. Large incisions into people's bodies are no longer necessary for many operations. Doctors are able to look inside people's bodies using fibre optic cables linked to monitor screens and use lasers to cut instead of scalpels and knives.

- The UK will have up to 100 or more TV channels using digital technology. Digital television can produce high-quality sound and pictures in wide screen format and link into the internet. Also, large flat screen 'Plasma' TVs are so thin they can be hung like a picture on a wall.

- Others; smart table clothes that know when to heat up to keep food warm; central heating boilers, garden sprinkler systems and other appliances that can receive instructions to turn on or off from electronic mail messages sent from a computer; voice-activated mobile phones as small as tie clips; DVD video and audio discs carrying digital quality sound and pictures.

1. How did Mattel develop the Barbie product in order to make more sales and reflect the changing tastes of consumers?

2. Can you think of any other products which have been 'kept alive' by regular changes in their design or advertising? In groups, discuss and make a list describing how each product and/or its advertising has changed over time.

All dolled up

Toys are a changing business in which last year's hit often becomes this year's turkey. All the more remarkable that a doll created in the 1950s should remain one of the toy industry's hottest properties.

Barbie, the world's best-selling doll, celebrates her 35th birthday at this month's New York toy fair, having sold 775 million of herself worldwide. There are few signs that she has reached maturity. Sales of Barbie and her accessories have more than doubled in the past five years, to more than $1 billion in 1993. Barbie has helped to make her owner Mattel, into America's biggest toy maker.

Barbie's secret according to John Amerman, Chairman of Mattel is that the product is regularly changed and freshened.' Barbie has been kitted out as a teacher, a doctor, a horsewoman, even a Presidential candidate. Barbie accessories include Ken, Barbie's partner, and a growing number of friends of different races. The latest success is a Barbie with floor-length hair that turns pink when sprayed with water.

These spin-offs mean that the average American girl owns eight Barbie dolls and buys two or three new ones every year.

The Economist 15.2.94

Improving customer services

A simple rule in business is that good products do not sell themselves. Only good products, with good customer service and marketing, sell. An organization that fails to provide good customer service could end up spending more effort and money dealing with customer complaints than selling goods and services. Its customers will be lost to organizations that can keep their customers happy.

Today, simply producing a good or service to sell to consumers is not enough to persuade them to buy. Suppose you are about to buy a new DVD player costing £400. Would you go ahead if you couldn't exchange it for another one if it was faulty, or couldn't have it repaired if it went wrong?

Consumers need to be confident that, if they change their mind, or if the products they have purchased are not satisfactory or need to be repaired at a later date, the firm will provide refunds, exchange faulty goods, and provide or arrange repairs with the minimum of fuss. These and other **customer services** are vital to the success of any organization selling goods or services to consumers.

Customer services provided by firms will include:

- Providing information and advice on goods and services

- Giving refunds and replacements

- After-sales care

- Catering for customers with special needs, for example, by providing wheelchair ramps

- Fast and reliable delivery service

Improving these services and persuading customers that they are better than other firms will attract custom, help increase market share, and boost sales revenues and profits.

In many organizations, customer surveys may reveal areas in which customer service needs to be improved. However, even if customer surveys suggest that customers are happy with the service they receive, improvements can and should still be made wherever possible. This is because:

- Not all customers will have participated in a survey of their opinions on service.

- Any organization that is in competition with other firms for customers must try to stay ahead of its rivals as they improve their services.

- Customers needs in terms of service are always changing. In general, customers are becoming more and more critical about the way they are treated by organizations.

Improvements to customer services can be made in many areas of business.

- **Reliability:** An organization that cannot be relied upon or trusted to provide goods or services that are of a high standard will fail to attract new customers or retain existing ones. Reliability is important to both individual and business customers. Goods and services should be reliable, and standards of customer service should be high. Agreed delivery times should be met, repairs carried out quickly, and complaints dealt with efficiently and promptly.

▼ An organization can improve its image and boost sales by providing good customer service.

Improving reliability – some suggestions

When looking at improving reliability, it is important to look at both the product and the service given.

Improvements in customer service may be achieved by more staff training in different aspects of customer care. Treating your staff better is often the best way to get them to treat customers better.

Improvements in the quality of the product may be achieved by contacting suppliers and providing them with information on the problems and faults experienced by sales staff, as well as customers. The supplier may then look at redesigning the product to correct the fault.

Reliability is also important when buying a service. A decorator who drops paint on your carpet, a financial adviser who loses your money, or a garage that fails to repair your car properly or overcharges you, are not providing a reliable service.

Each month, the Consumers' Association magazine *Which?* publishes reports on the reliability and other features of different goods and services. Consumers can study these reports before deciding where and what to buy.

Portfolio Activity 1.10

1. Why could the organizations featured in the article be described as 'unreliable'?

2. What could these organizations do to improve the reliability of their services?

TYRE FIRMS ARE PULLING A FAST ONE

MIRROR CONSUMER SPECIAL

DRIVERS risk getting dangerous advice on brakes and tyres at fast-fit centres, a damning report reveals today.

Six out of ten centres failed to spot all the brake defects on a car used in a secret survey.

And five out of six didn't look at the spare tyre, which had a deep cut capable of causing a blow-out at high-speed. The report in the consumer magazine Which?, follows a survey of 147 branches of Britain's eight leading fast-fit giants.

The eight firms involved in the ten-week survey were Halfords, Kwik-Fit, National Tyres and Autocare, Smiley Tyre and Exhaust Centrers, Charlie Browns, ATS and Hi-Q.

Halfords came top for both tyre AND brake advice. Charlie Browns were worst on tyres and often missed brake defects.

Daily Mirror 7.9.1995

● **Friendliness** is important to customers when making a purchase. They want to feel that their custom is valued, and that they are getting good advice and attention. Unfortunately, the trend towards bigger stores and quicker service has meant friendliness has been lost in some cases, and staff can seem abrupt because they are concentrating on speed of service.

Many stores are now retraining staff in how to be friendly towards their customers and serve them efficiently. Simple things like smiling and saying 'Hello' or 'Good morning', making eye-contact, saying 'Thank you' and 'Goodbye', can all help to make a good impression and encourage the customer to come back in future. However, staff who try to be too friendly can put off customers just as much as those who are too abrupt.

▼ *Over-friendly*

▼ *Too abrupt*

▼ *Just right*

● **Availability of goods and services:** No organization can stock everything that customers want. Many specialize in providing a narrow range of goods and services. For example, an electrical shop will concentrate on the supply of home appliances, such as microwaves, video recorders, and washing machines. However, nothing is more frustrating than to find out that a store does not have the item that you want. It is even worse if you telephoned first and were told that the goods were in stock.

Many large stores now have computerized stock control systems linked to bar code readers at the till. The bar code readers scan every item leaving the shop and automatically update the central stock records, so that at any moment the computer has a complete record of what is available in the store. In the most advanced systems used by large supermarkets, the computer is set to automatically generate an order for new stock when stocks fall to a certain level.

Sometimes consumers require a very wide range of goods and services. In this case it is important for an organization to operate a fast ordering and delivery service. However, it is pointless pretending to a consumer that a product can be obtained in a few days if it cannot.

Improving the availability of goods and services – some suggestions

There is no point trying to stock everything customers want. First, it would tie too much money up in stocks, some of which may remain unsold. Secondly, storage would take up too much space.

Some firms may successfully expand into other products in an attempt to offer customers more choice. For example, many Esso petrol stations also offer on-site supermarkets, and Blockbuster Video rent and sell computer games, soft drinks, crisps, and sweets, as well as hiring videos. However, before a business makes this decision it will need to use market research to find out more about what their customers want.

If an ordering and delivery service is introduced, it is important that it is simple for customers to use, and that sales staff are honest about how long products will take to be delivered.

- **Speed of delivery:** The time taken between a good or service being ordered and delivery is called the **delivery lead time**. There is increasing pressure on suppliers from their individual and business customers to reduce lead times. It is frustrating to wait a long time for something you have ordered to be delivered. A firm that is able to guarantee a short lead time between receiving an order and making delivery is likely to gain more customers than slower rivals.

Lead times will often depend on the type of good or service being supplied. For example, highly specialized items like hand-crafted furniture or industrial robots are likely to be made to order, and cannot simply be supplied from stock kept in a warehouse. Customers ordering a new Rolls-Royce will have to wait around two years for it to be delivered!

Business customers will often rely on delivery lead times being as short as possible. This is because many now operate Just In Time systems, where materials needed for production are ordered and delivered 'just in time' for them to be used. In this way, firms can keep their stocks of raw materials and components to a minimum to reduce storage costs.

Improving the speed of delivery – some suggestions

A business should always be honest with customers about expected delivery times. If delivery is delayed, the customer should be contacted in good time and alternative arrangements made. It is very annoying to wait for a delivery that never arrives!

The speed of delivery often depends on the time it takes for the supplier to process an order. Taking orders and receiving payment confirmation by phone, fax, or over computer links, can speed up the rate at which orders are turned around. Some organizations are even able to promise next-day delivery from their central warehouses, or a 24-hour emergency call-out service for service providers, such as car mechanics and plumbers, for an additional charge.

Delivery times may also be improved by changing the method used to deliver items – for example, using special delivery and courier services rather than first- or second-class post. Delivery by road may also be improved by planning in advance the best route to take. New technology such as routemaster programs can help drivers plan the most direct routes and warn them of any congestion along the way.

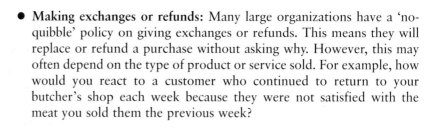

- **Making exchanges or refunds:** Many large organizations have a 'no-quibble' policy on giving exchanges or refunds. This means they will replace or refund a purchase without asking why. However, this may often depend on the type of product or service sold. For example, how would you react to a customer who continued to return to your butcher's shop each week because they were not satisfied with the meat you sold them the previous week?

- **Access to buildings:** Most of us take access to buildings for granted. We have little difficulty in entering, moving around, and leaving shops, cinemas, pubs, and other places. However, elderly people, parents with prams and pushchairs, and people who are blind, deaf, or disabled can find it very difficult to gain access to buildings and transport. The provision of ramps, lifts, and clear signs would help these people enter and move around buildings more easily. These facilities are an important aspect of customer care, and by providing them, firms can attract a whole range of potential new customers.

Improving access to buildings – some suggestions

Many people still have problems gaining access to buildings and different modes of transport. An organization may improve the accessibility of their premises and services by providing the following features:

- Ramps for wheelchairs and pushchairs that are neither too steep or too long

- Installing automatic doors to replace old or heavy doors that may be difficult to open

- Providing wide lifts and toilets for people in wheelchairs

- Signposting the layout of facilities in business premises

- Installing voice synthesizers in lifts to give details of floor numbers and warnings to stand clear of the doors

- Providing staff to help customers pack and carry their shopping and open doors for them

Many of these features can be 'designed into' new premises with ease. However, it may be more difficult adding them to old buildings.

Customer safety: Firms need to be aware of the safety of their customers when they visit their premises and when they purchase and use their products.

Firms are required by law to ensure customer safety at all times (see chapter 7). The safety of visitors, workers, and customers on business premises is covered by the Health and Safety at Work Act. Product safety is covered by the Consumer Protection Act and the Sale of Goods Act.

It is not enough for an organization simply to warn customers about risks to their safety. For example, notices on fairground rides saying that 'riders ride at their own risk' have no meaning in law. If someone is injured while using the ride, the fairground is still liable. All firms are required to accept responsibility for the safety of their customers, and to abide by the legal health and safety regulations – whatever the signs may say.

Injuries suffered by customers on business premises or through using a product can mean bad publicity for the firm, and many customers may be put off using them again. The injured customer may also start legal action, which could cost the organization a lot of money. Good customer safety is, therefore, an important aspect of customer service.

Improving customer safety – some suggestions

Product safety is an important issue for people who design and manufacture goods. For example, paints, dyes, and materials should be non-toxic; sharp edges should be removed; electrical appliances should have cut-outs if they overheat, and be earthed so that they do not give electric shocks. Products that comply with quality and safety standards set by the British Standards Institution will be awarded a kitemark to prove they are safe.

Improvements to customer safety on business premises may be made by regularly checking on health and safety practices and taking action where necessary. Key questions to ask include:

- Are warning notices displayed in prominent places for fire and other hazards?

- Are the signs clear?

- Would staff be able to evacuate customers quickly?

- Are staff trained in safety and First Aid procedures?

- Are there First Aid kits nearby?

- Are there any obvious hazards like boxes or other obstacles blocking fire exits?

- Are fire exits open or locked? s.

Portfolio Activity 1.11

The following tasks can be carried out in small groups or individually.

1. Investigate customer service in an organization of your choice.

   a Draw up a checklist of features of customer service you wish to investigate under each of the following headings:
   - Reliability
   - Friendliness
   - Availability of goods and services
   - Speed of delivery
   - Giving exchanges and refunds
   - Access to buildings
   - Care for the environment
   - Customer safety

   b If possible, visit your chosen organization as an 'undercover customer'. Make notes of your first-hand experiences on all the different aspects of customer service you listed in Task 1a.

   c Arrange to visit the organization with the business owners or managers in order to investigate the provision of customer service. During your visit, ask if you can interview a senior manager in order to find out:

   i How customer satisfaction is monitored

   ii What improvements to customer service the organization has introduced over the last few years.

   d Use your notes and a word processor to write up the first part of a short report on your findings. This should include descriptions of:
   - The organization and its activities
   - Customer services provided by the organization
   - How it monitors customer satisfaction

   You may also include evidence of customer satisfaction you have picked up from informal conversations with customers of the organization, and from your first-hand experience as an undercover customer.

2. a Prepare notes on:

   i How you think your chosen organization could improve its customer services in three of the key areas listed in Task 1a

   ii How the improvements to customer service you recommend could help to:
   - Attract more customers
   - Increase customer satisfaction
   - Secure customer loyalty
   - Enhance the image of the organization

   b Use your notes to complete the second part of the report you started in Task 1d. This should include your recommendations for customer service improvements and what you hope they will achieve.

How meeting business objectives can affect the firm

In all the examples above, money may be needed to pay for the additional work required. The money will have to come either from inside the business (from profits or by cutting back costs on other activities) or from outside the business (from business owners, banks or other lenders). It is the job of the Finance Department to raise the necessary finance for the business and the Accounts Department to record all the additional costs and sales revenues. Because more labour may be required, or workers with new skills, the Human Resources Department will also need to be involved. It will arrange job adverts, recruitment interviews and training programmes. This will be financed from the Finance Department and the Accounts department will arrange the payment of wages.

The next chapter looks in more detail at the organisation and work of the different functional areas or departments in a business.

▼ How a decision to make and sell a new product can affect all areas of a business

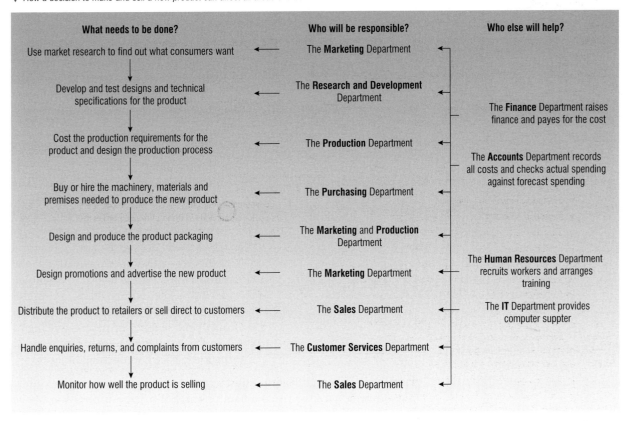

What needs to be done?	Who will be responsible?	Who else will help?
Use market research to find out what consumers want	The **Marketing** Department	
↓		
Develop and test designs and technical specifications for the product	The **Research and Development** Department	
		The **Finance** Department raises finance and payes for the cost
Cost the production requirements for the product and design the production process	The **Production** Department	
↓		The **Accounts** Department records all costs and checks actual spending against forecast spending
Buy or hire the machinery, materials and premises needed to produce the new product	The **Purchasing** Department	
↓		
Design and produce the product packaging	The **Marketing** and **Production** Department	
↓		The **Human Resources** Department recruits workers and arranges training
Design promotions and advertise the new product	The **Marketing** Department	
↓		The **IT** Department provides computer suppter
Distribute the product to retailers or sell direct to customers	The **Sales** Department	
↓		
Handle enquiries, returns, and complaints from customers	The **Customer Services** Department	
↓		
Monitor how well the product is selling	The **Sales** Department	

Section **1.5**

Evaluating business performance

Once a business sets its aims and objectives it needs to be able to measure how successful it has been at achieving them. For example, if Ford plc aims to increase profits by 10% by designing new features into their existing range of cars to increase their appeal and sales to younger drivers, then the company needs to be able to measure how successful it has been at doing so. If the company finds that it has not been as successful as it would like, it will need to reconsider its objectives and perhaps alter them to focus on selling cars to older people or alternatively change its advertising and marketing strategy.

Business performance can be evaluated by comparing business targets, for example, to increase sales or profits by a certain amount, with what actually does happen – for example, by

● **monitoring numbers of customers**

● **monitoring sales values and volumes**

● **monitoring repeat sales**

● **monitoring financial budgets**

▼ *Figure 1.2: Incoming vehicle movements at a London supermarket*

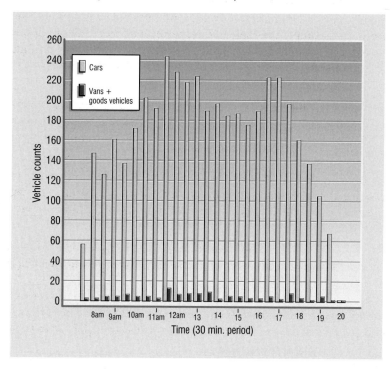

Monitoring the numbers of customers

An easy way to measure customers' liking of a business is simply to count the number of customers contacting or visiting it over a period of time. If customers are not satisfied with the service they receive, this will be reflected in low and falling customer numbers.

For example, Figure 1.2 shows the number of cars entering the car park of a large supermarket in London at different times of the day. The information was collected by placing an electronic sensor on the entrance road to the store. Every time a car drove over the sensor, a signal was sent to a computer which then added up the number of vehicles in every 30-minute period. The information is useful because it not only tells the supermarket about the number of people wishing to use the store, but can help it to plan car parking space and opening times.

People may contact or visit a business to make an enquiry, order or buy a good or service, or to complain. Clearly, if a large proportion of the people contacting or visiting a firm wish to complain, this is a good indicator of a low level of customer service. If a large number of people enquire about products but do not buy them, this might also indicate that sales staff are providing poor levels of service and are putting people off. On the other hand, if a large proportion of enquiries are converted into sales, then this indicates that sales staff are providing a high level of customer service.

When monitoring numbers of customers it may be useful to sort them into categories, for example, age, gender, marital status, etc. A clothes store could monitor the number of people of different ages entering to browse. If they found that an increasing number of older people were visiting the store, they could then change their product lines away from young fashions.

It is also useful to monitor the time of day at which customers contact or visit an organization. Extra staff cover can then be provided at peak times. For example, a bus company could monitor the number of passengers boarding and getting off different buses at different stops. This information would help the company to plan new bus routes and service frequencies at different times of the day.

Retail surveillance cameras are being used more and more by large retail organizations to count the number of customers in their shops and stores. Filming customers also allows stores to pinpoint customer reaction to staff, layout, new products, prices, and promotions.

Monitoring sales values and volumes

An organization can monitor sales values and sales volumes or both. The **value** of sales is simply the total amount of revenue from sales of goods and/or services. The **volume** of sales is the number of goods sold or units of service provided – for example, the number of haircuts given, cars cleaned, or mortgages confirmed.

If sales increase, this either means that existing customers are buying more, or that new customers are buying, or both. Rising sales provide a good indication that customers are happy with the service they are getting.

An important factor in obtaining a rising level of sales is the ability to persuade customers who enquire about products to buy them. This can be achieved by giving sales staff professional training in customer service techniques.

Sales may also increase due to special promotions or price reductions or display a seasonal pattern. For example, the sale of suntan lotions and ice cream rises during the summer. Toy purchases rise prior to Christmas. In fact, retail sales of all consumer goods and services peak in December every year. It is, therefore, important to compare sales in one period with the same period in the previous year to see if sales are higher or lower.

▼ Repeat sales can be monitored from customer orders, membership cards, and debit card sales.

Monitoring repeat sales

Finding out if the same customers are returning time after time to the same organization to buy goods and services can be difficult. For example, it is impossible to trace the sale of goods over the counter for cash unless customers are asked to give their names. This takes time, and some customers may not want to give details.

However, repeat purchases by customers who order and buy on credit are much easier to trace because their name and address are supplied with their payment details. These customers will include business customers placing orders with their suppliers, and individual customers who may telephone or post their orders through to mail order companies.

This form of monitoring is likely to increase with the introduction of 'home shopping' which will allow users to order goods and services direct by linking their personal computers to the telephone network via a modem (see chapter 5).

Some firms are also able to track repeat purchases by issuing membership cards to customers. Examples include Blockbuster Video, and 'loyalty bonus' cards like the Clubcard scheme introduced by Tesco. These cards contain details of the customer's name and address which can be read and stored by electronic tills.

Monitoring financial budgets

Each year business managers set financial targets for their firms to work towards. For example, a business might aim to expand production by 10%, increase market share by 5%, and/or raise profits by 20%.

▼ *Planning ahead is vital to the success of a business.*

Agreed business targets can effect future spending and revenues. For example, a firm that wants to increase production by 10% will need to buy more materials, use more power, and perhaps employ more workers and machinery. This means more money has to be spent. However, the firm will also have more goods or services to sell and so can earn more revenue.

Plans for spending and revenues linked to business targets are set out in a **budget**. A budget is simply a financial plan for the future prepared by business managers. Most budgets are for 12 months ahead, but some budget plans are drawn up for longer periods. For example, research and development may involve spending large amounts of money over many years.

The preparation of budgets is known as **budgeting**. This is a very important task for any business and is usually undertaken by the Finance Department (see chapters 2 and 8). By planning ahead a firm can make sure it has enough money in the future, by retaining profits from previous years, or by arranging loans from banks and other lenders.

In the same way, the UK Government prepares a budget at the end of every November for the whole economy. This is a statement of planned public spending and expected tax revenues for the coming financial year (see chapter 6).

Preparing budgets

The preparation of budgets is an important aspect of business planning. Budgets will help an organization to:

- **Examine alternative courses of action.** For example, identifying the costs and benefits of using more workers to raise output, buying new machinery, moving to new premises, using different materials, introducing computerized accounting systems, etc.

- **Examine the impact of unforeseen changes on the business.** For example, what will be the effect of rising prices, higher wage demands, falling consumer demand, etc.

- **Present information on incomes, expenditures, and expected profits** to potential lenders to raise finance.

- **Monitor business performance** by comparing actual results with plans

Drawing up a budget involves a number of steps. These are illustrated in Figure 1.3.

▼ Figure 1.3: Preparing a budget

SET AIMS AND OBJECTIVES

GATHER INFORMATION

PREPARE SALES AND PRODUCTION BUDGETS

PREPARE ALL OTHER OPERATING BUDGETS

PRODUCE MASTER BUDGET

Stage 1: Decide upon a budget period. Most budgets are produced annually. It is usual for an annual budget to be broken down into plans for each quarter or month.

Stage 2: Agree business objectives and set targets. In a large organization individual targets will be agreed for each factory or office, or each department, area, or product. Targets should be realistic: a firm that sets out to increase market share by 50% in three months is unlikely ever to achieve its target.

Stage 3: Obtain information on which to base budgets. For example, past information on costs and revenues, or new information from market research and quotes from suppliers.

Stage 4: Based on targets agreed, the business must now prepare key operating budgets for sales and production:

- The **sales budget** shows planned revenues the firm hopes to achieve each month. This is calculated by multiplying predicted sales volumes by the product prices the firm hopes to achieve.

- The **production budget** shows the amount of materials, labour hours, and machine hours needed to meet sales targets.

Stage 5: Based on the sales and production budgets, the next step is to prepare operating budgets for:

- labour

- materials

- capital, i.e. assets such as premises, machinery, vehicles, and other equipment

- overheads, i.e. administration, telephone, postage, heating and lighting, etc.

- inflows of cash from sales and outflows of cash to pay bills

- and all other items that give rise to expenditure or revenues

Stage 6: Draw up the master budget. This is a summary of all the incomes and expenditures identified in the operating budgets. It also shows expected profit.

Figure 1.4 shows a simple master budget prepared for a manufacturer of luxury chocolate bars for the first six months of the year (cash inflows and outflows are not shown). The target is to expand output by 20% by June. To do this, the owners have calculated they will need to expand the premises, buy new machinery, and take on extra staff. There will also be a need for more materials, power, and administration, etc. The simple master budget in Figure 1.4 lists all the revenues and costs expected from the business expansion. At the end of six months, the owners calculate that their plans will have resulted in an accumulated surplus revenue of £354,150. If at the end of the six-month period they find they have failed to achieve this, they can start to investigate why and make sure they do not make the same mistakes again. For example, they may have underestimated the cost of buying the extra machinery they needed, or overestimated the strength of consumer demand.

▼ Figure 1.4: An example of a master budget

	January	February	March	April	May	June
Output	100,000	100,000	105,000	110,000	115,000	120,000
Materials	£1,000	£1,000	£1,050	£1,100	£1,150	£1,200
Wages	£30,000	£32,000	£34,000	£35,000	£35,000	£35,000
Capital (premises, machinery, etc.)	–	–	£42,000	£28,000	£7,500	
Overheads	£7,000	£7,000	£7,300	£7,500	£7,500	£7,500
All other costs	£2,000	£2,000	£2,000	£2,000	£2,100	£2,200
Total expenditure	**£40,000**	**£42,000**	**£86,350**	**£73,600**	**£53,250**	**£45,900**
Unit price	£0.90	£1.10	£1.10	£1.25	£1.00	£1.00
Sales volumes	90,000	95,000	110,000	135,000	110,000	110,000
Sales revenues	**£81,000**	**£104,500**	**£121,000**	**£168,750**	**£110,000**	**£110,000**
Surplus(+)/Deficit (–)	**+£41,000**	**+£62,500**	**+£34,650**	**+£95,150**	**+£56,750**	**+£64,100**
Cumulative surplus/deficit	**+£41,000**	**+£103,500**	**+£138,150**	**+£233,300**	**+£290,050**	**+£354,150**

Monitoring budgets

If a business is to be successful it must always be aware of how well it is performing and its financial position. This can be done by comparing actual results with budget plans. **Budgetary control** is the process of setting targets, preparing budget plans, monitoring those plans, and then investigating why actual results may differ from what had been planned for.

A business that is **underperforming** is one that has not achieved its targets. Output and revenues may be lower than expected, and/or costs higher. In this case the financial position of the business will be getting worse because spending and revenues are not going according to plan. The firm may even run out of cash to pay its bills.

For example, consider the firm producing chocolate bars. In Figure 1.5 the managers of the business have plotted figures on sales from the master budget in Figure 1.4, against actual sales. Clearly, sales have not performed as well as planned, especially during April when sales are expected to be higher over the Easter period. Knowing this, managers may decide to cut product prices and/or launch a new advertising

Figure 1.5: Sales of chocolate bars, January-June

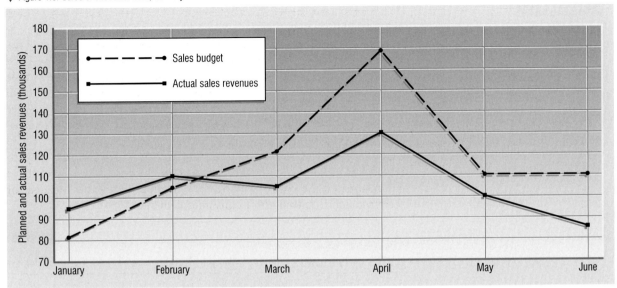

campaign in an attempt to raise sales of their chocolate bars. In addition, cutting the number of people employed and introducing new equipment could reduce costs so that profit targets are met.

A business that is **overperforming** is one that has achieved more than it had planned. Output and revenues will be more than expected, and/or spending less than had been budgeted for. The financial position of the business will be improving.

Portfolio Activity 1.12

The production budget for the first six months of the new tax year for a firm that assembles television sets is shown in the table opposite. The production budget gives details of planned outputs each month and the amount of materials, labour, and machine hours needed to produce the planned output. The production of each TV requires the following inputs:

– 2 units of materials

– 30 minutes of labour time

– 45 minutes of machine time

The next stage will be to work out how much the inputs of materials, labour, and machines will cost.

The table also shows what was actually produced each month. As you can see, things did not quite go according to plan.

1. Suggest what information the production budget may have been based on.

2. Calculate the difference between actual output and planned output each month. Is the firm under- or overperforming?

3. Explain what might have caused the large differences between planned and actual output.

Month	Planned output (TVs)	Planned materials hours	Planned labour hours	Planned machine hours	Actual output
April	1,000	2,000	500	750	800
May	1,000	2,000	500	750	910
June	1,200	2,400	600	900	1,150
July	1,500	3,000	750	1,125	1,400
August	1,500	3,000	750	1,125	1,700
September	1,300	2,600	650	975	1,500

4. Why is this information useful to business managers?

5. Suggest how the following events could affect the difference between planned and actual output in a firm:

● suppliers fail to deliver materials on time

● a strike by workers

● a power failure

● workers agree to work more overtime

● a flu outbreak among workers

Key words

Write down definitions and explanations of the following key words and terms to help you remember the things you learnt in this chapter.

Consumers	Demand	Consumer goods	Business objectives
Production	Expanding market	Durable goods	Monopoly
Producers	Contracting market	Non-durable goods	Public services
Inputs	Market share	Services	Private sector
Outputs	Profit/loss	Market	Public sector
Firms	Business aims	Domestic markets	Budgeting
Suppliers	Charities	International markets	Budgetary control
Business	Voluntary sector	Consumer needs and wants	Underperforming
Chain of productive activity	Customer service	Advertising	Overperforming

Test your knowledge

1 Which of the following is a non-durable good?
   A computer
   B office stationery
   C fax machine
   D telephone answering machine

2 Which of these is a consumer durable?
   A a motorcycle
   B a newspaper
   C food
   D soap

3 A private sector business is likely to have as a primary aim:
   A making as much profit as possible
   B increasing sales
   C being the best known product
   D having the greatest range of products on the market?

4 Before a business aims to enter a new market it is most likely to:
   A make more of its existing products
   B stop advertising
   C undertake market research to find out what consumers want
   D produce as much as it can of the new product?

5 A US-owned supermarket discount store has recently opened in the UK. In the first year of operation its main business aim is likely to be:
   A to gain market share
   B to reduce costs
   C to improve product quality
   D to maximize profits

6 What is the most likely aim of a small local grocers?
   A to get well-known among customers
   B to sell the best quality groceries
   C to try to survive competition from large supermarkets
   D to sell as many groceries as possible

7 What is likely to be the main aim of a government-owned organization?
   A to provide a service to the public
   B to grow as quickly as possible
   C to provide competition for private firms
   D to make as much profit as possible

Questions **8–10** share the following answer options:
A the speed of delivery
B friendliness
C customer safety
D the availability of goods and services

The following are extracts from customer complaints received by different business organizations. Which of the above aspects of customer service do you think need to be improved in each case?

8 'I sustained severe bruising to my left leg after I slipped on your highly polished floor'.

9 'Your member of staff then told me I would have to wait to be served until after he had finished his conversation with his friend'.

10 'On the phone a member of your sales staff told me the item I wanted was in stock. An hour later I arrived at your shop only to be told the item was sold out some days ago'.

11 Which of the following is unlikely to improve customer service in an organization?
A installing ramps for wheelchairs and prams
B reducing the range and amount of different goods for sale held in stock
C reducing the lead time between receiving an customers order and making delivery
D introducing more recycling facilities

12 A firm's market share is measured by the
A amount of product that it makes
B sales of its product
C product quality
D cost of its product?

13 The owner of a computer games shop finds that she is selling more games on CD than on cassette. What is the most likely reason for this?
A the market for games is expanding
B CDs take up less storage space
C CDs are cheaper than tapes
D the market for games is contracting

14 The UK firm XYZ Ltd has just opened new factories in Malaysia and China. What does this suggest about the type of market the business sells products to?
A it is a local market
B it is a domestic market
C it is a European market
D it is an international market

15 A large bakery making thousands of bread and cake products each week is experiencing a fall in sales and profits, yet its main rival in business is booming.
a What do you think the main business aim of the bakery is?
b What would you advise the bakery to do to try to restore sales and profits.
c Explain the reasons for the objectives you advised in **b** and the functional areas of the business are likely to be affected by them.
d How could the bakery check if the things you have advised it to do are working?

16 a Give three reasons why good customer service is important in business organisations?
b Write a short paragraph to show what you understand about each of the following aims of business activities:
   ● making a profit
   ● increasing market share
   ● increasing sales
   ● providing a public service
   ● business survival

chapter 2 *Inside a business*

What you need to learn

To make goods and/or provide services a business has to carry out a range of functions including **research and development, purchasing, production, marketing and sales, customer service, finance, administration, and human resources.**

Businesses organize their different functional areas in the best way possible to help them make decisions and carry out tasks to meet aims and objectives. In larger business organisations, staff will carry out these functions in **departments.**

How a business is organised is known as its **organizational structure**. The organisational structure shows all the different department and layers of **management** in the business. You will need to explain differences between a hierarchical business organisation and a flatter one, and understand how they can be shown on **organizational charts**, and how structure can affect communications in the business.

The **Production Department** will make goods or provide services. To do this it will need resources obtained by the purchasing and Human Resources Departments, such as:

- buildings and land – for example, offices, factories, shops and farmland
- equipment – for example, vehicles, computers and machinery
- people – for example, operators, managers, support staff and specialists
- materials – for example, raw materials and components

You will need to find out what kinds of resources business needs for production.

The **Marketing and Sales Departments** find out about customers' wants and then provide for them. Their activities include market research, promotions and sales. You will need to understand what marketing activities are carried out by business and why.

All businesses depend on their customers to buy their goods or use their services. In return customers expect goods and services to be available when they want them, to be safe and reliable, and offer value for money. To keep customers happy, businesses provide a range of **customer services** – for example, **providing information and advice, credit facilities, delivering goods and after-sale care**. You will need to investigate what makes a good-quality customer service

The **Finance and Accounts Department** manages all the money coming into and going out of the business. People who work in finance **prepare accounts, pay wages and salaries and obtain capital and resources for the business**. You will need to understand why and how business deals with financial aspects, and how they affect other functional areas.

Human Resources staff are involved in the **recruitment, retention and dismissal of employees, working conditions, health and safety, training and development**.

The **Administration Department** helps a business run efficiently and effectively from day to day. It carries out a variety of **clerical and maintenance tasks**. You will need to investigate what good administration is and why it is needed in business.

Section **2.1** **Organizational structures**

Organizational structure refers to the way in which a firm organizes its business activities to achieve its business aims and objectives (see chapter 1).

Any business organization, whatever its size, whether in the public or private sector, will need to organize its business activities and the employees who carry them out. Without a clear organizational structure, employees will not know what jobs to do, or what their responsibilities are. It would also be unclear who they should get their orders from, or give orders to.

It is vitally important that everyone in an organization knows exactly what they should be doing and what everybody else does. Unless this is the case, people can waste time trying to find out who can mend their machine, check the accounts, order materials, advertise new products, recruit new staff, and so on. Worse still, if individual employees cannot find the right person to perform a particular task, they may try to do something they are not qualified to do. An organizational structure makes all of these things clear. It will show:

- who does what job

- who is in charge

- who makes the decisions

- who carries out decisions

- how decisions and other information are communicated between employees

How to organize business activities

In any organization it makes sense to group people who do similar tasks together. For example, it would not be sensible for employees in selling and marketing to work with production workers operating noisy machinery. If people are grouped according to the jobs they do, it makes it easier for them to talk to each other about their work, decide who does what and how work should be done, and solve work-related problems. Groups of people organized together to carry out particular business functions, such as production, sales, and accounts, are known as **departments** (see 2.2).

In small organizations, everyone tends to 'muck in', doing whatever is necessary to keep the business running. However, some people in the business will spend more of their time doing some things rather than others, depending on their skills and qualifications. For example, a person with skills in bookkeeping is an obvious choice to keep accounting records. Others may be better employed in production or inselling the firm's products. That is, it makes sense if people in an organization **specialize** in the tasks or jobs they are best able to do. This is called **labour specialization**.

With large numbers of staff it is important that there are some people who can take decisions on who should do what. That is, organizations require **management**. Managers will need to identify the skills of different workers and give them tasks that are suited to them. Managers will also need to check with their staff to make sure tasks are being carried out to the right standard. In very large organizations there may be many different layers of management, each more senior than the one before.

Organization charts

The way in which activities and employees are organized in a business can be shown on an **organization chart**. This will show the relationships between different employees in an organization using lines and arrows. These are the **lines of authority**. Employees at the same level in a chart have the same amount of authority and responsibility over employees placed below them in the chart.

▼ Figure 2.1: An example of an organization chart for a small business

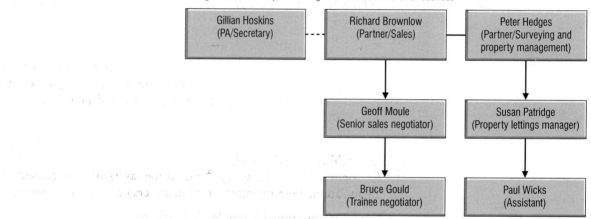

Figure 2.1 shows the organization chart for Brownlow Commercial, a small commercial property sales and management business. Richard Brownlow and Peter Hedges are the partners and senior managers of the business. They both have more authority and responsibility than any employee below them in the chart. They will pass instructions down to employees below them. That is, they will give employees under their command instructions on what jobs they should carry out. This is called **delegation**.

Line managers have the authority to delegate work tasks to the employees under their command. For example, Geoff Moule, the Senior Sales Negotiator in Brownlow Commercial, can delegate work tasks to his assistant. Geoff has the same level of authority as Susan Partridge, the Property Lettings Manager, and therefore appears at the same level in the chart, but he cannot delegate work tasks directly to her assistant, Paul Wicks.

In turn, employees are **accountable** to their line managers. Not only must they report back to them on work completed or any work-related problems, but they must also get their agreement to change their work tasks, take annual leave, etc. From Figure 2.1 it is clear that Bruce Gould is accountable to Geoff Moule who is, in turn, accountable to Richard Brownlow.

Gillian Hoskins is the personal assistant of Richard Brownlow. She is shown as being linked to him by a dotted line. This tells us she only ever reports to Richard Brownlow, but does not have the same level of authority as him despite appearing at the same level.

Portfolio Activity 2.1

1. Draw an organization chart for your school/college.

2. What departments can you identify in the structure?

3. Which employees in the structure have management responsibilities?

4. How many different layers of management are there?

5. Repeat Tasks 1-4 for a small business organization of your choice.

Choosing an organizational structure

Different organizations will be structured in different ways. There is no single 'correct' way to structure an organization. Each organization will choose a structure according to its objectives, and how it proposes to meet them.

Hierarchical organizations

The organizational **hierarchy** refers to the layers of management in an organization, from the most senior managers down to supervisors.

In any organizational hierarchy there will be:

- **A clearly defined management structure.** Everyone will have an official job title and know their precise responsibilities. Each employee only has one immediate line manager to take orders from and report back to.

- **A clearly defined salary scale.** The amount an employee is paid will tend to rise, the higher up the hierarchy they are.

- **Standard rules and procedures** on hours of work, arranging annual leave, job appraisal, promotions, discipline, etc.

- **Agreed rules and guidelines** on dress, arranging business meetings, the layout of business documents such as letters and memos (see chapter 4).

- **Agreed policy** on health and safety, equal opportunities, training, etc.

- **Common standards** of internal customer services (i.e. providing help and support to other parts of the same organization) and external customer services (i.e. to individuals and businesses who buy the goods and services of the organization).

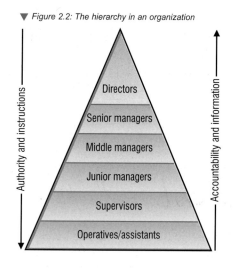

▼ *Figure 2.2: The hierarchy in an organization*

Authority and instructions →

Accountability and information →

- Directors
- Senior managers
- Middle managers
- Junior managers
- Supervisors
- Operatives/assistants

The structure of a **hierarchical organization** looks like a pyramid, as shown in Figure 2.2. It is narrow at the top with a small number of senior managers, wider in the middle to represent a larger number of middle managers, and widest at the bottom, showing a large number of employees who have little or no management responsibilities. These employees are called **operatives** or **assistants**, or are simply known as 'shop floor' workers (see 2.3).

In a large business there may be many management levels. Top management – directors or chief executives – are normally concerned with long-term plans for their business, and seeing that these are carried out. A senior manager will usually be placed in charge of each department, and will take decisions that affect the running of their department. Middle and more junior managers will be expected to put their decisions into practice, organize the day-to-day activities of shop floor workers, and report back on progress.

A clear **chain of command** runs in a line from the top layers of management down through each department in the organization to the 'shop floor'. The higher up a hierarchy, the more authority a manager will have over other employees. Orders are passed down the chain of command while information on which further decisions are based – for example, sales figures, revenues, output, staff turnover, etc. – is passed up the organization to senior managers.

In a small business there are unlikely to be many layers of management. For example, in a small one-person enterprise – a sole trader – the business owner is likely to be both manager and worker, making all the decisions and carrying them out.

The main advantages and disadvantages of having a hierarchical structure in a business organization are:

Advantages

+ Everyone knows what their job role is, who to accept work tasks from, and who to report to.

+ The authority and responsibilities of different employees are clear to all staff.

+ Senior managers are able to make all the decisions and control the whole organization.

Disadvantages

− Because there may be many layers of management, passing information up the hierarchy to inform senior managers can take a long time and slow down business decisions.

− Senior managers cannot possibly know enough about each department in a large organization to make the best decisions.

− If senior managers make all the decisions, it can discourage less senior managers and other employees from proposing new ideas and using their own initiative to solve business problems.

− There tends to be a lot of bureaucracy, i.e. too much paperwork and too many rules and regulations designed to make everybody work the same way. This can waste time and effort.

Flat or tall organizational structures?

Some businesses have many layers of management, each with a different level of seniority. This is called a **tall structure**. Organizations which have relatively few layers of management are said to have a **flat structure**.

▼ *Figure 2.3: The span of control within organizational structures*

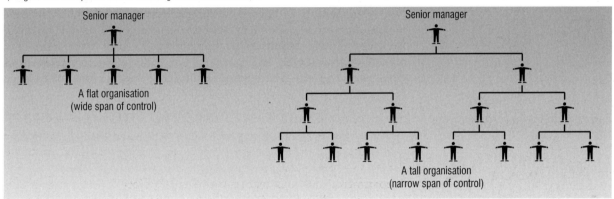

In a tall organization the chain of command is long, but the **span of control** of each manager in the hierarchy will tend to be narrow. This means that each manager will have relatively few employees to command. For example, if three middle managers report to a senior manager, the span of control of the senior manager is three. If each middle manager has five junior managers or supervisors reporting to them, then each middle manager would have a span of control of five.

In a flat organization the chain of command is short, with perhaps only one or two management levels. This helps communication between top managers and 'shop floor' workers. However, each manager may have responsibility over a relatively large number of staff. That is, their span of control is wide. For example, in a large supermarket the store manager may have control over 50 employees or more.

Figure 2.3 shows two simple charts for a tall organization and a flat organization. Each has the same number of employees. In the tall organization in the diagram, the span of control of each manager is two employees. In the flat organization the span of control is five employees.

The advantages and disadvantages of having a tall organizational structure with a narrow span of control include:

Advantages:

+ It enables managers to supervise their employees closely

+ Managers have fewer staff to communicate with, and so are able to communicate more easily with those they have under their command

+ It allows people to specialize in the tasks they are best at

Disadvantages:

− Because there are more managers, management costs are high

− Senior managers may find it difficult to manage large numbers of more junior managers

− Too much supervision in an organization may prevent staff taking the initiative and reduce their motivation to work hard

The advantages and disadvantages of having a flat organizational structure with a wide span of control will include:

Advantages:

+ Senior management decisions can be taken and implemented more quickly because fewer layers of management are involved

+ Because there are fewer managers, the cost of supervising staff is lower

+ Staff have greater freedom to make their own decisions and may work harder

Disadvantages:

− Staff may find that they have more than one boss to take orders from and report back to

− Senior managers will have less say in the control and future direction of their business

− Because each manager has more staff to deal with it becomes more difficult to get to know them all and supervise their work

Why are more firms becoming flat organizations?

A growing number of large modern firms in the UK and elsewhere are reorganizing the way in which they are structured, to cut out layers of management and bureaucracy (i.e. paperwork and strict rules and procedures which everyone has to follow). In these flatter organizations employees are given greater responsibility to make decisions and manage their own work.

Portfolio Activity 2.2

1. Why might a tall organizational structure be a problem for a firm working in a quickly changing consumer market?

2. How and why do you think the changes proposed to the IBM structure will help the firm to become more profitable?

3. Investigate the structure of a local business organization, for example, a supermarket, bank, or small factory. Draw an organization chart for the business and comment on whether you think the organization has a tall or flat structure, and the possible advantages and disadvantages of the chosen structure for that organization.

The shake up of Big Blues' army

IBM was once the largest and most successful computer firm in the world. Today the company faces falling sales and losses. Competition in the UK computer market is the fiercest in the world and IBM has been forced to change to survive.

The structure of the company has changed a great deal. Eight layers of management have been cut down to four. Early retirement and redundancy have reduced staff numbers from 18,600 in 1985 to 11,000 in 1993. 80% of the workforce now come face to face with their customers, compared with only 45% two years ago.

The firm is being split down into a number of smaller departments and the departments at headquarters will have to sell their services to the rest of the company. For example, if a part of the company does not wish to buy pension services from the head office finance department, they may buy these from any outside supplier.

▼ *IBM's U.K. headquarters*

In markets such as consumer electronics, where consumer wants change very rapidly, and new versions of products like camcorders and TVs are produced every few months, organizations need to keep in close touch with their customers. They cannot afford to wait until information has passed through many layers of management before developing new products. In these conditions a flat structure is better.

Quick decisions on new products, prices, and promotions are needed to attract customers away from rival firms. In a flat structure, these important decisions can be taken quickly by managers. Staff also tend to have more freedom to work without guidance or interference from managers. Many creative and innovative firms such as advertising agencies have flat structures in order to enable them to react quickly to changes.

Portfolio Activity 2.3

1. Look at the organization chart below for an organization that imports wines from all over the world to sell to UK retailers.

- How many layers of management are there?
- What is the average span of control of all the managers?
- Who is Sharon Slater's line manager?
- Can Raj De Souza give Sharon orders?
- Who should Sharon report to if a problem arises when her line manager is away?
- Has Sharon got more or less authority than Kiran Sojimi, Paul Raha, and Clive Young?

2. The organization is restructured as follows:

- Karina Plummer leaves to have a baby
- Paul Raha leaves to set up his own small business
- The white and red wine divisions in the sales department are merged

- Sue Bullen is appointed the sales department manager
- Raj De Souza retires
- Alison Frost becomes head of purchasing
- Andrew McKewan and Ken Jones leave for other jobs
- Customer accounts and wages staff now report directly to the manager of finance and accounts, Michael Anthony

Re-draw the chart to show these changes. Is the new structure taller or flatter than the original structure? Now answer the same questions as in Task 1 for the new organizational structure.

3. Do you think the re-organized structure meets the needs of the business better than the structure it had initially? In groups discuss the possible advantages and disadvantages of each structure to the organization. Make a note of your discussions to place in your file of work.

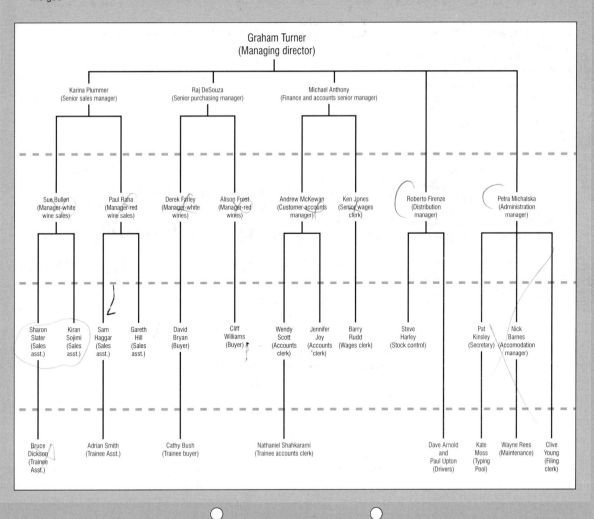

The matrix structure

In a **matrix structure,** employees with different skills will be borrowed from different departments within the organization to form project teams – for example, to create and launch a new product, or to install new computer equipment.

A matrix structure is different to the more usual hierarchical structure because members of staff can belong to a department, for example, marketing, and also to a project team working together to carry out a specific task.

▼ *Figure 2.4: An example of a matrix organization structure*

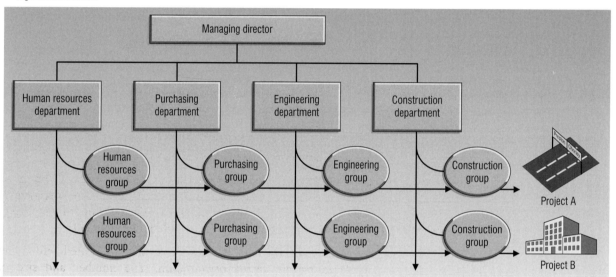

Ford maps out a global ambition

Ford, the world's second largest vehicle maker, is putting into place the biggest shake-up in its 92-year history. Under the title of Ford 2000, the group is trying to change itself from a multinational company organized into separate countries into a global car manufacturing business organized by the products it makes.

Ford aims to create a global company which will be the world's leading car company. But it has a long way to go. Ford is well behind General Motors, with sales of 6.64 million vehicles to GM's 8.33 million. In terms of quality, customers thought Ford were less than average in the USA last year.

In response to this, Ford has decided to redesign its organization to make more cars at a lower cost. The aim is to join up the companies operating in different countries around the world to form a global organization. The Chairman of Ford says, 'We cannot afford to waste time and money on making different car parts and engines all around the world to meet nearly identical customers' demands.'

Ford will create five vehicle centres around the world and each will be totally responsible for the world-wide development of particular cars and trucks. Ford will produce a new family car for sales all around the world using identical parts wherever it is sold.

Ford is creating a matrix structure. Instead of staff just belonging to a department like accounting or sales, they will be part of a team responsible for producing an entire car. The first loyalty of staff will be to their 'car team' rather than to their department. 'It's like a Formula One team: if a problem comes up, everyone will work on it. You always race to win, and it's no use saying afterwards that the chassis worked well, but it was a shame about the engine. If one part fails, the race is lost and the whole team fails.'

Ford has cut its layers of management from 14 down to just 7.

Figure 2.4 presents one way of changing the organizational structure of a large construction firm into a matrix organization. The organization has two special projects: project A, to widen a motorway for the UK government; and project B, to build a new office block in Hong Kong. A project manager is appointed to each project and is allocated staff with appropriate skills from all the other departments in the organization to complete the project. After the projects are completed the organization could change back to its original structure.

Matrix structures are becoming increasingly popular among large modern organizations. This is because by creating project teams, employees can concentrate their efforts on making, promoting, and selling one particular product. This may help a firm to increase the output, quality, and sales of that product.

Section **2.2**   **Departments in organizations**

What is a department?

Every organization must perform a number of functions if it is to be successful. Important business functions include:

● Research and development of new products and production processes

● Purchasing materials and equipment

● Producing goods and services

● Marketing

● Sales

● Distribution of goods

● Customer services

● Administration

● Finance and accounts (see chapters 8 and 9)

● Managing human resources (see chapter 3)

In medium-sized and large organizations employees will often be organized together into groups, so that each group can specialize in carrying out one of the functions above. Each group of employees carrying out one particular function is called a **department.**

Figure 2.5 shows all the main business departments you are likely to find in any large private sector organization. The number and size of individual departments will, of course, vary between different organizations. In small firms there are too few employees to divide up into specialized departments.

▼ *Figure 2.5: Business departments*

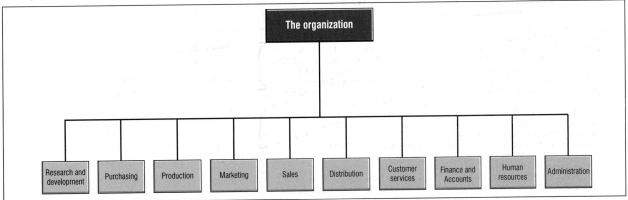

Production, sales, and marketing are usually considered to be the key operations in business. All the other departments, such as purchasing, human resources, accounts, and administration, provide **support services** for the production, sales and marketing departments. In practice, every department in a business organization will depend on work carried out by every other department. That is, they are **functionally interdependent.**

Other ways to form departments

Grouping workers into departments according to the business function they perform is just one way of organizing the structure of a business. Workers may also be grouped together according to the product they provide (such as in a matrix structure), the type of customers they deal with, or according to the region they serve or where they are located.

For example, consider the diagrams below which show the various ways departments in a large consumer electronics manufacturer might be organized:

- **Departments for different products/services:** An organization that produces many different products or brands may find it difficult to manage with each department working on all of them at once. Organizing staff into groups or departments working on one product each allows managers to group the resources needed to produce each product.

- **Departments for different customer groups:** Departments can be organized according to a firm's main customers. For example, most banks have specialized mortgage, foreign exchange, and small business departments.

- **Departments for different regions:** Departments can be created according to the place in which work is done, or by market areas. Most large organizations operate on a regional basis. Multinational organizations will have offices, factories, and often shops in different countries.

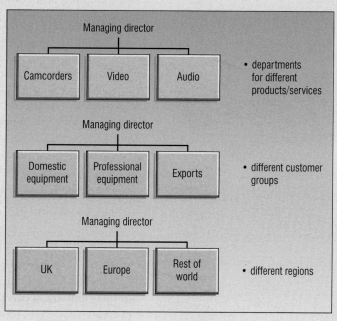

Portfolio Activity 2.4

1. For the types of organizations listed below, discuss in groups the main business functions employees will need to perform, and how departments could be organized:

- An international bank
- A department store
- A school/college
- A hospital
- An insurance company
- A hotel

2. a Choose three types of organization from the above list and investigate local examples. Try to find out:

- The main departments in each organization
- The main jobs performed in each department
- Which departments provide support for other departments

b Draw a simple organization chart for each local organization showing how departments are arranged. (There is no need to show individual employees in each department.)

c Write a short note explaining why each local organization has chosen to organize departments in the way shown in your chart.

▼ Meeting consumer wants for improved styling and better picture and sound quality of television sets has been made possible by research and development.

▼ Engineers at the Transport Research Laboratory conduct a motorcycle impact test with a prototype airbag.

The research and development (R&D) department

In a highly competitive business environment, research and development (R&D) is increasingly important to the success of business organizations. Each year, businesses spend many billions of pounds developing new products and methods of producing them. However successful a product is now, one day it will be replaced by a new or better product. For this reason, the future success of most businesses depends upon the work of the research and development department in coming up with new ideas and products which can be developed and sold in the future.

New products are being introduced all the time, especially in the highly competitive consumer electronics market. Every few months manufacturers of audio and visual consumer electronics equipment bring out new models with different features. Consider the development of television sets over the last few years. They have become slimmer, they can produce stereo sound, surround sound, and Dolby pro-logic sound from no less than 5 speakers. Screen size has increased, and widescreen TVs have now been introduced. The next generation of TV sets will be able to produce high-definition TV pictures (HDTV) as well as digital broadcast images. Each new development tempts the consumer to replace their old TV set with a new one.

Industrial and engineering design

Most firms work hard to stay ahead of competition from rival products and firms. This means finding out what consumers want, what they are likely to want in the near future, and developing ways to produce the products that are needed. The marketing department can advise R&D on the results of market research on consumer opinions about products and consumer wants.

Designing new products or improving existing products is called **industrial design**. People who work in R&D on industrial design matters will consider many features of different products including:

- Image
- Durability
- Smell
- Taste
- Texture
- Colours
- User-friendliness
- Packaging
- How easy it is to maintain/repair
- Safety
- Incorporated technology
- Shape

Product performance will also be very important. **Engineering design** considers how well a product does the job it is supposed to do. For example, does a washing powder work in low temperatures? Does it remove grease stains? Does it soften clothes and towels? Similarly, it will consider how many miles a car travels on each gallon of petrol, how it holds the road in wet conditions, and how many seconds it takes to accelerate from 0 to 60 miles per hour.

Industrial and engineering design are needed, whether the product in question is a highly technical personal computer, a new medicine, an industrial laser, or just a simple cake, children's toy, or choc ice.

The R&D department not only designs new products and re-designs old ones, but also advises the production department on the best way to produce them.

An extremely important consideration in product design is cost. That is, can the product be produced in the right quantities at a price the consumer is willing to pay? There is no point producing a good or service that consumers cannot afford or are unwilling to pay for. It is the job of research and development staff to work out if the product can be produced at a price consumers can afford.

Portfolio Activity 2.5

1. Make a list of all the features of the following goods and services which designers could change/improve so that they appeal more to consumers:

- Chocolate bars
- Motor cars
- Washing powders
- Computer game consoles
- Cough mixture
- A car wash
- Public transport
- Bank services

2. Using words and pictures, write a short report charting the development of any product or service of your choice over time. For example, you might like to consider the development of computer game consoles, from the very earliest machines which contained simple tennis games, through to the Sega Megadrive and Nintendo SNES that used cartridges, and finally to the new machines that play games CDs. Alternatively, you could choose something completely different, like toothpaste, oven-ready meals, medicines, or a make of motor car.

3. As a class, invite a industrial designer to give a short talk about his or her work. If the talk is able to go ahead:

   a Agree a list of questions you would like to ask beforehand

   b Take notes during the talk

   c After the talk, write a short paper on why research and development is so important in modern business, and the role of the industrial designer

4. As a class group, discuss how you think the work of the research and development department will depend on work carried out by the following departments:

- Marketing
- Human resources
- Finance

   Keep a note of the discussions for your portfolio.

Purchasing department

The purchasing department will specialize in buying in the goods and services that the firm needs in order to operate. Items purchased will include the raw materials used in production, paper and computer supplies used by office staff, new furniture, and any other items the organization needs. Services bought in from outside the firm may include cleaning, painting and decorating, and computer maintenance.

Purchasing staff need to carry out the following jobs:

- Advising other departments about the kinds of goods and services available, and how well these might meet their needs

- Finding and negotiating with suppliers

- Buying raw materials, components, and machinery for the production department

- Ordering other goods and services for the whole organization

- Taking delivery of goods

- Checking goods and services received against orders (see chapter 9)

- Arranging payment of invoices through the accounting department

Purchasing, therefore, involves buying materials and other goods and services of the right quality, in the right quantities, and at the right price. People who buy supplies will usually become specialists in the particular goods they buy. For example, Nescafé employs people who specialize in securing supplies of high quality coffee beans to make coffee. Marks & Spencer employs specialists to buy fashion ideas and clothing.

Large firms can often buy in bulk and obtain discounts from suppliers. However, this can take up valuable storage space. Because of this, many large modern organizations now use a purchasing system known as **Just In Time (JIT)** production. Under this system materials and components used in production are ordered and then delivered 'just in time' to be processed. This allows the purchasing organization to keep stocks to a minimum. For this system to work efficiently, suppliers must be reliable in terms of delivery times and product quality. If either is at fault, production will be held up.

Today many functions in purchasing are computerized. For example, computers can send and receive orders and invoices without the need for paper documents(see chapter 9).

Production Department

Production Departments are more normally a feature of manufacturing firms (see chapter 5). The role of the Production Department is to make goods of the right quality, in the right quantity, and at the least cost. To do this requires careful planning, monitoring, and control.

Production planning
It is essential that a business can supply enough goods to meet consumer demand. This requires careful planning of the whole production process, namely:

- How much should be produced and by when

- The method of production to use

- How much land and what premises are required

- What raw materials or components are needed and in what quantities

- What machinery and other equipment is needed

- How many workers are required and what skills they need

- The level of automation in production

- How the product will be packaged and packed for shipment

Production managers must work closely with staff from the research and development department, and sales and marketing departments. They will need to know what customers want, and how products can be made as attractive as possible to consumers. In addition, the sales department will advise production on how much of the goods or services should be produced to meet consumer demand; the purchasing department will buy the necessary materials and equipment to make the goods; and the human resources department will recruit production workers with the right skills (see chapter 3).

Cost is an important consideration in production planning. The cost of materials, equipment, and labour will largely determine the cost of each product and, therefore, the price at which it can be sold to make a profit. Resources must therefore be combined in the most efficient way, so as to keep the cost of producing each unit of output as low as possible. For example, employing ten people to operate only five sewing machines is clearly not the most efficient way of producing clothes. The cost of each garment would be less if the firm employed more machines and less labour.

Introducing new equipment in the factory, shop, or office has enabled many organizations to become more productive without having to employ more workers. New equipment can help workers complete tasks faster and with less waste than before, and even replace those workers altogether. The result is that more output can be produced with less labour input. This is called an increase in **productivity**.

▼ Productive   More productive

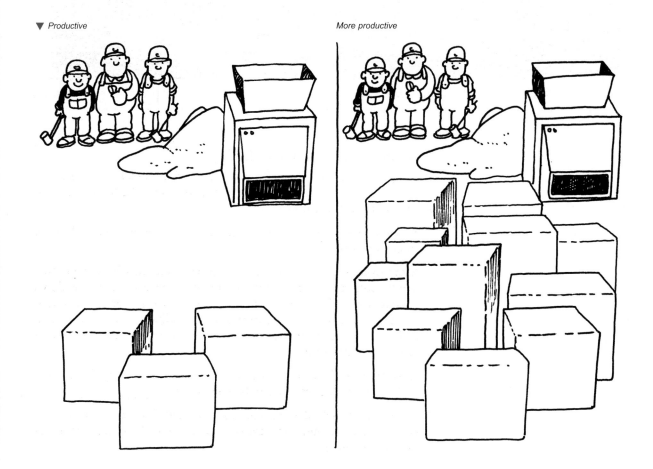

Methods of production

In general, there are three main ways production can be organized in a firm. These are:

1. Job production

This method is used for producing single or one-off orders where each order is custom built. For example, designer clothes, custom-built furniture, flower arrangements for weddings, even the building of ships and space rockets are all examples of job production.

2. Flow production

This method involves the manufacture of a product in a continuously moving process. Flow production is used to mass-produce identical products such as video recorders and cars on an assembly line.

3. Batch production

This method is used for producing a limited number of identical products to meet a specific order, for example, 1,000 calling cards, or 50,000 pre-recorded video cassettes of a particular film.

The precise method of production chosen will depend on the type of product, the level of consumer demand, and the size of the firm. For example, ships are built to individual specifications. They cannot be mass-produced like video recorders or toothpaste. Small firms will not have the capacity to mass-produce items, while clearly the market for designer jewellery is too small to make mass production worthwhile.

▼ *Job production*

▼ *Flow production*

▼ *Batch production*

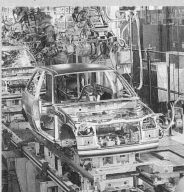

Monitoring and controlling production

It is important to monitor and control production to make sure there are no problems and that production targets and schedules are met. Production control will involve:

- **Scheduling** – working out the sequence, and time, in which jobs have to be performed

- **Monitoring** – checking that work is progressing on schedule and that production targets will be met. If any problems arise and slow down production, such as machine breakdowns or late delivery of materials, schedules will need to be rearranged. In addition, it is important to make sure that machines are not over- or underused and receive regular maintenance.

- **Cost control** – Information provided to the accounting department will allow production costs to be monitored.

- **Stock control** – Production will be interrupted if stocks of materials or components run out. The purpose of stock control is to make sure this does not happen.

- **Quality control** – This involves ensuring that the final product and its features entirely satisfy the consumer. It can be done by inspecting quality at every stage in the production process, including the quality of materials and components, work in progress, packaging, and the work of individual employees, even those in other departments such as sales, customer services, marketing, etc. This is called **Total Quality Management** or **TQM** (see 4.4).

A number of these controls can be computerized. For example, orders for more materials can be sent automatically by a computer when stocks fall to a pre-determined level; equipment can be used to check the size, weight, and ripeness of different fruits and vegetables; progress can be monitored from data automatically fed into a computer every time products move onto another part of an automated production line.

Firms might choose to require staff in every department to take repsonsibility for controlling quality or they might set up a specialist quality control department to check on the work of others.

Portfolio Activity 2.6

Arrange a class visit to a manufacturing plant. Take notes during your visit and gather enough information to produce a short report to discuss the following:

- The main functions of the production department
- The number of employees in the production department
- Examples of job titles in the production department
- The type of products made
- How much is produced each day, week, or month on average
- The method of production

- How quality is controlled in production
- The type of materials and components used in production
- The type of machinery used
- The level of automation in production
- The layout of the factory floor (include a diagram in your report to show where machinery, stores, etc., are located)
- How production depends on the work of other departments, especially R&D, purchasing, sales, finance, and human resources. Use a word processor to write up your report.

Marketing department

The main role of the marketing department is to identify what customers will be willing to buy and then to encourage them to buy the product at a price that will earn the organization as much profit as possible (see chapter 1).

There are four main functions of a marketing department in a firm:

- **Market research** – This involves finding out what different consumers want in terms of products and product features, what prices they are willing to pay, where they like to buy products, and how they respond to advertising. It can involve holding personal interviews, sending questionnaires through the post, telephone surveys, and consumer opinion panels.

- **Advertising** – This aims to raise consumer awareness of the firm's products. Firms can choose to advertise their goods and services through a variety of media, including newspapers, radio, TV, posters, and cinema (see chapter 1).

▼ *Camelot, the National Lottery organizers, expect to raise around £1 billion each year from the sale of instant tickets.*

- **Promotion** – This includes marketing methods such as exhibitions and trade fairs, competitions, money-off coupons, sponsorship or celebrity endorsement, special packaging, logos, etc. (see chapter 1).

- **Public relations** – This involves maintaining good relations with other organizations and the general public in order to give the firm a good, and high-profile, image. For example, organizations can sponsor local events and give donations to charities.

Many organizations pay outside firms that specialize in marketing to provide marketing services. These specialist agencies can plan and run public relations, advertising, and promotional campaigns, and carry out market research. To do this, they need the following skills:

- The ability to work in teams

- Creativity, and the ability to come up with attractive ideas and plans to promote products

- Presentation skills, to sell their ideas to clients

- Budgeting and financial skills, to keep accounts and control costs

- Writing skills, to produce scripts

- Graphic design and visualization skills to brief artists, designers, and photographers

- Technical skills, to use computer publishing, paint, drawing, and animation programs, and operate video cameras, sound equipment, etc.

- Negotiating skills, to negotiate with clients, sponsors, and to buy advertising space at the lowest cost

- Management skills, to see projects through to the finish

You will need to demonstrate similar skills to produce your own promotional materials.

▼ *Sponsorship is an increasingly popular method of promotion.*

▼ *Money-off coupons*

▼ *Charity raffle tickets*

Market Research

The importance of market research

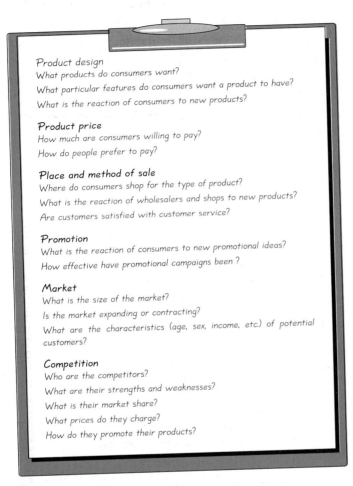

Product design
What products do consumers want?
What particular features do consumers want a product to have?
What is the reaction of consumers to new products?

Product price
How much are consumers willing to pay?
How do people prefer to pay?

Place and method of sale
Where do consumers shop for the type of product?
What is the reaction of wholesalers and shops to new products?
Are customers satisfied with customer service?

Promotion
What is the reaction of consumers to new promotional ideas?
How effective have promotional campaigns been?

Market
What is the size of the market?
Is the market expanding or contracting?
What are the characteristics (age, sex, income, etc.) of potential customers?

Competition
Who are the competitors?
What are their strengths and weaknesses?
What is their market share?
What prices do they charge?
How do they promote their products?

Methods of collecting market research information

There are many sources of information and collection methods a firm can use to gather market research information. Often, carefully designed customer questionnaires are used to obtain peoples' views and opinions.

- **Face-to-face interviews** using a pre-designed questionnaire are a popular method. Interviews are cheap and allow the researcher to target particular kinds of people.

- **Telephone surveys** allow market researchers to target particular consumers by area. However, some potential consumers may be ex-directory or not on the telephone.

- **Postal surveys** involve sending out questionnaires for people to complete and return by post. However, many people simply throw them away.

Other methods include:

- **Consumer panels,** where firms invite groups of customers to give their views on products and monitor their buying habits over a period of time.

- **Observation:** Simply observing the behaviour of consumers and rival firms can generate a great deal of useful information – for example, monitoring TV and radio audiences for particular programmes, counting traffic on roads and at car parks, and examining the products and promotions of rival firms.

- **Test marketing** a new good or service in a small area to monitor consumer reaction and sales. This allows an organization to test consumer reaction before launching the product on a national or international market.

- **Studying published information.** Useful data can be found in newspapers and magazines, government statistical journals, and the annual reports of rival companies. Internal business records can also provide useful facts and figures – for example, details of production costs, consumer complaints, and sales over time.

Sampling

When carrying out market research interviews or surveys, it is usually impossible to ask everyone who might buy the product. Instead, firms ask just a small number of consumers, called a **sample**. As long as the sample of people chosen for research have similar buying habits and tastes to all the other consumers in the market, then the sample will give a good indication of what most consumers want.

For example, if the customers of a business are mainly male aged between 15 and 25, there is little point in questioning women or males aged from 25 upwards. However, it might be worth asking the views of males aged between 15 and 25 who do not buy from the firm, because this may lead to an understanding of why they go elsewhere, and what the business can do to stop this.

Market research, therefore, needs to be planned, designed, and carried out carefully. Businesses will often employ specialist market research organizations who are experienced in questionnaire design and sampling.

The rules of questionnaire design

Questionnaires are a very useful way of collecting information about consumers' buying habits and tastes. However, a poorly designed questionnaire will gather poor or inaccurate information. Consider the example opposite. See if you can spot what is wrong with it.

A market researcher would not learn very much from these questions because:

- Questions 1 and 2 are embarrassing and may put people off.

- People are unlikely to know the answer to Questions 4 or 5.

- Question 8 may force people to reply 'Yes'.

- Questions 3, 6, and 9 may produce so many different answers it may be difficult to make any sense of them.

- Many of the questions are pointless!

The DO's and DONT's of questionnaire design

The bad questionnaire opposite provides a number of clues to how questionnaires *should* be designed.

Questions should...

- Be easy for people to understand

- Be to the point

- Be designed to limit the number of meaningful responses. For example, in Question 9 respondents could be offered alternatives and asked to tick their choice, e.g.:

  a less than £2

  b £2-£3

  c more than £3

Questions should not...

- Be personal or embarrassing

- Force people to give the answer the researcher wants rather than one that is truthful

- Ask people to make calculations in their heads

Questionnaire

1. When did you last use a toilet?
2. How often do you use a toilet?
   a More than twice each day
   b Twice each day
   c Once each day
   d Less than once each day
3. What brand of toilet paper do you use?
4. How many sheets of paper does each toilet roll of your current brand have?
5. How much water do you use when you flush your toilet?

   50 litres   100 litres
   150 litres   more than 150 litres

6. Where do you buy toilet rolls?
7. Do you think the price and colour of toilet rolls are important?
   a Yes
   b No
8. You would be interested in a new toilet roll with a pleasant fragrance, wouldn't you?
   a Yes
   b No
9. How much would you pay for a pack of four scented toilet rolls?

Sales department

In many organizations sales and marketing functions will be carried out by one department. However, selling is such an important activity that larger firms will normally have a separate Sales Department.

The role of the Sales Department is to create orders for goods and services. The sales department may control a salesforce whose job is to visit customers and persuade them to buy.

The Sales Department will be expected to carry out a number of functions fast and effectively. These include:

- Responding to requests for information on products, prices, delivery times, methods of payment, etc.
- Responding to customers' orders for goods or services (see chapter 9)
- Organizing deliveries with the distribution department
- Receiving payments by various methods, including cash, credit card, and hire purchase (see chapter 9) An organization will risk annoying their customers and losing their custom to rival firms if any of the above tasks are mismanaged or take too long. Good sales staff are essential to any organization engaged in selling.

The Sales Department will work closely with marketing in designing advertising material, and also with production in order to ensure that the right goods are available in the right quantities to meet customers' orders.

Distribution department

The role of distribution is to ensure that goods and services are available to customers when they want them. The Distribution Department must therefore ensure that the right goods are delivered in the right quantities at the time agreed with the customer, for the minimum cost. This is often called **logistics** – the science of storing and moving goods efficiently. Achieving this may involve the following tasks:

- Delivering supplies to other organizations
- Choosing delivery methods, e.g. by road, rail, air
- Vehicle maintenance
- Distribution of finished products to wholesalers, retail outlets, or direct to consumers
- Checking in goods received
- Storage
- Checking goods out
- Monitoring the movement of goods and work in progress within a factory
- Monitoring the movement of goods within a retail outlet (i.e. from the stockroom)
- Control of stock to ensure goods are available when they are required

▼ *Distribution*

Some firms run their own transport fleet to distribute goods, while others hire outside contractors to deliver for them. Distribution is an essential department, because no matter what the other departments do, if distribution does not get the right goods to the customer in time, then there will be no sale.

Distribution functions have been greatly helped by new technology. The use of barcodes on products and barcode readers means that stock records can be updated regularly and quickly.

Many large transport firms use 'routemaster' computer programs which produce a map for drivers showing the quickest route to a delivery address, taking into account the time of day and likely road conditions.

Customer services department

In addition to sales and marketing departments, many large organizations have a customer services department which specializes in assisting the public with enquiries about the firm's products and other matters.

Staff in customer services need to know a great deal about their firm and must also have good communications skills. They will also arrange after sales care for customers, such as repairs and refunds.

Good customer servicers are vital to business success today. Imagine you go into a shop and are made to wait 15 minutes while a sales assistant has a chat with a friend on the telephone. Then, when the assistant serves you, s/he is offhand and unable to give you a demonstration of the product, or to tell you much about it. You notice that the till area is also very dirty.

When you get the product home, you find out that the item you have bought does not work properly, and that parts are missing. You take it back to the shop, but the staff do not seem to care and are reluctant to change it or refund your money.

The chances are that you will think twice about buying from the business again. Not only will you not buy again, you will also advise others not to buy. The firm will lose your repeat custom, and it will lose new customers as well, because it failed to provide you with the standard of customer service that you expected.

More and more firms today are understanding the need for good **customer service**, and what it means for sales and profits. The horror story given above is unlikely to happen, but even if just one part of it occurs, customers may go elsewhere. The simple rule in business is that good products do not sell themselves. Good products, with good customer service and marketing, sell products.

Features of good customer service

An organization that fails to provide good customer service could end up spending more effort dealing with complaints than selling goods and services. Its customers will be lost to organizations that *can* keep their customers happy.

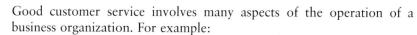

Good customer service involves many aspects of the operation of a business organization. For example:

- **Staff:** should be

  - friendly and provide a prompt service

  - helpful and polite

  - clean and tidy

  - dressed smartly

  - knowledgeable about products, methods of payments, the layout of the business premises and able to provide information and advice.

- **Premises:** should be

  - clean, tidy, and well presented

  - equipped for people with special needs, e.g. ramps for people in wheelchairs and parents with prams and pushchairs

  - easy to find your way around

  - well sign-posted

  - fitted with safety features, such as fire exits, wide doors, wide steps, handrails on stairs, emergency telephones in lifts, etc.

- **Products:** should be

  - reasonably priced

  - of good quality

  - safe

  - provided with clear instructions, if appropriate

  - guaranteed, if appropriate

- **After-sales care:** should aim to:

  - provide a prompt and reasonable repair service

  - deal with customer complaints quickly and sympathetically

  - exchange goods and provide refunds

- **Other services:**

  - customer orders should be fulfilled quickly

  - delivery services should be prompt and reliable

  - product catalogues, price lists, and information leaflets could be provided free of charge

  - provide loans, hire purchase and other credit payment options for customers (see chapter 9)

Clearly not every organization will offer customers all the same features of customer service. For example, you would expect to find a customer toilet in a restaurant, but not in a record shop. Similarly, you would not expect car mechanics providing a service in a car repair centre to be smartly dressed or very clean. In fact you may be put off taking your car there if they were!

Portfolio Activity 2.7

1. Using the checklist of good customer service features above, investigate customer service in a business organization of your choice. For example, this could be:

- A retail outlet, such as a shop, bank, sandwich bar, or hairdresser's

- A service provider, such as a window cleaner, car mechanic, painter and decorator, or bus and rail company

- An office, such as a Jobcentre, council office, or government department

- A factory

- A local hospital, school, or college

You may need to adapt the checklist to suit the particular activities of the organization you choose. For example, the product features above would not apply in a factory, hospital, school.

In some cases you may have to ask permission to be on the organization's premises. In other cases, you will simply be just another member of the public looking around.

2. Write up your findings in a short report using a word processor. Your report should contain:

- An introduction describing your chosen organization, its name, and location

- Your impression of customer service in the organization, i.e. how well you think it lives up to the features of good customer service listed above

- What the organization could do to improve its customer service

The benefits of good customer service

Increasingly, business organizations are becoming **customer-focused**. This means that their goods and services are designed to meet the changing needs and wants of their customers (see 10.1). There are four main reasons for doing this:

1. To gain and retain customers

2. To improve customer satisfaction

3. To build customer loyalty

4. To improve the organization's image

1. To gain and retain customers

Most of the goods that we buy are offered by a wide range of businesses in competition with each other. In fact, the government encourages this by taking legal action against any firm that appears to be the only supplier of a good, if it can be proven that the firm takes advantage of its position against the consumer in a harmful way.

Businesses are in competition with each other for customers' money. However, many of the products offered for sale today are fairly similar, such as washing powders, soaps, margarines, even cars and televisions. Therefore, to make their business stand out from the crowd and appear to be better than the others, it pays a firm to provide a good customer service.

2. Improve customer satisfaction

If customers feel satisfied with their purchase and with the level of service provided, they are more likely to buy the same or other products from the organization again. If, however, premises appear dirty, staff are unhelpful, delivery is slow, and/or no after-sales care is provided, customers will be put off and take their custom elsewhere.

3. To build customer loyalty

If customers can be encouraged to feel loyal to an organization and/or its product, they may stay with that firm and not buy from competitors. In fact, they may even be willing to pay a higher price for a product if they feel it is better than the rest. A firm that provides good customer service can make its customers become loyal, because they know they will always receive good and fair treatment.

4. Improving an organization's image

The products, activities, and general behaviour of a firm all combine over time to build an image in the public mind. If the general image of an organization is good, consumers will be more willing to buy from that firm. If the image of an organization is poor, consumers are less likely to try their product – even it is a very good one.

Providing a good customer service is one way a firm can enhance its image. If customers feel they have received good service from an organization and have been treated well, they are more likely to recommend that organization and/or its products to their friends.

However, the image of a organization can also be damaged very easily by bad publicity. For example, news items on television or in the press about customers taking companies to court; investigative reports on consumer affairs programmes such as *Watchdog*; or poor product test reports in magazines such as *Which?* – all these can seriously dent a company's image.

Portfolio Activity 2.8

1. What was the purpose of the vouchers scheme launched by Boots?

2. How might the Boots vouchers plan have damaged the company's public image?

3. What evidence is there that it might be cheaper to keep existing customers loyal than to spend money on attracting new ones?

4. Conduct a survey of businesses that you know. Make a list of all of the customer loyalty schemes that they operate, for example, club cards at many supermarkets. How effective are they? Can you think of any others that could be introduced?

Rewards for the loyal shopper

Boots the Chemist was this week putting a brave face on what must be judged at the very least a public relations embarrassment. Its 'vouchers for sports equipment' scheme highlights some of the dangers in the current rush to create consumer loyalty schemes and reward regular spenders. Between September and November, Boots issued 36 million vouchers to customers – one for every £5 spent at its stores – which could be exchanged by schools for sports equipment. A total of 22,000 schools throughout the UK registered for the scheme, and started eyeing equipment in the Boots catalogue, for which they hoped parents would collect tokens.

Unfortunately the vouchers were worth so little individually that consumers threw them away, and when the required volume of vouchers failed to get through to schools there was a stream of complaints. Boots has recently announced that it will halve the number of vouchers needed for each piece of equipment. This is just one of the traps to be avoided by companies seeking to join the customer loyalty industry. Existing schemes range from Air Miles, now believed to be collected in one in ten households, to tie-ups between petrol stations and retailers. Premier points are, for example, collected at Mobil petrol stations and redeemed at Argos.

Many firms are now finding it cheaper to keep existing customers loyal rather than to advertise in order to recruit new customers. The longer the life' of a customer, the more the initial recruitment costs will be spread. If 80% of customers stay loyal each year, a firm's group of customers will need renewing once in every five years. But, by increasing the loyalty rate to 90%, the customer base will only need to be renewed once every 10 years. A recent study by the Cranfield School of Management, published this week, which looked at shopping centres across the UK, found that loyal shoppers spend up to four times more in their first-choice store than those who shop around.

Finance and Accounts Department

The key business activities of controlling finance and keeping accounts are usually carried out by the Finance and Accounts Department(s). Chapters 8 and 9 look at these activities in more detail.

Finance

It is the job of the financial managers to make sure the organization has enough capital, either from its own funds and/or from borrowing, to finance its operations. This will include obtaining money to pay for new projects, such as buying new premises, investing in new machinery or a computer system. The financial managers will calculate if the new project is worth undertaking by comparing the predicted revenues (or cost savings) from the investment with the cost of the project.

In addition, wages and salaries will often be paid from the financial division of the Finance and Accounts Department.

Accounts

Accounts staff are responsible for recording and analysing all the different financial transactions in the firm (see chapter 9). They will keep track of all of the cash entering and leaving the business, as well as the amount of credit given to customers and amounts owed by the firm to suppliers. Information about these day-to-day financial activities is recorded in a financial accounting system, which is usually held on computer.

- **Financial accountants** use accounting records to prepare business accounts. These will include the end-of-year accounts which summarize how much the business is worth and how much profit it made (see chapter 8). These accounts will be made available to the tax authorities and business owners.

- **Cost accountants** will monitor business costs, including those directly related to production, such as materials and machine hire, and costs which arise due to activities such as sales, marketing, human resource management and even the accounting department itself.

- **Management accountants** are expected to provide the managers of the firm with up-to-date financial information to show how well the firm is doing at any moment in time, and to predict how well it is likely to do in the future.

Small organizations may buy in the services of a self-employed accountant or an accountancy firm. Large firms can often afford to employ their own full-time accountants.

The accounting department will work with every other department in the organization. It will need information from sales on the amount of money coming into the business, and from purchasing and production on how much they are spending. The accounting department will also set budgets for each department, and will monitor how actual business performance compares to financial plans (see chapter 1).

Human Resources Department

The most valuable resource in any business organization is its people, or **human resources**. The success of a business will depend on the quality of its workforce.

The size of the human resources (or personnel) department will vary according to the number of people employed in the firm – and often with the importance a firm attaches to keeping its staff happy. The larger the firm, the larger the department tends to be, and the more specialists it can afford to employ with skills in human resource management.

All departments in an organization will rely on the human resource department to carry out the following functions:

- The recruitment and selection of staff with the skills and experience the organization needs
- Providing employment advice and information
- Providing terms and conditions of employment to new employees
- Managing changes in working arrangements, for example, due to the introduction of new technology, changes in organizational structure, etc.
- Developing and promoting induction courses and training for employees
- Handling staff promotions and transfers
- Developing and handling staff appraisal procedures
- Developing and handling grievance procedures and complaints by staff
- Handling employee discipline and dismissal
- Dealing with redundancies and redundancy pay
- Administering pay and conditions of service, such as holiday entitlements and maternity pay
- Taking part in negotiations with trade unions and employee representatives on pay and conditions
- Looking after staff welfare, which can include (particularly in larger organizations) employing a staff nurse, and supervising canteen and sports facilities
- Ensuring health and safety at work guidelines are followed
- Keeping staff records on every employee

The functions of a human resources department are considered in detail in Chapter 3.

Administration Department

It is the job of the Administration Department to support all the other departments in a business by providing a range of services for the whole organization. These can include:

- Staffing a reception
- Operating the switchboard
- Providing typing/word processing services

▼ *A company canteen*

- Photocopying
- Data processing
- Filing
- Running the mailroom
- Internal deliveries and collections of post
- Arranging security and cleaning services
- Planning and managing relocations
- Providing staff telephone and office number directories
- Maintaining the premises (i.e. furniture, air conditioning systems, decorations, etc.)
- Main
- Maintaining computer systems

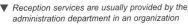

▼ Reception services are usually provided by the administration department in an organization

Some of these services may be provided by other firms employed by the administration department, for example, cleaning, computer maintenance and security, are often contracted out to other suppliers.

The size and importance of the Administration Department in an organization will vary considerably. Most departments in modern organizations employ their own clerical and administration staff to provide a number of the above services, such as photocopying and filing, rather than having these jobs done centrally.

Members of the Administration Department will include clerical, office and secretarial staff, messengers, cleaners, and the office manager. In a limited company, the company secretary may oversee the work of the administration department. S/he will also have responsibility for making sure the company meets legal requirements, arranging board of directors' meetings, and communicating with shareholders (see chapter 6).

It is often easy to overlook the importance of administrative tasks in business and why good administration is needed to help meet business aims. For example, imagine the problems that would arise if an office had no photocopying facilities or up-to-date files, of if waste was never cleared from a factory and lightbulbs never replaced, or if a bank had no security.

Departments in public sector organizations

Public sector organizations will also be organized into departments based on the very different functions they perform compared to many private sector organizations. Departments will differ because most public sector organizations:

- Provide a service
- Do not aim to make sales revenues or profit (see chapter 1)
- Are responsible for advising on, implementing, and managing government policies

For example:

- Central government is divided into around 20 different departments, including Health, Education and Employment, Trade and Industry, etc (see chapter 6). Each central government department is an entire organization in itself. For example, the Department for the Environment, Transport and the Region (DETR) is an organization with some 12,000 employees in England and Wales. In turn the DETR is divided up into many different departments with different responsibilities for roads, railways, buses, shipping, aviation, housing, landuse, plus more familiar ones for human resources, purchasing, and finance.

- Local authorities may have separate departments for housing, economic development, parks and leisure, environmental health, legal advice, finance, and administration.

- Schools and universities have departments based on the subjects they teach and research, including business, economics, chemistry, engineering, biology, mathematics, computing, etc.

- Hospitals may be organized into departments for different medical conditions and types of treatment, such as physiotherapy, maternity, cardiology, audiology, paediatric, geriatric, etc.

Many public sector organizations tend to have tall structures in which decision-making is centralized. This is because many of the decisions made will involve spending taxpayers' money and can affect individuals and businesses in the local and national economy.

Portfolio Activity 2.9

1. In which departments are you likely to find the following jobs?

Data processor	Secretary	Security guard	Production planner
Engineer	Cleaner	Shipping clerk	Advertising executive
Technician	Welfare officer	Wages clerk	Messenger
Scientist	Despatch clerk	Maintenance engineer	Accounts clerk
Training officer	Machine operative	Draughtsman	Statistician
Accountant	Clerical assistant	Sales assistant	Customer liaison officer
Quality controller	Public relations manager	Purchasing clerk	Management accountant
Mechanic	Credit controller	Recruitment consultant	
Buyer	Warehouse supervisor		
Receptionist	Designer		
Personnel manager	Chief cashier		

2. Produce a short report using a word processor describing the main functions performed by each department in a business organization of your choice. Also include a list of at least three examples of different jobs in each department.

Section **2.3**

Job roles in organizations

When you start work, or go on work experience, you will notice that even in the smallest business, workers have different jobs to do. That is, workers specialize in particular jobs in order to make the best use of their individual talents and abilities.

By specializing in particular jobs, workers not only use their existing skills, but they can get better through practice. You may also notice that in all but the smallest of organizations, different workers have different levels of responsibility and authority, from the most junior staff, to middle managers, and finally to senior managers. Typical job roles at different levels in an organization are shown in Figure 2.8. You will remember from Section 2.1 that organizations with a pyramid-like structure are called hierarchical organizations. The pyramid-like structure tells us that the organization has more staff at lower levels than it does at senior management levels.

▼ Figure 2.8: Typical job roles at different levels in an organization

Levels of responsibility in an organization

Most jobs in business can be grouped into one of three levels. These are:

● Senior-level jobs

● Middle-level jobs

● Junior-level jobs

Staff at senior levels will have more responsibility than employees at lower levels in an organization. Senior staff will also have more authority than employees at lower levels. They will have the authority to tell staff below them what tasks they need to carry out, and the targets they will have to meet.

How many people there are working at each level depends upon the structure of the particular organization (see 2.1). Organizations with flat structures tend to have fewer middle and senior staff than tall structures. A worker cooperative is a totally flat organization in which all the workers will have the same level of responsibility (see chapter 6).

Staff at senior levels

The **managing director** or **MD** is normally the most senior member of staff in a limited company, followed by the board of directors.

In public sector organizations, the most senior member of staff is usually called the **chief executive**. In a central government department the most senior post is called the **permanent under-secretary of state**.

Senior managers tend to focus on setting policy and on the overall direction of the firm rather than on the day-to-day details.

Depending on the firm and their exact job role, managers can be senior or middle-ranking staff. Managers running large departments like finance, production, and marketing are generally thought of as senior managers. A manager running a section within a department – for example, an invoicing section within a Finance Department – is most likely to be a middle manager, or in a supervisory role.

Staff at the middle level

Middle managers and supervisors are considered to be at the middle level in an organization. They both have management responsibilities over more junior staff. As such, they are considered to be the 'first line' of management in an organization. Middle managers tend to work closely with supervisors, production operatives, and junior staff. The main role of middle managers is to carry out the instructions of more senior management, to pass them down to more junior staff, and relay information up to senior managers. Giving instructions to junior staff requires good management and communication skills. A middle manager is unlikely to earn the respect of his or her junior staff, or get them to work willingly, if s/he talks down to them or simply blames them if anything goes wrong or if targets are not met.

Because information technology enables information to be communicated quickly and effectively, many middle management posts in large organizations have disappeared in recent years. This has led to flatter organizations with fewer layers of management.

Staff at the junior level

Junior staff include production operatives and some support staff, including administrative and filing clerks, cleaners, security guards, drivers, sales assistants, etc. Any staff below the level of supervisor are considered to be junior staff.

Junior staff work on the 'shop floor', which means they are the people who actually produce goods and services and are often the people seen by the public at the point of sale. The 'shop floor' simply refers to anywhere junior staff carry out their work tasks – in a factory, office or shop.

Junior staff receive instructions from middle and senior managers and in turn provide them with production, sales, cost, and other information about the performance of the business. Their chief responsibility is to organize and carry out their own allocated tasks well.

Portfolio Activity 2.10

Read the articles and discuss the following questions in your class group with your tutor. Take notes of the discussion to include in your portfolio.

1. Why do you think middle managers have been removed from some organizations?

2. What has changed in the years between the writing of the two articles?

3. What might the value of middle managers be?

4. Can, and should, a firm have self-managing teams *and* middle managers as well?

Management experts see middle managers, the product managers and department heads as being people who separate the boardroom from the shop floor. At first sight, middle managers seem to be in the way of everything to do with progress. Successful companies seem to want to give responsibility to self-managing teams, but middle managers make their living by controlling the flow of information up and down in the firm.

Yet suddenly, experts are having second thoughts. There is growing evidence that when middle managers are cut and the size of organizations is reduced, firms lose important expertise and experience. Many firms who slashed layers of middle managers now find that they have no real gain in performance.

Middle managers, it now appears, bring what might be called a 'middle level perspective' to a company's work. Top managers think big strategic thoughts, but have only a vague idea of what is happening on the ground. Frontline workers know their own jobs but have no idea of how they fit into long-term company plans. Middle managers act as go-betweens: they know enough about both the shop floor and their customers to see how a strategy can be turned into new products.

The Economist 4.2.95

'The Death of Loyalty'

The job losses among the world's largest companies continue to grow. Recent job cuts have been at firms earning good profits. Jobs are going not just on the factory floor, but among the middle managers and professionals who usually manage to keep their jobs. Because of foreign competition and new technology, many firms are removing layers of middle managers and giving more responsibility to self-managing staff teams further down in the organization. The idea is that by giving workers lower down in the firm more responsibility, it will cut out the need for middle managers, and so be cheaper. The theory is that workers will be better motivated and so will work harder.

The Economist 3.4.1993

Job levels in departments

Most medium-to-large organizations are organized into departments in which staff carry out a narrow range of specialist roles – for example, managing human resources, accounting, sales and marketing, production, etc. (see 2.2).

Each department within an organization will have its own hierarchy. For example, the sales department in an organization is likely to have a sales director and/or senior sales manager in charge. Middle managers and supervisors in sales may have particular responsibility for given areas of sales, for example, UK sales, European sales, and sales to the rest of the world. They will pass on instructions to junior sales representatives. Similarly, all other departments will tend to have their own senior, middle, and junior levels.

Career progression

Jobs at different levels will be graded according to the experience and qualifications needed to do them. Extra allowances are often paid for seniority, length of service, and performance. In different departments, jobs at junior, middle, and senior levels are likely to be graded in the same way. In this way, the different levels in an organization are said to provide a career path, or ladder, for competent employees to climb up.

Career progression involves working your way up through the different levels within an organization to reach more senior positions which have more responsibility and attract a higher level of pay. The level at which a new entrant joins an organization will depend upon their previous experience and qualifications. Generally, the better qualified an applicant, the higher up the career ladder they will start.

Age is not necessarily a good guide to seniority in an organization. You might think that most young people would be lower down the career ladder. But not everyone wants to rise to the top of an organization and have all the responsibility of a senior position. Also, younger people with drive and ambition may progress up the different levels in an organization quite quickly.

Job levels in the Civil Service

People who work in government departments are called **civil servants**. It is their job to provide support and advice to government ministers and to put their policies into practice.

Each government department is headed by a senior civil servant called the **permanent secretary** – a grade 1 post in the civil service career structure. A permanent secretary in the civil service is broadly equivalent to being the managing director of a large company.

As you can see in the diagram, below grade 1 in the Civil Service is a clear hierarchy of less senior posts. Most people with management potential enter the civil service at **executive officer** or **higher executive officer** level. Some may even progress to become a permanent secretary one day.

Civil Service posts...	and their company equivalents:
Permanent secretary (Grade 1)	Managing director
Deputy secretary (Grade 2)	Directors
Under secretary (Grade 3) Senior principal officer (Grade 5)	Senior managers
Principal (Grade 7) Senior executive officer (SEO) Higher executive officer (HEO)	Middle managers
Executive officer (EO) Administrative officer (AO) Administrative assistant (AA)	Junior staff

Portfolio Activity 2.11

1. Investigate job roles at different levels:

● in your school/college

● within an organization of your choice.

2. Draw a diagram for each organization in Task 1 to show typical career paths for their staff.

Job roles

We will now consider in more detail the different tasks and responsibilities of the main job roles you can expect to find at different levels in a typical medium-to-large company.

Directors

Directors are chosen or elected by shareholders – the people and/or firms who own the company. All limited companies must have at least one director.

Most companies have more than one director. Individual directors are often in charge of particular departments in the firm, for example, the sales director or human resources director. They are responsible for setting the long-term targets for their departments and ensuring that these targets are met.

All the directors of a company form the **board of directors**, which is collectively responsible for the long-term planning and the overall strategy of the firm.

The board of directors has a number of responsibilities, some of them laid down in law. These are:

● Setting business objectives

● Deciding long-term policies and plans to achieve set objectives

● Monitoring business performance

● Controlling company activities

● Making important financial decisions

● Safeguarding funds invested by shareholders

● Determining the distribution of profits

● Preparing and publishing an annual report

● Protecting the company against fraud and inefficiency

The board of directors of a company will meet regularly in a boardroom. Two types of director will be present at these meetings:

● **Executive directors** are employees of the company who are full-time members of the board of directors.

▼ *A board meeting*

- **Non-executive directors** are not employees of the company. It is their job to provide the benefit of their experience and specialist knowledge to the business. Being non-executive, these directors have no management responsibility for particular parts of the business. They may provide useful links with other organizations because of directorships they hold in other companies.

The directors are responsible for the overall running of the company. They must ensure that it is well managed. All directors are accountable to their shareholders – the people who own the company. Every year, directors must report on the progress of the firm to the shareholders at the **annual general meeting (AGM)**. If shareholders are dissatisfied with the performance of directors, they can vote to replace them. This means that a major job role of directors is to ensure that shareholders are kept happy. Some directors may be also be owners, or shareholders, of the company as well (see chapter 6).

In large companies, directors tend to leave the day-to-day running of the business and decision-making to the managing director. The **managing director (MD)** is responsible for ensuring that decisions made by the full board of directors are carried out. That is, the managing director is both a director and a senior manager. The MD is usually seen by the workers in the firm as 'the Boss'. In some organizations the MD is known as the chief executive.

Specific duties and responsibilities of a managing director will include:

- Appointing senior managers

- Implementing company policies designed to achieve business goals

- Supervising and coordinating day-to-day activities within the company

- Meeting, and taking part in negotiations on major issues with, important trade union and government officials, key suppliers, and customers

▼ *Inside a boardroom*

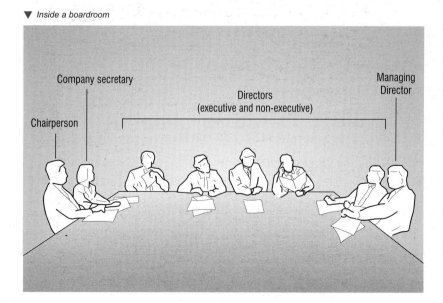

Chairperson

Company secretary

Directors
(executive and non-executive)

Managing Director

Managers

A manager is not a director. His or her main responsibilities will be to carry out the plans made by the directors and take care of the day-to-day running of the organization. For example, the directors might decide that an electronics firm should make DVD players and aim to have a 25% market share at the luxury end of the market by the end of the year. But the managers will decide how to organize the staff, materials, and machines to produce and promote DVD players in order to achieve that target.

Managers influence all aspects of modern organizations. Production managers run manufacturing operations that produce goods to satisfy customer wants and needs. Sales managers organize sales teams to sell goods and services. Human resources managers recruit staff.

Senior managers may be heads of department, supported by middle managers and supervisors who look after individual sections within a department.

Managers have the following responsibilities:

- Carry out the instructions of their directors

- Allocate work tasks to staff

- Motivate staff to increase work effort

- Make sure staff are doing their work properly and are meeting targets and deadlines

- Sort out day-to-day problems

- Staff appraisal

- Identify staff training needs

- Keep directors informed of progress and any major problems

- Inform staff of directors' decisions on long-term plans for the organization (if they are not confidential)

- Administrative duties

All organizations – businesses, government departments, charities, even sports teams – need good managers to achieve their objectives. Whether or not an organization meets its objectives in terms of output, sales, profit, and/or costs largely depends on the quality of its management.

Portfolio Activity 2.12

Make a list of all the different tasks managers must perform in an organization and the qualities you think they need to carry out their tasks successfully. To help you, use these job adverts for managers and your own observations of managers in organizations you are familiar with, either in your school/college, place of work experience, etc.

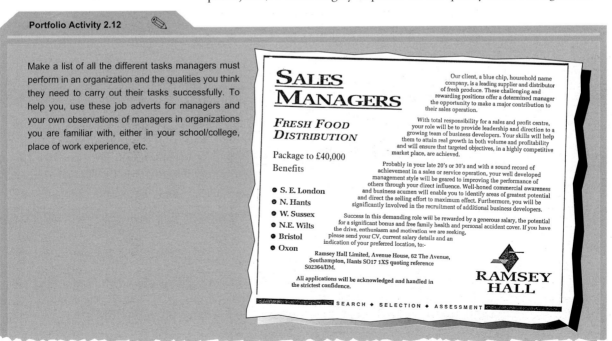

SALES MANAGERS

FRESH FOOD DISTRIBUTION

Package to £40,000
Benefits

- S. E. London
- N. Hants
- W. Sussex
- N.E. Wilts
- Bristol
- Oxon

Our client, a blue chip, household name company, is a leading supplier and distributor of fresh produce. These challenging and rewarding positions offer a determined manager the opportunity to make a major contribution to their sales operation.

With total responsibility for a sales and profit centre, your role will be to provide leadership and direction to a growing team of business developers. Your skills will help them to attain real growth in both volume and profitability and will ensure that targeted objectives, in a highly competitive market place, are achieved.

Probably in your late 20's or 30's and with a sound record of achievement in a sales or service operation, your well developed management style will be geared to improving the performance of others through your direct influence. Well-honed commercial awareness and business acumen will enable you to identify areas of greatest potential and direct the selling effort to maximum effect. Furthermore, you will be significantly involved in the recruitment of additional business developers.

Success in this demanding role will be rewarded by a generous salary, the potential for a significant bonus and free family health and personal accident cover. If you have the drive, enthusiasm and motivation we are seeking, please send your CV, current salary details and an indication of your preferred location, to:-

Ramsey Hall Limited, Avenue House, 62 The Avenue, Southampton, Hants SO17 1XS quoting reference S02364/DM.

All applications will be acknowledged and handled in the strictest confidence.

RAMSEY HALL

SEARCH ◆ SELECTION ◆ ASSESSMENT

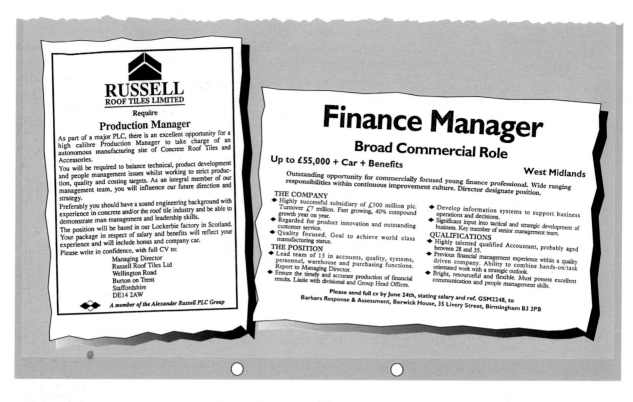

RUSSELL
ROOF TILES LIMITED

Require

Production Manager

As part of a major PLC, there is an excellent opportunity for a high calibre Production Manager to take charge of an autonomous manufacturing site of Concrete Roof Tiles and Accessories.

You will be required to balance technical, product development and people management issues whilst working to strict production, quality and costing targets. As an integral member of our management team, you will influence our future direction and strategy.

Preferably you should have a sound engineering background with experience in concrete and/or the roof tile industry and be able to demonstrate man management and leadership skills.

The position will be based in our Lockerbie factory in Scotland. Your package in respect of salary and benefits will reflect your experience and will include bonus and company car.

Please write in confidence, with full CV to:

Managing Director
Russell Roof Tiles Ltd
Wellington Road
Burton on Trent
Staffordshire
DE14 2AW

A member of the Alexander Russell PLC Group

Finance Manager

Broad Commercial Role

Up to £55,000 + Car + Benefits

West Midlands

Outstanding opportunity for commercially focused young finance professional. Wide ranging responsibilities within continuous improvement culture. Director designate position.

THE COMPANY
◆ Highly successful subsidiary of £500 million plc. Turnover £7 million. Fast growing, 40% compound growth year on year.
◆ Regarded for product innovation and outstanding customer service.
◆ Quality focused. Goal to achieve world class manufacturing status.

THE POSITION
◆ Lead team of 15 in accounts, quality, systems, personnel, warehouse and purchasing functions. Report to Managing Director.
◆ Ensure the timely and accurate production of financial results. Liaise with divisional and Group Head Offices.

◆ Develop information systems to support business operations and decisions.
◆ Significant input into tactical and strategic development of business. Key member of senior management team.

QUALIFICATIONS
◆ Highly talented qualified Accountant, probably aged between 28 and 35.
◆ Previous financial management experience within a quality driven company. Ability to combine hands-on/task orientated work with a strategic outlook.
◆ Bright, resourceful and flexible. Must possess excellent communication and people management skills.

Please send full cv by June 24th, stating salary and ref. GSM2248, to Barkers Response & Assessment, Berwick House, 35 Livery Street, Birmingham B3 2PB

Supervisors

Supervisors are sometimes known as **first line managers**. They are often employees who are able to lead a team because of their long experience in the job. However, some supervisors may be new recruits to an organization who have a degree or other useful qualification and have been identified as likely future managers.

The responsibilities of a supervisor are similar in many ways to those of managers. However, supervisors will tend to be far more involved with day-to-day operations and shop floor workers than their line managers.

Supervisors are rarely involved in decision-making about long-term planning or strategy.

For example, supervisors will be expected to:

● Make sure their staff get things done

● Sort out any mechanical problems or other hold-ups

● Make sure the working area of their staff is kept clean and tidy

● Make sure supplies of materials are readily available for their staff

● Look after staff welfare and morale

● Enforce discipline

● Organize overtime working and leave arrangements

Increasingly, firms are replacing supervisors with team leaders or self-managing teams. The aim of this is to give workers more power over the organization of their work and so improve their motivation and efficiency.

Portfolio Activity 2.13

Using the two job adverts for supervisors in different organizations below, make a list of the tasks a supervisor could be expected to perform, and the qualities they should possess. Also draw on any personal experience you have of supervisors, or junior managers, in organizations you are familiar with.

SCAFFOLDING SUPERVISOR/ESTIMATOR

MG Scaffolding is a well established scaffolding contractor, and we wish to continue our expansion in the Cambridge area by appointing an experienced Scaffolding/Estimator to join our management team.

To be considered for this position you must be able to demonstrate the following attributes:-

★ Minimum of 5 years experience in the Scaffolding Industry.
★ Proven skills in the planning, motivation and control of labour, and materials planning.
★ The ability to achieve demanding operational and financial targets.
★ Flexible and enthusiastic approach to work.

We offer an attractive remuneration package, including competitive salary, performance related bonus scheme, and Company car.

Please apply in writing enclosing a C.V. to:

The Operations Director
MG Scaffold Limited, Industrial Estate
Stanton Harcourt, Oxford OX8 1SL

Croner Publications Ltd, the country's leading publisher in business information is seeking a

SUPERVISOR

to join our Electronic Product Help Desk to promote quality customer care in the developing field of electronic publishing.

As Supervisor, you will be responsible for providing front-line support to subscribers over the telephone, supporting a team of executives and producing a variety of management information and statistics.

A sound educational background to GCSE level (or equivalent) is necessary, together with a working knowledge of PCs, ideally Wordperfect and Lotus spreadsheet packages.

Previous supervisory experience, preferably with a telephone/customer service environment, is essential, together with a mature and flexible approach to work.

As a progressive company, Croner Publications Ltd offers a competitive salary and an attractive benefits package including life assurance, a pension scheme (subject to qualifying conditions), 28 days' holiday and medical cover. Hours of work are normally 35 per week as appropriate, within an 8am - 6pm framework.

Applicants should write, with a CV and details of current salary, to Moira Jevons at:-

Croner Publications Ltd
Croner House, London Road,
Kingston-Upon-Thames, Surrey KT2 6SR

Tel: 020 8547 3333
Fax: 020 8541 1733

Closing date: Friday 7 October 1994

NON-SMOKERS PREFERRED

▼ *Production operatives at work*

Production operatives

A production operative is a worker who operates machinery and equipment to make or assemble goods, or to supply a service. For example, production operatives can be found in manufacturing organizations such as car assembly plants, using machines and tools to build motor vehicles. Production operatives may also be found bolting together scaffolding around buildings so that it can be cleaned or repaired. They may also drive forklift trucks in a warehouse, grill burgers in a fast food restaurant, type in data to a computer, drive a combine harvester on a farm, or fit double-glazed windows to your house.

▼ Support staff provide a variety of useful functions in an organization from cleaning (above) to highly trained advisors and consultants (below).

Production operatives may be skilled or semi-skilled, and will usually have no responsibilities for managing other people. They are expected only to make day-to-day decisions concerning their particular job. If they work in teams, they will be involved in group discussions but are unlikely to be team leaders (see 6.2).

Support staff

If staff do not work in the production department of an organization, they are likely to be providing a support function to those who do. Employees in other departments, such as accounts, human resources, sales or marketing provide a wide range of services, both to employees within the organization and to external customers. All these employees, whether senior managers or junior staff, are known as **support staff**.

Support staff services are designed to ensure that the organization runs smoothly. Services provided internally might include administration, purchasing materials, advertising, staff recruitment, caretaking, security, computer maintenance, cleaning, canteen services, etc. Services provided to customers might include dealing with customer enquiries and after-sales service.

Support staff may be very junior or very senior. Senior support staff may include highly trained legal executives providing advice on the law, or computer systems analysts writing computer programs.

Portfolio Activity 2.14

In small groups, discuss and list the production operatives and support staff you might expect to find in the following organizations:

- A large construction company
- A coal mine
- A leisure centre
- A supermarket
- A hospital
- Your school/college

  Is there any similarity between the lists for the different organizations? If so, why do you think this is?

Investigating job roles, activities and tasks

Lightning Computers Plc – a case study

This section presents case studies on different people with different job roles at different levels in an organization called Lightning Computers Plc – a manufacturer and supplier of personal computers. Read them and learn about the different activities and tasks they carry out and the skills they need to do them successfully. Then answer the questions that follow in Portfolio Activity 2.15 on page 101.

Case Study 1

Jack Douglas, Managing Director

'I am responsible for running the whole business. With the board of directors, I make decisions about long-term policy for the firm, and it is my job to see that these policies are carried out. In the end, the shareholders will judge how well I run the company, and if they do not like what I do, they can fire me.

'An important part of my job is knowing what is going on in the business. I keep in contact with employees at all levels in the firm so that I know their concerns and worries. It is also important that staff feel able to contribute ideas and suggestions about how best to improve the working of the firm. I try to be approachable and interested in my workers.'

A typical day for Jack

8.30 am: Jack starts the day with a meeting with the marketing director in order to discuss the latest sales figures and the plans for launching a new and improved Pentium multimedia computer.

11 am: Jack meets with the director of human resources in order to see how recent discussions with the trades union shop steward over pay bargaining went. The human resources director warns that the union may threaten a strike if planned

redundancies go ahead. Jack suggests the company offers an extra 2% in pay this year in order to avoid problems with strikes and lost production.

2 pm: The early afternoon is spent with a group of major shareholders explaining plans for building a new computer assembly plant, and the ways in which it might be financed. Jack gives the shareholders a tour of the existing plant, explaining the problems caused by lack of space and storage areas.

5 pm: In the late afternoon Jack tours the assembly plant, chatting with workers, and then spends ten minutes talking with customer services staff finding out about the kinds of complaints received recently.

7.30 pm: Jack attends a local business function organized by the Chamber of Commerce.

Case Study 2

Callum McFarlane, Director of Human Resources

'I am in charge of recruiting, training, and disciplining staff at all levels in the firm. I report directly to the managing director. I work closely with all of the other managers on staff matters.

'My job is to ensure that we have the right people, with the right skills for the jobs that need to be done. I get involved in organizing training, interviewing for promotions, and also in disciplinary procedures when these arise. I have to be approachable by staff and sensitive to their needs and the needs of the company.'

A typical day for Callum

8.45 am: Callum starts his day with a meeting with the production manager to review health and safety matters on the factory shop floor. It was agreed that the firm needs to increase the number of trained First Aiders on the production line, and that Callum would select staff to attend training.

10.30 am: A meeting with departmental heads to plan the recruitment needs of the firm over the next six months. This is followed by a meeting with the two human resources assistant managers in order to brief them on the kinds of posts that the firm needs to fill and the terms and conditions that the firm wishes to offer these new staff.

1.30 pm: Callum meets with the training manager to review plans to train production staff in the operation of new computer assembly methods.

3.45 pm: A meeting with two staff who have recently passed their NVQ qualifications in electronics. Callum praises them for their efforts. Photographs are taken for the in-house company magazine.

Case Study 3

Helen Vining, Production Manager

'It is my job to ensure that the computers are produced in the right numbers, to the right quality, and at the right time. I supervise all of the production workers and junior managers. My boss is the production director, and I work closely with the sales manager, who keeps me informed about what customers want and what they think about the quality of our products. I also work closely with the purchasing manager. Together we agree the best materials, and the prices at which we would like to buy, in order to produce the computers.

'If there are any problems with the speed or quality of production, it is my job to sort them out. Like all of the managers in this firm, I try to ensure that the views of production workers are listened to and that their ideas to improve the working of the firm are taken seriously.'

A typical day for Helen

6 am: Helen arrives at work with the first shift of production workers. There is a problem on the production line because they are running out of disk drives to install in the new computers, and the supplier has failed to deliver on time. Helen talks to the production director at home who telephones the supplier to threaten that all future business will go elsewhere if supplies are not delivered today.

11 am: Helen meets with a group of production supervisors to hear their ideas for improving the way work is done on the production line. They request more training for certain staff, and Helen agrees to put this to the human resources department.

2.45 pm: Helen attends a meeting with the human resources director to consider what to do about an employee accused of producing poor quality work. It was agreed to issue a formal warning and also to arrange a two-day retraining course.

4 pm: The managing director talks to Helen about why production figures for new computers were below the target set for the month.

Case Study 4

Linda Potts, Marketing Manager

'My job is to ensure that the public find out about our products and then to persuade them to buy. There is a lot of competition in the computer industry and so marketing is very important in making our products stand out in the mind of the customer. I report to the marketing director who, together with the board of directors, sets our overall marketing policy. My job is to manage the marketing department to carry this out.

'My team is made up of 30 staff. Some are responsible for placing advertisements in national computer magazines. Others are responsible for working with advertising agencies to come up with new adverts and promotional methods. The remainder take customer orders and answer queries from the public.'

A typical day for Linda

9.15 am: Linda starts the day with a meeting with Paul Isaacs, the in-house artist. Paul has designed a new range of logos and ideas for posters to advertise computers. Linda likes the advertisement designs but is a little worried that they may be expensive. She arranges a meeting between Paul, herself, and the finance director for later in the week to discuss budgets.

11 am: Linda attends a meeting with the managing director and production manager to discuss why sales of new computers are below target. She explains that the market is very competitive at present and she recommends that prices are cut and advertising spending increased. The managing director agrees to this and Linda immediately arranges a sales team meeting to work out a strategy to relaunch the products at a lower price using double the amount of advertising.

2.30 pm: Linda meets with the editor of a new computer magazine who is keen for Linda to place adverts for Lightning PCs in the magazine. Linda pushes hard to arrange a discount and succeeds in getting a four-page advert at 60% of the usual price as an introductory offer.

Case Study 5

David Osgood, Central Services Manager in Administration Department

'Central services provide a wide range of background services which are needed by other departments so that they can get their own work done. We provide some of these services "in-house", for example, computer maintenance, security, and cleaning. Other services, such as catering, we buy in from private contractors. In a company like this, which produces a large number of valuable computers, it is essential that we have tight security.

Central services ensures that security guards are on duty 24 hours a day and that the site is patrolled at night. Cleaning is also important because dust and dirt damage delicate computer components and can also be dangerous in the workplace. We employ our teams of cleaners who work in shifts every six hours to keep the site clean and tidy. We prefer to employ our own staff rather than hire an agency to do it because that way we can train them ourselves and have more control over who we get.

'I have to work closely with all of the other departmental managers to ensure that I know what kind of services they need and how happy they are with existing provision. My line manager is head of the administration department, which also provides office services, such as filing and photocopying to all other departments.'

A typical day for David

9 am: David starts the day by walking around the factory and checking that it is clean and well maintained. He finds some areas that have not been cleaned and contacts the cleaning supervisor and demands that the early morning cleaning team is sent back to the areas that need further work.

10.45 am: Later in the morning Helen, the production manager, calls and is angry because burglars have broken in and stolen computer parts from the stores. She wants to know why this was not picked up by the security staff. David suspects that the guards were watching TV in another part of the building. He demands that the head of security meet with him immediately.

2.40 pm: In the afternoon the catering company sends in a representative to talk about renewing their contract and David pushes very hard to keep the cost low.

Case Study 6

Annette Pitcher, Telesales Operative

'My job is to take enquiries from customers over the telephone. We advertise our computers in national magazines and most of our sales are made by phone. I help customers to choose the right kind of machine for their needs, so I have to keep up to date with all of the details about our products.

'When customers telephone through with complaints, I have to deal with them as quickly as possible and try and keep the customer happy. It can be a difficult and demanding job, but I enjoy talking with the public. I also earn commission on every sale made.'

A typical day for Annette

10.30 am: Annette works Flexitime and so arrives for work at 10.30. Immediately she sets about taking calls from customers to answer their enquiries and entering details about their orders for computers and accessories into her computer.

2.30 pm: After lunch the telesales team leader asks Annette to follow up some of the customer complaints received that day with the production department. This takes Trudi until 6 pm when she leaves to go home.

Case Study 7

Robert Kemp, Administration Assistant

'I left school last year and this is my first job. I work with 20 other staff, around half of whom are recent school leavers. My job is to do clerical work around the office. Sometimes I am asked to file copies of invoices or customer orders. Sometimes I am required to word-process letters or type sales figures into a spreadsheet. My work is quite varied, and the human resources manager has arranged for me to take an NVQ in business on a part-time day-release basis when I finish my probation.'

A typical day for Robert

8.30 am: On arrival at work Robert is given a large amount of urgent photocopying to do.

9.45 am: The machine breaks down and Robert is authorized by his supervisor to go the printers in the High Street to finish his photocopying.

11 am: Robert is asked to complete the filing of copy invoices sent out the previous day. This takes until lunchtime.

2 pm: Robert does some word processing and entry of sales figures into a spreadsheet.

4.30 pm: Robert leaves work to enrol at his college for an evening class.

Case Study 8

Gareth Williams, *Shipping Clerk*

'I work in the distribution department. My job is to keep careful records of the computer parts and finished computers that we hold in stock. If we run low on any components I inform the distribution manager, who will work with the purchasing department to re-order the components.

'I also work with other warehouse staff in despatching computers to customers. Our job is to ensure that finished computers are carefully packaged and despatched by courier as quickly as possible to the customer. If we do not do our job properly, we will let down all of the other departments. Customers are rightly upset if they are sent the wrong machine, or if it is damaged, or late arriving.'

A typical day for Gareth

7.30 am: Gareth starts work and checks the consignments ready to go out that morning. He makes sure that the private courier signs for them before leaving the depot.

9 am: The rest of the morning is spent ensuring that the right machines are packaged and despatched to the correct customers.

11 am: The telesales team pass on some complaints from customers who say they have not received their machines, and Gareth spends most of the afternoon tracing the paperwork to go with these orders, in order to establish what has happened to the computers.

Case Study 9

Akhtar Khan, Production Operative

'I work in a team with 5 other people. There are about 15 teams on the factory floor. It is our job to assemble computer parts and test the final products before they are sent off to be packed.

'My team has been allocated its own work area, and we have been able to lay out our work benches and equipment in a way that best suits us. We have a target number of different computers to assemble and test each week. We have not missed a target yet, although some weeks we have just scraped through.

'We work well as a team. We help each other in our work and try to solve any production problems together.'

A typical day for Akhtar

4 pm: Akhtar clocks on for his evening shift from 4 pm through to 12 pm. Some weeks he will be on an early shift and others the nightshift. After having a chat with some members of another work team, he starts work with his own group.

6.30 pm: Akhtar's welding gun has burnt out and will not work. Output will be down if he cannot get it fixed. He telephones the maintenance crew for help. They are busy and cannot send someone to look at the welding gun until 8 pm at the earliest. To get around the problem until then, the team reorganizes their assembly line so that Akhtar can share a welding gun.

9.40 pm: A new batch of 50 monitor casings that have been delivered to their work area display hairline cracks. Team members discuss whether they can still be used. They agree that there is a risk that in use heat given off by the monitor could expand these tiny cracks into major faults. They discuss the flaw with their supervisor who agrees to take it up with Helen Vining, the production manager.

12 pm: The end of a long day. Time to go home, watch a late-night movie, and then go to bed!

Portfolio Activity 2.15

Now that you have read about some of the different people who work for Lightning Computers Plc, complete the following exercise:

1. For each employee, suggest what level their job role is in the organization – senior, middle, or junior?

2. What is the main business activity each employee is involved in?

3. For each employee try to find examples where they:

- Have planned ahead
- Made a decision
- Tried to solve a problem
- Were involved in setting or achieving targets
- Provided a supporting role to other staff
- Undertook non-routine tasks

Where you are unable to find examples of these tasks from the case studies, try to think of other examples of tasks they are likely to carry out in a 'typical day'.

4. What would you say are the main differences between the job roles of directors and less senior staff in Lightning Computers Plc?

5. Which levels of staff are most likely to deal with customers? What skills in communication will these members of staff need?

6. Why do you think Lightning Computers Plc employs so many young staff in its administration department? What kind of skills might be useful for a young school leaver to have who wished to work in administration?

Key crossword

Use the clues below to complete the key words and terms in the crossword

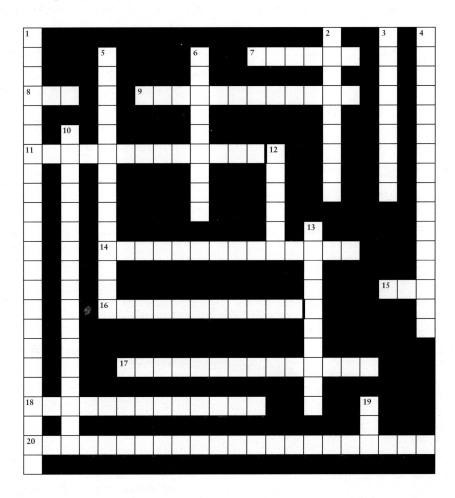

Clues across

7. A firm that has this type of structure will organize employees from different departments to form project teams (6)
8. A company will hold one of these each year to allow shareholders to vote on who should manage their company and company policy (1,1,1)
9. These senior staff have authority to manage and delegate tasks to staff below them (4,8)
11. Managers in a flat organisation will tend to have authority over a 'wide' range and number of staff (4,2,7)
14. Finding out about customer wants and buying trends (6,8)
15. To keep stocks and the need for storage space low, the production department in a business will depend on supplies of materials arriving as and when it needs them. What is the name for this in short? (1,1,1)
16. Functional areas in a business will be organized into these (11)
17. The most senior manager in a business (5, 9)
18. This type of organization will have a long chain of command (4, 9)
20. A function in a business that explores and evolves new products (8,3,11)

Clues down

1. The way in which a firm organizes its business activities (14,9)
2. All businesses have this. It describes the pyramid like chain of command in an organization (9)
3. Making sure the right goods reach the right customers at the right time at the least cost possible to the business (9)
4. Another name for the most senior manager in a business (8,8)
5. This is the line of authority that runs down from the top layers of management in a business, through middle managers to the 'shop floor' (5,2,7)
6. A junior member of staff (9)
10. These two business functions involve promoting and selling products (9,3,4)
12. This is a handful of people picked by an organisation to answer questions about their customer wants (6)
13. This department turns materials into semi-finished and finished goods (10)
19. In short, quality control across the whole business (1,1,1)

Test your knowledge

1 What is the main role of the managing director of a company?
  A managing a particular department
  B marketing products and winning sales
  C long-term planning
  D controlling budgets for all departments

2 What is the main job role of a departmental manager?
  A deciding on long-term policy for a company
  B controlling the work of staff in a particular department
  C managing the work of other departmental managers
  D sitting with the board of directors

3 A main responsibility of the distribution manager in a firm is to ensure that:
  A production targets are met on time
  B customers want what the firm produces
  C customers receive the right goods at the right time
  D sales targets are met

4 The first line manager of a production team is:
  A a production operative
  B a member of support staff
  C a company director
  D a production supervisor

Questions 5–7 share the following answer options:

  A managing director
  B human resources manager
  C purchasing manager
  D customer services manager

Which of the above will take responsibility for:

5 Overall control of the company?

6 Meeting target reductions in the number of customer complaints?

7 Organizing staff training?

8 Who has the responsibility for getting customers to buy a company's products?
  A the marketing director
  B an administration assistant
  C a production team supervisor
  D a sales manager

9 a What is a pay slip?

  b List at least five things that would be recorded on a pay slip.

  c Explain the difference between gross pay, taxable pay, and net pay.

Questions 10–12 share the following answer options:

  A to gain and retain customers

  B to increase customer satisfaction

  C to make customers loyal

  D to improve the image of an organization

Which of the above benefits of good customer service do you think each of the following business activities is chiefly designed to achieve?

10 A supermarket that introduces a free bus service for customers

11 A petrol station issuing membership cards to allow regular customers to receive discounts on petrol, or money-off vouchers for other products

12 A manufacturer refusing to buy chemicals that have been tested on animals

13 What kind of organizational structure has only a few layers of management?
  A hierarchical
  B tall
  C matrix
  D flat

14 Which of the following is an advantage of a flat organizational structure?
  A employees feel that their managers are a long way away in the organization
  B communications are fast between the top and bottom of the firm
  C there is a need for a great deal of paperwork
  D managers have less control over their staff

15 A production department makes finished products. Which department delivers the goods to the customer?
  A human resources
  B distribution
  C finance
  D marketing

16 The role of the accounts department is to:
  A keep records of financial transactions and manage payments and receipts
  B choose raw materials for the production department
  C design new products
  D look after staff

17 From the diagrams below, which organization has a structure which could be described as matrix?

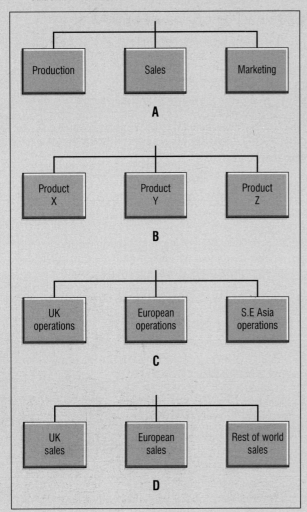

Production | Sales | Marketing

A

Product X | Product Y | Product Z

B

UK operations | European operations | S.E Asia operations

C

UK sales | European sales | Rest of world sales

D

18 In a matrix organization structure:
A employees work in separate departments
B employees work on their own
C employees work as members of project teams as well as members of departments
D employees work from home

19 In a hierarchical organization structure, each employee has:
A one line manager
B no line managers
C no clear job role
D no other employees reporting to him/her

20 a. What is an organizational structure?

b. Draw two simple organization charts to shows layers of management in a tall hierarchical structure and a flatter organization.

c. Make a list of the main departments you are likely to find in a large organization that makes video recorders and sells them all over the world.

d. Explain how the work of the production department in an organization that manufactures cars will depend on the work carried out by purchasing, human resources, and accounting departments in the same firm.

chapter 3 *Managing human resources in business*

What you need to learn

Businesses try to make sure that people in the business can work effectively and safely. Staff in the **Human Resources Departments** are involved with:

- **recruitment, retention and dismissal**
- **working conditions**
- **health and safety**
- **training, development and promotion**
- **employee organisations and unions**

You will need to understand how these activities are carried out and how they affect people working in business.

Employees and employers both have rights and responsibilities toward each other. These rights and responsibilities are safeguarded by employment laws as well as by employee organisations and unions.

You will need to know about employment laws, including:

- **The Employment Rights Act 1996**
- **The Sex Discrimination Act 1975**
- **The Race Relations Act 1976**
- **The Disability Discrimination Act 1995**

Section **3.1** # Recruiting, selecting and dismissing employees

What does a human resources department do?

The most valuable resource in any business organization is its people, or **human resources**. There is a direct relationship between the quality of the workforce and the success of a business. Many medium and large businesses create **a Human Resources Department** to try to make sure that the people in the business can work effectively and safely.

The size of the Human Resources Department will vary according to the number of people employed in a firm and often with the importance a firm attaches to keeping it's staff happy. The larger the firm the larger the larger the department tends to be and the more specialists it can afford to employ with skills in human resource management.

All departments in an organisation will rely on the human resource department to carry out the following functions:

- the recruitment, selection, retention and sometimes, dismissal of staff
- providing terms and conditions of employment to new employees
- looking after working conditions
- ensuring health and safety at work guidelines are followed
- providing training, development and promotions
- dealing with trade unions and employee representatives

The recruitment and selection of staff

A vital role for the human resources department is to encourage people to want to work for the business and then to employ the right kinds of people and keep them. This involves two stages known as **recruitment and selection.**

Recruitment is the first part of a process to fill a job vacancy. It refers to the things that the Human Resources Department does in order to encourage people to apply for jobs. Selection is the next stage, where the human resources department makes a choice between those people applying for jobs and offers employment to those it thinks are best.

Job analysis

The first task of recruitment is to identify that a vacancy needs to be filled. The next stage is to find out what the job involves, that is, the tasks, skills and training a person needs to carry out the job effectively. This is called **job analysis.**

▼ Figure 3.1: How to recruit and select

Identify the job vacancy

What does the job entail (job analysis)
Write a job description

What type of person is needed to fill the job?
Write a person specification

Advertise the job and send out details
and application forms on request

Compare job applications with the person
specification to select a shortlist of the best
applicants to interview

Send invitations to attend interviews to
job applicants who were shortlisted

If the applicant is not shortlisted,
send a letter of regret

Prepare and conduct job interviews

Select the best applicant, and make a
formal job offer in writing

Draw up a contract of employment

Portfolio Activity 3.1

Look at the jobs pictured. For each one discuss and list:

1. the various tasks and activities involved in the job

2. the skills the job holder should have

3. the ways that could be used to work out how much the job should be paid

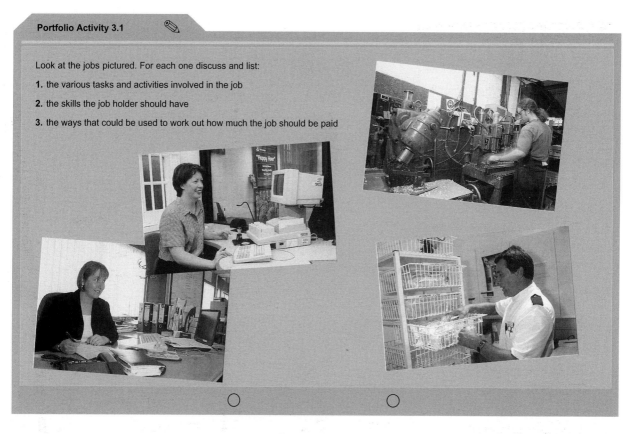

The job description

Once a business has decided what a job involves it is necessary to prepare a **job description**.

Every job in a business will have a job description, usually written before a new employee starts work. A job description tells job applicants what is expected of them. Once in post, the performance of the worker can be judged on how well they carry out the tasks listed in their job description.

What's in a Job Description?

General information

- job title
- position in the organizational structure, e.g. director, manager, supervisor, etc.
- department the job is in
- name and location of employing firm
- working conditions, salary details and other benefits

Job Content

- main tasks and responsibilities (can be in order of priority)
- the administrative arrangements in the employee needs to be familiar with

- specific tasks, e.g. produce a report purpose of tasks, eg. to design a new sportswear range
- methods involved, e.g. use EXCEL computer spreadsheet, etc.
- supervisory/management duties

Performance criteria

- for example, dates for the completion of certain tasks, quality standards, etc.

Special competencies

- qualifications and skills considered vital to the post, for example, a degree in chemistry, a clean driving licence, fluency in German, etc.

Some examples of job description

Job title: Business Assistant

Responsible to: Group Financial Director

Main responsibilities and activities
- gathering and recording financial information
- keeping a computer database of financial data
- prepare monthly cashflow forecasts
- assist in preparing annual accounts
- setting up and implementing administrative procedures for the above

Specific responsibilities

1. Staff
- no staff currently reporting to Business Assistant

2. Planning
- plans and manages own time to achieve mutually agreed delivery schedules
- provide advice and input into financial reporting process

3. Confidential information
- access to customer information database
- access to group financial information of a confidential nature

4. Contacts
- Liaison with group accounts and sales managers
- Liaison with financial managers at regional offices

Working conditions
- based at group head office in Warrington
- occasional foreign travel
- salary approx £23,000+ p.a
- 37.5 hours per week (flexitime: Core hours 1000 – 1600 Mon–Fri)
- additional benefits (subject to medical qualification)
  - PPP private health insurance
  - permanent health insurance to 75% of salary
  - life insurance 4 times salary

Job title: Personal Assistant

Reports to: Director of Human Resources

Hours of work: 0830 – 1700 Mon – Fri

Significant Working Relationships:
- All managers and secretaries
- All Staff Division

Overall Purpose:
- To provide an administrative and secretarial function to the Human Resources Director and her Department

Principal Responsibilities:
- Managing the HR Directors office and diary
- Typing and filing business correspondence
- Organising and arranging meetings
- Receiving visitors and providing hospitality required
- Making travel arrangements as necessary
- Send outgoing faxes
- Mail distribution
- Order and control stationary
- Other support tasks necessary to ensure the smooth running of the office and department

Training:
- Word processing package
- Graphics package

Qualifications and Personal skills:
- Good office management and communications skills
- Typing and shorthand
- Word processing
- An ability to speak French is desirable

Job title: Sales consultant

Reports to: Store Manager

Objectives: To provide effective sales support services

Specific duties:
- Greet and assist customers
- Provide product information
- Sales
- Produce invoices
- Make records of stock movements
- Stock-retrieval

Working conditions:
- Hours of work: 09.00 – 17.30,
- 5 days per week, Mon – Sat
- Leave entitlement: 4 weeks paid
- Wage: £4.20 per hour

Skills:
- Operation of computerised till
- Handling money and credit card payments
- Good communications

The person specification

A **person specification** describes the skills, qualifications, abilities and personal qualities a person will need to do a particular job as described in a job description. The specification will be used to select the most suitable job applicant to fill a vacant post.

What's in a Person Specification?

What's in a Person Specification?

Previous experience and qualifications

- is experience required or will training be given?
- evidence of previous experience and qualifications, if necessary, eg. HGV drivers licence, references from former employers
- formal education and training qualifications required, eg. GCSEs, A levels, BTEC, NVQs and GNVQs, university degrees, postgraduate studies etc.

Special aptitudes

- for example, is the person able to work under pressure? Is s/he flexible and adaptable? Has s/he a good memory?

Personal qualities and motivation

- for example, is the person willing to take on responsibility? Is s/he ambitious and able to work independently? A 'self-starter'? Reliable and personable?

Special circumstances

- for example, will the person need to travel, and/or work unsociable hours?

(*For some jobs, physical attributes will also be specified. For example, a minimum height for people wishing to join the Police).

Some examples of person description

Job title: **Business Assistant**

Physical Attributes

Minimum
- Good health record. Few absences from work. Tidy appearance.

Desirable
- Smart appearance, creates good impression on others

Mental Attributes
- Above average intelligence, good communication skills

Qualifications

Minimum
- Higher education in a business discipline eg. business administration

Desirable
- Further education in Public Relations and Marketing

Experience, training and skill

Minimum
- Experience from positions involving similar duties
- Experience using PCs as part of daily work eg. word processing, spreadsheets

Desirable
- Conversational ability in German and French

Job title: Sales assistant

Qualities/Skills:

- Neat and tidy appearance
- personable , able to get on with people
- reliable and trustworthy
- numerate
- physically fit
- age 16+

Training given:

- operation of till
- stock taking and ordering procedures

Attracting suitable applicants for a job

If vacancies exist, then it is up to the Human Resources Department to find suitable employees to fill them. If employees are unsuitable, the jobs will not be done well, business costs may be higher than they need be and output lower: business aims will not be met. Dismissing unsuitable staff and recruiting new ones is also very costly and time-consuming, so it is far better to employ the right people first.

Some job vacancies may be filled by looking for suitable employees already in the business. Staff may be promoted into more senior positions or may want to move into other departments. This is known as **internal recruitment**, but it will leave other vacancies in an organization to fill.

External recruitment involves recruiting and selecting employees who do not already work for the business. Adverts can be placed in local or national newspapers or local employment service offices to attract them.

External recruitment

Choosing the best method of attracting external job applicants will often depend on the type of job and type of employee a business wants.

- **Unsolicited applications**: A business will sometimes receive applications from people who either call personally looking for work or write letters of enquiry. Their applications can be placed on file until a suitable vacancy arises.

- **Links with schools and colleges**: Many employers maintain links with schools, colleges and universities. For example, the 'milk round' involves companies visiting universities around the country each year with the aim of getting final-year students interested in applying for their jobs.

- **Professional associations**: A business can use these if it needs to find employees with very specialized skills. For example, professional bodies, such as the Institute of Chartered Surveyors or British Medical Association, have an employment service for their members.

- **Employment and recruitment agencies:** These business organizations specialize in recruiting and selecting suitable employees on behalf of other organizations. Businesses will often use their services to fill temporary vacancies. Some well known agencies are Office Angels, Reed Employment, Brook Street and Kelly Services.

- **Government agencies:** It is in the interest of the UK Government to help people get jobs to keep unemployment low. The Government, therefore, provides a number of free services to people looking for work and to employers who want to fill vacancies. The **Careers Service** collects information about local job vacancies and distributes them to local schools/colleges and training establishments etc. **Jobcentres** will advertise posts on behalf of employers and select suitable candidates for interview. The service is free and most useful for advertising skilled, semi-skilled and unskilled manual and clerical jobs. Employers may also fill some vacancies with people from **government-supported training schemes.** The cost of employing a trainee can be paid for or heavily subsidized by the Government.

- **Headhunting:** A business in need of very senior and experienced people may approach top staff in other organizations and offer them more money and other perks to come and work for their firm.

- **Advertising:** The most popular method of recruitment is to advertise the vacancy and invite candidates to apply to a business.

Job advertisements should aim to attract a small number of well-qualified job applicants quickly and cheaply. It is therefore important for a business to make sure that the right advertisement is placed in the right place at the right time. For example, it would not be a good idea for a hospital to advertise for doctors in a *The Sun* newspaper or to broadcast the vacancy on Kiss FM radio. Adverts for jobs, just like adverts for goods and services, should be aimed at their target audience (see chapter 4).

Advertising: A job well done

It is important for job advertisements to attract the right people for the advertised job, quickly and cheaply. The following guidelines will help a human resources department to do this.

- Job adverts should be clear, accurate, honest, and to the point. They should contain enough information for people to know what the job involves and if they would make a suitable candidate or not:
    - a job title and brief details about the job tasks
    - experience, skills and qualifications required
    - pay and working conditions
    - a brief description of the organization, including location
    - if the business has an equal opportunities policy
    - how to apply

- Choose the right place in which to advertise. This will depend on the type of job vacancy, how many vacancies there are, and cost. Where a large number of vacancies exist, for example, for trainee nurses or army cadets, mass advertising in national newspapers or on TV may be worthwhile, although expensive. Some newspapers print specialized job supplements devoted to different types of job on particular days each week. For example, *The Guardian* advertises jobs in computing every Thursday.

- Examine how good the response to the advert was. How many people applied? Were the applicants suitable candidates for the job? This will help a business to plan and design future job advertisements.

You are head of human resources at Flinchem Plc, a major UK manufacturer of kitchen appliances which are sold all over the world. You have asked a professional recruitment agency to help you find a new Finance Director for the company. The agency has produced two adverts for the job. One is a good advert, the other is not.

1. Use the good advert to produce a check list of all the things a job advert should contain.

2. Compare your list from task 1 to the poor advert. What is wrong with the advert? How could it be improved? Use a word processor program on a computer to redesign the advert.

3. Suggest where you to advertise the job. Give reasons and try to find out how much it will cost.

Finance Director

c£65,000

Dynamic kitchen appliance maker seeks an experienced finance director. She will be a key member of the board and work closely with the Chief Executive.

To apply you must be a graduate and qualified accountant with a minimum of 2 years experience of finance and marketing, and the ability to work under stress. You will be required to manage the financial reporting process, establish internal controls and procedures, co-ordinate planning and company administration, and assess the potential for e-commerce.

If you are interested in this exciting opportunity contact
High Profile Search Associates on 01894 715354

Finance Director

London

c£65K + benefits

An outstanding opportunity for an entrepreneurial, commercially biased person to join a dynamic listed white goods company. The company, established 3 years ago, has an innovative new product due for market launch next year in the UK and thereafter across Europe, The United States and Asia. The successful candidate will be a key member of the Plc Board of directors and work closely with the Chief Executive to create a company that will generate growth over the next five years of trading.

The Role

- Manage monthly financial reporting against agreed budgets
- Establish internal controls and procedures
- Define the IT framework
- Co-ordinate planning against the agreed basis
- Monitor and summarise product variable costs.
- Manage cash planning against agreed basis
- Establish company book-keeping procedures and ensure key issues such as banking, payment of payroll etc. have back-up processes
- Co-ordinate the activities of all company administration procedures to ensure a smooth flow of key business data
- Address the opportunity for electronic commerce

The Person

- A graduate, qualified accountant
- A minimum of 2 years experience as the Finance Director of a company with a turnover of at least £20M
- A background in consumer goods or where retail product marketing is strategically important
- Be fully conversant with UK statutory and tax legislation
- Demonstrate a proven ability to work under pressure, often with limited resources
- Possess an optimistic outlook and demonstrate a "can do" attitude
- Desire to be a proactive, key member of the executive team
- Have an ability to build strong relationships across all levels, both internally and externally
- Age 30 to mid 40's

▼ *Skilled, semi-skilled, or unskilled labour?*

Skilled or unskilled labour?

Manual work can require either **skilled, semi-skilled, or unskilled labour,** depending on the nature of the work. For example, an electronic engineer might be considered as skilled, a bricklayer semi-skilled, and a farm labourer who undertakes a variety of tasks on a farm to be unskilled.

Similarly non-manual work can be either skilled – for example, a computer programmer – or unskilled, such as an office messenger. However, it is difficult to draw a hard-and-fast line. Doctors, nurses, teachers, accountants, lawyers, and computer programmers are clearly highly skilled people. But a farm labourer will also need skills to operate farm machinery and drive tractors. Secretaries must be able to use computers and have good communication skills.

In general, a worker is considered skilled if s/he needs to undergo intensive education and/or training in order to carry out his or her job.

The demand for skilled workers is increasing all the time. Firms want people who are able to do their jobs well and can also adapt their skills to a variety of tasks. Technological change also means that the demand for skills by business is always changing. For example, the introduction of computers created a demand for workers with skills in programming. Workers must continually update their skills through education and training if they want to keep their jobs. It is the job of the human resources departments to help them (see 3.3).

Skill needs in Britain

A survey of employers' needs for workers with different skills is carried out each year by the Department for Education and Employment. In 1998, 1 in 5 employers interviewed said they were having problems recruiting new employees with the right skills. The hardest-to-fill vacancies were in:

- skilled engineering and machine operations in manufacturing
- distribution and customer services
- finance and business services
- transport and public administration

Portfolio Activity 3.4

1. Draw up a table with the following column headings:

- Job advertised
- Type of employment (full-time or part-time)
- Type of contract (permanent or temporary)
- Manual or non-manual
- Skilled, semi-skilled, or unskilled
- Skills, qualifications required
- Hours of work
- Wages/salary
- Other benefits (e.g. holidays, free medical insurance, pension, etc.)

Now in groups, select at least 20 different job adverts from local papers and complete your table with brief details about each job.

Also consider how far the wages or salary for each job reflects other aspects such as skills and qualifications needed, level of responsibility, hours of work, etc.

2. Find out how many different types of employment exist in a medium-sized organization of your choice, and in comparison with your school. For each organization draw a pie-chart to show percentages employed in each of the following categories:

- full-time permanent employees
- full-time temporary employees
- part-time temporary employees
- part-time permanent employees
- others

Selecting the right employee for the job

There are a number of ways of asking people to reply to a job advertisement. These include:

- complete an **application form**
- prepare a **curriculum vitae (CV)**
- write a **letter of application**

These will be used by the Human Resources Department, working with the managers of the other departments where the job vacancies exist, to select people for job interviews. Information provided by job applicants to business organisations in an application form, letter or CV, must be treated confidentially.

The application form

Staff in the Human Resources Department will receive phone calls and letters from people who are interested in an advertised job. An application form, along with job details, will be sent to every person who asks.

The application form is used by a business organization to make sure job applicants provide important information about themselves. Comparing details on each job applicant is also made easy because all applicants must complete the same questions.

Portfolio Activity 3.5

1. Select 5 – 10 different job advertisements from local and national newspapers for posts at different levels within organisations in different industrial sectors. Check that each advertisement requests the applicant to apply for an application form.

2. Apply for the application forms in writing to the advertised addresses or by telephoning.

3. Compare the application forms you have received. Make a list of the main requirements you think a good application should have. Which of the application forms you have received do you think is **a** the most, and **b** the least, effective. Give reasons.

The layout and design of an application form will depend on the purpose for which it is being used, namely the type of job and level of information required. However, in general, an application form will request the following details;

- **Personal details:** name, address (permanent and temporary if applicable), telephone number, date of birth, marital status
- **Title of the job** applied for
- **Education history:** schools, colleges, universities attended and dates
- **Educational and professional qualifications;** exam grades, dates taken
- **Employment history/previous experience;** names and addresses of former employers, previous jobs and tasks, dates, reasons for leaving
- **Medical history:** any serious illnesses and disabilities, but only if relevant to the job

▼ Figure 3.2: An example of a job application form

JOB APPLICATION FORM

Please complete this side of the form in BLOCK CAPITALS

Surname (Mr/Mrs/Miss/Ms)   Forenames

Address (including postcode)   Previous name
                                              (if applicable)

Telephone number   Date of birth

Names and addresses of schools/   Dates attended
colleges since age 11   From   to
                                     From   to
                                     From   to

Examinations taken or about to be taken

GCSE	Date	Grade	GCSE	Date	Grade	A & A /S levels	Date	Grade

Please list any other courses and qualifications taken
or about to be taken

Course/examination	Date	Grade

If you have shorthand/typing
qualifications please indicate
speeds

Shorthand   wpm
Audio   wpm
Typing   wpm

Please give details of any work experience you have had, including Saturday
and holiday jobs

Employer's name and address	Dates of employment	Duties

Please complete this side of the form in your own handwriting unless unable to do so
because of physical disability

Indicate your interests and activities – include involvement in voluntary work, clubs and
societies, hobbies and sport

Inside school   Duties

Outside school   Duties

Provide examples of where you have worked as part of a team. What was your role/
contribution?

Please give details of special achievements and/or positions of responsibility (e.g. prefect,
Duke of Edinburgh's Award)

Outline any activities you have planned and organised, and how you achieved your results

Please indicate why you are interested in this post, the reasons why you consider yourself
suitable and how you see your future with this company

Signed   Date

- **Ethnic origin**: the Commission for Racial Equality code of practice recommends that employers include on application form questions about the applicants ethnic origin to allow monitoring

- **Interests:** leisure-related and work-related

- **Other information**: such as positions of responsibility, for example, prefect at school, treasurer of local football club. Why is the applicant interested in the job? What qualities do they think they have that are suited to the job?

- **Referees**: the names and addresses of two people, usually someone who has employed or taught the applicant, or someone who knows the applicant very well. The Human Resources Department in a business may ask these people to provide **references** on how suitable they think the applicant is for the advertised job, his or her personal qualities and skills. References are normally only required for a candidate who is being considered for appointment or who has been shortlisted for interview.

An application form should make clear who to send the completed form to and the closing date for applications to be received.

The curriculum vitae (CV)

Much of the information on an application form could be provided from a **curriculum vitae**. A CV is designed and written by a job applicant and will summarize his or her personal details, education, and career achievements to date. It is good practice to send a covering letter with a CV when applying for a job.

An example of a job applicant's curriculum vitae

Curriculum Vitae

Personal details:
Name: Dawn MARTIN
Date of Birth: 6 September 1982
Address: 69 Westbank Road, Tayworth, Herts, TY5 9ER
Telephone: 020 8530 0123

Education history:
1993–1998: Tayworth Girls School, Fillers Tay Road, Tayworth, Herts
1998–2000: Tayworth College of Further Education, Tayworth, Herts.

Qualifications:

GCSE Subjects:	Art	A
	Biology	C
	English Language	B
	French	A
	History	B
	Mathematics	C
GNVQ Subjects:	Intermediate Business	Merit
	Advanced Business	Distinction
	Advanced Art and Design	Pass

Work experience (Vacation and temporary posts):
June–Sept 1998: Sales Assistant, Kendalls Store, Tayworth
June–Sept 1999: Receptionist, Hotel Antoinette , Tayworth
Nov–Dec 1999:   Work Placement at Nutmeg UK assisting the
                       manager of the design studio

Positions of responsibility:
1995: Captain of hockey team
1997: Fifth form prefect
1998: Editor of student magazine

Interests:
Watercolour painting, tennis, swimming, rock music, reading

Other information:
Typing (90 wpm) using Word
User experience of Microsoft Excel
Full driving licence for 7 months
Oral and written French good

References:

Academic:	Mrs B Sure
	Department of Art and Design
	Tayworth College of Further Education
	Tayworth TY1 2AQ
	Tel: 020 8566 4661
Work Experience:	Mr D Jones
	Nutmeg UK
	Tayworth Trading Estate
	Tayworth TY7 8XX
	Tel: 020 8947 6666

A carefully prepared CV, preferably typed or word processed, is the means by which a job applicant can advertise themselves to employers. It is often the first contact between an applicant and prospective employer and if it fails to make an impact then the effort and opportunity will have been wasted.

A CV should be no longer than 2–3 sides of A4 paper, well presented, and include the following headings:

- Personal details
- Education history and qualifications
- Training and Professional qualifications
- Employment history and posts held / Work Experience
- Positions of responsibility
- Interests
- Other information
- References

Portfolio Activity 3.6

1. Produce an up to date CV for yourself using a word processor. Also ask a friend to produce one.

2. Swop your CV with the CV of your friend and then answer the following questions about each one:
   - is the content and coverage right?
   - do major achievements stand out?
   - is it concise and to the point?
   - is spelling and grammar correct?
   - is layout pleasing?
   - is it easily understood?
   - does it create an overall good impression?

   Why do you think these questions are important in human resource management?

3. If possible, ask an employee in Human Resources Department of a large business to look at and comment of your CVs. Failing this, ask a careers adviser in your school/college to comment.

Sometimes job applicants may simply be asked to write and submit a letter of application. However, more usually an applicant will use this as a covering letter for a completed application form or CV.

Many employers will prefer letters of application to be handwritten. Good handwriting is a needed for many jobs, particularly in office work.

Writing a letter of application probably requires more skill than filling in an application form, or preparing a CV. A Human Resources Department will look for well written letters of application which contain the following information:

- what job they are applying for and where and when they saw it advertised
- reasons for applying for the job
- the skills and knowledge the applicant has that are well suited to the advertised job
- details of relevant experience and qualifications (if not already provided in a supporting CV)

Portfolio Activity 3.7

You have been sent the following letter of application for the job advertised. You have rejected the application.

1. List what you think is wrong with the letter and why.

2. How would you improve the letter if you were applying for the job?

Data processor
Salary circa £13,500
Depending on experience

Established medium-sized company seeks a full time data processor to record and analyse purchase and sales information from UK and overseas subsidiaries.

You will probably be aged between 18 and 28 years of age, a self-starter and educated to Advanced GNVQ standard or equivalent with some experience of computing and database manipulation. Good communication skills and the ability to work as part of a team are essential.

For further details and an application form contact

Margaret Liddel,
Head of Human Resources,
The Computer Search Agency
17 Stanley Street, Sheffield
Tel: 01367-890345 Fax: 01367-0009867

---

57 Whey Close
Trumpton
Cambridge
CR2 1B3

Ms M Liddell
Human Resoures
Dear Miss Lidel

I would like to apply for the job you advertise. I am very interested in computing and think it would be very interesting and rewarding job that I am well suited to carry out.

I am 18 and have been at college for the last two years. I have just competed GNVQs in Business and Leisure and Tourism. Computer studies was my best subject at school and I got a grade B in the GCSE. I have just enrolled at my college for part-time evening study in A level Computer studies.

I was a fifth form prefect at school and captain of the football team. I am currently working part-time at a local library. this allows me time to persue pursue my hobbies of photography and looking after my aquarium. At the library I have to check incoming and outgoing books, collect fines, order and shelve books and advise customers on library colections.

I am currently preparing my CV and will send this to you within the next few days. Should you require a reference you should contact Mr A Young, Head of Computer Studies at Milton High School.

Many thanks.

Yours faithfully

D J Moore
D J Moore (Mr)

Shortlisting applicants for job interviews

Sometimes many tens, hundreds or even thousands can apply for an advertised job. It is the role of the Human Resources Department to sift through all the applications and select those people who appear to be best suited to the job and the organisation. This sifting process is known as **shortlisting** and turns job applicants into candidates for the job. Shortlisted candidates will usually be invited for job interviews before final appointment is made.

Shortlisting begins with human resource managers comparing individual applications with the person specification for the job to look for applicants who closely match the skills, qualifications and qualities required. From this comparison managers can make a list of those candidates who will be invited for interview and those who will be rejected and sent a letter of regret.

Interviewing shortlisted job applicants

The final stage of the job selection process is usually the interview of shortlisted applicants. Interviews involve a face to face meeting between a job candidate and his or her prospective employer. An interview is designed to include questions to test communication skills, knowledge and past achievement at work.

A well-conducted job interview should fulfil five main aims:

- to discover information about the applicants reasons for wanting the job

- to observe the behaviour of the applicant to find out about their personality

- to check factual information already supplied by the applicant

- to inform the applicant about the job applied for and the business

- to be fair so that each candidate feels they had an equal chance and leaves with a favourable impression of the business organization

Whether or not an interview fulfils these aims depends on the skill and judgement of the interviewers and the questions they ask.

There are three main types of selection interview:

- a **one-to-one interview** between the job candidate and an interviewer. The interviewer is likely to be someone senior from the Human Resources Department in the business

- a **panel interview** involving several interviewers, for example a senior manger, departmental manager and human resources manager. Panel interviews have the advantage that each interviewer can ask different questions, and all the interviewers can help choose which person is the best one to employ

- a **board interview** with many more representatives of the business. For example, boards of over twenty interviewers are not uncommon in the selection of very senior civil servants. The board interview is a useful way to reveal the behaviour of the job candidate under stress. However, having large numbers of interviewers can make the final decision of who to employ very difficult.

Sometimes, a job candidate may have more than one interview for the same job. Each time the list of people invited back to attend a further interview will be shorter. Job applicants may also be asked to sit written and practical tests to demonstrate the skills they would need for the job.

Interview preparation checklist

It Poorly planned and structured interviews can give a business organization a bad image and may result in the selection of an unsuitable person for a job. It is, therefore, important for the human resources department to plan and conduct interviews carefully. The following steps can be followed:

1. Decide (a) is a test required ? (b) is interview to be one to one or panel?

2. If a panel interview is chosen, select and invite members.

3. Organize a room and facilities for the interview. Make sure the room is quiet and private. If necessary, check access arrangements for any disabled candidates

4. Send clear instructions to each candidate and interviewer about the time, date and place of the interview to candidates and panel members. Allow enough time for each interview (around 30–40 minutes is common) and short break in between.

5. Make sure interviewers know the job description and person specification for the job

6. Compare the written application form or CV of each candidate with the job description so that the interviewers can decide where more information may be needed.

7. Make a note of questions to ask each candidate. Some questions should be common to all candidates to help make comparisons between them. These might include problem-solving questions or more open questions such as; 'what qualities do you think a good manager should have?', 'why do you want to work here?', 'what were your favourite subjects at school?'.

8. Agree list of questions with interviewers.

And on the day of the interviews …

1. Before the start of interviews check the arrangements and facilities are satisfactory. For example, check the seating plan, lighting and refreshments. Make sure the room will not be disturbed.

2. Begin each interview with a few remarks and questions to welcome the candidate and to calm their nerves. For example, a candidate may first be asked 'Did you manage to find your way here all right?'

3. Explain the purpose of the interview to the candidate. For example, will selection be made for the job on the basis of this interview or is it part of a sequence of interviews

4. Ask probing questions. Don't always accept candidates replies at face value. If an applicant says s/he was responsible for a particular activity or has operated a piece of machinery before, further questions should be asked to find out whether they really did.

5. As a rule of thumb, in an interview lasting 30 minutes the candidate should be expected to talk for around 20 minutes. During this time interviewers should look interested in what the person has to say, and if necessary make occasional comment to encourage him or her to say more.

6. Observe each candidate during interview. Body language can provide vital clues about the applicants honesty, personality and level of stress. For example, observe how they are they sitting, their eye movements and eye contact, and their arm and hand movements.

7. At the end of the interview ask the candidate if they would like to ask any questions about the job or the business.

8. Find out whether, if offered the job, the candidate would still want it and when they could start work.

9. Finally, indicate when the interview is over, thank the candidate for attending and tell them what the next step will be. For example, will the candidate be contacted by letter or telephone, and how long they can expect to wait for a reply.

10. Write down any notes about each candidate for future reference after the interview. Making notes during interview may unsettle the candidate.

Ethical and legal obligations in recruitment and selection

Matching the right person to the right job is essential if an organization is to achieve its business aims and objectives. However, despite careful planning and conduct the recruitment and selection process the wrong person for the job may still be chosen. This may be for a variety of reasons. For example, the most suitable candidate may have been very nervous at interview, or was just having a bad day due to a stomach ache.

Studies have shown that most interviewers make up their minds about a job applicant within the first few minutes of interview. Sometimes interviewers may base their views on prejudice and judge people on factors which may be unrelated to the job – for example, how the applicant speaks, their school and social background, physical attraction, etc. It is important for interviewers not to let these factors cloud their judgement on how well an applicant could fill the job vacancy.

The recruitment and selection process relies on both the job applicant and the employer being fair, honest and providing accurate information. A job advertisement must provide an accurate description of both the job and person required. If the job involves weekend work, for example, it must say so. Similarly, information supplied by an applicant on application forms, CVs or during interview should be truthful. Failing to disclose, or giving false, information could lead to disciplinary action and even dismissal if discovered.

Care must also be taken by a business to make sure recruitment and selection procedures follow employment laws on discrimination. Equal opportunity laws make it an offence to discriminate in recruitment on grounds of sex, race, religion, disability, age, trade union membership or against ex-offenders. Job advertisements, application forms and interviews should be carefully worded to avoid asking discriminatory questions. However, it is legal to advertise for a person of a particular sex or race if it is a genuine requirement of the job – for example, a male attendant for male toilets, an Asian actor to appear in a TV programme.

Appointing a new employee

The Human Resources Department will help with or be responsible for the following tasks once the selection process to fill a job vacancy has been completed.

- **Making the decision** – Once all the interviews have taken place the interviewer or panel must make their decision on which applicant to appoint to the job vacancy. They will compare notes and all the information they have collected on each candidate.

- **Sending a letter of confirmation:** The successful candidate selected to fill a vacant post should be informed promptly, usually by telephone and/or letter. This should confirm essential details such as start date, wage rate/salary, hours and holidays. Offers of employment may be made subject to satisfactory references or may be conditional on passing a medical exam or educational qualification if the person is still at school or college. Applicants who were unsuccessful will be sent letters of regret, and may be offered the chance to discuss why they were not selected.

- **Drawing up the contract of employment:** Under UK employment law a new employee is entitled to a written statement of the main terms and conditions of their employment within 13 weeks of appointment .

- **Making sure the right choice was made:** The progress and behaviour of the newly appointed employee should be monitored from time to time as they perform their job.

The contract of employment

When a person is offered a job, the offer will be subject to certain **terms and conditions**. These may be explained to that person at an interview and will usually be set out in a letter confirming your appointment. Figure 3.3 shows an example of a letter confirming the appointment of a new employee.

Employers are required to provide both full-time and part-time workers with a written statement of their terms and conditions of employment within 13 weeks of their starting a job.

▼ *Figure 3.3: A letter confirming employment*

Leigh Limited
12-18 Green Street
Newtown
Newshire NX4 7YY

Ms K Jennings
34 Saunders Close
Newtown
Newshire NX7 8RG

14 May 200X

Dear Karen

Appointment as Receptionist

We are pleased to confirm your appointment for the above post. The terms and conditions of your appointment are given below.

1. The job will start on 1 June 200X.
2. You will be paid a salary of £15,000 per year, payable monthly in arrears into your bank account.
3. Your work performance against targets set by your manager will be reviewed every six months. Salary will also be reviewed at the same time.
4. Hours of work are from 8.15 am to 5.30 pm from Monday to Thursday and from 8.15 am to 4 pm on Friday. You will also be required to attend a special sales evening for our customers at the factory every two months. Hours will include attendance at this evening between 6 pm and 10 pm. The date of each sales evening will be given one month in advance and will be paid at a rate of £8 per hour as overtime. This sum may be reviewed at the six-monthly salary review.
5. The appointment is subject to two weeks' notice in writing.
6. Your line manager will be the head of administration.
7. This appointment is subject to a one-month probationary period. If performance is satisfactory after this period, the probationary period will end. If performance is unsatisfactory, the probationary period may be extended or the employment may be terminated at the discretion of your line manager.
8. Sickness must be notified as early as possible, ideally at least one hour before start of work. Sickness of up to five working days requires a self-certification form. A longer period of sickness requires a doctor's certificate. Statutory Sick Pay (SSP) will be paid where appropriate for a period up to 20 weeks in a year. After that period, any entitlement to SSP will be paid by the Department of Health and Social Security.
9. Holiday entitlement accrues at one day per month in the first year of employment and one and a half day's per month thereafter. Holiday entitlement may be taken after three months' employment and notice of at least three weeks is required.
10. At all times, conduct befitting a representative of our firm when dealing with the public will be expected.

Any grievances relating to this employment should follow the company grievance procedure. Grievances in the first instance should be referred to your line manager, thereafter to the managing director in writing.

Please sign and return the enclosed copy indicating your acceptance of these terms and conditions.

Yours sincerely

Allan Salt

Allan Salt
Administration Manager

1. Study the letter in Figure 3.3 on page 123.

   a What are the expressed terms in the offer of employment?

   b What implied terms do you think Karen will be expected to work to in her job?

2. In the first few months of her appointment Karen is asked to do the following:

- Wear more business-like clothes in reception instead of jeans and tee-shirts. Karen has agreed in order to pass her probationary period, but intends to wear what she likes once this period is over.

- Pop out to the local Chinese takeaway to get the managing director some lunch because he is too busy to do it himself. Karen refuses because she is meeting someone for lunch.

- Wash the senior sales manager's car during a quiet period when she has little to do. Karen refuses point blank.

- Attend a sales evening in four weeks' time. Karen has already booked to go to a concert that night and refuses to attend. The company has offered to reimburse her ticket if she is unable to sell it to someone else.

- Attend a three-day training course in customer care. Karen does not want to go because the training centre is 50 miles away and would involve a long train journey. Her employer will pay the cost of the travel.

- After two months' employment, Karen has asked to take two days' holiday in three weeks' time. It is a busy period for the firm and her request is refused. Karen feels this is an injustice and intends to discuss the matter with the senior human resources manager.

Discuss whether the organization was right to ask Karen to do these things, and if Karen was right to refuse or feel aggrieved.

Terms and conditions

A contract of employment is drawn up by the employer and signed by the employee. It is a legally binding agreement and can be enforced in law. A contract can contain any details, but as a minimum it must contain the following:

* Name of employer and employee
* Date on which employment started
* Date on which employment will end if the contract is for fixed term only
* Job title
* Rates of pay, payment intervals, and method of payment
* Normal hours of work and related conditions, such as meal breaks
* Holiday entitlement, holiday pay, and public holidays
* Conditions relating to sickness, injury, and maternity pay
* Pension arrangements
* Length of notice to quit to and from employee
* Disciplinary rules and procedures
* Arrangements for handling employee grievances

Other conditions may cover topics such as trade union membership, dress codes, the need for confidentiality, work locations, etc.

All of these are called the **expressed terms** – that is, terms which are openly agreed between employer and employee. Because the range of expressed terms can be enormous, some organizations will not provide full written details in a contract, but will instead direct employees to company handbooks, where the rules of the company and other matters are set in out in more detail.

In addition, there will be unwritten **implied terms** which are assumed to be part of a contract. For example, employees will be expected to work towards the achievement of organizational goals, obey reasonable orders from their managers, wear suitable and acceptable clothing, and produce good quality work. Both employer and employee are expected to be trustworthy, act in good faith, and exercise due care to ensure health and safety in the workplace.

Disciplinary action and dismissal

Employers are entitled to discipline and to sack workers if necessary. To do so, they must draw up a **disciplinary procedure**, and employees must be made aware of it.

A disciplinary procedure usually involves a series of steps including verbal warnings, a written warning, and, if the offence persists, a final written warning. Dismissal will follow if the final written warning is made within twelve months of the first. Alternatively, if an employee is involved in a serious breach of company rules (such as theft or a deliberate and dangerous action which breaks health and safety rules) s/he may be suspended (with or without pay) or dismissed immediately. The employee should be given the right to appeal and independent assessment at any stage throughout this procedure.

Figure 3.4 shows a typical disciplinary procedure used in organizations.

▼ *Figure 3.4: A typical disciplinary and dismissal procedure*

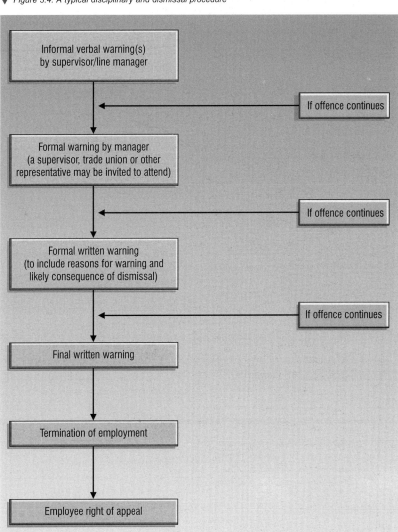

125

'Fair and legal' dismissal

In law there are only five main reasons for dismissing or sacking an employee which are considered 'fair and legal'. These are:

- **Redundancy** – when employees are no longer needed, perhaps due to a decline in business, the introduction of new technology, or a business reorganization. Employees who have worked for the same organization for more than two years have a right to receive compensation for the loss of their job. This is called a **redundancy payment**, and its size will usually depend on the length of their service and how much the employee earned each month or year.

- **Gross misconduct** – drunkenness, theft, fraud, disobedience, frequent lateness or absence, giving out confidential information, sexual harassment or negligence which involves a breach of contract

- **Incompetence** – when the worker is clearly not able to do their job and produces sub-standard work

- **If continued employment breaks laws** – for example, if a heavy goods vehicle driver has been banned for drink driving

- **Important other reasons** – such as an employee or group of employees refusing to accept changes in working practices.

Portfolio Activity 3.9

1. **In small groups:** You are a group of senior managers in a large organization. Below is an assortment of offences committed by employees. In each case discuss whether the employee needs to be disciplined and if you decide disciplinary action is necessary, which of the following actions you will take:

A an informal verbal warning

B a formal verbal warning

C a formal written warning

D a final written warning

E instant dismissal

If you choose C or D as the appropriate action, then you must warn your employee of one of the following punishments:

- Suspension with pay pending a disciplinary investigation
- Suspension without pay
- Transfer to another job in the organization
- Demotion to a more junior position
- Dismissal

Which punishment do you think is appropriate in each case? Give reasons for your decisions.

An office worker has left confidential papers about future product developments on her desk overnight. They should have been locked away in a secure filing cabinet.	An employee is found drunk at work. His wife has recently died and he is of previous good record.

A production worker is caught stealing computer parts.	A supervisor who has already received a verbal warning and a written one for continual lateness is late again without a reasonable excuse.	A sales manager is accused of sexually harassing his secretary. She has reliable witnesses within the firm to confirm the harassment.
The police inform the organization that they have detained one of their van drivers for drink driving while making deliveries.	An employee who has been verbally warned for incompetence at his job has recently failed to meet his work targets and has caused a whole section of staff to underperform.	A newly promoted manager clearly cannot cope with the demands of his new job and has lost the respect of his staff.

Section **3.2**

Working conditions, laws and regulations

Why do people want to work?

Most people go to work or seek work to earn money to pay for the goods and services they need and want. People will supply their labour in return for wages or salaries.

However, other aspects of working are also important to people. Many people want the opportunity to mix with other people, be creative, and have responsibility over an area of work, or for caring for others – for example, nurses and charity workers. Others such as directors of large companies, or politicians want the **status** certain jobs give them. Often workers are attracted to different jobs by other benefits such as free medical insurance or a company car.

All of the above factors give people **satisfaction** in their jobs. When choosing between different jobs, people will naturally take into account how much they pay and the amount of job satisfaction they think they will get from them.

What makes a job satisfying?

- Good wages and other benefits, e.g. pension, company car
- Generous holiday entitlement
- Pleasant working environment
- Challenging and interesting tasks
- Variety in the working day
- Opportunities to learn and try new ideas
- Availability of training
- Working as part of a team
- No discrimination at work

- Job security
- Being consulted on management decisions
- Having responsibility
- Regular feedback on performance
- Recognition for good work through pay bonuses or promotion
- Good social relationships inside and outside of work with work colleagues
- A healthy and safe workplace

Portfolio Activity 3.10

Conduct a survey of at least five employees you know. Prepare a short questionnaire in order to find out what they like and what they dislike about their work and the organizations they work for.

Write up a short report of the findings from your survey. Conclude your report by suggesting what you think are the main factors that give workers job satisfaction.

In choosing between different jobs, people will also consider how long it takes them to travel to and from work to home and the cost of travelling. For example, it would not be sensible to spend over two hours travelling each day at a cost of over £10 if the job is for three hours each evening part-time at £5 an hour! Some firms may help their employees with the cost of their travel by giving them allowances or interest-free loans to buy season tickets.

However, in some cases the work itself may involve travelling long distances. For example, sales representatives will often have to travel around the country or even abroad to promote their products. Couriers and hauliers often carry goods for delivery over long distances. Business managers may have to attend meetings with other organizations at home and abroad. Some people are attracted to particular jobs because of the prospects of travel and are usually able to claim travelling expenses from their employers.

The journey to work

Greater London residents in full-time employment made 1.7 million trips from home to work during a typical weekday in 1991, according to the 1991 London Area Transport Survey.

Sixty-three per cent of trips from home to work in London were less than 5 miles. Of these, 45% were by car, 31% by public transport, and 17% on foot. Less than 1% of trips from home to work were over 30 miles long.

A new survey will take place in 2001. What do you think this will show about travel to work in London?

What are working conditions?

When people go to work they will expect to receive a number of benefits from their employers and to work in environments that are both pleasant and safe.

The main **working conditions** of any type of employment are:

- The hours of work, including any overtime
- Level and method of payment, and other benefits
- Entitlements to holidays
- Job security
- The physical conditions of the workplace, which should be both healthy and safe to work in
- Opportunities for career progression
- Training opportunities

If working conditions are unreasonable, the job satisfaction of workers will suffer. The firms responsible will find it difficult to keep existing staff and to recruit new workers. It is, therefore, the job of a Human Resources Department to make sure working conditions are satisfactory and meet legal requirements where necessary.

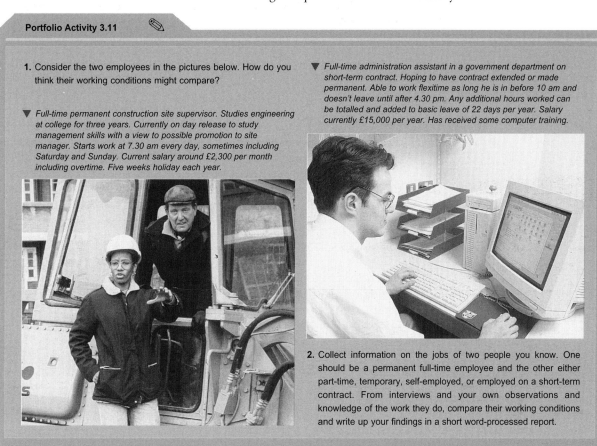

Portfolio Activity 3.11

1. Consider the two employees in the pictures below. How do you think their working conditions might compare?

▼ *Full-time permanent construction site supervisor. Studies engineering at college for three years. Currently on day release to study management skills with a view to possible promotion to site manager. Starts work at 7.30 am every day, sometimes including Saturday and Sunday. Current salary around £2,300 per month including overtime. Five weeks holiday each year.*

▼ *Full-time administration assistant in a government department on short-term contract. Hoping to have contract extended or made permanent. Able to work flexitime as long he is in before 10 am and doesn't leave until after 4.30 pm. Any additional hours worked can be totalled and added to basic leave of 22 days per year. Salary currently £15,000 per year. Has received some computer training.*

2. Collect information on the jobs of two people you know. One should be a permanent full-time employee and the other either part-time, temporary, self-employed, or employed on a short-term contract. From interviews and your own observations and knowledge of the work they do, compare their working conditions and write up your findings in a short word-processed report.

Hours of work and holiday entitlement

All employees will have agreed hours they are expected to work each day, week, month or year, depending on the precise form of agreement. The basic working week in the UK is 37.5 to 40 hours each week for manual workers and 35–38 hours for non-manual workers. However, due to overtime, many workers work longer than the basic week, especially in manual occupations.

Actual hours and days worked will vary between jobs. Some employees – for example, staff in shops – may have to arrive and leave work at the same time every day to coincide with opening and closing times. Many shop workers are also obliged to work some Saturdays and Sundays in return for days off during the week. Most office staff work what is considered the 'normal' working week from 9 am to 5.30 pm Monday to Friday each week. **Shiftwork** and **flexitime** also mean hours of work can vary widely between industries and occupations.

How the times are changing

In the past, employment contracts would often require workers to work a fixed number of hours, usually around 38 each week, between set times – for example, 9am to 5pm. However, a large number of employees are now working different patterns.

- **Shiftwork** involves working blocks of hours each day in order to keep a factory, shop or office running 24 hours each day. Each day is usually divided into 3 shifts of 8 hours each. Staff may be able to vary which shift they work each day

- **Annualized hours systems** set the total number of hours an employee will work over each 12 month period. It is then up to the employer and employee to agree when, how long and how often to come to work

- **Flexitime** enables an employee to choose what time to start and leave work each day around agreed core hours they must be at work, say between 10 am and 4pm

The **European Working Time Directive** was introduced to European Union members countries, including the UK, in 1998. It limits the number of hours an employee can be required to work each to an average of 48. However, workers can choose to work more than 48 hours each week if they wish, and some workers are exempt, e.g. doctors and army personnel.

The EU Working Time Directive also requires workers to receive a minimum of four weeks paid holiday each year. Many employers give their workers more holiday than this because they know the amount of annual leave their workers are entitled to is an important working condition for them. Good workers may leave a business if another firm offers them longer holidays.

The European Working Time Directive

European and UK law introduced the following rights and protections for workers in October 1998:

- a limit of an average of 48 hours a week a worker can be required to work

- a limit of an average 8 hours work in 254 hours which nightworkers can be required to work

- a right for nightworkers to receive a free health assessment and free health insurance

- a right to a minimum 11 hours rest a day

- a right to uninterrupted rest of 24 hours once every 7 days (or 48 hours over 14 days)

- a right to take rest periods of at least 20 minutes if the working day is longer than six hours

- a minimum of 4 weeks annual paid leave

Pay

Wages and salaries
Wages and salaries are payments made to workers.

- Workers who receive a **salary** normally receive the same amount of money each month, regardless of the number of hours they work each day, week, or month. Monthly payments will simply be calculated as 1/12th of an agreed annual salary. The amount received by a worker is only likely to change if they are promoted, demoted, or receive a pay rise. Workers in clerical, managerial, and professional occupations tend to be paid salaries.

- Workers who receive **wages** are normally paid by the hour at the end of each week or month. The more hours they work per day, week, or month, the more pay they will receive. Often, work outside of normal hours, for example, early in the morning, late in the evening, or at weekends, will be paid at **overtime** rates which are 1.5 times or twice the normal hourly wage rate. Manual workers are usually paid an hourly **wage rate** and are required to 'clock on and off' as proof of the number of hours they have worked.

Additional payments

Some workers on a basic wage or salary may also receive additional payments. For example:

- **Piece rates** are paid per unit of output produced. The more an employee makes, the more money s/he will be paid.

- **Commission** is often paid to employees involved in sales, such as insurance and double-glazing salespeople, financial advisers, and travel agents. Commission is based on a percentage of the value of sales they achieve.

- **Bonuses** may include one-off bonuses paid at Christmas as a token of goodwill or profit-sharing schemes which pay employees bonuses when profits are good

- **Performance-related pay (PRP)** rewards an employee for good work. Some organizations hold staff appraisal interviews each year with all their employees. An employee who is thought to have performed well will receive a high appraisal mark and PRP.

- **Fringe benefits** are 'payments' to employees in a form other than money, for example:

  – An **occupational pension scheme** allows the employer to make pension contributions on behalf of an employee. This is paid in addition to the state retirement pension.

  – **Occupational sick pay** is paid in addition to statutory sick pay, so that employees do not suffer any loss of earnings while they are off sick

  – **Holiday pay** ensures that employees do not lose earnings while they are taking time off. Most employees receive between 4-6 annual leave weeks depending on their job, length of service, and level of seniority.

  Other fringe benefits include **company cars, subsidized meals, and free private health insurance.**

Gross and net earnings

The total earnings of an employee each week or month will consist of wages plus any overtime and other payments such as bonuses. It is usual for an employer to deduct income tax and national insurance contributions from the gross earnings of their employees before they are paid. Payments after these deductions have been made are known as **net earnings**. Self-employed workers are responsible for paying their own taxes direct to the government tax authority, the Inland Revenue.

Deductions from pay

By law, employers are only allowed to make the following deductions from an employee's wage or salary:

- Statutory deductions required by law, i.e. national insurance and income tax

- Voluntary contributions agreed in writing by an employee, e.g. trade union subscriptions, give-as-you-earn donations to charities, subscriptions to clubs and societies, additional pension contributions, etc.

National insurance contributions (NICs): All employees, unless they are on very low wages, have to pay NICs. These allow them to claim government benefits such as:

- Jobseeker's allowance (unemployment benefit)
- Retirement pension
- Child benefit
- Statutory sick pay (SSP)
- Statutory maternity pay
- Widow's benefit
- Industrial disability benefit

To make sure people only claim what they are entitled to, everyone is issued with their own national insurance number by the Department of Social Security (DSS).

Unless a worker is self-employed, the employer will calculate and deduct NICs from the employee's weekly or monthly pay, details of which will be recorded on their pay slip (see chapter 8).

Income tax: Income tax is paid by both employed and self-employed people, the amount depending on how much they earn in a tax year (from 6 April one year to 5 April the next). Employers are responsible for calculating the amount of income tax each employee is liable for and then deducting this amount from their weekly or monthly pay. This is known as the **Pay-As-You-Earn (PAYE)** scheme.

Wage protection for employees is provided by the **Wages Act 1986**. This sets out conditions for payments to workers, excluding redundancy payments, expenses or loans, and deductions.

Wage protection is also covered by the **Equal Pay Acts of 1970/1983**. These state that an employee doing the same or broadly similar work to a member of the opposite sex in the same organization is entitled to the same rate of pay and conditions, for example, relating to duties, holidays, overtime, and hours.

A 1983 amendment to the Equal Pay Act allowed female employees to claim equal pay for work of 'equal value' to that done by a man, in terms of effort, skills, and type of decision-making required.

Job security

Most employees today want to work in a secure job where they can plan ahead knowing they are unlikely to be made redundant. But in practice this is becoming increasingly rare.

Temporary employment, for example, in summer and holiday jobs, is perhaps the least secure form of employment. But even permanent jobs

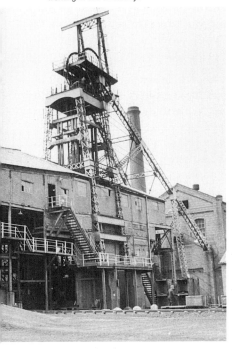

▼ *UK coal mines were once thought to offer their employees jobs for life. Few mines are still working in the UK today.*

cannot be entirely safe in an ever-changing business environment. For example, many years ago, people living and working in coalmining towns and villages in the UK thought they had jobs for life. Fathers, sons, and even grandsons worked in the local pits. Today, few coal mines exist and most mining jobs have disappeared due to advances in mining technology, competition from cheaper coal imports from overseas, and a switch in household demand towards cleaner sources of fuel, namely electricity and gas (see chapter 5).

Changes in technology, competition from rival firms at home and overseas, changes in consumer demand – can all lead to changes in numbers employed in different industries and occupations. However, some jobs are less affected by these changes than others. For example, traditionally secure jobs include:

- **Teaching** – because there will always be schoolchildren and students who need to be taught

- **Doctors** – because people will always get ill

- **Emergency services** – such as the police and fire brigade

In the past, office jobs in the public sector were often considered to be among the most secure. Civil servants in government departments provide advice to whichever political party forms the UK government. They do not have to make a profit, nor are they affected by competition or consumer demand. However, more recently jobs in the civil service have become less secure as the UK government has cut staff numbers in a bid to reduce costs. Personal computers have also done away with a number of tasks which in the past were carried out by office workers.

▼ *Secure jobs?*

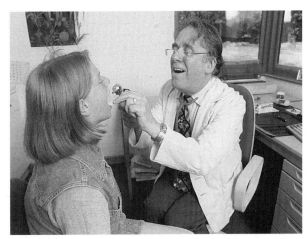

The working environment

Working conditions vary greatly from industry to industry and from organization to organization. For example, consider the physical aspects of an office compared to a large iron and steel foundry. The office is probably air-conditioned, carpeted, attractively decorated, and quiet. The steel plant is likely to be hot, dirty, smelly, noisy, and potentially hazardous to workers' health.

▼ Pleasant working environment?

▼ Unpleasant working environment?

Even within the same industry working conditions can vary widely. For example, contrast the worker on an outside market stall with the assistant in a plush department store, or the policeman on the beat with an inspector in an office, or machine operators in a large modern computer-aided manufacturing plant with those in an old run-down factory.

In a typical week in the UK, around nine workers are killed as a result of accidents in the workplace. Many more receive injury or suffer health problems related to working, from stress to breathing disorders. It is not surprising that firms are required by law to provide, as far as possible, a healthy and safe environment for their workers and customers. A firm that fails to take into account the health and safety of its workers will not only find it difficult to recruit and retain its staff, but will fail to meet targets for output, sales, and profits.

Measures that can make a workplace safer, healthier, and more pleasant to work in include:

- Providing protective clothing, goggles, breathing masks if appropriate
- Providing ear protectors against excessive noise
- Training staff in health and safety matters
- Maintaining safety equipment and clothing
- Allowing breaks for lunch and tea so that workers do not become tired
- Providing First Aid kits and medical officers
- Controlling workplace temperatures
- Installing filters to reduce air pollution
- Refurbishing offices and canteens

How necessary these measures are will depend on the materials and processes being used and the nature of the environment. For example, office workers will need to be aware of fire drills and precautions relating to the prolonged use of computer screens, the movement of office furniture, etc. In contrast, many manufacturing plants are by their very nature noisy, smelly and potentially hazardous places to work in, and stricter health and safety measures will be needed.

▼ Health and safety at work

Sick as a building

BLOCKED OR stuffy nose, dry eyes, dry throat, headaches, and lethargy are some of symptoms of Sick Building Syndrome.

How to Deal with Sick Building Syndrome: Guidance for Employers, Building Owners and Building Managers is the first published HSE guidance on the subject.

Solutions can be simple and cheap and employers are advised to do the simplest things first. For example:

- look for the obvious such as a breakdown in the air-conditioning system;
- check the symptoms, to see how widespread they really are, or whether they are confined to a particular group or area;
- ask staff if they know of any problem or likely causes; and.

- if this doesn't solve the problem, the building services and the maintenance and cleaning procedures should be checked

Employment Gazette April 1995

Health and safety policy

Every employer should produce a written statement of their policy on health and safety, including details of how the policy should be carried out. This will include details of safe working practices, how accidents should be reported, First Aid representatives, etc. All employees should be made familiar with these details and are expected to comply with them.

Large organizations can also set up **safety committees** to discuss health and safety issues and how improvements can be made. Senior and junior staff are usually represented on these committees, including any trade union safety representatives who are able to check on the day-to-day operation of the policy. This will include inspecting safety equipment and other possible hazards, investigating accidents and employee complaints, and talking with Health and Safety Executive inspectors.

Portfolio Activity 3.12

1. From the article, suggest why it is so important for employers to develop and promote health and safety measures in their workplace.

2. What does the article suggest an employer should do to reduce the risk of accidents and ill health at work?

▼ *Daily Mirror 2.8.1995*

£12bn lost by accident

POOR SAFETY COSTS FIRMS £50 A SECOND

ACCIDENTS and work-linked ill health are costing British industry a fortune.

Around 30 million working days are lost through illness and injury, costing £12 billion a year – £50 a second.

The cost of incidents is reflected in the level of claims paid by employers' liability insurers.

Latest figures show that about £3 billion was paid out in claims over the past four years because employers failed to provide a safe, healthy workplace.

As well as these claims, businesses also face hidden costs, says the Association of British Insurers.

These include retraining, the costs of any investigation and clearing up environmental damage. And machines may also have to be shut down, hitting production.

Not all accidents are avoidable, but most firms could do more to minimise the risk.

Doubt

Nearly a quarter of accidents are caused by falls from a height, and about one-third involve being struck by a moving vehicle or moving or falling object.

By IAN MILLER

By law, most employers must insure for a minimum of £2 million for claims arising from any one incident.

Firms should check with their insurers if they are in doubt over their cover. The following five-point checklist should help firms avoid disaster:

- LOOK for hazards and ask employees for their views on dangers.
- DECIDE who might be harmed and how. Don't forget about cleaners, contractors and visitors who are not there all the time.

- EVALUATE the risks. Where a hazard is spotted, assess whether the risk is high, medium or low and ensure that you stay within the law.
- RECORD the findings – businesses with more than five employees must record significant findings to show proper checks are made.
- REVIEW the assessment regularly. As your business grows or work practices change, further changes may be needed if new hazards develop.

Health and Safety Laws

The 1974 **Health and Safety at Work Act,** which requires employers to 'ensure as far as is reasonably practicable, the health, safety, and welfare at work of all staff.' The Act requires:

- Firms to provide all necessary safety equipment and clothing free of charge
- Employers to provide a safe working environment
- Union-appointed representatives to have the right to inspect the workplace and investigate the causes of any accident

The Act also requires employees to take reasonable care to avoid injury to themselves or to others by their work activities, and to cooperate with employers and others in meeting statutory requirements. Employees must not interfere with or avoid anything provided to protect their health, safety, or welfare.

There are also a number of European Union regulations on health and safety at work. These cover the provision and use of work equipment, including the use of computer keyboards and screens, the provision and availability of protective clothing, manual handling operations, and workplace conditions.

Health and safety laws and regulations are enforced in the UK by the **Health and Safety Executive (HSE).** The HSE is a government organization.

Career progression

It is the role of the Human Resources Department in a business to provide good workers with career opportunities and to develop them so that they can gain new skills and take on more responsibilities and challenges. Many workers will want to develop their careers by getting promotion to more senior jobs with more pay. A business that provides few opportunities for career development and promotion will frustrate their workers who are worthy of promotion. If workers are dissatisfied, their work may suffer and they may seek career opportunities with other firms. A business could lose its best workers and fail to recruit new ones, and will eventually be unable to meet its aims and objectives.

Defining what is meant by a 'career' is difficult. Simply working in the same job or a number of different jobs during your working life would not normally be thought of as a career, especially if those jobs involve mundane, repetitive work.

A career normally means working your way up an organization, gaining more experience, and taking on more responsibility in return for more pay. However, not everybody wants to progress in this way. Some people prefer to try out new things, and move from one department to another within the same organization – for example, from production to marketing to finance – broadening their experience as they go. Sometimes, a person's career prospects can be limited by the number of jobs available, or because they are not thought to be suitable for promotion. In other cases career moves may be ruled out because the job involves too much travelling, or because the employee is not able or willing to relocate.

Careers in banking – an example

Management Grades

After Grade 5, the next step is a managerial position, either in a branch, starting with a small one and working your way up, or as a manager of a department undertaking a specialist role, such as personnel, marketing and sales, business finance, auditing and credit control, international, or IT.

Grades 4–5

By this stage, an employee will be working closely with the management team and probably supervising a small team of people. Dealings with customers will become more complex and could involve analysing balance sheets and lending propositions, and preparing reports.

Grade 3

When an employee reaches this grade, they will take on supervisory duties and support more junior members of staff. An employee might be responsible for buying and selling foreign currency and traveller's cheques, assisting customers, and even granting some loans.

Grade 2

Most jobs at this level involve meeting customers – perhaps as a cashier or receptionist – maintaining cash-dispenser machines, processing standing orders, issuing cash cards, and closing accounts.

Grade 1

In this trainee grade you will be expected to undertake basic clerical duties such as inputting records on to computers, filing, faxing, photocopying, and handling routine customer enquiries.

Jobs in banking are graded according to how difficult they are, how much responsibility they carry, and how much experience they require.

Portfolio Activity 3.13

Investigate and report on career opportunities in a business sector of your choice, such as catering, construction, manufacturing, insurance, or retailing.

As a guide, here are some questions you might need to research if you choose health care provision as your business sector:

- What types of jobs are available?
- How can people apply to be a hospital porter or ambulance driver?
- How can people become nurses?
- What qualifications and experience will they need to be promoted to a sister or matron?
- What qualifications and training do people need to become doctors?
- What areas can doctors and nurses specialize in – for example, radiology, physiotherapy, maternity?
- How can doctors become consultants and surgeons?
- What are the main responsibilities of each job?

Opportunities for training

Training workers to improve their existing skills and learn new ones can be very important to a business. Training workers can improve the amount and quality of work they do.

Often training is linked to new developments to give workers the skills to operate new production processes and equipment. A worker may also undergo training – for example, in keeping business accounts – in order to take on a new role in the firm. Training, therefore, is especially important in career development and can increase the satisfaction workers get from their jobs.

However, training can be expensive. Firms will tend to restrict training to what is entirely necessary and will often only train employees who are likely to stay with the firm for a long time. Permanent full-time workers will, therefore, tend to receive more training than their temporary and part-time colleagues. Training for these workers will tend to be short lived and 'on the job'. It will also focus only on the skills they need to carry out their immediate tasks, such as operating an electronic cash register, and on essential health and safety matters.

Types of training

New employees are often introduced to their organization through a programme of **induction training**. This involves learning about the way the business works and what other staff do. For example, it may contain information about:

- The history and development of the business
- On-site facilities, such as canteens and toilets
- Rules and safety procedures
- Relationships between different jobs
- Employee benefits and services

Once in a job, an employee may receive training to develop their work skills. This can be **on-the-job** or **off-the-job** training.

When training is on-the-job, employees are trained while they are carrying out their normal duties at their place of work. This can take a number of forms:

- **Shadowing** – when a new worker is shown what to do by an experienced worker. It can vary from simply sitting next to a machine operator or attending meetings with another office employee.

- **Job rotation** – involves a employee training to do different jobs over short periods of time, either to become multi-skilled or simply to gain knowledge of the way in which the whole company functions. This is often an important element in the training of management trainees.

- **Apprenticeships** – here, the training is normally sufficiently long and thorough to ensure that very little extra training will ever be necessary, apart from some occasional updating of worker skills and knowledge.

Off-the-job training will involve employees attending courses and training programmes away from their normal jobs:

- **In-house courses** are run by firms for their own employees. Some large organizations, like banks and building societies, even have their own residential training centres or colleges offering a variety of courses run by specialist training officers.

- **External courses** may be run by another employer or at a specialist training centre, or with a supplier of new equipment who is willing to train workers how to use it.

- **Vocational and professional courses** are provided by colleges, universities, and increasingly schools, as a means of supporting what is learnt in the workplace. Vocational courses, such as NVQs, provide training in competencies or job-related skills. Professional courses, for example, in accountancy, engineering, or law, are normally completed by university graduates entering these professions in order to develop their careers.

Investors in People

The **Investors in People (IiP)** award is a national training standard set up by the government to help British business get the most from its employees. In order to qualify for the award a firm must:

● Make a public commitment to develop all employees to achieve its business objectives

● Regularly review the training and development needs of all of its employees

● Take action to train and develop staff on recruitment and throughout their employment

● Regularly check training to assess achievement and make improvements

INVESTORS IN PEOPLE

Portfolio Activity 3.14

Look at the pictures below.

1. For each one suggest:

  i What knowledge or skills are being taught?

  ii What kinds of training methods are being used?

  iii What types of business organization would you expect to use these training methods?

  iv What other forms of training could be used to train the workers in each case?

2. Investigate the training available to two employees you know, preferably in different occupations and industrial sectors. What methods are used to train them? What skills are they trained in? What are the benefits of training to the trainee and to their employers?

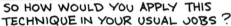

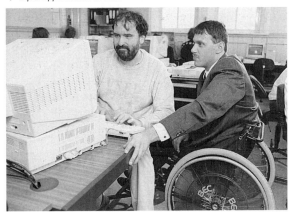
▼ *Equal opportunities at work*

Equal opportunities at work

All employees have a right not to be discriminated against at their place of work. It is the responsibility of an employer to make sure that equal opportunities laws are observed in all aspects of their relationship with employees. This means that the wording of job adverts, the selection of new employees, wage and salary levels, attendance on training programmes, selection of employees for promotion, dismissal, must all be free from discrimination on grounds of sex, marital status, race, religion, or disability.

Types of unlawful discrimination

Discrimination at work can take a number of forms. Few are legal:

- **Direct discrimination** occurs when a person is treated less favourably than another because of their sex, race, religion, disability, etc. For example, this may occur when a pregnant woman is selected for redundancy, or a West Indian person is overlooked for promotion or paid less simply because of the colour of his or her skin.

- **Indirect discrimination** occurs when certain people would find it hard to meet a specific requirement. For example, advertising a job for people who are over six feet tall or who have red hair.

- **Victimization** occurs when a person is treated less favourably after claiming they have been discriminated against repeatedly. For example, a female worker could claim she has been victimized if she is made redundant or moved to a less well paid job because she had complained that her boss was sexually harassing her.

Legal discrimination

Discrimination is only legal where it involves a 'genuine occupational qualification'. This means it is possible to advertise, recruit, train, promote, and dismiss employees on grounds of their different skills, performance, and behaviour at work.

Discrimination on grounds of age is not illegal in the UK, although it is considered to be unfair by many people.

Job advertising

It is legal for an employer to express a preference for one type of person over another in a job advert if there is a genuine occupational qualification for the job concerned. For example, advertising for the following is legal:

- For a coloured actor to appear in a TV programme
- For a female housemistress to work in a girls' boarding school

- For a male attendant for a male toilet
- For male applicants for jobs in countries overseas which may have laws or customs that prevent women doing some types of work
- For a West Indian person to communicate with, and understand the needs of West Indian people in a community project

Equal opportunities at the BBC

'The BBC is committed to equal opportunities for all, irrespective of race, colour, creed, ethnic or national origins, gender, marital status, sexuality, disability, or age.

'We are committed to taking positive action to promote such equality of opportunity, and our recruitment, training, and promotion procedures are based on the requirements of the job.'

Equal opportunities policy

Although not required to do so by law, many firms have written their own equal opportunities policies which attempt to remove discrimination in the selection, payment, training, and promotion of their workers. Leading public and private sector organizations, such as Rank Xerox, Shell UK, British Airways, the BBC, and government departments have all adopted these type of policies.

Anti-discrimination legislation

A number of laws have been passed by the UK government to protect workers rights not to be discriminated against. The main laws are:

- **The Disability Discrimination Act 1995** makes it illegal for an employer to treat a disabled person less favourably than someone else because of their disability. It requires schools and colleges to provide information for disabled people. It also allows the Government to set minimum standards so that disabled people can use public transport more easily. The Act set up the National Disability Council to advise the Government on discrimination against disabled people.

Under the Act, employers and people who provide goods and services to the public must take reasonable measures to make sure that they are not discriminating against disabled people. For example, this could mean removing physical obstructions (by, say, widening doors, fitting ramps) to enable disabled people to use their services. Firms providing services are not allowed to charge a disabled person more to meet the cost of making it easier for them to use their services. People who sell or let property for rent ensure that they do not unreasonably discriminate against disabled people.

If a disabled person feels that they have been unfairly treated in the provision of goods and services or selling of land, they can go to court to seek damages for any financial loss or injury to their feelings. There is no upper limit on the amount of damages that can be paid for injuries to feelings.

- **The Race Relations Act 1976** states that is illegal for an employer to discriminate on grounds of colour, race or ethnic origin in employment, education, training and the provision of housing and other services.

- **The Sex Discrimination Acts 1975/1986** makes it illegal to discriminate against a person on grounds of sex or marital status whether in job adverts, interviews, selection, training, promotion, dismissal and terms of employment. The 1986 act removed restrictions on the hours women could work each week.

- **The Fair Employment (NI) Act** in Northern Ireland contains much of the same legislation as the above laws.

Any employee who feels discriminated against can take their case to an employment tribunal. They can also ask for the help of the Equal Opportunities Commission (EOC), a government body set up in 1975 to

- promote equal opportunities through codes of good practice
- investigate complaints of discrimination
- provide legal advice and financial help when a case goes to court or employment tribunal
- monitor the pay gap between men and women
- review the Equal Pay Act
- issue notices preventing an organisation from discriminating

---

Section **3.3**

Resolving disagreements at work

Why do disagreements between employees and employers occur?

For a wide range of reasons employees (as individuals or as a group) can become unhappy at work. If workers are unhappy because they feel that they are not being treated properly, then they may lose motivation, work less well and eventually leave. This is not in the interests of the firm or the workforce.

▼ *Poor facilities?*

▼ *Harassment?*

Both employers and employees in an organization may have grievances which need to be sorted out if the business is to meet its aims and objectives. The role of the Human Resources Department is to anticipate situations that might cause problems between workers and their employers and to take steps to prevent these from happening and damaging the business.

Employee grievances may also arise due to:

- Incorrect calculation of pay
- Being overlooked for promotion
- Unfair allocation of overtime
- Poor physical working conditions
- Not being allowed time off
- Sexual or racial harassment
- A line manager being rude or unreasonable

However, the most common grievance against employers is unfair dismissal. Dismissal of an employee under the following circumstances is illegal in the UK:

- The employer failing to give the required period of notice as set out in the contract of employment in the case of redundancy
- The employee for going on strike, when others who have done the same have not been dismissed
- The employee for joining or refusing to leave a trade union
- On grounds of the employee's sex, race, or religion
- The employee's illness or pregnancy

Many organizations have a formal **grievance procedure** to deal with complaints from individual employees. A typical grievance procedure will allow both sides in a dispute to present their case to their department manager. The manager will examine the facts and then present his or her decision on what action should be taken, if any. If the employee is not satisfied with the decision they can take their case to more senior managers, or in some cases even a joint consultative committee of unions and management representatives. If the employee is still not satisfied with the outcome, they can apply to have the case examined by an industrial tribunal.

Industrial disputes

Sometimes disagreements can arise between an organization and its entire workforce. Such large-scale disputes can occur for a number of reasons:

- **Pay:** Employees will often demand higher wages if the cost of living is rising or if other groups of workers are getting larger pay rises. Employees may also demand higher pay if their firm is making large profits, or if management are giving themselves large pay rises. A business may be reluctant to pay higher wages if output and sales have not increased, because it will reduce profits.

- **Changes in working practices:** Disputes may occur if employers attempt to change the way in which work is done without consulting employees, or if workers feel that the new arrangements are not as good as before. For example, an employer may introduce shiftwork in an attempt to reduce overtime working. Employees may try to resist these changes.

- **Changes in hours and conditions of work:** Employees will also tend to push for a shorter working week and longer holidays. This again will reduce output and raise costs for an employer, and may be resisted.

- **Redundancies:** Sometimes employers will cut the size of their workforce in an attempt to reduce their costs. New technology may be introduced which requires less labour input. Employees who risk being made redundant may fight to keep their jobs.

Resolving disputes

There are a number of ways employers and employees can attempt to settle their disagreements. These include:

- Negotiation between employers and trade unions

- Seeking the help of the **Advisory, Conciliation, and Arbitration Service (ACAS)**

- Taking the dispute to an **employment tribunal**

- Seeking **civil legal action**

- Appealing to the **European Court of Justice**

We will now consider these options in more detail.

Trade union negotiation

A **trade union** is an organization of workers whose main purpose is to represent the interests of its members (workers) in the workplace. Unions play a key role in resolving disputes between employers and individual employees and with their entire workforce.

Employees in many organizations, whether production operatives or managers, can belong to a trade union. Many trades unions for professional and managerial workers prefer to call themselves **staff associations.**

Several unions or staff associations can represent the interests of workers in the same workplace. For example, teachers and other staff in schools or colleges may belong to the National Union of Teachers (NUT), the Professional Association of Teachers (PAT), or the National Union of Public Employees (NUPE), among others.

Employees who belong to a trade union can seek the help and advice of union officials if they feel they have been unfairly treated or harassed by their employer or by another member of staff. The union official will be able to present the views and rights of the aggrieved employee to representatives of the employer.

Collective bargaining

The process of negotiating over pay and working conditions between trade union and employer representatives is called **collective bargaining**.

Collective bargaining may be organized so that a negotiated settlement determines pay and conditions for all firms in a particular industry, or in local agreements between particular companies and their own workers.

In addition to bargaining on wages and conditions, unions and employers will also negotiate about redundancies and the introduction of new technology.

What happens if negotiations fail?

If a union and an employer fail to reach agreement, they may enlist the help of the **Advisory, Conciliation, and Arbitration Service (ACAS)** to resolve the dispute.

If these further negotiations with unions and ACAS fail, and if one side feels that the other has broken the law, the dispute may be taken to a court of law or to an informal type of court for settling employment disputes called an **employment tribunal**.

Finally, both parties can appeal to the highest court in Europe for a decision, the **European Court of Justice.**

Industrial action

When negotiations fail, trade unions may resort to the following types of industrial action to put pressure on their employers:

● **Overtime ban** – when workers refuse to work more than their normal hours. Many firms rely on overtime to meet production targets and deadlines.

▼ *Striking workers picketing their place of work*

The Trade Union Reform and Employment Rights Act 1993 made unofficial strikes illegal, insisted that strikes could only be considered official if workers had been able to vote for it by postal ballot and allowed employees to claim damages or business losses suffered as a result of industrial actions from those unions responsible

- **Work-to-rule** – when workers comply with every rule and regulation at work in order to slow down production
- **Go slow** – working deliberately slowly
- **Sit-in** – when workers refuse to leave their place of work, often in an attempt to stop their firm from being closed down
- **Strikes** – when negotiations between unions and employers fail, a trade union may recommend that their members withdraw their labour and refuse to work. A strike can be **official**, if it has the backing of the union, or **unofficial** if it is called by workers without the support of their union.

Workers on strike may **picket** their firms by standing outside trying to persuade other people – fellow workers or members of other unions not involved in the dispute – not to enter the premises. However, going on strike will mean a loss of wages for workers, and can result in them losing their jobs if the firm is forced to reduce production as a result of lost customers and profits.

In extreme cases, an employer may retaliate by locking workers out of the firm with no pay.

Employee and employer associations

The aims of trade unions

The trade union movement started more than a hundred years ago. Workers, dissatisfied with poor pay and working conditions, organised themselves into groups to negotiate with 'one voice' against powerful employers. The main functions of trade unions are largely unchanged today being

- To defend employee rights
- To secure improvements in working conditions, including health and safety
- To secure adequate pay for their members
- To secure improvements in sick pay, pensions and industrial injury benefits

- To provide education, training, and recreational and social amenities for members
- To encourage firms to increase worker participation in business decision making

Membership of trade unions in the UK has been declining. In the late 1970s over 50% of people in work belonged to a union. By 1998 this had fallen to just 31%, around 8 million workers. Union membership has declined as employment in manufacturing industries has fallen. Participation in unions is now highest in professional and lowest in sales occupations.

▼ **Trade unions in Great Britain, 1976 – 1997**

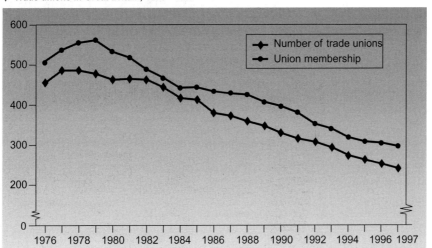

Labour Market Trends, July 1999

Types of Trade Union

There a number of different types of trade union:

- General unions represent workers from many different occupations and industries. For example, the Transport and General Workers Union (TGWU) represents all sorts of clerical, manufacturing, transport and commercial workers.

- Industrial unions represent workers in the same industry, for example, the Communications Workers union (CMU) and the Iron and Steel Trades Confederation (ISTC).

- Craft unions are often small and few in number today. They usually represent workers with the same skill across several industries, such as the Graphical, Paper and Media union (GPMU) and the Amalgamated Engineers and Electrical Union (AEEU).

- Non-manual unions and staff associations represent workers in professional and commercial jobs. For example, National Union of Teachers and Royal College of Nursing. UNISON is the largest union in the UK with 1.4 million members representing local government, health service, and other public sector workers.

Many large firms have a single union agreement with their employees. This means one union will represent all the workers in their place of work. Employers benefit by only having to negotiate on wages and working conditions with one a single union rather than many.

The structure of a trade union

Every union in the UK is entirely independent and self governing, but many are affiliated to the Trade Union Congress (TUC). The TUC represents the union movement in discussions with employer associations, the media and the UK and European Union Governments.

The TUC is headed by the general council, which is the TUCs executive decision making body. It meets every year to discuss and establish policy. Each union can send delegates to the meeting, to debate and vote on policy.

The internal structure trade unions varies widely, but there is a typical pattern extending from full-time union officials in the union headquarters to union members in factories, shops and offices.

The Typical Structure of a Trade Union

- **General Secretary** – Head of a Union

- **National Executive** – Policy making group. An important role of the executive is to negotiate pay and conditions with employers

- **Full-time Officials** – Union members at headquarters who assist local branches

- **Union Branches** – These co-ordinate the affairs of union members at a localised level

- **Shop Stewards** – Conduct day to day business of the union in their places of work as well as carrying out the job they were employed to do

What are employers associations?

These organizations exist to provide employers with help and advice, for example, on legal matters and calculating tax, and to represent their views in discussions with trade unions and Government. For example, the National Farmers Union (NFU) represents the views of farm owners and managers. Other examples include the Society of British Aerospace Companies and the Federation of Small Businesses.

Many employers associations belong to the Confederation of British Industry (CBI) along with many trade associations and over 250,000 different companies. The CBI is a very influential national organization representing the interests of many different employers in discussions with unions and Governments. It also collects and publishes up-to-date information on industrial trends, such as wage costs and sales, and on how well UK firms are performing.

Portfolio Activity 3.15

In groups of four, act out the following roles in an industrial dispute between an employer and a trade union. Your job is to try to find a settlement both sides in the dispute are willing to accept.

Characters in the dispute

Union representatives

1. The shop steward

2. A machine operator

Management representatives

1. The managing director

2. The work study engineer

UNION THREATENS ACTION OVER NEW MACHINERY

The Association of Metalworkers are today threatening to undertake industrial action if the decision to install new computer-assisted metal shaping and grinding machinery in AK Metals Plc Sunderland plant is taken without assurance on pay and redundancies. The local branch of the union has asked for a 5% wage increase to operate the new machinery.

'Any strike could damage the company considerably,' explained Mr Graham Stone, managing director of AK Metals (North). A large overseas order has boosted the company's prospects recently and they are keen to fulfil it. Any disruption could threaten their international reputation. The management are also keen to avoid any increase in wage costs.

Workers are claiming that the new technology requires a higher level of skill and concentration and compensation is sought. They are also seeking management assurances that there will be no redundancies as a result of the new machines.

The two sides in the dispute have agreed to meet and negotiate today.

The union brief

The machine operators want a pay rise for operating more complex and demanding machinery. You also want to set an example for the future. You do not want the management to think that every time it introduces new ways of working it can overlook its workforce. What you want is a share in the increased profits that will come from the new machines.

You also fear that redundancies may follow as machines replace workers, and you want to limit the number of jobs lost.

You both know that the firm has recently received a large order from abroad, so you need to be careful that you do not cause the firm to lose the business. Losing the order could mean losing jobs.

Your tasks before negotiations

Before you enter negotiations, write a brief report for all your union members to read, pointing out your demands and the management's position. This should include answers to questions like:

- What is your pay claim?
- Why have you made this pay claim?
- What has been the management response?
- What forms of action could the union take, if necessary?
- Why are both you and the management keen to avoid a strike?

Your tasks after negotiations

Write a report highlighting the results of negotiations, that is, what agreements were reached, if any?

If no firm agreement was reached, do you advise your members to accept or reject the management's offer? What will the union do next?

The management brief

The work study engineer has concluded that the machines require no more effort to operate than the old ones. In fact, you feel that they ease pressure on the skilled operator. No pay rise is necessary to compensate.

As the managing director, you fear that any cost reductions from the increased output from specialist machinery may be lost if workers push for higher wages. It may even allow lower-cost competitors to undercut your prices. Also, if you are unable to cut the number of jobs, your plant will be overmanned and wage costs will be much higher than they need to be. However, you do not want to lose the goodwill of the workforce at a critical time, with an overseas order to fulfil.

Your tasks before negotiations

Write an information sheet for the other management staff, including answers to such questions as:

- What wage claim has the union asked for?
- Why are you keen to meet this claim?
- Why are you keen to avoid a strike?
- What will be discussed with the union?

Task after negotiations

Prepare another management document to report on agreements reached and their effects on the company. Outline the action that will be taken if negotiations break down and no firm agreement is reached.

The negotiations

The four people taking part in the roleplay should try to negotiate an agreement acceptable to both sides. If you cannot reach an agreement perhaps your tutor can join in to act as an independent commentator, or ask for the meeting to take a short break while you work out what to do next.

The Advisory, Conciliation, and Arbitration Service (ACAS)

If negotiations between employer and employee representatives fail to reach a settlement that is acceptable to both sides, they may ask for the help of the **Advisory, Conciliation, and Arbitration Service (ACAS)**.

ACAS is an independent organization set up by the government in 1975 to help settle disputes between employers and unions. It publishes a code of good practice which employers may wish to follow when dealing with their employees.

The main aim of ACAS is to improve relations between employers and employees by bringing opposing parties together and attempting to find solutions to disputes.

When employers and employees are unable to agree, they may wish to talk with an independent organization like ACAS. In its conciliation role, ACAS will listen to both sides in a dispute and look for possible common ground. When asked to arbitrate, ACAS will listen to all the people involved in a dispute and make a decision for both sides on what to do. Sometimes both sides in a dispute may agree in advance to accept whatever ACAS decides.

ACAS in Northern Ireland is known as the **Labour Relations Agency**.

ACAS tries to bring opposing parties together

Employment tribunal

If an employee, or group of employees, feels that an employer has treated them unfairly and broken employment law, they can take their case to an **employment tribunal**.

An industrial tribunal is rather like a court of law. It is less formal than the type of court you often see on television, but it has the authority to settle cases under a range of employment laws, such as wrongful or unfair dismissal or discrimination.

Each tribunal is made up of three people – a legally trained chairperson, plus one employer and one employee representative. They will listen to each side in the dispute and then make their recommendations. They can either reject the claim or make one of three decisions in favour of the employee, which the employer is legally bound to abide by. These are that:

- The employee is to be given back their old job
- The employee is to be given another job
- The employee is to be compensated

Both employer and employee have the right to appeal against a decision by the employment tribunal.

The Employment Rights Act 1996

This law simplifies the work of employment tribunals and allows them different ways to solve industrial and employment disputes. To speed up the process of settling disputes an employment tribunal can decide a case without a full hearing or in some situations, without a formal hearing at all.

In addition, the Employment Rights Act enables the Arbitration, Conciliation and Arbitration Service to provide an arbitration scheme to settle unfair dismissal disputes without using the law and without going to an employment tribunal. The Act also encourages employers and employees to use the internal appeals systems within their organisations to resolve unfair dismissal cases. It allows financial awards in settlement of cases of unfair dismissal to be reduced if the employee failed to use the procedures of the business, or raised if the employer failed to use them.

Civil legal action

Instead of going to an employment tribunal, an employee may decide to seek compensation for unfair dismissal by taking their employer to court. However, this can be expensive because it involves employing a solicitor, and sometimes a barrister as well. If the employer wins the case, then the employee may have to pay both sets of legal costs.

Because court cases can involve bad publicity, employers may sometimes wish to make an out-of-court settlement with a former employee, or suggest that both parties go to arbitration with an independent body deciding the outcome of the case.

The European Court of Justice

The **European Court of Justice** is run by judges from the member countries of the European Union. The role of the court is to settle cases where European Union laws or directives are concerned.

An employee, or employer, can appeal to the European Court if they believe that British courts have failed to apply European laws correctly.

The European Court is often used as a last resort to settle a disagreement between employees and firms if they have failed to reach a satisfactory settlement in a UK court.

EU directives

The European Union has passed a number of directives which aim to give workers in member countries the same basic employment rights. These include:

- A maximum working week of 48 hours
- Freedom to join unions and take strike action
- Equal treatment for part-time and full-time workers
- Access to appropriate training and re-training opportunities
- Equal treatment for men and women
- The right to be consulted on changes in organization, new working methods, mergers, and redundancies
- Protection of rights of pregnant women, with working hours and conditions to be adapted if the job endangers health
- Freedom to move between EU member states for work and to enjoy the same terms and conditions of employment, such as pay and holidays, as native workers, and have equal recognition of qualifications

You are the head of the Human Resources Department in a large manufacturing plant making electric irons. Paul Downie, a union shop steward, has been asked by a team of workers to make an official complaint about their treatment by a production supervisor, Mr Frampton

'I have been asked by the members of my union to make a formal complaint against Mr Martin Frampton, one of the production supervisors. Let me say before we begin that my members understand perfectly well that the company is under a lot of pressure to bring its new range of products to the market. We understand that this means that staff will be under stress and pressurized.

'However, Mr Frampton has been abusive to my members. He has called them lazy and stupid when they have failed to meet targets. One worker was told off publicly in front of his workmates and shouted at as if he were a child. Mr Frampton expects us to produce twice as much as we did before, in under half the time. It cannot be done – these targets are unreasonable. We cannot work in the way demanded by Mr Frampton. I am sure that if this treatment continues, some of my members will become so stressed that it will affect their health and work attendance. If this happens we will fall behind even further.

'We all want the firm to be a success, but it takes time to learn to produce a new range of goods, and staff must be treated like adults.'

You listen carefully to Paul's views and agree to follow up the complaint by talking to the supervisor. A short while later, Mr Frampton comes to your office…

'Perhaps I have been pushing too hard, but we all know that if we don't get the new range out by the end of the month, we'll lose our customers – and they may never come back. What with the redundancies last year and the financial mess the firm's in, I've tried to ensure that we all keep our jobs by pushing the men to get the job done by the deadline.

'Management have said we need to get the goods in the shops in the next four weeks. The production manager said we'd be able to produce the first batches in two weeks' time. At present we're at least a week behind target. The men are working too slowly, and taking too long to learn how to produce the new range. I shouldn't have shouted in public, and I will apologize, but we must keep the pressure up. We can't have staff threatening to go off sick if they are asked to meet reasonable deadlines.'

1. a You have now heard both sides of the disagreement and must come to a decision. Do you agree with Paul or his supervisor? Or do you think a compromise is better? What are the reasons for your decision?

b What further action could Paul take if he is not satisfied with your decision?

c What could be the effect of the dispute on the organization?

2. a Find out about the grievance procedure of your school/college and one other organization of your choice.

b What trade unions, if any, represent the interests of employees in your school/college and other organization?

3. Using desktop publishing software, prepare a fact sheet advising employees what to do if they feel they have been unfairly treated. To do this, you will need to investigate:

- The grounds on which employees can claim unfair treatment in terms of, for example, discrimination, harassment, dismissal, redundancy, and unequal pay

- The role of industrial tribunals, ACAS, civil courts, and the EU Court of Social Justice, and how to apply to them

You listen carefully to Paul's views and agree to follow up the complaint by talking to the supervisor. A short while later, Mr Frampton comes to your office…

Section **3.4**

The rights and responsibilities of employees and employers

Legal obligations

If employees and employers are to cooperate with each other, it is important that both parties live up to what is expected of them. When you start work you will expect your employer to pay you correctly, to make sure your workplace is clean and not hazardous to your health, and to treat you fairly.

Your employer will also have expectations of you. You will be expected to turn up for work on time, follow the rules and regulations of the organization, cooperate with your colleagues, make good use of your skills, and be honest and trustworthy.

Many of the expectations of employees and employers are influenced by laws passed in the UK. Employment laws and health and safety regulations give employers and their employees certain legal rights and obligations which must be observed.

Employers' rights
An employer has the following main legal rights in the UK:

● Employees are expected to comply with the terms and conditions of their employment contract

● Employees are expected to comply with health and safety regulations

● Employers may take appropriate disciplinary action against an employee who does not comply with the terms of their contract or health and safety regulations, or who commits an offence against fellow workers or their organization (for example, stealing)

● Employers have the right to defend their actions at ACAS, an employment tribunal, and the European Court of Justice (see 3.3)

More employee rights

In addition to the main legal rights employment laws also give employees the following rights immediately they start work:

* The right not to suffer unlawful deductions from pay
* The right to work in a safe and healthy environment
* The right to receive statutory sick pay (SSP) during illness
* The right to itemized pay statements
* The right to return to work after illness
* The right to time off work for public duties, for example, jury service
* The right not to be dismissed, made redundant or subjected to any other detriment for refusing to work on Sundays
* The right of women to receive equal pay as men for work of equal value
* The right of women to maternity leave and reasonable time off for ante-natal care
* The right of women to return to work after maternity leave

After two years of continuous employment for the same employer, employees also qualify for the following rights:

* The right of women to receive maternity pay
* The right not to be unfairly dismissed
* The right to redundancy payment
* The right to time off to look for work or arrange training in a redundancy situation

EU directives

The European Union has passed a number of directives which aim to give workers in member countries the same basic employment rights. These include:

- A maximum working week of 48 hours
- Freedom to join unions and take strike action
- Equal treatment for part-time and full-time workers
- Access to appropriate training and re-training opportunities
- Equal treatment for men and women
- The right to be consulted on changes in organization, new working methods, mergers, and redundancies
- Protection of rights of pregnant women, with working hours and conditions to be adapted if the job endangers health
- Freedom to move between EU member countries for work and to enjoy the same terms and conditions of employment, such as pay and holidays, as native workers, and have equal recognition of qualifications

Employer responsibilities

Employers have the following responsibilities to look after their employees:

- To explain business aims and objectives (see chapter 1)
- To offer and facilitate training
- To implement equal opportunities at work
- To comply with health and safety regulations
- To calculate their pay and any deductions (remuneration)

Employee responsibilities

Employers can expect their employees to have the following responsibilities:

- To comply with the terms and conditions in their contract of employment
- To meet health and safety regulations
- To meet the aims and objectives of the business
- To provide good customer service (see chapter 1)
- To maintain standards of quality in their work

We will now consider the responsibilities of both employers and employees in more detail.

Portfolio Activity 3.17

Look back through this chapter to remind yourself of the different laws and regulations that protect the rights of employers and employees. Which laws do you think provided protection in the following situations and why?

CAR FIRM FOR 'WOMEN ONLY' GUILTY OF BIAS

A firm which sacked its salesmen to create an all-woman team was found guilty yesterday of 'blatant' discrimination. Swithland Motors denied discrimination, admitting that the majority of the sales staff at its 19 sites were woman, but that they were selected purely on merit.

Daily Mail, 21.6.1994

Officers bullied pregnant PC

A policewoman won a sexism battle yesterday against bosses who blocked her promotion to sergeant.

PC Suzanne Box claims senior officers intimidated and bullied her in her struggle to climb up through the ranks. She applied for promotion while six months pregnant but felt totally intimidated during an assessment hearing with a chief inspector.' He was abrupt and I realised that I wasn't getting a fair hearing' she said in her statement. She had already been told that she was not ready for promotion by a detective chief inspector because she was pregnant.

Daily Mail, 7.2.1995

MUFFLING THE SOUND OF JUSTICE

A council employee has won damages worth £100,000 against his local authority for loss of hearing and stress caused by tinnitus. Justin Cayse worked as road maintenance crew for 5 years and regularly used pneumatic drills and cutting machines to construct and repair road and pavement surfaces. He claimed the council consistently failed to provide adequate ear protection and information on the dangers to hearing of high levels of noise. The council claimed that warning posters had been placed in council locker rooms and workers only had to ask for protectors if they needed them.

Union liable for £250,000 damages

Bracken Engineering Ltd. has successfully sued the Amalgamated Engineers and Electrical Union (AEEU) for damages caused by a wildcat strike at its plant by AEEU members for 10 days during February last year. Workers had claimed the plant was too cold to work in during the bad spell of weather experienced last winter. Managers at Bracken presented evidence of independent temperature readings during prior to and during the strike and claimed the unofficial action resulted in lost orders which would have kept the plant fully employed for 7 months.

Your turkey is well and truly stuffed!

Carol Smith is certainly not in the festive mood this Christmas. Not only have bosses told her and fellow workers that there will be no bonus payments this year but they have deducted £20 from their November pay packets to pay for the office party. 'They never even asked us' said Carol. 'So just for that we want our money back and intend to party somewhere where the bosses are not invited!'

ON THE WRONG TRACK

Graham Hartson has been confined to a wheelchair since a car accident five years ago. He has recently moved into purpose-built accommodation which has given him the freedom to be independent for the first time since he left hospital after his crash. But there is one problem with his new-found freedom. To catch a train from his local railway station he needs to descend seven stairs. No ramp is provided. Railtrack, the owners of the station, intend to provide a ramp but not for another 18 months. A spokesperson for Railtrack said they intend to discuss with Mr Hartson what alternative travel arrangements they might be able to assist with until the ramp is in place.

Key words

Write down definitions and explanations of the following key words and terms to help you remember the things you learnt in this chapter;

Human Resources Department	Letter of application	Annualised hours systems	Equal Opportunities Commission
Recruitment and selection process	References	EU Working Time Directive	ACAS
Job analysis	Shortlisting	Gross and net earnings	Employment tribunal
Job description	Panel interview	Wages Act	European Court of Justice
Person specification	Board interview	Equal Pay Acts	Collective Bargaining
Internal recruitment	Contract of employment	HSE	Trade unions
External recruitment	Terms and conditions of employment	Health and Safety at Work Act	TUC
Careers service	Disciplinary procedures	On the job training	Single union agreement
Headhunting	Redundancy	Off the job training	CBI
Jobcentres	Working conditions	Induction training	Employment Rights Act
Job application form	Shiftwork	Disability Discrimination Act	
CV	Flexitime	Race Relations Act	
		Sex Discrimination Act	

Test your knowledge

1 Which of the following external sources of recruitment is a business seeking an experienced financial manager most likely to choose?
   A a local employment service office
   B the university 'milk round'
   C a professional recruitment agency
   D a trade union

2 Employers often like job applicants to submit a letter of application for an advertised job because:
   A it reveals information not included in an application form
   B it is more personal
   C it makes shortlisting easier
   D it reveals handwriting ability?

3 A person specification is designed to:
   A analyse the authority and responsibility involved in a job
   B identify the qualities of a worker needed to do a specific job
   C set performance criteria for a job
   D identify the various tasks involved in a job?

4 A job selection interview should fulfil all of the following functions **except**;
   A inform candidates about the job and the organisation
   B allow the assessment of the candidates personality
   C check factual information provided by each candidate
   D agree terms and conditions of employment?

5 A company has expanded into new premises and is seeking additional employees. Which of the following represents the usual order of recruitment and selection procedures?
   A advertise; applications; shortlist; interviews; appoint
   B advertise; shortlist; interviews; applications; appoint
   C applications; interviews; shortlist; advertise; appoint
   D advertise; applications; interviews; shortlist; appoint

6 A job description should include the following information **except**:
   A job title and position
   B job tasks and responsibilities
   C personal qualities and attributes
   D job performance criteria?

Questions 7–9 share the following answer options:
   A Equal Pay Act
   B Health and Safety at Work Act
   C Race Relations Act
   D Sex Discrimination Act

Which of the above laws would an organization be breaking if it:

7 Failed to give workmen working with chemicals protective clothing?

8 Sacked a woman because she was pregnant?

9 Advertised a job for 'English male drivers only'?

10 The role of ACAS is to:
   A help employers in settling disputes with trade unions
   B help trade unions in settling disputes with employers
   C make decisions which are legally binding on employers and employees
   D from an independent standpoint, assist employers and employees to reach agreement

11 Which of the following reasons for dismissing an employee would be unfair?
   A for joining a trade union
   B for redundancy due to a fall in sales of the product
   C for very poor time-keeping
   D for sexual harassment

12 What is the main advantage to employees of having a contract of employment?
   A it guarantees that you can never be sacked
   B it guarantees that you will be promoted
   C it explains how to behave at work
   D it clearly states your rights and responsibilities as a worker

13 Callum is in dispute with his manager about how much holiday he can have. Where should this be written down?
   A equal opportunities law
   B job description
   C contract of employment
   D employment law

14 Which of the following is the most likely reason for instant dismissal?
   A illness for a few days confirmed by a medical note
   B serious theft
   C being late back from lunch
   D attending a union meeting after work

15 Which of the following is a legal responsibility of an employer?
   A to ensure that health and safety standards at work are met
   B to give staff regular training
   C to provide a quiet place to rest during breaks
   D to ensure that food can be bought on the premises for staff

16 Under health and safety legislation, who has a legal responsibility to report any health and safety hazards?

   A both employers and employees

   B employees only

   C company owners

   D customers

17 Which of the following does an employer have a legal responsibility to deduct from an employee's wages?

   A union membership fees

   B income tax

   C season ticket loan repayments

   D subscriptions to a social club

18 About which of the following matters do employers have the right to be consulted by employees?

   A if they want to join a trade union

   B if they want to join a social club

   C if they want to take evening classes

   D when they want to take annual leave

19 Which of the following details are given in the remuneration section of a contract of employment?

   A holiday entitlements

   B main duties

   C trade union membership

   D pay

20 A friend of yours claims she has been unfairly dismissed by her employer because she is pregnant. What would you advise her to do?

   A take her case to the European Court of Social Justice

   B nothing

   C write to her employer demanding redundancy pay

   D take her case to an industrial tribunal

21 a Describe three benefits to a firm from cooperation between the employer and employees.

   b Suggest three reasons why a dispute between an employer and an employee may occur.

   c What is an industrial tribunal and why may an employer or employee use one?

22 a. Explain how the following legislation affects the rights and responsibilities of both employer and employees at work:

   • equal opportunity laws

   • health and safety law

   b. An employee has a right to receive a contract of employment. Describe five terms and conditions that are likely to appear in a contract of employment.

chapter 4 Business communications

What you need to learn

People working in a business have to communicate with each other and with people outside the business such as customers and suppliers.

Oral communications include face-to-face meetings, telephone calls and video-conferencing.

Written communications include **letters, memos, notices, financial documents** and **advertisements**. Written documents should conform to an accepted business style and layout and be free from errors of spelling and grammar.

Information communications technology can be used to send **electronic mail** and **fax transmissions**.

You will need to find out the different methods of communication used in business and what they are for.

Section **4.1**

Why do businesses need to communicate?

Keeping people informed

Communication is the process by which information is passed from one person or organization to another.

When we talk to each other or write letters and notes to other people, we are communicating information to them. Communication is very important in business. All businesses need to communicate with customers, other organizations and employees on a daily basis. A business that fails to communicate the right messages at the right time to customers, other businesses, and employees will not be successful.

Portfolio Activity 4.1

1. The following situations arise from day to day in many business organizations. All of them will involve communication. In each case write down:

- Who the communication is with
- Why you need to communicate with them
- What message you need to communicate
- What is the best way of getting the message to them

i A customer has sent an e-mail to your company asking for information about your products. How would you reply?

ii You take an important phone call for a work colleague who is out of the office. You do not know if your colleague will be back before you leave for a meeting. How would you make sure your colleague gets the phone message?

iii Some new fire fighting equipment has been installed in your office. How would you make sure people know how to use it in an emergency?

iv You have to cancel a meeting with other staff in your department at short notice. How would you make sure they know it has been cancelled, and let them know about alternative arrangements?

2. Investigate the purpose and methods of oral, written and electronic communications in a business organization of your choice:

- Why do they need to send and retrieve information?
- Who do they send to, and retrieve information from?
- What types of information do they send and retrieve?
- What documents does the business use to record, send, and retrieve information?

Collect examples of business documents used by the organization (Remember to ask the business owner's or manager's permission to use them).

Write up your findings in a short report using a word processor. Include, if possible, examples of business documents you have collected.

v A customer has written in to complain about late delivery of goods ordered from your company. How would you reply?

vi An employee is consistently late for work and has ignored all verbal warnings. How would you tell them that if they do not start on time in future they are likely to get the sack?

vii The goods inward department has taken delivery of the office equipment you ordered. How could they notify you?

There are a number of reasons why businesses need written communications:

● **To communicate with customers:** The main purpose of any commercial business is to sell goods and/or services to customers. A business that fails to communicate the right information at the right time to customers is in danger of losing them to rival firms.

To an external customer a member of staff is the organization they are dealing with. Because first impressions last, it is very important the first communication between an organization and a customer leaves a good impression.

Sometimes a business may write to potential customers advertising its new goods or services. However, it is often the customer who first contacts a business – for example, to find out about products and prices. Some may write to complain about a product, while others may write to say how pleased they are with the product. In all cases a business should reply quickly to customers with the information they want. For example, in the case of a complaint, the firm should send a letter of apology and offer either a refund or a replacement.

● **To communicate with other businesses:** A business will need to make regular contact with other business organizations if they are customers or suppliers.

A business will have dealings with many different suppliers. Banks, insurance companies, employment agencies, solicitors, accountants, advertising agencies – are all suppliers of business services. Others will provide materials, component parts, fuel, machinery, and other equipment. As a customer of these organizations, a business may write to make enquiries, complain, or thank them for their services.

A business will also need to communicate with government organizations such as the Inland Revenue, Customs and Excise department, Health and Safety Executive, Environment Agency, etc.

● **To communicate with colleagues:** Everyone in a business works as part of a team to achieve the firm's objectives (see chapter 1). Communication between work colleagues is therefore very important. For example, managers will need to communicate business objectives to the workforce, negotiate wages, and inform them of changes to working practices. More informally, employees may need to take phone messages for colleagues, or arrange business and social meetings.

▼ *All businesses need to communicate with customers, other organizations, and employees on a daily basis.*

Types of communications

Business employees communicate with each other and with their suppliers and customers using a wide variety of methods, including:

- Oral communications
  - face-to-face meetings
  - videoconferencing
  - using the telephone

- Written communications
  - letters
  - memos
  - notices
  - financial documents
  - advertisements

- Electronic communications
  - e-mail
  - fax transmissions

McDonald's staff told not to mince their words

McDonald's, the fast food chain, has found that its service with a smile is proving too much to chew on for the British stiff upper lip. The company which brought American 'Have a nice day' culture to nearly every high street in Britain has told its restaurant managers across the country to serve customers the way they like best. A senior spokesperson for McDonald's said a survey of staff and customers found that people had become unhappy with the 'robotic' service in McDonald's restaurants.

She told *Personnel Management Plus* magazine: 'A lot of customers felt we were too machine-like. Customers wanted more warmth over the counter. It was only through our research that we discovered they thought we were a bit brash and a bit arrogant.' Staff were also uncomfortable and complained about having to say 'Thank you, please call again' to every customer.

McDonald's is now training its 500 managers to be more flexible to local needs. If thought fit by managers, McDonald's customers may be greeted in future by phrases such as 'Eh-up, chuck,' or 'Get that down your neck,' or 'Here's your Big Mac, whack'.

Financial Times 17.10.1994

| Section | 4.2 | Oral communications |

It's good to talk

The easiest way to communicate is simply to talk to people. Today people can talk to each other all over the world using a telephone. However, oral or verbal communication is often complemented by facial expressions, such as frowning at another person's suggestion, and body language, such as shrugging shoulders as an indication of indifference. Non-verbal forms of communication such as pictures, graphs and letters, may also form the topic of verbal discussion. Therefore, to be truly effective, verbal communication requires both sound and vision.

We all speak to people every day and so should all have good spoken skills However, the kinds of formal spoken skills needed at work are different to those we may be used to. People sometimes find it difficult to speak to people who they have never met before or whom they are quite junior to in age, experience or position. These skills come with practice.

A person with good oral communication skills will:

- have the confidence to talk to people they do not know

- have a clear voice (regional accents make no difference as long as they are not so broad that people from other regions do not understand)

- listen and not interrupt other people while they are talking

- give the impression that they want to hear what the speaker is saying

- not tap their fingers, not look at the clock or their watch

- use the name of the person they are talking too, to make the listener feel recognised and important

- speak neither too quickly nor too slowly

- not use words that the listener does not know

- not use slang words

- not make the listener feel threatened or inferior

- always give the other person, or listener, an opportunity to ask questions in order to clarify their own understanding

- understands the messages people give with their body language and

- put people at their ease.

- use eye contact when talking to someone face to face, without staring

In business, it is very important to establish a good relationship with work colleagues, suppliers and customers as quickly as possible and to find out what their needs are. For example, customers are more likely to buy products from firms where they feel that their needs have been listened to, and where the firm is genuinely trying to provide for their needs rather than simply trying to persuade them to buy a product which may not be exactly what they want. Similarly, colleagues will be more ready to help good commmunicators at work, and suppliers may be willing to offer a better service, perhaps even giving organizations with good communication skills priority over others.

Face-to-face communications
These takes place when you meet work colleagues, suppliers or customers in person. You will be able to tell how they react to what you are saying by their body language.

Meeting and greeting
Greeting the customer is very important. In large retail stores a few words of welcome and a smile will be enough because so many customers will be first time visitors.

In organizations which supply goods and services by order customers should be greeted with a handshake, especially the representatives of business customers. On first meeting you should give your name and remember theirs. Exchanging business cards will help. Regular customers should be greeted by name.

Some customers will tell you their needs – for example, to make a purchase or receive information – and ask how you intend to respond. Others may need to be asked some questions by you to find out their needs, particularly if they are not sure themselves. For example, customers browsing in a clothes shop may need help if they are unsure of their size or the colour they want.

One chance to make a first impression

Because the way staff greet and say goodbye to customers is so important to the success of an organization, the retail subsidiary of a well known American film company provides the following guidelines to staff on acceptable greetings and goodbyes to use with customers:

In addition to the greeting, staff are encouraged to:

- Tell them some trivia about the organization
- Ask open-ended questions to establish customers' needs
- Incorporate product information
- Talk about current in-store promotions
- Acknowledge something special about the guest

'Good morning and welcome'

'Hi, how are you?'

'Hello'

'Hi, is this your first visit to the store?'

'Have fun.'

'Don't hesitate to ask if you need any help.'

'Hello, how are you today?'

'Goodbye'

'Goodbye, please call again.'

'Goodbye, have a great day.'

'Bye, safe journey.'

'Goodbye, hope to see you soon.'

'Goodbye and take care.'

Business meetings

Many meetings in business are informal – for example, work colleagues stopping to discuss their work as they pass each other in the corridor or a customer approaching a sales assistant in a shop for advice. However, many meetings in business are formal, whereby people are invited to attend a meeting at a given time and venue to discuss particular issues. Staff at all levels in an organization will be involved at some time in a meeting. However, meetings among managers tend to be the most frequent.

Internal business meetings are the most common means of attempting to agree business plans, resolve difficulties and find solutions to problems. Typically, managers will use meetings to:

- set business objectives

- monitor progress and business performance

- discuss new ideas

- plan for the future

- discuss and make decisions

Well-run meetings usually require the following key ingredients:

- a strong chairperson who is able to keep people to the point and encourage everybody to have their say, yet at the same time prevent certain individuals from dominating.

- an **agenda** issued in advance of the meeting, with a clear list of topics for discussion

- a group of people who are capable of keeping to the point and who are willing to listen to each other, make compromises and reach a solution.

- someone who is able to take notes of points and matters arising from the meeting for future reference. These notes can be used to produce the minutes of the meeting.

▼ Figure 4.1: An Example of An Agenda for a Business Meeting

KRB FOODS PLC

Notice of Meeting: **Regional Sales Divisions**
Date: 26 March 200X
Time: 2.30 pm
Venue: Head Office, London

Agenda

1. Apologies for absence

2. Minutes of last meeting

3. Action points – budget allocation for IT

                 – new promotion campaign update

4. 'Paris' project: tender proposals for research

5. AOB (Any Other Business)

6. Date of next meeting

▼ *Videoconferencing can be used for face to face communication between people separated by long distances*

Cascading will often follow senior management meetings at which decisions have been made. This involves setting up a series of meetings to tell lower level managers, supervisors and operatives the senior managers' business decisions and ideas and how they will be put into effect.

External business meetings will involve people from other organizations. These may be representatives of major business customers or suppliers.

Meetings with customers will typically be used to discuss their customer wants, present new products, agree prices, and generate sales. However, they may also be used to discuss and resolve customer complaints.

Meetings with suppliers will typically be used to discuss what they can do for your business: the goods or services they can provide, their delivery times and prices. A business may meet with several suppliers before it chooses one to supply a particular good or service for example, to supply materials, or to provide computer maintenance, or construct or rent a new building the business can expand into.

Video conferencing

Modern communications technology can transmit sound as well as pictures very quickly over very long distances. This means people in different places can talk to each other and see each other on TV or computer screens. **Videoconferencing** can link two or more people in this way and offers a quicker and cheaper way of having face-to-face meetings than having people travel over long distances.

'Take a look at the problem – Video conferencing helps decisions'

Keith Platt, who runs a £3 million turnover insurance business, has been using British Telecom desktop video conferencing for just over a year to link six sites around the country. 'We did it because we were looking for a competitive advantage in a market where direct sales of insurance are cleaning up the business'.

Platt is based in Wakefield and a two hour meeting in London effectively meant writing off a whole day. Now, by linking up on the video phone, he can save hours at a time – and the cost of travelling. He uses the facilities for board meetings, management meetings, presentations and training.

You can resolve a lot more things by talking face to face. You can see the body language, negotiate and come to quick decisions" says Platt who has spent around £40,000 on video communications equipment.

The cost of video communications is coming down all the time. Whereas five years ago it was strictly for the multinationals, who has hundreds of thousands to invest in large systems with expensive, dedicated transmission lines, the entry cost of video phones is now just a few thousand pounds.

The Daily Telegraph 8.11.1994

Telephone communications

The telephone is an important piece of communications equipment in business. It allows an organisation to talk to it's employees, customers and suppliers anywhere in the world. However, using the telephone in business requires skill.

Using a telephone in a business context is very different to using one to speak to family or friends. Even though the person you are talking to cannot see you, s/he will still be able to tell a great deal about what you are thinking from your tone of voice, the words you use, and from your breathing. The way in which you say things is as important as what you say.

Many businesses now issue **mobile phones** to staff who need to travel away from their offices. This allows them to keep in touch and up-to-date on the latest developments in their business. They can also keep in touch with their customers.

Voice messaging is available to the customers of telephone service providers such as Vodafone and British Telecom. The service allows telephone users to record a message and have it delivered to an electronic 'mailbox'. The user dials the mailbox and uses a personal identification number to listen to the messages. Voice messaging systems are used by business people who travel or who are away from their offices. The advantage of voicemail is that it is useful for communicating out of office hours and between countries where there are time differences.

Telephone courtesy: some golden rules

- Try to answer the phone in less than four rings.
- Be enthusiastic and friendly when you answer, and try to make callers feel welcome.
- Hold the transmitter directly in front of your mouth when speaking.
- State the name of your organization and department and offer your help.
- Be prepared to smile: people can often sense a smile in your tone of voice and will warm to this.
- Make sure the customer has plenty of opportunity to tell you what they want.
- Always double-check that you have recorded the important details correctly on paper.

- Before placing a caller on hold, ask their permission to do so.
- Make sure the caller is on hold before you discuss their enquiry with others.
- Do not keep callers on hold for too long.
- If you cannot provide an answer immediately, take down the caller's name and phone number, and follow up their call as soon as possible.
- Always be sure to let the caller or customer know what will happen next. For example, will you phone them back with information? If so, when?
- Always let the person who telephoned you end the conversation.
- At the end of the conversation, thank the caller for contacting your organization.

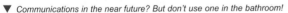

▼ *Communications in the near future? But don't use one in the bathroom!*

With new technology, telephones in the near future will also have video screens and people will be able to see the person they are talking to, and respond to their facial expressions. This will mean that good communication skills will be even more important for business employees.

Portfolio Activity 4.2

In pairs, roleplay the following situations to examine how well you handle face-to-face and telephone communications with customers.

Face-to-face communications:

- A customer enters a large store and asks the sales assistant for directions to the electrical department.

- A customer asks the sales assistant to provide product details and give a demonstration of a video recorder (or other electrical good of your choice. It would be useful if you could demonstrate with an actual product).

- A work colleague asks a member of the purchasing department to provide information on the types and prices of computer printers available to buy

Telephone communications:

(These are best carried out if you face away from each other, so that you cannot see the other person's facial reactions.)

- A work colleague telephones to ask you if you will be able to come to a sales meeting next week

- A supplier telephones you to check some details on your order for stationery

- A customer telephones to complain that the items they ordered have not yet been delivered.

- A customer telephones to ask if an item is in stock. This enquiry will take some time to check on the computer database.

Take it in turn to be the person making a request and the employee responding. Either take notes of your conversations or better still, make audio or video recordings.

After each conversation discuss and note how well you both thought the business representative responded to the customer. How could the responses be improved in each case?

Section **4.3**

Written communications

The safest way to make sure that the right information reaches the right people is to write it down. Unless details of conversations, phone calls or meetings are written down, information passed between the people who are talking may be forgotten or misunderstood.

People in business organizations use a variety of documents to communicate with other people and firms. The main routine non-financial business documents are:

- Business letters
- Memos
- Notices
- Financial documents
- Advertisements

Copies of the most important documents can be placed on file in case they are needed again.

Business letters

By far the most important means of sending information to customers and other business organizations is by a formal **business letter**. It is very important that business letters are well presented and accurate.

Business letters can be used for many different purposes. Below are just a few examples:

- Arranging and confirming meetings

- Asking job applicants to attend interviews

- Offering jobs to successful applicants

- Providing details of prices or cost estimates for work

- Making complaints to suppliers about poor delivery times or faulty goods

- Asking banks to check the creditworthiness of a customer

- Advertising details of new goods or services to customers

- Making enquiries or seeking information and help from other organizations

- Recording the main points of business conversations

- Writing to members of parliament on matters of concern

- Notifying employees that they are no longer required

- Responding to customer enquiries and complaints

How to write a business letter

The layout and style of business letters will vary greatly between organizations. However, there are some golden rules all organizations need to follow. If a business letter is to be effective and get its message across, it must be well presented, to the point, tactful, accurate, and addressed correctly.

Spelling and grammar in a business letter must also be correct. Poor spelling, bad grammar, and any other errors can give a poor impression. Careful preparation, drafting out the letter first, and getting the agreement of others in your organization, perhaps a manager, are very important before sending out a business letter.

Most business organizations use headed notepaper for their letters. This will usually show the name of the organization, address, phone numbers, and, if available, fax and e-mail numbers. The notepaper may also show the organization's logo and the names of business owners or company directors.

Figure 4.2 presents an example of a business letter from Pantera Computing Limited, a provider of computer training courses, in response to an enquiry by a potential customer.

Most business letters are typed on one side of an A4 sheet of headed or plain paper. The style used is what is known as **fully blocked, open punctuation**. This means that all words including addresses, dates, and titles start at the left margin. No line indents are used. With modern word processors the text can be justified against both the left and right margins. This means words on each line start and end in the same place – at the margins.

▼ Figure 4.2: An example of a business letter

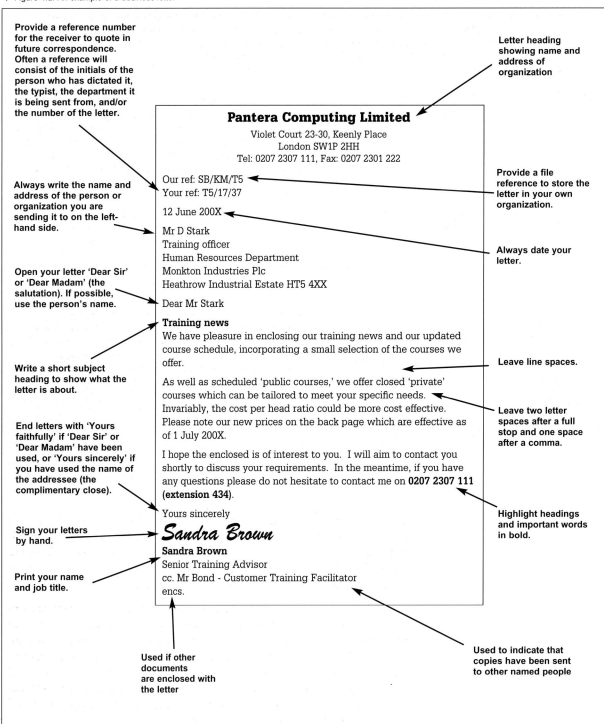

Provide a reference number for the receiver to quote in future correspondence. Often a reference will consist of the initials of the person who has dictated it, the typist, the department it is being sent from, and/or the number of the letter.

Letter heading showing name and address of organization

Always write the name and address of the person or organization you are sending it to on the left-hand side.

Provide a file reference to store the letter in your own organization.

Open your letter 'Dear Sir' or 'Dear Madam' (the salutation). If possible, use the person's name.

Always date your letter.

Write a short subject heading to show what the letter is about.

Leave line spaces.

End letters with 'Yours faithfully' if 'Dear Sir' or 'Dear Madam' have been used, or 'Yours sincerely' if you have used the name of the addressee (the complimentary close).

Leave two letter spaces after a full stop and one space after a comma.

Sign your letters by hand.

Highlight headings and important words in bold.

Print your name and job title.

Used if other documents are enclosed with the letter

Used to indicate that copies have been sent to other named people

---

Pantera Computing Limited

Violet Court 23-30, Keenly Place
London SW1P 2HH
Tel: 0207 2307 111, Fax: 0207 2301 222

Our ref: SB/KM/T5
Your ref: T5/17/37

12 June 200X

Mr D Stark
Training officer
Human Resources Department
Monkton Industries Plc
Heathrow Industrial Estate HT5 4XX

Dear Mr Stark

Training news

We have pleasure in enclosing our training news and our updated course schedule, incorporating a small selection of the courses we offer.

As well as scheduled 'public courses,' we offer closed 'private' courses which can be tailored to meet your specific needs. Invariably, the cost per head ratio could be more cost effective. Please note our new prices on the back page which are effective as of 1 July 200X.

I hope the enclosed is of interest to you. I will aim to contact you shortly to discuss your requirements. In the meantime, if you have any questions please do not hesitate to contact me on **0207 2307 111 (extension 434)**.

Yours sincerely

Sandra Brown

Sandra Brown
Senior Training Advisor
cc. Mr Bond - Customer Training Facilitator
encs.

Portfolio Activity 4.3

Preparing business letters to customers and other external organizations is a very important task. Letters must always be clear and to the point, courteous, accurate, have a pleasing layout, and contain no spelling errors, abbreviations, jargon, or slang.

When preparing a letter:

- Check that you have all the information you need.

- Decide on a suitable reference, heading, opening, and conclusion.

- If the subject matter is confidential, add the word 'CONFIDENTIAL' at the very top of the letter and on the envelope that contains it.

- Always prepare the letter in draft first.

- If you are replying to a letter (or fax) you have received, start your letter with '*Thank you for your letter/fax of (date) concerning (subject) ...*'

- If the letter follows a telephone conversation with the addressee, then start your letter with '*Following our recent telephone conversation regarding (subject) ...*'

- Conclude your letter appropriately. For example:

  – '*I look forward to hearing from you...*'

  – '*I hope this information will be helpful to you...*'

  – '*Please let me know if I can be of any further assistance...*'

  – '*Please do not hesitate to contact me should you have any further queries...*'

- Read through your draft letter to check spelling, grammar, accuracy, and tone. Make sure you have not used jargon, and that no important information has been omitted.

Imagine now that you work for a large bank. You have received three written communications to which you must reply in the form of a business letter. Using the guidelines above, prepare draft letters first, and ask your tutor and fellow students for comments, before producing final versions for your portfolio using a word processor.

1. A customer has written to complain that she has been overcharged for banking services. She has had to pay £25 for being overdrawn, although her bank account was only in debit for one day, and the amount of the overdraft was only £15.75. Because she is a valued customer and has held an account with the bank for many years, you agree to refund her the money. You apologize for the charges and explain that they are automatically deducted from the account by computer once a negative balance is recognized.

2. You have received an enquiry from a student currently studying for his GNVQ business qualifications. He would like to know if the bank can offer him a work experience placement. You reply that the bank is unable to offer any further work experience places this year, but that you will keep his letter on file if a place becomes available next year. You also wish him luck with his studies.

3. Your bank manager, Sheila Jones, has asked you to arrange a meeting with Peter Smith, the financial director of Fretton Foods Ltd, Unit 75, Hogton Industrial Estate, Hogton, HT5 7DB. The meeting will take place at the bank at 10.00 am in ten days' time, and a car parking space will be made available for him at the rear of the building. Mr Smith is to contact the bank if he has a problem with these arrangements.

Standard business letters

Not all business letters are written from scratch. Most organizations have a range of standard responses to enquiries and complaints by customers. **Standard letters** are often stored on computer with gaps left to fill in the particular details of individual customers and their enquiries or complaints. Alternatively, details can be entered by hand.

Business letters which are standard and routine are often preprinted to save time and money. Modern computer word processors means that standard letters can be stored and 'personalise' them with individual names and addresses prior to printing them off. This is very important to a business that wants to send out the same letters to many people but still wants to give the impression that each letter is a personal correspondence. This makes it much less likely that the person receiving the letter will simply throw it away without reading it.

Increasingly organisations are promoting their goods and services by sending out personalised letters to thousands of customers. These letters are known as **circulars**.

▼ *An advertisement for services and a request for payment – two examples of the type of standard business letters used by firms*

QUANTIME

Quantime Ltd

Maygrove House
67 Maygrove Road
London NW6 2EG

Tel: 0207-625 7222
Fax: 0207-624 5297

June 200X

Dear Client,

Because the world's best survey software deserves the best support

It is in our interest as much as yours that you should use our software to the best of its capabilities. Therefore, I am happy to enclose a leaflet giving full details of the Quantime Support Service, which is available to all Quantime's clients.

The leaflet gives the contact numbers and opening hours of the three international service centers and details the various support methods offered. I hope you will find it informative and useful. I am also enclosing a label for you to attach to your computer or telephone, thus ensuring the Quantime Support Service contact numbers are always close at hand!

Please do not hesitate to contact me should you have any further questions about the Quantime Support Service, or any of the other services mentioned in the brochure. Further copies of the brochure or label are available via your Account Manager.

Yours sincerely,

Madeleine Ashbery

Madeleine Ashbery
Support Director

Badger Builders Ltd
Unit 49A
Marsh Lane Industrial Estate
Marsham
Newshire
Tel: 01334–5073
Fax: 01334–5077

Our Ref: 4703/ACC/AM/RAD

7 June 200X

Radcliffe Ltd
14 Brambledown Road
Watford
Hertfordshire

Dear Sirs

OVERDUE PAYMENT FOR BUILDING SERVICES

We are again contacting you about your cheque number 207893 for £750.75 which was returned to us because of insufficient funds. We wrote to you once before about this matter, but you have not responded.

Within 10 working days from the date of this letter, we expect to receive payment in full. If you are unable to send payment for the entire amount, please call me to explain the circumstances and work out a payment solution.

You have been a good customer and we don't want to lose you. Please respond today.

Yours faithfully

A Morrison

A Morrison
Accounts Representative

P.S. If your remittance is already in the post, please accept our thanks and disregard this notice.

Business memos

Businesses often use **memos**, or **memoranda**, for short important messages when there is no time for a formal letter. Memos are generally for internal use only, and are often handwritten on small pieces of paper which are sometimes pre-printed with the word 'Memo' at the top of each sheet.

Memos can be used for a variety of internal messages. For example:

- Making a specific request or query

- Providing information

- Notifying people of a change of date, time, or venue for a meeting

- Notifying people who are arranging a meeting that you are not able to attend

- Arranging more informal meetings – for example, a lunch

- Notifying people that a letter or parcel has arrived for them

Figure 4.3 shows an example of a memo cancelling a business meeting.

▼ *Figure 4.3: An example of a memo*

MEMO

To: All senior managers
From: A Bowmer MD

Date: 12.2.0X
Ref: AB/CG

Subject: Meeting on 15.2.200X

Meeting cancelled. Rescheduled to 23.2.00 at 2 pm. Venue unchanged.

Please phone Clare Biggs (x6783) to confirm attendance.

Apologies for inconvenience.

AB

Most business organizations use pre-printed memo forms. The layout and content of these forms will vary between organizations, but will usually contain the following headings:

To – the name of the person(s) the memo is intended for

From – the name of the person sending the memo

Date – the date the memo was prepared

Ref: – a filing reference

Like business letters, memos should also have a clear subject heading, so that people immediately know what the communication is about.

The word 'urgent' may also be added to the memo if it is very important and needs to be read quickly. It is usual to finish a memo by writing or typing your initials. Memos are never signed in full.

Portfolio Activity 4.4

1. In groups, prepare memos for the following messages. These can be handwritten, typed, or produced using a word processor. (You can make up names, and other details, for the people and business organizations involved in each case.)

● The managing director has had to rearrange the date and time of the next board meeting.

● Your line manager asks for sales figures for the last quarter.

● You provide your line manager with the latest sales figures as requested.

● The goods inward department notifies you that the new computer equipment you ordered has arrived and is ready to collect.

● You notify the sales and marketing department that a new photocopier has been installed for their use on Floor 3 near the lifts.

2. Swap the memos you have produced between fellow students in your group. Discuss each one in terms of:

● Spelling and grammar

● Style and layout

● Whether the message is clear

3. From your discussions in Task 2, compile a list of 'do's and don'ts' for memo-writing.

Notices

Business letters, memos, and invitations are personal communications which are only meant to be read by the people they are sent to. Notices, however, are meant to be read by everyone – or at least, those interested in the messages they contain. Examples include bus timetables provided at bus stops, or health and safety regulations in factories. Notices will contain largely factual information and can therefore serve many purposes.

If notices are to attract people's attention, they must be placed somewhere they can be seen easily. They should also be short, to the point, and easily understandable to all the different people who might read them. Attractive layout will catch the attention of people passing by. They will also usually be dated so that people will know if the information contained in the notice is new or old.

Sometimes businesses will place notices in newspapers to reach a wide audience. For example, notices may be used to advertise the sale of shares in a public limited company, or to recall faulty electrical goods, or to notify local residents that planning permission has been granted to develop an area of land.

▼ *Notices can contain important information.*

THE LEIGH CITY TECHNOLOGY COLLEGE

IN CASE OF FIRE:

1. IF YOU FIND A FIRE, RAISE THE ALARM IMMEDIATELY BY PRESSING THE NEAREST ALARM, OR BY SHOUTING "FIRE". THEN EVACUATE THE ROOM, FOLLOWING THE PROCEDURES BELOW.

2. WHEN THE FIRE ALARM SOUNDS, EVERYONE SHOULD LEAVE THE BUILDING, IMMEDIATELY, BY THE NEAREST ROUTE.

3. STUDENTS SHOULD FILE OUT OF THE ROOM IN SILENCE, LEAVING ALL BOOKS AND BAGS BEHIND. ON THE TEACHER'S INSTRUCTION, STUDENTS SHOULD PROCEED, IN PAIRS, TOWARDS THE NEAREST FIRE EXIT.

4. ENSURE THAT THE DOOR OF THE CLASSROOM IS CLOSED.

5. WALK BRISKLY, AND IN SILENCE, KEEPING TO THE RIGHT SIDE OF THE CORRIDOR OR STAIRS.

6. ONCE OUTSIDE, PROCEED TO THE NEAREST ASSEMBLY POINT, WHERE STUDENTS SHOULD LINE UP IN SINGLE FILE, IN REGISTER ORDER, AND WAIT IN SILENCE WHILE THE TEACHER CHECKS THAT ALL ARE PRESENT.

7. ASSEMBLY POINTS:

   EAST CAMPUS - YRS. 7, 8 AND 9 ON THE COURT BEHIND TECHNOLOGY
   YRS. 10, 11 AND 12 ON THE COURT BEHIND THE SPORTS HALL

   WEST CAMPUS - ALL YEARS ON THE NETBALL COURTS BEHIND THE GYM

8. STUDENTS MAY NOT BE DISMISSED TO RETURN TO THEIR CLASSROOMS UNTIL THE SENIOR MEMBER OF STAFF IS SATISFIED THAT ALL ARE PRESENT, AND THAT THE FIRE DRILL HAS BEEN CARRIED OUT AS QUICKLY, EFFICIENTLY AND SAFELY AS POSSIBLE.

9. STAFF SHOULD USE THEIR MARK BOOKS TO CHECK ATTENDANCE. OFFICE STAFF WILL BRING OUT THE VISITORS' BOOK AND THE SIGNING OUT BOOK SO THAT ABSENCES CAN BE CHECKED.

IMPORTANT NOTICE
RECYCLING BINS FOR ALL CANS AND TINS

Please can all staff use the recycling bin provided at this teapoint for can and tins. This bin should not be used for general rubbish/waste disposal, as there is another bin provided in this location for this purpose.

Should you have any queries on this matter or any other energy or environmental issues, please contact Ursula Smith on 020 7219 5999 (Internal X 5100)

Servus Facilities Management (21 July 1999)

Portfolio Activity 4.5

1. Draw a table like the one below with enough rows for at least ten business notices.

Examples of business notices

Place	Information	Intended audience
Bus timetable	Bus departure times	Customers/passengers
Factory floor	Safety procedures	Employees

2. Identify at least ten different notices used by different business organizations in your local area. For each one write down in your table where you would expect to find them, the messages or information they contain, and who they are intended for. The table already contains two examples of business notices to help you.

3. Design an invitation using a word processor or desktop publishing program to invite an important business customer to a party to celebrate your firm's 25th year in business. Make up your own business name and details of the date, time, and venue for the celebration.

▼ Figure 4.4: A pre-printed telephone message form

Post-it™ Telephone Message Pad 7660

To _____

Date _____ Time _____

WHILE YOU WERE OUT

M _____

of _____

Phone No. _____

TELEPHONED	PLEASE CALL
WAS IN TO SEE YOU	WILL CALL BACK
WANTS TO SEE YOU	**URGENT**
RETURNED YOUR CALL	

Message _____

_____

_____

_____

FT-5001-6785-1   Operator _____

Messages

People working in busy organizations will often need to take messages for their colleagues or even to remind themselves to do things. Messages can be personal – for example, to tell someone that his wife rang while he was out of the office – or work-related.

Messages may be written down following:

- A phone call

- A conversation with a work colleague

- A conversation with a supplier or customer

Messages will usually be jotted down on a pad or Post-it note, which can then be stuck in a position where the person is most likely to see it, for example, on their computer screen. If you cannot give them the message in person, it is often useful to contact them later to make sure that the message has been received and understood.

In all cases, a message should be simple, clear and to the point, accurate, and marked 'urgent' if necessary. The date and time the message was taken should also be recorded.

It is vitally important that the person receiving the message is able to understand it and has all the information he or she needs. You may need to question the person leaving the message. For example, you might ask them what their full name is, what the message concerns, and where can they be contacted. A good way to check that you have written down the right message is to read it back to the caller.

To help people take accurate messages over the phone, business organizations often provide their staff with pre-printed message forms (see Figure 4.4).

Hello. This is Key Motors. I am trying to contact Richard Sambora. He asked us to prepare an estimate for repair to accident damage to his car. We want to know if he would like us to go ahead and carry out the repairs based on our estimate. If he could let us know by 3 pm today we can get the parts ordered for delivery tomorrow, otherwise it will take another day to get them. Could you ask him to give me a ring on 0208 901 0001? Thank you.

Financial documents

Businesses must keep accurate and up to date records of the goods and services they buy and sell, who they buy them from or sell them to, and how much money they receive in revenue and pay out for costs. To do this businesses use a variety of **financial documents** (see chapter 9). Financial documents must be clear and easy to fill in otherwise people who complete them may make mistakes.

The following financial documents are used in business and can be completed by hand or on a computer screen and then printed out.

Key Financial Documents

- **order forms** are used to order goods and services from suppliers
- a **goods received note** lists the goods delivered to a customer
- an **invoice** will be issued by a supplier to a customer. It tells the customer how much to pay for the goods and services received and when to make payment
- a **remittance advice note** advises customers payment is due for items received
- a **credit note** is issued to a customer if they have been overcharged for goods or services supplied. A credit note can be used against future purchases
- a **debit note** is issued to a customer if they have been charged too little for goods or services supplied and must pay more
- a **receipt** is issued when a customer pays for goods or services. It is a proof of purchase

- **cheques** are used to make payments instead of using cash. A cheque will allow a supplier to draw the payment from the customers bank account
- **statement of account**: customers who make regular purchases from a supplier may hold an account. Each month they will receive a statement of all the items they have purchased and the total amount of money they owe. For example, banks and credit card companies issue statements of account to all their customers
- **paying-in slips**: businesses use these to record the amounts of notes, coins and cheques they pay into their bank accounts. It allows businesses and their banks to keep a record of what has been paid in and when

Section **4.4**   ## Electronic communications

Information communications technology

Information communications technology refers to the modern equipment and networks which are able to transmit and carry huge amounts of information – words and numbers, still and moving pictures, and sound – over vast distances, if required, at very high speed without loss of quality. The technology includes telephone and satellite communication networks and the phones and personal computers linked into these networks which allow the use of electronic mail and access to the internet. New digital technology means far more information can be transmitted without loss of quality and faster than ever before.

Electronic transmission

Imagine that the New York office of your organization has asked you to prepare a report on UK sales figures for the last three months. You prepare the report containing text, tables, and graphs using desktop publishing software. The New York office wants a **hard copy** (i.e. paper copy) of the report and a copy of the computer file. You store the computer file on a floppy disk, print out the report, and send both by special delivery to New York. However, there is a much easier and quicker way of doing this without the need to send paper or disks over long distances.

Electronic mail (e-mail) is an increasingly popular means of sending information and business documents without the need to send paper. Computers linked to the telephone network can send and receive computer files containing business documents to and from other computers all over the world. E-mail can be sent via computers either within the same organization or between different organizations.

To send E-mail, all you have to do is to call up a file on your computer or input a letter or message. You then type in the e-mail 'mailbox' address

▼ *Figure 4.5: How electronic mail works*

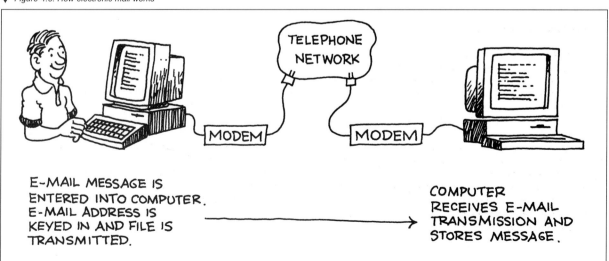

TELEPHONE NETWORK

MODEM   MODEM

E-MAIL MESSAGE IS ENTERED INTO COMPUTER. E-MAIL ADDRESS IS KEYED IN AND FILE IS TRANSMITTED.

COMPUTER RECEIVES E-MAIL TRANSMISSION AND STORES MESSAGE.

of the computer terminal of the person or organization you are sending it to. An e-mail address code is very similar to a phone number except that it will consist of letters and symbols as well as numbers. For example, 'bigbreakfast@planet24.co.uk' is the well known e-mail address of Channel 4's Big Breakfast TV studios.

Once the E-mail address has been entered, the computer will transmit the document over the phoneline to the other computer, often in just a matter of seconds, even for large amounts of information. The cost of sending the document is charged for in the same way as an ordinary phone call and often costs only a few pence, although the cost will be higher for international transmissions.

A computer at the e-mail address will receive the transmission. The person or organization to whom the computer belongs can then save their file onto their own hard disk or floppy disks, and print out the document.

The advantage of e-mail is that a large number of people at different e-mail addresses can be sent the same message at the same time. Once sent, the message will wait in an electronic mailbox in a computer for the user to access it.

Why e-mail?

- It saves stationery and paper costs
- It allows workers to tele-work from home
- Transmission is rapid
- It reduces the need to talk over the phone and cuts bills
- It can be integrated with other systems, for example, the Internet
- Incoming and outgoing messages can be held in a 'mailbox'
- The time and date of incoming messages are automatically recorded
- Addresses can be stored and recalled
- It has a multiple addressing facility
- Messages can be printed out

The information superhighway

You have probably heard of the Internet. This is a worldwide network of computers linked via telephone lines, often called the 'information superhighway'. Information is free on the Internet – only the use of the telephone is charged for. 'Surfing the net' refers to browsing through all the information it has to offer.

Many companies are now linked via the Internet system, and sending e-mail has become even easier. Commercial uses of the Internet are also increasing as businesses are finding it a useful means of contacting customers and advertising their products (see chapter 5).

Facsimile transmissions (FAX)

Fax machines are small desktop machines connected to a telephone line. To operate the fax, the user types in the fax number of the recipient of the message. The sender's fax then rings the receiver's fax and establishes contact (this may be heard as a series of screeching tones). Once contact is made, documents placed in the sender's fax machine are read through one page at a time and the details are sent via the phonelines to print out as an exact copy at the receiver's fax machine.

Fax machines are a useful way of sending pictures, drawings, and many other very urgent documents. Sometimes fax machines may be engaged with other incoming messages or documents, although modern machines often have automatic re-dial facilities. The quality of the printout from a fax machine may also be poor on occasions. You will know yourself from talking on the phone to your friends that phonelines are not always very clear. For the fax machine, this means that transmissions may be faulty. Because of this, it is often better to write or type information you intend to send by fax using larger letter and number sizes.

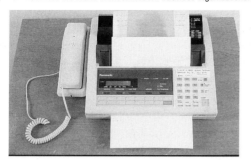
▼ *Fax machines are found in most modern business organizations.*

A fax machine is an essential piece of modern business equipment. Prices started at around £120 in 2000 – an affordable amount even for the smallest of businesses. Using a fax is also relatively inexpensive. For most modern machines it will take about one minute to fax ten A4 pages – the cost of a one-minute phone call plus some electricity to power the machine. Larger documents sent by fax and international faxes will clearly be more expensive.

Section	4.5

Advertisements

Everything a business says, prints or does will communicate information about the business to existing and potential customers. For example, a sales assistant in a shop who is slow or unable to respond to customer enquiries will send a message to that customer suggesting that he or she may be better off shopping elsewhere. However, in this section we are concerned with communications designed specifically to communicate positive messages to people and firms about businesses and their products. These communications are called **advertisements**.

Persuasive or informative communications?

A great deal of information needs to be communicated quickly and clearly to customers about the goods and services provided by organizations. They will often use the services of professional designers and printing firms to produce these communications, including leaflets and brochures. Many are in colour and have two main objectives – to be informative and persuasive to get customers to buy.

▼ *An informative promotion*

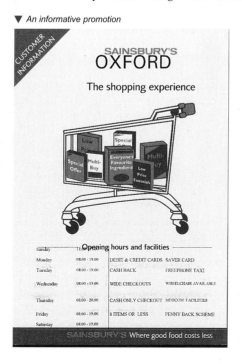

▼ *A persuasive promotion*

Advertising is a very powerful form of promotion. If firms can identify the type of consumers who are most likely to buy their products, they can then design promotional materials that will appeal to them. That is, different promotional messages can be targeted at a different groups of consumers called **target audiences**. For example, the target audience for promotions of pop and rock magazines are primarily young people aged between 12 and 24. The target audience for promotions for baby foods and clothing are new parents and proud grandparents.

The type of message communicated will depend on the organization and the product being promoted. For example, government organizations will tend to be informative; banks will inform you about their range of services and try to persuade you that they offer good rates of interest on loans and savings and are financially secure; face-cream manufacturers will try to convince you that their products will give you healthy, younger-looking skin.

Messages that are designed to inform are generally obvious – for example, messages about train departure times, special offers, road safety, pop group tour dates, directions to superstores, etc.

Persuasive messages tend not to be so obvious. Many are subliminal, which means that they enter your thoughts subconsciously. For example, the imaginative use of colour, product names, packaging materials, logos, symbols, and music can all help to create persuasive images which stay in the mind. This can be done in a number of ways:

▼ *Names for products are chosen carefully to give the right image.*

▼ *Perfumes in distinctive packaging can persuade consumers to buy.*

- **The use of colour:** Women tend to prefer to buy products packaged in pastel colours, while men prefer to buy products packaged in darker colours. Bright colours are often used to attract children and teenagers. Dark, rich colours are often used to suggest elegance and high quality. For example, which television would you think was better quality – one that had a black casing, or one that was bright pink? By carefully choosing the colour of packaging, firms are sending a message to their customers about who should buy their products.

- **Product names:** The name of a product can also be chosen to communicate messages. For example, 'Comfort' fabric conditioner and 'Flash' liquid cleaner convey strong messages about the properties of these particular products. Similarly, many perfumes for women have been given names to make them sound romantic or sexy, such as 'Obsession', 'White Linen' and 'Beautiful'. These are called **brand names**.

- **Packaging:** Chocolates packed in a plain brown cardboard box are unlikely to attract much attention. Placing the same chocolates in a box with embossed gold lettering, tied up with ribbons, will suggest that the contents of the box are luxurious and exotic. Perfumes also tend to be sold in distinctive bottles and boxes to make them stand out from competing products.

- **Logos and symbols:** Organizations will also use logos, symbols, and distinctive product designs to promote awareness of the organization and its products. Every time a consumer sees the logo, symbol, or packaging they will recall past messages about the organization and the product. In this way, the logos and symbols become messages in themselves. For example, the 'St Michael' trademark on products sold in Marks & Spencer stores is recognized by many consumers as a symbol of quality. Under the Trademark Act, it is illegal to copy or use the logos or trademarks of other organizations or products.

- **Music:** Promotions on TV and radio advertisements may also use distinctive music. For example, in 1999 the Levi Strauss clothing company used a yellow puppet called Flat Eric and a record by Mr Oizo called 'Flat Beat' to advertise their jeans and stay press clothing. The record went to number one in the UK Similarly, product elegance and quality may be suggested by using classical music to appeal to older people.

Most major film releases use pop records to help promote them to young people – the main cinema-going audience. For example, 'Everything I do, I do for you' sung by Bryan Adams from the film *Robin Hood, Prince of Thieves* stayed at number one for 13 weeks in the UK in 1991. More recently the films *Titanic* and *Wild, Wild West* were promoted using chart-topping songs by Celine Dion and Will Smith respectively.

Evaluating a promotion (1)

The success of a promotion in communicating a message to a particular audience can be measured by asking the following questions:

– Who was the audience for the promotion?

– Did the audience get the message? Has the firm checked this with customers?

– Were the messages appropriate? For example, were they too technical? Did they offend people?

– Which parts of the promotion were least successful and which were most successful?

– How could the promotion be altered to become more successful?

– Could the promotion have been made at a lower cost?

Old brands top lists of nation's shoppers

THE British have often been accused of being stuck in their ways and clinging to tradition.

And a new study has found that as far as their grocery shopping is concerned it is true.

Research into shoppers' habits showed that although people are willing to try new products, they quickly return to the brands they know best.

The study, by market research company AC Nielsen

and Checkout magazine, found that of the country's 100 top selling brands, 39 per cent have been on the market for 50 years or more. The study also found only nine per cent have been launched in the past ten years.

Robert Buckeldee, spokesman for AC Nielson, said with more than 20,000 brands to chose from on supermarket shelves a new product must make a big impact to succeed.

THE COUNTRY'S FAVOURITES

These best-selling brands, all introduced at least 50 years ago, are a marketing man's dream:

- Coca Cola soft drink
- Walkers crisps
- Nescafé coffee
- Persil washing powder
- Andrex toilet roll
- Heinz tomato soup

- Pepsi soft drink
- Heinz baked beans
- Brooke Bond PG Tips tea
- Kit Kat chocolate
- Anchor butter
- Tate & Lyle sugar
- Kellog's Corn Flakes cereal
- Weetabix cereal
- Mars chocolate bars
- Kleenex tissues
- Wrigley's chewing gum

- Cadbury's Dairy Milk chocolate
- Birds Eye frozen peas
- Kit-e-Kat cat food
- Typhoo tea
- Colgate toothpaste
- Bisto gravy mix
- McVites Homewheat biscuits
- Oxo stock cubes
- Shredded Wheat cereal
- Tampax tampons

Portfolio Activity 4.7

1. Choosing a name for a product is often as important as what is said about it in an advert, or its price and quality. What type of products are these brand names for? What message do they give the consumer about the product?

Aquafresh	Citrus Spring	Brillo
Black Magic	Parazone	Gold Blend
Imperial Leather	Flora	Crunchie
Pampers	Radox	Impulse

2. Some products have such well known trademarks or logos that it is possible to promote them without using word or pictures at all. How many of the following do you recognize? What products/organizations do they promote?

What can advertising do for a business

Advertising is used to create sales

This is the main aim of most promotional activity. The whole point of creating awareness, interest, and desire is to persuade consumers to purchase. An advertisement that just creates interest without converting this into sales is a failure. Sales may be achieved by advertisements that convince consumers that the product is new, or that it is somehow better than competitors' products, or that the consumer will benefit from buying the product, either through the features of the product or by 'buying into' the image of that product.

Evaluating a promotion (2)

The effectiveness of a promotional strategy to create sales can be measured by asking the following questions:

– What increase in sales was expected as a result of the promotion?

– What increase in sales was experienced?

– Did sales increase only because of the promotion or would they have risen anyway? What evidence is there for this?

– What could have been done to increase sales more?

– What reasons did those consumers not buying the product give for their decision?

– Which aspects of the promotion could be changed to further raise sales?

▼ Promotional images can influence consumers' perceptions of the lifestyle they can lead if they buy the product.

Advertising is used to influence customers' perceptions

Persuasive advertising is designed to persuade consumers to do things they might not otherwise do, in particular to buy a product that they might not otherwise buy. One way to do this is to change their attitudes, opinions, and perceptions of the organization and/or its product.

Consumers' perceptions of a product can be changed by creating a **brand image,** and using a distinctive brand name, logo, humorous catchphrase, or visual treatment to make it stand out from its competitors. It does not particularly matter whether the product really *is* different: what matters is whether or not customers *think* it is. For example, most soap and washing-up powders are quite similar except for their colouring and smell. Yet soap producers spend vast sums of money attempting to create brand images and make the products appear different so that they will appeal to particular kinds of consumers.

Brand imaging is successful because firms realize that consumers not only buy products, but also buy images associated with the ownership and use of those products. If consumers desire the lifestyle promoted by a product, they may believe that buying the product will give them the same lifestyle – even if only in a small way. For example, Bounty advertisements have shown young, attractive, and carefree people enjoying life on a tropical beach, while Volkswagen recently ran an advert showing typical VW drivers as being attractive and well-off. Some consumers will be influenced by this image, and may buy the product for the image as much as for the features of the product itself.

Advertising can also be used to create a better image for an organization – for example, one that is more caring towards the environment – or to make it more attractive to young people.

Has advertising changed consumer perceptions

The success of an advertising promotion in influencing consumers' perceptions can be judged by asking the following questions:

– In what ways was it intended to influence consumers' perceptions of the product?

– What were consumers' views and perceptions of the product and/or organization *before* the promotion?

– What were customers' perceptions of the product/and or organization *after* the promotion?

– How successful was the promotion in achieving the desired change in perceptions?

– What could have been done better?

Portfolio Activity 4.8

Slogans and catchphrases are used in a variety of promotions to send messages about products and organizations to consumers. What organizations or products used the following slogans in promotions? What messages do they convey about the product or organization? Try to think of at least 5 other slogans used in promotions.

- 'The world's favourite airline'
- 'Wecome 2 your world'

- 'Every little helps'
- 'Everything we do is driven by you'
- 'Helps you work, rest and play'
- 'It's you'
- 'Probably the best lager in the world'
- 'Pure genius'
- 'Your flexible friend'
- 'No FT. No comment'

Advertisements are used to provide information

An important feature of promotion is to provide information about products, to let people know what is available, or give instructions.

In order to provide the information, the promotion must attract the attention of the consumer, and great skill is required in doing this. Images should be attractive and eye-catching, otherwise people may not bother to look at the promotion at all. Any written information must be big enough to read, accurate, and understandable.

Simple informative messages can often be promoted on television, especially if a strong image is needed. Examples include campaigns by the government to make children use the Green Cross Code and to make people aware of AIDS. Retail outlets will often promote information about opening times and dates for sales. Information may also be combined with persuasive messages in these promotions.

▼ *Some advertisements are designed to provide information.*

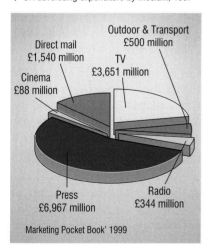

▼ *UK advertising expenditure by medium, 1997*

Direct mail £1,540 million
Outdoor & Transport £500 million
TV £3,651 million
Cinema £88 million
Press £6,967 million
Radio £344 million

Marketing Pocket Book' 1999

Where to advertise?

Business organizations can choose from a variety of **advertising media** through which to promote their products and image. These include newspapers and magazines, TV, radio, the cinema, and posters. Adverts for products can also be placed on the packaging of other products, for example, on the back of matchboxes, on carrier bags and T-shirts, even on hot-air balloons.

Advertising is important because it can create a brand image for a product in the eyes of the consumer. For example, in the past Volvo always emphasized their image as a producer of safe family cars, targeting their advertising at people who might buy a family car, and who rate safety as an important feature. More recently they have found that their advertising actually encouraged people who prefer cars to have sporty features to choose other makes! Because of this, Volvo have recently launched an advertising campaign showing their cars being used in dangerous situations by stuntmen. The purpose of this has been to use advertising to create a slightly different brand image involving excitement, danger, and speed.

THE ESSENCE OF GOOD ADVERTISING

The British Code of Advertising Practice states all advertisements should be:

* Legal, decent, honest, and truthful

* Prepared with a sense of responsibility to the consumer and to society

* In line with the principles of fair competition generally accepted in business

No advertiser can make a claim about their product that cannot be proved.

Because advertising is so powerful, firms are willing to spend many billions of pounds each year producing and showing adverts to consumers. If successful, advertising can make a big difference to sales and profits.

▼ Advertising to the advertisers

If you thought the Government controlled consumer spending in the UK- THINK AGAIN

GOOD HOUSEKEEPING READERS CONTROL:-

£1 in every £8 of total household income
£1 in every £9 spent on cosmetics
£1 in every £10 spent on food
£1 in every £7 spent on holidays

HIGHEST CIRCULATION EVER

501,654

ABC Jan/June 1994 **POWER BEYOND THE PAGE**

 THE NATIONAL MAGAZINE COMPANY LIMITED
National Magazine House, 72 Broadwick Street, London W1V 2BP. 071 439 5000
70 Years of Excellence   A Subsidiary of The Hearst Corporation Since 1910

Newspapers and magazines

There are over 11,000 different newspapers and magazines available in the UK, ranging from national daily newspapers to free local newspapers and specialist magazines of limited circulation.

Different kinds of people tend to read different national newspapers, and so advertising can be targeted at different groups by finding out which papers they read. In 1997, 53% of all adults read a daily newspaper, and 40% of all males read either *The Sun* or *Daily Mirror*.

Most areas of the country receive free local newspapers paid for by advertising. Because these free newspapers are delivered to everyone, it is harder to select a particular target market using them. However, advertising in the local press is a lot cheaper than in the national papers.

Trade journals are magazines targeted at people working in specific trades or professions. There are also a wide variety of car buyers' guides, yachting, camera, video, and computing magazines published monthly and weekly.

Television

Television is an ideal means of advertising to reach mass markets using the benefits of movement and sound to promote a product.

There are an increasing number of commercial TV stations in the UK due to increasing sales of digital satellite and cable systems. Because their market is still relatively small, the cost of advertising on these channels tends to be much lower than on ITV and Channel 4, where a single showing of a 60-second peak-time advert could cost as much as £100,000 in 1999.

Different kinds of audience watch television at different times of the day. By choosing the time of day in which to advertise it is possible to target a particular group of consumers who might be interested in a particular product. For example, a toy manufacturer might choose to advertise on TV on Saturday mornings in the hope of reaching large audiences of young people. Different adverts can also be shown in different regions of the country.

Radio

There are many hundreds of local and national radio stations in the UK. Commercial stations are funded by sales revenues from advertising. Different kinds of radio station attract different kinds of listener. For example, Radio One tends to attract young people, while Radio Four attracts middle-aged and middle-income groups. Organizations can target their advertising by placing it on stations listened to by the kind of people most likely to buy their products.

Local radio provides a relatively cheap and effective means of advertising for many medium-sized and even smaller firms.

Cinema

In 1993 there were over 113 million cinema admissions in the UK – the highest number since 1978. Over 14 million people alone watched the film *Jurassic Park*. Because of the growth in cinema audiences, advertisers have begun to increase their use of cinema advertising and are designing adverts specially for cinema release. Adverts are also being included on video cassettes for rent or sale.

Posters

Large posters placed in highly visible sites can be a relatively cheap and effective means of grabbing people's attention as they pass by. Most major roads have billboards alongside them which can be used to show posters of pictures and slogans. Electronic billboards are also increasingly popular. These use changing neon displays to show different advertisements during the day.

Similarly, smaller posters can be placed on the side of buses and taxis, on railway stations, and in airports, where they can be seen by as many people as possible. Posters are also often placed on hoardings at sporting venues.

The main drawback of posters is that they cannot contain much information. Most people may only glance quickly at them as they walk or drive by.

▼ *Posters can be an inexpensive way of grabbing the consumer's attention.*

▼ *Choosing advertising media*

Advertising media	Plus points	Minus points
National newspapers	Coverage is national Reader can refer back to advert Product information can be provided Many use colour Can be used for mail order replies	Use of colour limited Smaller adverts tend to get 'lost' among others Readers often ignore adverts
Regional /local newspapers	Adverts can be linked to local conditions Can be used for test marketing before national launch	Reproduction and layout can be poor Average cost per reader relatively high due to more limited circulation
Magazines	Can use colour Adverts can be linked with feature articles Adverts can be targeted in specialist magazines	Adverts must be submitted a long time before publication Competitors' products often advertised alongside
Radio	Can use sound and music Relatively cheap to produce Growing number of stations Audiences can be targeted	Non-visual Message usually short-lived Listeners may switch off or ignore adverts Reception may be poor
Television	Creative use of moving images, colour, and sound Can use visual endorsements by well known personalities Repeats reinforce message Growing number of channels	High production costs Peak time can be expensive Message short-lived Viewers may ignore or switch over during adverts
Cinema	Creative use of images, colour, and sound Adverts can be localized Adverts can be targeted at age groups for different films After decline during 1980s, audiences increasing again	Limited audiences compared to other media Audience restricted to mainly younger age groups Message may only be seen once due to infrequent visits to cinema
Posters	Good cheap visual stimulus Can be placed near to point of sale National campaigns possible	Only limited information possible Susceptible to vandalism and adverse weather
The Internet	Easy and relatively cheap to set up web pages Can contain moving images and sounds Adverts can be interactive Internet is worldwide and 'open' 24 hours a day	Not everyone has access to a computer or the Internet Web pages need to be updated regularly and quickly

The Internet

Modern information communications technology can store and transmit visual images, text and sound over the telephone network to anyone who has a computer linked by modem to the 'world-wide web' or **Internet** (see chapter 5).

People can use the internet to visit the 'web sites' of many different organizations for information on the goods and services they offer. Advertising on the internet can be informative or persuasive. Web pages can also be interactive. This means the user can select different options and the web site can react to their choices, for example, by advertising other products or offering price discounts.

Some organisations also provide secure web sites so that people can enter their credit card and address details to order goods and services. Buying and selling over the internet is called **e-commerce**, and is becoming increasingly popular.

Portfolio Activity 4.9

Put your feet up in front of your television and watch some adverts.

1. Watch a sample of around 20 different adverts at different times of the day. Try to decide whether each advert :

- Is informative

- Is persuasive

- Makes meaningless statements

- Promotes a brand image

- Has a slogan or catchphrase

- Appears to suggest that buying the product will improve your quality of life

- Is sexist, racist or offensive in any way

Draw a table like the one started below. Mark each column with a tick if you think the heading applies to the advert you are watching:

2. Are any patterns evident from your completed table? Are most adverts on TV persuasive? Do most promote a brand image? etc.

3. Look through some newspapers and magazines. Select at least five adverts you like. For each one write down:

- What it is advertising

- Why it grabbed your attention

- What messages it contains

- What images it uses

- Which groups of consumers it is aimed at

Product advertised	Informative?	Persuasive?	Meaningless?	Brand image	Slogan	Quality of life	Sexist/racist
Washing powder		✔		✔		✔	✔

Other communications with customers

In addition to advertisements, business organizations will communicate messages and information to customers at the point of sale via direct mail, on instruction manuals, price lists, guarantees, statements of account and safety notices.

Point of sale promotions

The **point of sale** is the shop or place where goods are actually sold. Promotions at the point of sale may include:

- Product display cabinets and stands

- Posters in shop windows and on walls

- In-store audio and video announcements, perhaps telling people about new products and special offers

- Free samples

- Food and drink tastings

- Illuminated signs and displays

- Working models

- Celebrity book and CD signings

- Cardboard cut-outs, for example of famous film stars or characters from cartoons and children's books

▼ *Some point of sale promotions*

Retail outlets are even able to buy specially manufactured fragrances to release in different parts of the store. For example, perfumes can be sprayed around the cosmetics counter, the fragrance of coconut oils can be released near to suntan lotions to make people think of holidays, and the smell of freshly-baked bread can be wafted around food stores and in-store bakeries. All this is designed to communicate the message 'buy me' to consumers.

Point-of-sale promotions can be very effective. This is because the customer is in the shop with the product, and is likely to be carrying enough money either in cash or credit cards to be able to buy the product, if persuaded. Sales staff are also on hand to assist customers to choose products, and their role can be crucial. If they fail to provide accurate information, or are rude, or look scruffy, they may put the customer off making a purchase. Sales staff can also give out product leaflets and other promotional literature to passing customers.

Direct mail
Retailers and manufacturers can contact customers directly by post to advertise their products, and invite them to make a purchase by mail or telephone order

In the past, **direct mail** was often regarded as 'junk mail' because firms would send out identical letters to many thousands of homes. Today, firms build up a careful picture of consumer wants based on their past purchases and on the filling-in of product guarantee cards which ask a series of questions about tastes and buying habits. By storing this information on computer databases, firms can target mail at just those people likely to buy. Most word processors today have a mailmerge facility which enables a word processor to pick names and addresses off a database and then print out personalized letters with individual details. Modern computer technology has made this much easier, and even small firms can afford to send mailshots to many thousands of homes.

Hitting the target audience

Direct marketing's ever-closer targeting of individuals is one of the reasons why junk mail is less of a problem than it used to be: what might be junk to one person could be a welcome correspondence to another. The industry's improving reputation is also due to the fact that it appears to be sticking by and large to a system of self-regulation, says the Advertising Standards Authority. Rules which were introduced in 1992 require companies to make sure their information is up to date and consumers know why it is being collected.

Says the ASA: 'If a company intends to pass on information to anyone else or use it for a different purpose, consumers should be given an opportunity to say no. If a company decides to use information it already has for a different purpose, it must get permission first. Companies must comb their records for consumers who have stated that they do not want to receive mailings before sending them out. These rules also apply to press advertisements featuring response coupons.

Financial Times 15.9.1994

Product information

Products are goods and services (see chapter 1). Customers usually want to see and read about products at their leisure and compare details of different products before deciding what to buy or use. Most firms communicate information about their products to customers in carefully designed leaflets and brochures.

The more attractive a leaflet or brochure, the more likely it is to lead to a sale. Many products come with leaflets and booklets explaining how to assemble them, look after them, and/or use them safely. Instructions should always be clear and easy to understand.

Prices

Customers will be particularly keen to compare the prices of different products before they decide to buy. For example, restaurants will display their prices on menus placed outside or in their window. Price lists will also be on display in many other shops and may be printed as advertisements in newspapers. Most stores, however, rely on printed price tags to give price information on individual items.

Statement of account

Customers who buy products on credit from an organization are sent a **statement of account** at the end of each month (see chapter 9). This gives a summary of the goods purchased by the customer since the last statement, the money the customer owes, any payments which have been received, and the total balance owed by the customer to the firm.

▼ *Product information is provided in brochures, leaflets, and user instructions.*

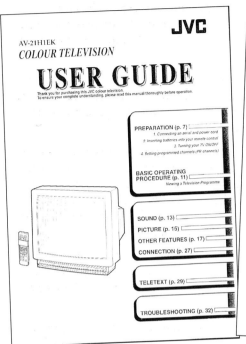

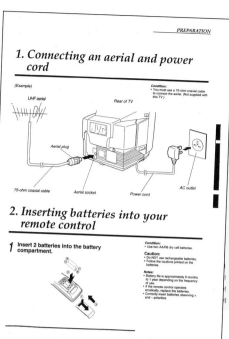

▼ *A customer guarantee certificate and registration card*

JVC

CONSUMER GUARANTEE CERTIFICATE

Subject to the conditions stated on the guarantee card, JVC (UK) Limited guarantees this equipment through its authorised dealership, only against defects in workmanship or materials of its mechanical and electronic component parts (excluding styli, battery cells, magnetic tapes, and re-chargeable batteries) for the period of one year from the date of purchase. No charge will be made during this period for labour or for replacement parts for the consumer goods related to this guarantee.

JVC (U.K.) Limited

CONSUMER CARD	MODEL AV-21H1EK	SERIAL NO. 08985886	DATE OF PURCHASE
		DETACH HERE	
PART 1 REGISTRATION CARD	MODEL AV-21H1EK	SERIAL NO. 08985886	DATE OF PURCHASE

Dealer's Name
Address

WE WOULD BE GRATEFUL IF YOU WOULD COMPLETE THE FOLLOWING BEFORE RETURNING THIS CARD FOR REGISTRATION.

☐ MALE   ☐ FEMALE   AGE( )

1. WHAT TYPE OF STORE?
☐ RADIO TV GENERAL
☐ HI FI AUDIO SPECIALIST
☐ MULTIPLE
☐ DEPARTMENT
☐ MAIL ORDER
☐ OTHER

2. WHEN YOU PURCHASED THIS EQUIPMENT DID YOU COMPARE WITH OTHER MODELS?
☐ YES   ☐ NO
MAKE
MODEL
PLACE

3. WHERE DO YOU PLAN TO USE IT?
☐ LIVING ROOM
☐ DINING ROOM
☐ STUDY
☐ RECREATION ROOM
☐ BEDROOM
☐ OTHER

4. HOW DID YOU LEARN OF THIS PRODUCT?
☐ AD OF MAGAZINE PAPER
☐ EDITORIAL IN MAGAZINE
☐ AD ON HOARDING
☐ AD ON TV OR RADIO
☐ DISPLAY IN STORE
☐ CATALOGUE
☐ OTHERS

5. WHAT PERSUADED YOU TO BUY THIS UNIT?
☐ TRUST IN BRAND NAME
☐ HIGH QUALITY
☐ PRICE
☐ DEALER'S RECOMMENDATION
☐ FRIEND'S RECOMMENDATION
☐ TECHNICAL SPECIFICATION
☐ APPEARANCE AND DESIGN
☐ SIMPLE CONTROLS

6. IS THIS UNIT YOUR
☐ FIRST OWNED?
☐ REPLACEMENT?

7. PLEASE IDENTIFY OTHER EQUIPMENT IN YOUR HOME
TYPE   MAKE
COLOUR TV
MONO TV
MUSIC CENTRE
AMPLIFIER
TUNER
TUNER/AMP
TAPE DECK
SPEAKERS
VIDEO RECORDER
VIDEO CAMERA

8. YOUR COMMENTS IF ANY

THANK YOU
Printed in UK
BT 20060
0288

Statements of accounts are covered in detail in chapter 9.

● **Guarantees:** Consumers are unlikely to buy expensive durable products, such as televisions and camcorders, unless they get a guarantee with them. If the product goes wrong, they want to know that they will be able to exchange it or get it repaired at little or no cost. Otherwise why take the risk of buying an expensive item?

Many durable products come with a one- or two-year parts and labour guarantee. Often a registration card is enclosed which the buyer is asked to complete. If the card is not returned, consumers are still entitled to their legal rights if they have a problem with the product.

Firms often use the warranty card as an opportunity to undertake market research, by including on it a number of questions which the buyer can fill in if they wish. The data received is then fed into a database and used to provide a customer list for further marketing and mailshots for future products.

A number of firms also offer consumers the opportunity to purchase an additional extended guarantee, usually up to five years, for a set fee.

Safety precautions

WARNING:

TO PREVENT FIRE OR SHOCK HAZARD, DO NOT EXPOSE THIS
APPLIANCE TO RAIN OR MOISTURE.

CAUTION:

TO ENSURE PERSONAL SAFETY, OBSERVE THE FOLLOWING RULES
REGARDING THE USE OF THIS UNIT.

* Operate only from the power source specified (AC 220–240 V, 50 Hz) on the
  unit.
* Avoid damaging the AC plug and power cord.
* Avoid improper installation and never position the unit where good ventilation
  is unattainable.
* Do not allow objects or liquid into the cabinet openings.
* In the event of a fault, unplug the unit and call a service technician. Do not
  attempt to repair it yourself or remove the rear cover.

* When you do not use this TV set for a long period of time, be sure to
disconnect the power plug from the AC outlet.

WARNING:

DO NOT cut off the mains plug from this equipment. If the plug fitted is not suitable for the power
points in your home or the cable is too short to reach a power point, then obtain an appropriate
safety approved extension lead or adaptor or consult your dealer.

If nonetheless the mains plug is cut off, remove the fuse and dispose of the plug immediately, to
avoid a possible shock hazard by inadvertent connection to the mains supply.

If this product is not provided with a mains plug, or one has to be fitted, then follow the instructions
given below:

IMPORTANT
DO NOT make any connection to the larger terminal which is marked with the letter E or by the
safety earth symbol ⏚ or coloured green or green-and-yellow.

The wires in the mains lead on this product are coloured in accordance with the following code:
    Blue   Neutral
    Brown   Live

As these colours may not correspond with the coloured marking identifying the terminals in your
plug proceed as follows:

The wire which is coloured blue must be connected to the terminal which is marked with the letter N
or coloured black.

The wire which is coloured brown must be connected to the terminal which is marked with the letter
L or coloured red.

When replacing the fuse only a correctly rated approved type should be used and be sure to re-fit
the fuse cover.

How To Replace The Fuse
Open the fuse compartment with a blade screwdriver, and replace the fuse.

IF IN DOUBT — CONSULT A COMPETENT ELECTRICIAN.

(The power plug is either type A or type B.)

Type A

Type B

● **Safety notices:** Some electrical and mechanical products can cause injury if used incorrectly. Some manufacturers therefore include safety notices with the user instructions for their goods. Customers also need to be advised about the use of certain chemicals and medicines they can buy.

Similarly, business premises can be dangerous places and must be carefully managed in order to protect staff and the public. There are a wide range of laws relating to health and safety, designed to protect customers and employees in the UK.

Firms communicate information on health and safety using a wide range of **safety notices**. For example, fire notices giving instructions on what to do in the event of a fire are usually displayed all around most business premises. 'No Smoking' signs are also widely used, as are a wide variety of other warning notices. The key issue with these kinds of notices is that they must be easily seen and clear to those reading them.

The **Safety Signs Regulations 1980** requires that all safety signs are made in either red, blue, yellow, or green, and that they are either rectangular, triangular, or circular. This helps people to recognize safety signs when they see them.

Sometimes firms put up signs saying that management bears no responsibility in the event of accidents. These signs have no legal effect. Firms are required by law to take steps to ensure the health and safety of their workforces, and the law holds them responsible for this, regardless of any disclaimer signs that may be put up.

Portfolio Activity 4.10

1. Investigate and collect examples of how the following organizations communicate information on products and prices to customers:

* A holiday company
* A mail order organization
* A school or college
* A department store
* A leisure centre
* A video rental shop
* A DIY warehouse

   In each case, suggest how the style of the different brochures, leaflets, and other literature you have collected reflects:

* The image of the organization
* The type of goods and services it provides
* The particular needs of customers

2. Collect examples of safety notices and signs used in the following organizations:

* A hospital
* A school or college
* A shop
* A manufacturing plant
* A DIY warehouse
* A local authority park
* A bus or train service

   How effective do you think the notices and signs are in each case?

   You may need to ask the permission of a manager in each of the above organizations to draw or take pictures of their notices and signs.

3. Design safety notices or signs for the following potential hazards:

* A kettle provided in the staff kitchen which spits out hot water and steam if it is over-filled
* A set of revolving doors to your business premises which can trap trailing clothing, bags, and children's fingers
* A set of sharp blades on a new lawnmower for sale

   If possible, use a desktop publishing package to help produce your designs.

Producing written communications

Does it look good, and can you understand it?

If a business document is to do the job it is intended to do, it must be produced with care. In a business environment, it will not always be possible for someone to check the documents you have written, so you will have to learn to evaluate them yourself.

You can evaluate a document in terms of its:

- **Appearance** – style and format
- **Language** – spelling, grammar and tone

Simply by looking at other business documents you receive at work you can learn a lot about the do's and don't's of producing business documents.

Appearance

This is simply what the document looks like. Is it pleasing to look at? Is it neat or scrappy-looking? Is it too cluttered with text, or clear and easy to read? In all cases, documents should be well presented. Every business will have its own business style for documents. This will include the type of paper they are written on, which may be thick, display a company logo, be embossed, and/or coloured. Thick embossed paper with an eye-catching logo can promote a good image for the business.

Style also includes the way documents are addressed. For example, some business organizations may insist that internal documents always show the first name as well as the surname of the people to whom they are sent; that they are listed in terms of their seniority if there is more than one addressee on the same document; that information such as the date and a file reference is positioned in a certain way – and so on.

Format refers to the layout of a document. This will include paper size, margins, line spacings, the use of headings, block paragraphs, size and type of characters, and so on. Clearly, style and format are closely related. For example, a business letter which filled the page with a mixture of fancy typefaces would not only demonstrate a poor layout but also a lack of style.

Many business organizations have set rules on style and format that all employees must follow when preparing business documents. This is called their **house style**.

Language

Language refers to how the document is worded. Does it make sense? Are words spelt correctly? Is it grammatically correct? Are sentences and/or paragraphs too long? Are commas and full stops used in the right places? Is the tone appropriate? For example, in response to a customer complaint, is the letter apologetic or aggressive?

Grammatical errors and spelling mistakes are unprofessional and can create a bad image for a business, and for individual members of staff.

Writing documents by hand

Before the invention of typewriters and word processors, all correspondence had to be written by hand. Many letters are still handwritten today, especially if the message is short and simple, because handwriting is a relatively quick and easy method. It also makes a message more personal.

It is also common for draft documents to be handwritten before they are typed or word-processed. Often one person will prepare the draft and another person will type it out or input it to a computer – for example, a manager drafting out a business letter for his or her secretary to produce and send out. Preparing a draft beforehand allows any changes to be made before the final version is produced.

If final versions of documents such as business letters are to be handwritten, then the writer should bear in mind:

- Not everyone can write neatly

- Mistakes cannot easily be corrected

- Tippex or correction fluid to correct mistakes can look messy and unprofessional

- It is time-consuming to write out the document again once a mistake has been made

- A photocopier will be needed to make copies

For these reasons most business organizations prefer to use typewritten or word-processed documents.

▼ *Two handwritten memos*

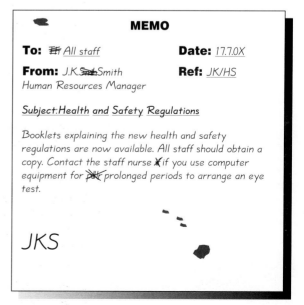

MEMO

To: All staff   **Date:** 17.7.0X

From: J.K. Smith   **Ref:** JK/HS
Human Resources Manager

Subject: Health and Safety Regulations

A booklet explaining the new health and safety regulations concerning the use of computer equipment is now available from Cathy Burke in room 137 (extension 7893).

All staff should be aware of the new regulations. If you use computer equipment for prolonged periods contact the staff nurse in room 304 (x3333) to arrange an eye test.

JKS

Right

MEMO

To: ~~The~~ *All staff*   **Date:** *17.7.0X*

From: J.K. ~~Smit~~ Smith   **Ref:** *JK/HS*
Human Resources Manager

Subject: Health and Safety Regulations

Booklets explaining the new health and safety regulations are now available. All staff should obtain a copy. Contact the staff nurse ✗ if you use computer equipment for ~~pub~~ prolonged periods to arrange an eye test.

JKS

Wrong

▼ *Using a computer word processing program*

Word processing (WP)

Many people now have access to a personal computer in their place of work. Special programs can be loaded on to computers to provide word processing functions.

Word processors can be used for producing all types of business documents, but are mainly used for writing letters, reports, and notices.

The latest versions of word processing programs such as Microsoft Word and WordPerfect are very like **desktop publishing (DTP)** programs. DTP allows users to design complex page layouts using columns, boxes, diagrams, and pictures in the same way as a newspaper or magazine. Using programs such as Aldus Pagemaker, Ami Pro, and Microsoft Publisher, even the smallest businesses can produce high-quality business documents and other publicity and marketing materials.

What word processing can do for you

▼ *A popular word-processing program*

- Provide many different typefaces and sizes
- Provide mathematical notation and symbols
- Count the number of words
- Automatically line up (justify) text at each margin
- Cut and copy text
- Correct spellings
- Suggest alternative words in a thesaurus
- Number pages automatically
- Create tables
- Import graphs and tables from other packages
- Make multiple copies
- Print on paper and slide transparencies
- Save and retrieve files

▼ *Printing in the past*

Voice recognition software is likely to revolutionize the way in which people use computers over the next few years. Computers are able to recognize spoken words and commands so that people can write messages without having to use a keyboard to input letters and numbers.

Before computer technology became miniaturized and affordable, businesses that needed multiple copies of business documents either had to use a photocopier or, if better quality was required, to have copies printed commercially. Traditionally, this would require raised metal blocks to be produced for each letter, line, and number. Typeset blocks of each page would then be printed on to paper. This was a slow and expensive process.

Nowadays a wide variety of business documents can be input into a word processing or desktop publishing package and downloaded directly to a printer linked to the computer. Multiple copies of the same document can then be printed out, in colour if necessary. The user will often have a choice of print quality: 'draft' for draft documents, 'letter quality', and 'near-typeset quality' for reports and published documents.

▼ *Printing today using computers*

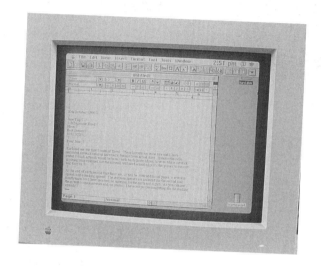

Modern printers linked to computers can be used to print out multiple copies of the same document to send to different people and to place on file.

If a business letter is sent to a great number of people, it can be very time-consuming for the person sending it to sign each copy individually. However, in the same way that photographs can be scanned and turned into digital images, it is possible to scan in the signature of a person sending a letter. The computerized image of the signature can then be incorporated at the end of a word-processed business letter. Every time the letter is printed out it will contain the signature of the writer.

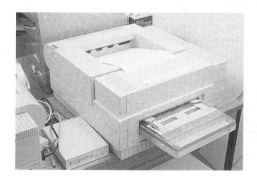

How good are business communications?

Communication breakdowns

Despite spending a lot of time and money on improving the quality and speed of their communications many businesses may still fail to communicate effectively with their customers, staff and suppliers for a variety of reasons:

- **Poor management.** Some people in business may be unprofessional and allow clashes of personality with other staff to affect communications with them. Also, some managers may not recognize their need to motivate employees by allowing them time to consult and become involved in business decision making. Managers may not always explain the reasons for their decisions very well.

- **Poor design.** Communication may be badly designed or be out of date. For example, a business on more than one site might find it very difficult to maintain good communications and good staff moral if it relies on the postal service for communication. Alternatively, a business might outgrow its existing communications network and find, for example, that its existing computer network regularly breaks down because of work overload.

- **Differences in language or culture or large geographical distances** between staff in a firm. Many large firms have customers and suppliers who are located overseas and may not understand the English language and customs. The same firms may even locate factories, offices and shops in more than one country.

- **Poorly explained or presented messages** can cause confusion and misunderstanding.

- **Prejudices.** Sometimes people interpret a message according to their prejudices. That is they see or hear what they want to and not what is actually being communicated.

- **Internal politics.** Some staff may compete with each other and may hold grievances. In doing so they may attempt to distort communications by spreading rumour and gossip in order to further their own aims rather than those of the business.

- **Physiological barriers.** Some people in business may be partially or totally blind or deaf. Communications can be adapted to the needs of people with special needs. For example, sign language is commonly used to communicate with deaf or hard of hearing workers.

Braille is used to communicate written text and numbers to blind people. Words and numbers are represented by a series of raised dots on paper or other surfaces, for example on lift buttons. Computers programs are now available to convert text directly into braille and special keyboards have been made for the blind with braille keys.

- **Overuse of jargon.** Not everyone can understand business jargon or technical terms.

Questions all businesses should ask about their communications

Because of the rapid pace of technological change and the pressure to compete with other firms, business organizations are continually reviewing their communications requirements. There are many questions a firm should ask to judge how good it is at communicating, but the most important is:

- **Does the communication meet business objectives?** For example, if a business finds that its sales are falling, its products are always out of date, and that it is usually beaten to the market by rival firms, this may indicate that communications with customers – letters, advertisements, telephone calls – are not very good. Alternatively, a survey of staff morale and motivation can reveal a great deal about the operation and workings of internal communications within the business.

Other questions include:

- **Was the communication made at the lowest cost possible?** Exchanging information is now faster than ever before and accuracy has improved requiring less time, effort and power. For example, a large printed business report may take several days and cost several pounds to send by post, whereas e-mail can send it in a matter of seconds and cost only a few pence on the telephone bill to do so.

- **Is it value for money?** Compared to its cost, how well does the communication do its job? Are there much cheaper ways of communicating which would work just as well? For example, there is little point in a small firm investing thousands of pounds in building a computer network for e-mail if is not going to be used to send and receive messages.

- **Does it provide accurate information?** It is essential that information sent and received by a business is error-free. For example, detailed faxes may not always be very easy to read and the receiver may have to interpret words and figures – or a supplier may deliver the wrong quantity of materials to firm in response to an illegible faxed order.

- **How easy is it to use and access information?** Communication will be of little use if users find operating equipment, like computers and fax machines, too difficult.

- **What is the speed of access?** Paper-based communication is slow – for example, sending a letter or data by internal mail or external post. Technological advance has allowed us to send and receive information from anywhere in the world in just a matter of minutes – for example, via electronic mail.

- **What is its impact on information exchange?** Because of improvements in the speed and cost of data exchange, interaction between individuals and business organizations has increased. For example, firms are able to learn of conditions in world markets, such as strikes or wars in countries supplying raw materials, and be able to react immediately to minimize the impact on their business.

- **What is its impact on users?** Prolonged use of computers screens and keyboards can result in poor eyesight and repetitive strain injury (RSI) in users fingers and wrists. Increasing demands on users to up date their computer skills and to operate a variety of equipment may cause stress.

- **Do staff need training?** To ensure that full and effective use is made of new communications equipment a business also needs to make sure that users are adequately trained. No matter how user-friendly computers and other equipment are today some basic training will be necessary if employees are to use them to send and receive information.

Portfolio Activity 4.11

Investigate communications in a business of your choice and produce a report covering:

- the types of communications used
- what they are for and why
- how they are produced, and the reasons why they are produced in this way
- how good the communications are, in terms of presentation, accuracy, cost, speed of delivery, and meeting their objectives
- how communications could be improved

1. With the permission of the owners or managers collect and/or record examples of oral, written and electronic communications used by the firm to communicate with staff, customers and suppliers.

2. Produce an evaluation of each document in terms of each of the questions above – meeting objectives, value for money, accuracy, ease of use, speed of access, etc. – and suggest how each one might be improved.

3. Use your evaluations from question 2 to report on communication in and by your chosen business. How effective is communication in the business and with customers and suppliers. How could communication be improved and how could this benefit the firm?

4. Present in draft a copy of your report to the business owners or managers. Ask for their comments. Discuss these with them before your produce your final report.

5. Finally present the findings of your report orally to your class. Use overhead slides in your presentation to list key points including the name of your business, the types of communications used and what they are used for, your evidence of good communications, and any thoughts you have on how communications in the business could be improved.

Portfolio Activity 4.12

Investigate functional areas, job roles and business communications in a business organisation of your choice using the all the things you have learnt from chapters 1 to 4. Write a report to describe

1. The name and size of the business (by employment, sales turnover, profit)

2. The main business aims and objectives

3. The goods and/or services it produces and the resources it needs to produce them

4. The organizational structure (and draw a organisation chart to illustrate)

5. The main functional areas in the business, including human resources

6. How these functional areas work together to achieve business aims

7. Typical jobs roles and tasks in each functional area

8. How staff in the functional areas communicate with each other on different matters, and with suppliers and customers

9. How the organizational structure of the business helps or hinders communications (you may like to interview staff at different levels in the organization to get their opinions first)

10. Why good communications are needed in the business to achieve business aims

Remember to list information sources you used in compiling your report. For example, business reports accounts, newspaper articles, the names of key personnel in the business, internal business communications

---

Key words

In your own words, write down explanations and definitions for the following key words and terms in this chapter:

Business communications	Business letters	E-mail	Point of sale
Internal business meetings	Memos	Fax transmission	Direct mail
External business meetings	Circulars	The Internet	Desk top publishing
Agenda	Notices	Advertisements	Word processing
Videoconferencing	Financial documents	Target audience	
Mobile phones	Information communications technology	Brand name	
Voice messaging		Brand image	

Test your knowledge

Questions 1–3 share the following answer options;

    A to communicate with customers
    B to communicate with other businesses
    C to communicate with colleagues
    D to keep records

Which of the above purposes will the following business documents serve?

1 Writing a memo to remind managers within a business that the time and venue of a meeting has been changed

2 Producing a standard letter to advertise the services of a new business

3 Writing a letter to a supplier to confirm arrangements for deliveries

Questions 4 – 6 share the following answer options;

    A standard business letter
    B invitation
    C memo
    D personal business letter

Which of the above business documents would you use in the following situations?

4 To reply to a customer who has complained about receiving the wrong order

5 To attach an urgent request for photocopying to a business report

6 To ask important customers to attend a Christmas party

7 Handwritten business messages have the following advantages except:
    A they are personalized
    B errors cannot be corrected easily
    C short messages can be written quickly
    D they do not require electronic equipment?

8 Sending documents by electronic mail has all of the following advantages except
    A it saves stationary and paper costs
    B transmission is rapid
    C the cost of sending documents is relatively cheap
    D you need a personal computer linked to the telephone network?

9 **a** List three routine documents a business may use.
    b What are the main purposes of the routine business documents you have listed?
    c Suggest three ways you can produce these business documents.

10 **a** Suggest three main advantages of using a word processor to produce a business letter compared to typing.
    b What is electronic mail?
    c Suggest three main advantages of sending a business document by electronic mail compared to sending a fax.

How Businesses Develop

About this unit

In this unit you will look at the different ways of describing what businesses do and what influences their decisions and activities.

Every business organization operates in a wider business world in which there are many different influences. Businesses cannot always control these influences, but they have to find ways of responding to them.

You will investigate different businesses to find out about their type of ownership, what they do, and how they are developing in response to different external influences. You will need to understand where these businesses fit into the wider business world and which influences have the most effect on them.

unit 2

chapter 5	*Business activities*
chapter 6	*Types of business organization*
chapter 7	*The business environment*

chapter 5 Business activities

Businesses can be described as belonging to one or more **industrial sectors** depending on the activities they carry out, and the types of goods and services they produce. Businesses can carry out one or more activities. As you investigate selected businesses you will need to decide what their core activity is, and how changes over time have affected them.

Primary industries, such as farming, forestry, fishing and mining, produce natural resources.

Secondary industries, such as **manufacturing** and construction use natural resources to produce **capital goods** and **consumer goods**.

Tertiary industries provide personal and commercial services, such as health care, banking, insurance, leisure, transport, communications, wholesaling and retailing.

The importance of primary industries in terms of employment and output in the UK has declined over time. Many workers have also lost their jobs from manufacturing industries. Services now employ around 75% of all workers in the UK and account for around 70% of total output. You will need to understand the main differences between these industrial sectors and find out about changes in them over time.

Section **5.1**

Causes of change in business activity

Types of business activity

Most business organizations specialize in one particular broad business activity. Some key business activities are:

- agriculture, forestry, fishing and mining
- manufacturing
- retailing, including the wholesale trade, shops and e-commerce
- transport and communications
- other services, such as hotels and restaurants, banking and insurance, sport, education and health care

In the UK and many other countries, some of these business activities are becoming more important in terms of the number of people they employ and the amount of output they produce, while others are declining in importance. These changes are the result of changing patterns of consumer spending over time, technological advance and increasing competition to supply goods and services from business organizations overseas.

Consumer trends

Consumer demand and the way people shop is always changing. Over time, the demand for some goods and services may fall, while the demand for others rises. Products that were popular ten years ago, or even just last year, may no longer be wanted by today's consumers. Business organizations – those who make and sell goods and services – must try to predict what consumers will want next, and provide it before their competitors do, otherwise they risk failure. A firm that does not produce what consumers want, or produces it too late, will not be successful. A **trend** in consumer demand refers to the general direction of change over time. Trends can operate in both directions. If sales are rising, this suggests an upward trend in demand. If sales are falling there is a downward trend.

▼ *Figure 5.1: How to recognize a trend in consumer demand*

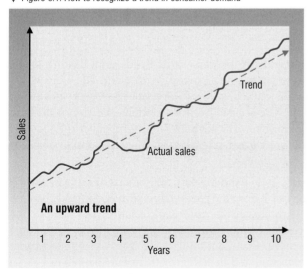

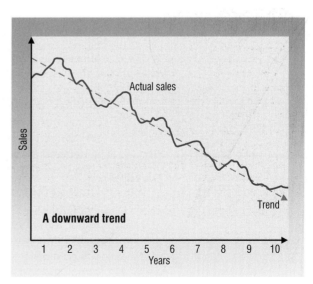

Long-term trends

Some trends may be established over a period of many years. For example, there are now around 27 million cars and light vans in the UK, compared to just over 6 million 30 years ago. The trend towards greater car ownership is likely to continue into the future as incomes increase. On the other hand, sales of cigarettes in the UK have declined consistently over the last 25 years.

Changes in consumer demand which continue in the same general direction for two to three years or more are usually considered to show a long-term trend. A long-term downward trend in consumer demand for particular goods and services can spell trouble for those firms that produce them. Firms may be tempted to switch production to those goods and services which show a continuing upward trend.

▼ *Figure 5.2: Long-term growth in car ownership in the UK*

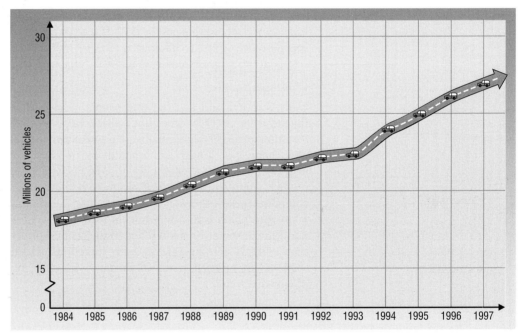

Transport Statistics 1999

Short-term trends

Other changes in demand can be very short-lived, some lasting for as little as a few days, such as the increase in demand for flowers on Mothers' day each year, or tickets for a pop concert. Other short-term changes in demand may be seasonal – for example, the rise in demand for suntan lotion for three to four months each summer, or the increase in demand for toys before Christmas each year. All are examples of short-term trends in consumer demand.

Other short-term trends in demand for particular goods or services may be observed for a year or two before the general direction of demand changes. Many will be to do with changes in tastes and fashion. For example, the early 1990s craze for Ninja Mutant Turtle toys was short-lived. By the time you read this book, a more recent, but similar craze for Pokémon computer games and toys may be over, and demand for them may be falling.

Square eyes

The graph below shows the percentage of the population who watch television at various times during the day. There is a rising trend in viewing numbers from 6 pm to 8 pm. After this, numbers of viewers start to fall away again. This two-hour growth period in viewing figures is a short-term trend. Not surprisingly, TV adverts are more expensive to show at this time than at any other time.

▼ *Radio and television audiences throughout the day*

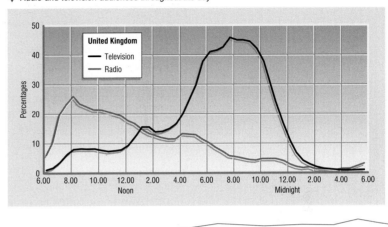

Some short-term trends in consumer demand

You will be able to think of many different examples of short-term trends in consumer demand for different goods and services. Here are just a few:

- Sales of tickets to a pop concert
- Sales of Christmas cards

- Sales of special editions of newspapers and magazines
- Sales of foreign holidays during the summer
- Sales or rentals of a new video film release
- The surge in demand for electricity at around 6-7 pm when people get home from work

Long-term trends in demand usually occur for all the products in the same market. For example, there has been a steady growth in the number of compact discs purchased over time, while the demand for vinyl LPs has fallen so markedly that few record companies make them. Now, sales of DVD music and video discs and players seem likely to overtake CD sales in the next few years.

On the other hand, short-term changes in demand often relate to a particular good or service, rather than the entire market. So, for example, pop groups may decline in popularity through time and sell less CDs, despite the growth in sales of CDs in general. Similarly, despite the long-term decline in demand for cigarettes, sales of a brand called 'Death' cigarettes increased after they were launched, but the increase was short-lived.

Short-term trends in consumer demand may move in a different direction to the long-term trend. For example, more and more tourists are visiting the UK each year. However, during the Gulf War in Kuwait in 1990, the number of tourists visiting the UK fell sharply – a short-term downward trend – because of the fear of terrorist attacks on American planes. Similarly, tourist numbers tend to fall during the winter compared to the summer despite a year-on-year rise in numbers.

Past trends

Some trends in consumer demand have developed over many years. For example, in the UK over the last hundred years, there has been a steady trend towards more home ownership and less private renting of accommodation. At the same time, there have been trends towards increased car ownership and more holidays abroad. Most homes now have a television, refrigerator, and telephone. Thirty years ago, very few homes had these items. The reasons for these observed long-term trends in consumer demand are many. Some of the most important are:

- **Most people in the UK now have more money to spend.** This has enabled them to spend more of their incomes meeting their wants – for example, on video recorders, jewellery, holidays. The increased use of credit cards to boost our spending also reflects a change in people's attitude towards debt.

- **People work fewer hours than many years ago.** This has given them more time for leisure activities, and has increased demand for holidays, sport centres, DIY and garden centres, restaurants, and pubs.

- **Social attitudes have changed.** More women now go out to work and have less time to look after their families. This has caused an increase in demand for time-saving appliances such as microwave cookers and dishwashers. Also, less people go to church today. Until the late 1990s, shops had been prevented from opening on Sunday because of pressure from churchgoers.

- **Couples are marrying later and having fewer children.** This has meant a growing number of single people, an increase in the number of households, but a fall in their average size. This has helped to increase the demand for household furnishings and appliances. Some large retail outlets have even introduced 'singles shopping nights' where people can meet.

- **People have become more health-conscious.** We now take more exercise, smoke fewer cigarettes, eat less fatty foods, and drink more fruit and herbal drinks.

- **There is growing concern for the environment** – so-called 'green consumerism'. This has affected the way many goods and services are produced and the types of products stocked by many shops. It has increased the demand for products which are not tested on animals and do not release harmful pollutants into the air.

- **Technology has advanced rapidly.** This has meant that once high-cost products such as televisions, CDs, computers, and video recorders have come down in price and can now be afforded by many more people.

Portfolio Activity 5.1

1. Look at the graphs and tables. What past trends in consumer demand can you identify?

2. Suggest possible reasons for the trends in consumer demand you have identified above.

3. Give examples of the kinds of firms that might use the information on trends in consumer demand, and explain how they would do so.

4. Choose one particular product from those shown, and suggest whether you think the past trend in demand will continue into the future or is likely to change direction. Give reasons for your answer.

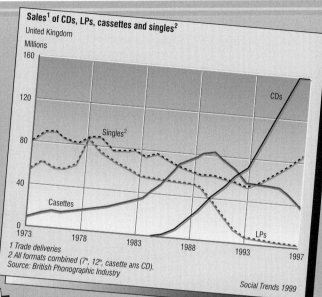

Sales[1] of CDs, LPs, cassettes and singles[2]
United Kingdom
Millions

1 Trade deliveries
2 All formats combined (7", 12", casette ans CD).
Source: British Phonographic Industry

Social Trends 1999

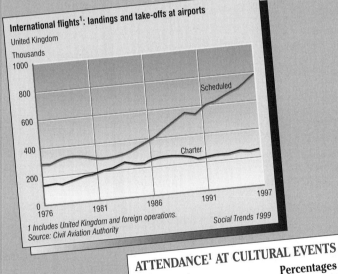

International flights[1]: landings and take-offs at airports
United Kingdom
Thousands

1 Includes United Kingdom and foreign operations.
Source: Civil Aviation Authority

Social Trends 1999

Number of pets
United Kingdom
Millions

Source: Pet Food Manufacturers Association Ltd

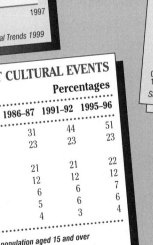

ATTENDANCE[1] AT CULTURAL EVENTS
Great Britain — Percentages

	1986–87	1991–92	1995–96
Cinema	31	44	51
Plays	23	23	23
Art galleries exhibitions	21	21	22
Classical music	12	12	12
Ballet	6	6	7
Opera	5	6	6
Contemporary dance	4	3	4

1 Percentage of resident population aged 15 and over attending 'these days'.
Source: Target Group Index. BMRB international.

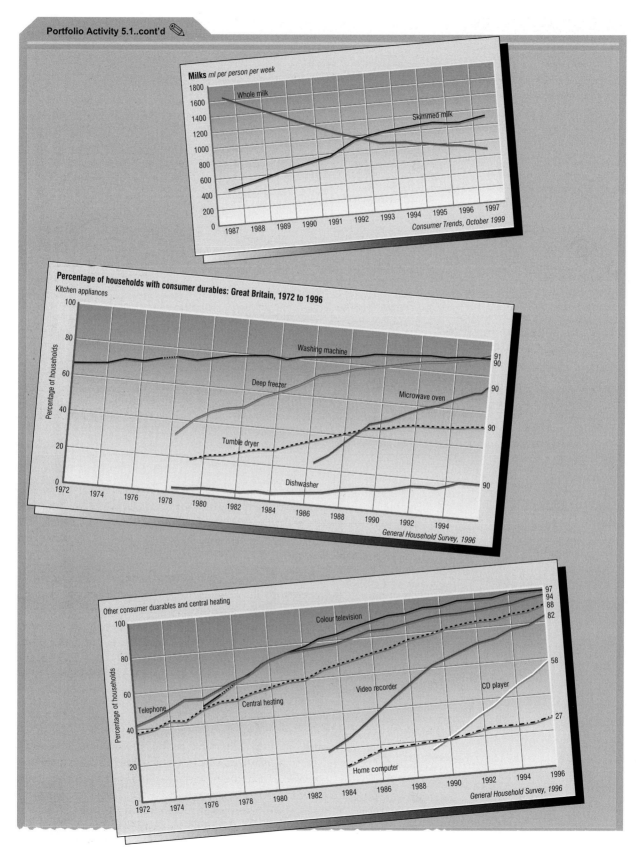

Milks *ml per person per week*

Whole milk

Skimmed milk

Consumer Trends, October 1999

Percentage of households with consumer durables: Great Britain, 1972 to 1996

Kitchen appliances

Percentage of households

Washing machine

Deep freezer

Microwave oven

Tumble dryer

Dishwasher

General Household Survey, 1996

Other consumer duarables and central heating

Percentage of households

Colour television

Video recorder

CD player

Telephone

Central heating

Home computer

General Household Survey, 1996

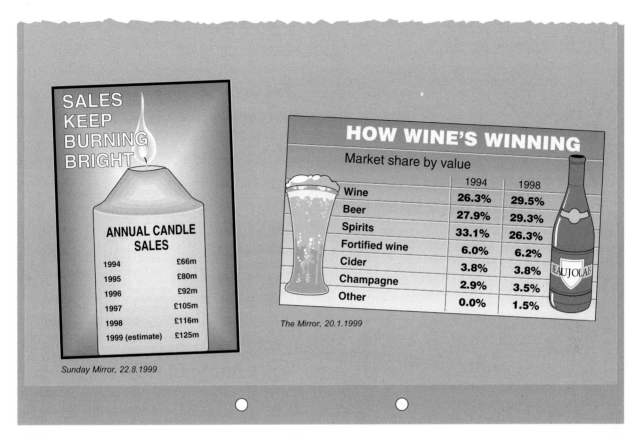

SALES KEEP BURNING BRIGHT

ANNUAL CANDLE SALES

1994	£66m
1995	£80m
1996	£92m
1997	£105m
1998	£116m
1999 (estimate)	£125m

Sunday Mirror, 22.8.1999

HOW WINE'S WINNING
Market share by value

	1994	1998
Wine	26.3%	29.5%
Beer	27.9%	29.3%
Spirits	33.1%	26.3%
Fortified wine	6.0%	6.2%
Cider	3.8%	3.8%
Champagne	2.9%	3.5%
Other	0.0%	1.5%

The Mirror, 20.1.1999

Future trends

Firms investigate past trends in demand in order to predict what might happen in the future. For example, sales of tobacco in Western countries have been falling for many years, and it is likely this long-term trend will continue. Tobacco firms have responded by trying to sell more cigarettes in Third World countries.

Sales of computer PC-DVD drives have been growing steadily recently, and again it seems reasonable to guess that this trend will continue. However, guessing at the future using the past can be dangerous, because the future may be completely different. Some experts suggest that the Internet will make text, sound, and video available to all homes on demand in the near future, and that this will make CD and DVD discs redundant. If this were to happen in the future, demand for DVD products could quickly fall.

It is possible to identify a number of current trends in consumer demand which are likely to continue into the future. For example, the growth of the 'green consumer', healthy diets and eating, more computers, and increased cinema attendance are sales trends which have all been growing in recent years. However, technology, fashions, and tastes are changing all the time, and this can lead to new and unexpected changes in demand in the future. Businesses will use market research to try to predict future trends in consumer demand and shopping patterns (see chapter 2).

Causes of change in consumer demand

Read all the newspaper articles. For each one write down:

- What has caused consumer demand to change
- Which goods and/or services the change in demand has affected
- How the change in demand is likely to affect those firms that produce and sell the goods and services

How times have changed

In 1947 the typical working man took home around £2 a week, but his hours were longer and he usually worked six days so it would take him around half a day to earn half a crown (25p) to pay for a basket of groceries.

Nowadays the average working man's wages are £21,000 a year – around £420 a week – so it would take less than half an hour to earn enough to pay for the same amount of groceries today, even at their higher prices.

Festive spirit surge

SHOPPERS stocking up on festive spirit stripped supermarket shelves bare as booze sales surged, according to drinks bosses.

Spirits sales more than doubled in the week before Christmas, drinks giant Allied-Domecq revealed last night.

Price-cutting and an advertising push provided a boost, but a rush to beat Budget tax rises also helped.

Divorce rate sparks surge in toy market

Britain's toy market is booming thanks to the soaring divorce rate. As one in three parents split, the number of 'guilt gifts' given by separated mums and dads is growing.

Despite the growth of video and computer games, sales of small, portable toys which can be taken by children from one parent's home to another are increasing. According to market researchers Mintel, the divorce generation's 'portable kids' are being lavished with new portable toys. Mintel say sales of small cheap toys like Polly Pockets, Mighty Max, Trolls, and Monster In my Pocket boosted toy sales in Britain by £1.57 billion last year.

The Independent 30.6.1994

Sales boom in high street

HIGH STREET sales are rising at their fastest rate for 18 months, official figures showed yesterday. Clothes and shoe shops and household goods stores saw the strongest rises.

Sales in the three months to the end of July increased by 1.3 per cent on the previous 3 months. The Office for National Statistics said the figure represented the biggest rise since February 1988.

Some economists said the boom in sales showed that interest rates had been cut too far. Low interest rates and price inflation have increased disposable incomes, while rising house prices and low unemployment have helped to boost consumer confidence.

Adapted from Metro, 19.8.1999

It's a £1.6bn cracker

Biscuit firms will make £1.6 billion this year as sales boom.

Britons eat their way through a staggering 25 pounds of biscuits each year. That works out at £1.36 per person a week on biscuits.

But bosses are spending £18.5 million on TV ads to get people eating even more. 'The only way to grow is to get more people to eat more biscuits,' says McVitie's marketing director, Andy Rush.

Changes in demand

Business organizations have little control over the factors that cause short-term or long-term changes in consumer demand for their goods and services. We can divide up the factors that influence consumer demand into two main categories:

- Price
- Non-price factors

Price

As the price of a good or service rises, consumers will tend to buy less of it, simply because they cannot afford to buy so much at higher prices and because cheaper alternatives may be available.

As prices fall, consumers can afford to buy more of a product and may switch from more expensive alternatives.

Technological advance in electronics has reduced the cost of producing high-technology products such as video recorders, compact disc players, camcorders, and computers. Falling production costs have allowed manufacturers to lower their prices without cutting their profits. As the price of these products has tumbled, sales have increased.

Non-price factors

These are factors that cause consumer demand for a good or service to change regardless of the price charged. These factors are considered in detail below.

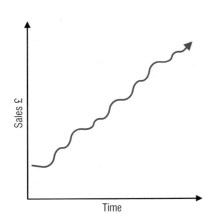

- **An increase in consumer demand:** If demand is rising, consumers will be buying more products. Sales revenues and potential profits will increase. Firms will expand their production to meet demand, especially if the increase in demand is long-lived.

  An increase in demand for a particular good or service may occur because:
  - Consumers have more money to spend
  - The price of other goods and services has increased
  - Consumers have more confidence to spend
  - Consumer needs and wants have changed in favour of the product
  - Advertising has persuaded them to buy

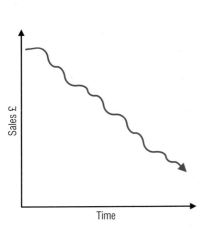

- **A fall in consumer demand:** Falling demand for a good or service, if prolonged, may spell trouble for a business. Stocks of finished goods will build up and may have to be sold off at a lower price. Production may have to be cut, otherwise stocks of unsold goods will build up again. Workers may lose their jobs. Suppliers of machinery and materials will also suffer a cut in their orders.

  A fall in demand for a particular good or service may occur because:
  - Consumers have less money to spend
  - The price of other goods and services has fallen
  - Consumers have less confidence to spend
  - Consumer needs and wants have changed in favour of other products

What causes demand to change for goods and services?

'Changes in income'

Both long-term and short-term changes in demand can occur if people have more or less money to spend. The amount of money people have to spend is called their **disposable income**. This is the amount of money they can spend and/or save after they have paid income tax and national insurance contributions.

In general, the more disposable income people have, the more they spend and the stronger is the demand for certain goods. Increases in income tax and national insurance can, therefore, reduce disposable income and cut consumer demand.

The cost of living

Between 1960 and 1999, UK household disposable income increased from around £18.5 billion to over £570 billion. But this does not mean we are over 30 times better off now than we were in 1960. At the same time the prices of the goods and services we buy have increased. That is, the **cost of living** has gone up.

Prices tend to rise for two main reasons:

i People demand more goods and services than firms can supply. This will tend to force up the prices at which firms sell their products.

ii As the cost of wages, machinery, and/or materials increases, firms' profits will be squeezed unless they can pass on these costs to consumers as higher prices.

Measuring inflation

Between 1960 and 1999 the cost of living in the UK, as measured by the **Retail Prices Index (RPI)**, increased by 13 fold! This suggests that the prices of all goods and services increased on average by around 6.8% per year over this period, so something that may have cost £1 in 1960 may now cost £13. A sustained increase in prices is called **inflation**.

Figure 5.3 below shows how the rate of price inflation in the UK, as measured by the RPI, has changed each year since 1960. It shows that the largest annual increase in prices was in 1975, at just under 25%. The lowest rate of increase in prices was recorded in 1993 when prices increased, on average, by less than 2%.

The RPI is calculated by working out the average price of some 600 different goods and services each month. It is, therefore, not a true cost of living measure, because it does not include all the things we spend money on, nor does it tell us the change in the quality of the items we buy over time. However, as new products such as camcorders and computer games are developed, these are added to the 'basket of goods' measured by the RPI.

Purchasing power and inflation

Inflation reduces the purchasing power of the money we spend. For example, if you spend £100 each week you could buy 10 items at £10 each. If prices were to double, your £100 would buy only 5 items at £20 each. Because of inflation, £1 in 1960 is now worth the equivalent of around 7 pence in purchasing power.

As long as our incomes increase faster than prices, we can afford to buy more goods and services. Between 1981 and 1999, prices increased on average by around 4.3% per year. Over the same period, average weekly earnings, including any overtime and bonus payments, increased by almost 5% each year. This means that, in general, people in work have managed to increase the amount of money they have to spend faster than prices have increased.

However, inflation hits people on low or fixed incomes the hardest. People who are unemployed or old age pensioners may find it hard to keep up with rising prices.

▼ Figure 5.3: Retail Prices Index, percentage change over 12 months

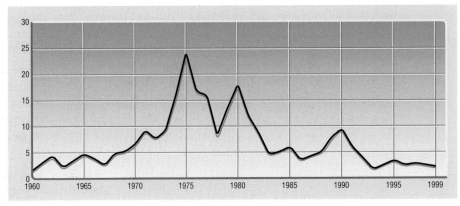

1960

1999

"The pound in your pocket is now worth only 7 pence compared with how much it could buy at 1960 prices."

One of the main reasons for the long-term growth in the demand for products such as homes, cars, electrical appliances, overseas holidays, financial services, and many more, is the growth in disposable income over time. Between 1960 and 1999 the total disposable income in the UK increased from £18.5 billion to over £570 billion.

However, not all goods and services have experienced an increase in demand as disposable incomes have risen. For example, we do not buy more salt or newspapers simply because our incomes have gone up.

Some products are called **inferior goods,** because as our incomes increase, we tend to buy less of them in favour of more expensive, but still affordable products. For example, more people have bought cars as incomes have increased instead of using public transport. Bus and train passenger numbers have fallen over time. Similarly, our demand for overseas holidays has increased at the expense of holidays in the UK. Other factors affecting demand for goods and services include:

● **Unemployment:** During periods when unemployment is rising, disposable income and consumer demand will tend to fall because less people are at work earning money.

● **Interest rates:** The amount of money people have to spend will also depend in part on how much they borrow from banks and building societies. When interest rates are high, borrowing money becomes more expensive and people will tend to borrow less. An increase in interest rates will also make buying goods on hire purchase more expensive, and consumers will tend to buy less using this method.

Incomes, and therefore the purchasing power of consumers, are unequal. Some people have more money to spend than others. In general, firms will aim to produce goods and services for consumers who have enough money to buy them. People on low incomes may be unable to afford holidays overseas, new cars, fashionable clothes, and hi-tech household goods.

Confidence to spend

Consumer confidence has a large impact on the spending decisions of consumers. For example, if unemployment is rising, consumers may worry that they might lose their jobs in the future, and so may wish to cut their spending now and put more aside in savings. If, however, unemployment is falling, consumers may feel more confident and raise their spending in the belief that their jobs are safe.

Changing needs

All people have the same basic needs for food, water, and shelter. However, people also have other needs which will differ according to their particular lifestyle, health, and age. For example, an old person may need more medical attention and warmer clothes than a younger person. A disabled person may need a wheelchair and waist-level plug sockets and light switches fitted in their home.

Many people might argue they need a car to get to and from work each day because there is no regular bus or train service. Similarly, new parents will need baby clothes and nappies.

▼ *Consumers have different needs.*

The most dramatic change in your needs will probably occur when you leave full-time education. If you have not already opened a bank account, it is likely you will need one so that you can receive your pay each month. You may need to buy overalls or a suit to wear to work. As you grow older, you may want to buy your own home and will need the services of a solicitor and building society to do so.

Private sector businesses will only provide the goods and services we need if they can be produced at a profit (see chapter 1). Some people cannot buy the goods and services they need because they cannot afford to pay for them. In some poor countries, many people cannot even afford to buy food.

In the UK, the Government will often provide goods and services people need but cannot afford. For example, schools and hospitals are provided for people who cannot afford private education or healthcare. Benefits are paid to people who are disabled or out or work so that they can buy the basic items they need.

Changing wants

In addition to income, one of the most important factors causing short- and long-term changes in demand for products is the changing wants of consumers. Our wants change much quicker than our needs. Our wants as consumers are also endless compared to our needs.

Most people do not have enough money to buy everything they want. When buying goods and services, they have to prioritize and make choices. In general, consumers will buy those products that give them the most satisfaction. Some of the main factors affecting consumer wants are:

● **Fashion and tastes:** Tastes and fashions can change rapidly. This is true of many products, not just clothes.

▼ Fashions and our wants for different clothes change rapidly.

▼ Good advertising can create wants and persuade consumers that the advertised product is better than the rest.

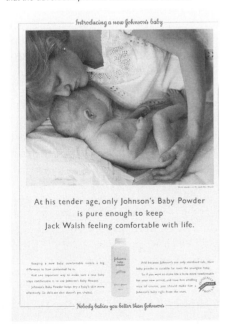

Introducing a new Johnson's baby

At his tender age, only Johnson's Baby Powder is pure enough to keep Jack Walsh feeling comfortable with life.

Nobody babies you better than Johnson's

People in the UK now buy more wine than they ever did before, because they have acquired a taste for it from holidays abroad. We have also developed a taste for more healthy eating, and food manufacturers are now keen to advertise that their products are low in fat. Rabbit disappeared as a favoured meat many years ago, to be replaced by chicken. Organic food is now growing rapidly in popularity as people have become concerned about modern intensive farming methods.

More people now want their own personal computer, mobile phone, and widescreen digital TV. More people also want to eat out at restaurants, go abroad for their holidays, and use environmentally friendly products.

- **Social and cultural factors:** The British spend more leisure time at home than other nationalities and are more willing to spend money on consumer electronics goods. This reflects, in part, cultural and social differences between consumers in Britain and consumers overseas.

More females are going to work now than ever before; women are also getting married later, and having fewer children. These important changes in UK society have affected the demand for many goods and services. Supermarkets and other shops have had to adapt by staying open later in the evening. Shops have also successfully campaigned to open on Sundays.

Cultural differences between people in different regions of the UK will also affect the regional pattern of demand. For example, did you know that men in the North and North West drink twice as much beer as men in East Anglia?

- **Advertising:** Business organizations can influence the demand for their goods or services through advertising. Advertising not only tells a consumer that particular products exist, but can also create powerful images for products on posters, radio, and TV, to persuade people to buy them (see chapter 4).

Advertising may try to prevent demand for an old product falling by telling consumers that it has been 'improved'. Alternatively, firms will often advertise their new products heavily to encourage people to believe that they need them. For example, until Sony invented the Walkman, most consumers had never thought of having portable personal music-players. However, strong advertising persuaded many people to buy them. Portable mini-disc, CD, and DVD players are now a common sight.

A firm in competition with rival organizations to sell very similar products, such as washing powders and biscuits, will make great use of advertising to persuade consumers that their particular product is better than all the others. Here, advertising is used not only to create a want for their product, but also to attract customers away from rival firms.

- **Other factors:** A whole host of other factors can explain why our wants change over time. For example, changes in the seasons affect our demand for goods and services. We want Christmas trees and decorations in December, while in the summer we want T-shirts, ice creams, and holidays.

Section **5.2**

Industrial sectors

What is an industry?

Business activities are often classified by grouping together firms producing the same goods or services into industries. An **industry** consists of all those firms producing the same good or service. For example, the construction industry consists of all those firms engaged in building homes, offices, shops, factories, roads, hospitals, or even small garages or patios. The oil and gas industry consists of firms like Exxon, BP Amoco, and British Gas that extract and sell fossil fuels. The retailing industry consists of firms that operate shops, mail order catalogues, home shopping channels on TV, and outlets through which consumers can buy products. One of the most important developments in retailing in recent years has been the introduction and growth of **e-commerce**, or shopping via the Internet (see 5.3)

Industrial sectors

Because there are so many different types of industry it is often useful to divide them up into three broad **industrial sectors**, or groupings.

UK Industries

The **British Standard Industrial Classification (SIC)** groups industries into 17 groups based on broadly common business activities.

Broad structure of SIC (1992)

Section	Description
A	Agriculture, hunting, and forestry
B	Fishing
C	Mining and quarrying
D	Manufacturing
E	Electricity, gas, and water supply
F	Construction
G	Wholesale and retail trade; motor vehicle repair, motorcycles, personal and household goods
H	Hotels and restaurants
I	Transport, storage, and communication
J	Financial intermediation
K	Real estate, renting, and business activities
L	Public administration and defence; compulsory social security
M	Education
N	Health and social work
O	Other community, social, and personal service activities
P	Private households with employed persons
Q	Extra-territorial organizations and bodies

The primary sector

The primary sector consists of firms which produce natural resources by growing plants, like wheat and barley, digging for minerals like coal or copper, or breeding animals. Primary firms are grouped into **primary industries**.

Primary industries
Farming
Fishing
Mining
Quarrying
Oil and gas extraction
Forestry
Water supply

Primary means these industries are the first stage in most production chains, as many of the raw materials grown or dug out of the ground are used to produce something else. Primary industries are sometimes called **extractive industries**, because they extract natural resources from the earth (see section 5.3).

The secondary sector

Secondary firms use natural resources provided by primary industries to make other goods. For example, a dairy will take milk provided by a farm and turn it into cheese and yoghurt. Iron ore is turned into iron and steel. Oil is refined into petrol and other fuels, and is also used in paints and plastics. Oil, coal, and gas are used to produce electricity.

Using raw materials to make other goods is known as **manufacturing** (see section 5.3). Firms involved in manufacturing, and those engaged in construction, are known as **secondary industries**.

Some secondary industries

Aerospace
Clothing
Vehicles
Steel
Electricity
Computers
Processed foods
Furniture
Construction
Metal goods
Food products

The tertiary sector (or service sector)

A great many firms do not produce physical products but provide services instead. Firms in the service sector are grouped together as **tertiary industries**.

It is usual to divide tertiary activities into two groups:

- Firms that produce **personal services**, such as doctors, hairdressers, window cleaners, tailors, teachers, and gardeners.

- Firms that produce **commercial services** for other business organizations, such as selling goods in their shops, transporting them, business banking, finance and insurance, advertising services, and communications.

Because retailing – selling goods and services to final consumers – is such an important commercial service on which other firms rely, people often make the mistake of thinking that tertiary industries provide the final link

Some tertiary industries

Education
Banking
Insurance
Wholesaling
Retailing (Shops etc)
Public Administration
Leisure
Health
Distribution
Advertising
Transport
Communications

in the chain of production for most goods and services. In fact, retailing is only one of many tertiary industries. Without a great many other commercial services like banking and insurance, transport or advertising, many primary, secondary, and other tertiary firms would find it very difficult to produce anything at all (see chapter 1).

Developments in industrial sectors

Significant changes have taken place in the industrial make-up of the UK over time. We can examine these changes in terms of the number of people employed and the amount of output from each of the major industrial sectors.

Figures 5.4 and 5.5 show how the proportion of total employment and total output accounted for by each sector has changed since 1971.

▼ *Figure 5.4: Employment by main sector of business activity 1971-1999*

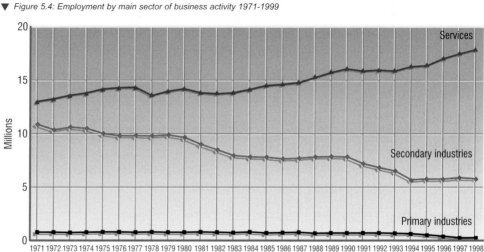

▼ Figure 5.5: Value of output in manufacturing, as a % of total UK output 1982-1999

The decline of the primary sector

Many years ago, most people in the UK relied on farming and other primary industries, such as coal and tin mining, for jobs and incomes. Today, the picture is very different.

During the Industrial Revolution in the UK, which is thought to have started in 1760, millions of workers left farming and mining to get jobs in the new factories producing textiles and clothing, rolling stock for the new railways, ships, and industrial machinery.

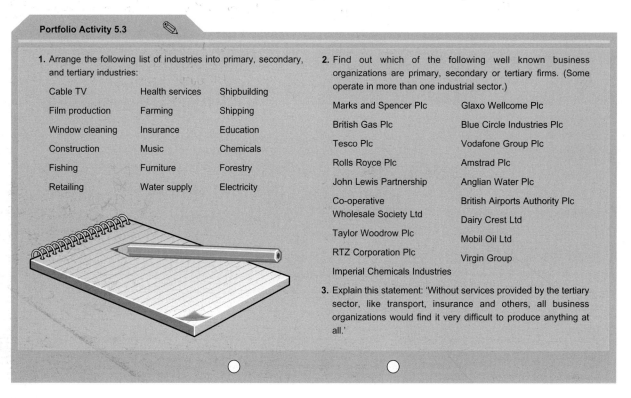

Portfolio Activity 5.3

1. Arrange the following list of industries into primary, secondary, and tertiary industries:

Cable TV	Health services	Shipbuilding
Film production	Farming	Shipping
Window cleaning	Insurance	Education
Construction	Music	Chemicals
Fishing	Furniture	Forestry
Retailing	Water supply	Electricity

2. Find out which of the following well known business organizations are primary, secondary or tertiary firms. (Some operate in more than one industrial sector.)

Marks and Spencer Plc	Glaxo Wellcome Plc
British Gas Plc	Blue Circle Industries Plc
Tesco Plc	Vodafone Group Plc
Rolls Royce Plc	Amstrad Plc
John Lewis Partnership	Anglian Water Plc
Co-operative Wholesale Society Ltd	British Airports Authority Plc
Taylor Woodrow Plc	Dairy Crest Ltd
RTZ Corporation Plc	Mobil Oil Ltd
Imperial Chemicals Industries	Virgin Group

3. Explain this statement: 'Without services provided by the tertiary sector, like transport, insurance and others, all business organizations would find it very difficult to produce anything at all.'

The new manufacturing industries consumed large amounts of raw materials such as coal for power, iron and steel, wood, and rubber. An increasing amount of these raw materials were imported from cheap sources overseas.

Because an increasing number of people no longer worked the land to provide their own supply of food, there was an increase in the demand for food from workers employed in factories. Despite the falling number of farm workers, new farming technology and cheap food imports from overseas ensured that an ever-increasing supply of food could be provided for the growing number of manufacturing workers in towns and cities.

By 1999 primary industries employed around 500,000 workers – just 2% of all workers in the UK. This compares to 3.8% of workers employed in primary industries in 1971.

The value of goods and services from the primary sector has grown over time, but has fallen as a proportion of the total value of output from all industries in the UK . This is because the output of secondary and tertiary industries has increased faster than output from primary industries. In 1971 primary sector output accounted for just 4% of the value of total UK output. This share had fallen slightly by 1999.

The decline of manufacturing

Despite the strong growth in UK manufacturing employment and output during the eighteenth and nineteenth centuries, this industrial sector is now in decline. Many jobs have been lost from manufacturing industries and their contribution to the total UK output of goods and services has fallen.

Between 1971 and 1999, almost 4 million jobs had been lost from manufacturing industries in the UK. Over the same period the proportion of the total value of UK output provided by these industries fell, from 41% in 1971 to around 20% in 1999.

▼ *Declining*

▽ *Growing*

The growth of services

With the rapid growth in the incomes and wealth of many workers in the UK over the last 70 years, many people have been taking more leisure time and have used more of their money to spend on consumer services. Many millions of people now work in shops, offices, transport, communications, financial services, and other tertiary sector jobs.

Between 1971 and 1981, services like banking and insurance created a total of 1.8 million jobs. By 1981, around 61% of all employees in the UK were employed in the service sector.

Between 1981 and 1999, services had created almost 4 million jobs. By 1999, some 18 million people were employed by the service sector – around 75% of all UK employees. The service sector now produces around 70% of the total value of UK output, up from 55% in 1971.

Portfolio Activity 5.4

1. Below is a jumbled group of reasons for the rapid increase in the importance of the tertiary sector in the UK and other developed countries. Match up each reason for growth with its possible effect on the service sector in the economy.

   Reasons for growth

   - Rise in consumers' incomes, allowing them to spend more on luxury goods, e.g. TVs, videos, cars
   - Increase in peoples' savings as incomes have risen
   - Increase in number of tourists, as people can afford to travel more
   - Increase in number of people wanting to own their own home
   - Reduction in the number of hours many people work each week (the average working week of full-time employees in the UK in 1999 was 38.2 hours)

   Impacts on service sector

   - More solicitors, building societies, estate agents, and insurance services
   - Increase in demand for leisure activities and leisure centres
   - Increase in number of large shops and shopping centres
   - More holiday shops, restaurants, and hotels
   - Increase in banking and financial services

2. What evidence is there of growth in the service sector in your local town? Conduct a local business survey using business telephone directories, and from your own observations. Your local authority, Chamber of Commerce, and Business Link office may also provide useful information.

The next section looks at some of the more recent changes in the activities of a number of UK industries.

What does the future hold?

It is difficult to predict what will happen to the industrial sectors of the UK in the future, but a number of trends seem likely:

- Continued growth in services
- Technological advance in services and manufacturing, which will make production rely more on machinery and equipment and less on workers

- Workers will need to update and change their work skills to keep pace with the new technology

- High unemployment, especially among older manufacturing workers

Between 1984 and 1999, the total number of people in work or looking for work (i.e. the total workforce) in the UK increased from 27.3 million to 29.2 million. Although the number of jobs in services increased at the same time, there were not enough jobs for everyone looking for work, including those people who had lost their jobs from manufacturing industry. As a result, the number of people unemployed in the UK increased.

▼ *Figure 5.6: Unemployment in the UK*

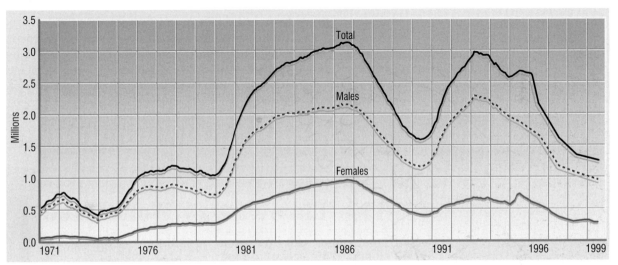

ONS Labour Market Trends

The total number of people in the UK registered as unemployed increased from 693,000 in 1971 to peak at over 3 million in 1985 (see Figure 5.6). Despite falling back to around 1.7 million in 1990, unemployment increased again to nearly 3 million people in 1992. However, since 1993 unemployment in the UK has been on a downward trend. In 1999 just over 1.2 million were counted as unemployed.

High levels of unemployment may continue as technological advance means more and more workers' jobs are replaced by machines and the skills they have become out of date. Service industries rely heavily on the use of computers and other office equipment, and do not require large numbers of employees.

UK industry and jobs continue to face aggressive competition from firms overseas, especially from developing countries like China, Malaysia, and Taiwan, where output is high but wages remain low. Firms in these countries are, therefore, able to produce similar goods and services to UK firms but at a much lower cost and final price to consumers.

Prominent trades in 1900	Declining trades in the 1990s (why?...)	Growth areas in the 1990s (why?...)
Ash collectors	Air couriers (electronic mail)	Advertising (TV and Internet)
Starchers	Insurance claims assessors (computers)	Security devices and services (rising crime)
Blood driers	Bailiffs (electronic credit freezes)	Sports equipment (more leisure time)
Mourning hat band makers	Checkout staff (image recognition software)	Cable manufacturers (more TV and computer networks)
Lamp black makers	Cash register suppliers (computers)	Computer programmers
Lamplighters	Coal merchants (electricity)	Recycling (tighter controls on waste)
Ice merchants	Secretarial services (voice recognition software)	Career consultants (rising unemployment)
Soot merchants	Layout artists (computer templates)	Dating agencies (less time for personal contact)
Whale oil refiners	Factory cleaning (intelligent robots)	Telemarketing (wider access to consumers)
Saddlers	Typewriter manufacturers (word processors)	Stress managers (pressures of everyday life and work)
Livery stable keepers	Draughting equipment makers (computer aided design)	Cruise companies (rising incomes, business travel)
Soap makers	Notaries and commissioners of oaths in courts (video recordings)	
	Film processors (video and digital technology)	

Adapted from the New Scientist 16.4.1994

A number of people have argued that the only way for UK manufacturing to recover is to concentrate on making high-quality products which many foreign countries are unable to produce. Successful UK examples of using this strategy include Rolls Royce in the production of cars and engines for civil and military aircraft and BAE Systems in the production of aircraft wings and aircraft parts.

Portfolio Activity 5.5

1. What does the article suggest is happening to employment in car manufacturing?

2. What are the causes of these changes in employment?

3. What kind of industrial sectors might these unemployed workers look at when searching for new jobs? What problems might they find when looking for jobs in other sectors?

4. What evidence is there of the decline of manufacturing industries in your area? (For example, how many manufacturing firms are located in your area? How many people do they employ? How many have closed down recently? How many job vacancies exist in local newspapers and job centres for manufacturing firms?)

The Throwaway Workforce

You could call it 'junk labour'. This seems a good description for what could develop into one of the most important changes at work since Ford started the moving production line 80 years ago.

For the first time, large firms are saying that their workers should not expect to have a job past middle age. This is because when technology and new ways of doing things are developed, older workers may be too difficult to train and so will need to be replaced. Well educated young people, straight from school are easier to train for high technology production lines. Young workers are also cheap.

The Chairman of Fiat Cars says he 'fears' for the future of any car workers aged over 40. Fiat is opening a new car factory in Italy. The factory will cost £1.5 billion and will be built using the latest technology. The average age for all the Fiat workforce is 45. The average age for workers in the new factory will be just 26. The firm is taking on workers with no previous experience in car production. Some experts say that these workers will have a short working life, being replaced by other young workers when more new technology is introduced in the future.

Some experts say that in future, there may be no factory workers at all. This is because of the introduction of robot-based car plants around the world. These are cutting employment opportunities for both managers and workers.

London Evening Standard 11.10.1993

Section **5.3**   **Investigating business activities**

The production of natural resources

Some business organizations produce and supply natural resources such as foods, timber, coal and other minerals, metal ores, crude oil and gas. There have been great changes in the scale and importance of these activities in the UK over time.

Portfolio Activity 5.6

Look at the information below. What long term trends can you identify in agriculture, fishing, mining and crude oil production in the UK. Why do you think these changes have occurred?

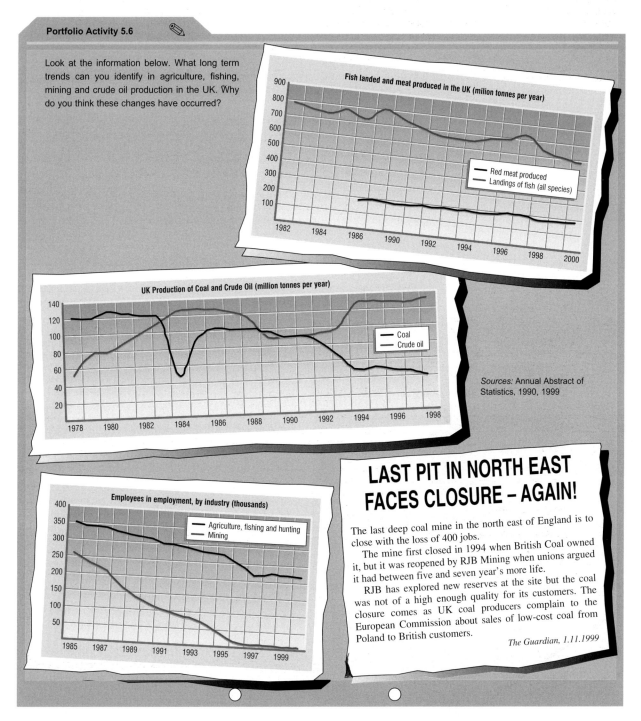

Sources: Annual Abstract of Statistics, 1990, 1999

LAST PIT IN NORTH EAST FACES CLOSURE – AGAIN!

The last deep coal mine in the north east of England is to close with the loss of 400 jobs.

The mine first closed in 1994 when British Coal owned it, but it was reopened by RJB Mining when unions argued it had between five and seven year's more life.

RJB has explored new reserves at the site but the coal was not of a high enough quality for its customers. The closure comes as UK coal producers complain to the European Commission about sales of low-cost coal from Poland to British customers.

The Guardian, 1.11.1999

Mining and the extraction of crude oil and gas

The **mining** of coal, tin and other metal ores, and clay was once a major activity in the UK. There are very few mines still working in the UK today.

In 1947, 718,000 miners produced 150 million tonnes of coal each year. The UK coal mining industry was nationalized following the second world war to protect jobs and a valuable source of power (see chapter 6). The British Coal Corporation ran and managed the coal mines in the public sector. However, the demand for British coal fell significantly over time because:

- major customers for coal, such as the iron and steel industry, ship and railway locomotive builders, have also declined

- coal was burnt to produce coal gas to supply to homes and businesses. This has been replaced since the early 1970s by natural gas from under the North Sea

- fewer and fewer people needed to burn coal for heat in their own homes and instead installed central heating run on gas or electricity

- more power stations have been built to burn cleaner fuels like natural gas

- cheaper supplies of coal became available from overseas

In 1998, there were fewer than 9,000 coal miners in the UK and output was down to 40 million tonnes. Many of the remaining coal mines were closed in the first half of the 1990s and the few left working were sold to private sector organizations.

▼ Oil and gas rigs in the North Sea

However, since 1979 the UK has become a major producer of crude oil from natural oil reservoirs deep below the surface of the sea bed of the North Sea. This followed the discovery of vast supplies of natural gas under the southern part of the North Sea in the 1960s.

Crude oil and gas is pumped ashore in pipelines from oil and gas rigs which drill into the natural reservoirs in the rock below the sea bed. Gas is piped under pressure to our homes or burnt in power stations to produce electricity. Crude oil is refined into oil and petroleum products such as kerosene, petrol and diesel oil. Many of these products are sold overseas. The value of UK exports of oil and petroleum products was almost twice as much as the value of UK imports of similar products in 1999.

Employment in oil and gas extraction has increased over time as production has expanded. In 1999 around 35,000 people were employed by this activity, and a similar number in oil refining.

Agriculture

Agriculture involves producing fruit, vegetables and cereals, rearing cattle and other animals for their meats, milk and skins, and providing seeds and manure. Business organizations that are active in agriculture are usually called farms. In 1998 around 18.6 million hectares, or 77% of the land area of the UK was used for agricultural activity.

Portfolio Activity 5.7

What recent trends in agriculture can you identify from the articles below? What are the reasons behind these changes? How are these trends likely to affect the activities of many farmers and the types of food products stocked by many shops?

Produce a short report on changes in UK agriculture using the following headings;

- Long term trends in agriculture

- Recent trends in the agricultural sector

- Reasons for change

- The likely impact of these changes on farmers and food shops

Are our farms dying?

British farming is in crisis. Farm incomes have dropped by 75% in the last two years and many farmers are earning next to nothing for the crops and livestock they raise. The situation is so bad that some farmers have dumped sheep at animal sanctuaries because they cannot afford to keep them, or even to have them slaughtered. The Government has now agreed to give farmers £150 million in emergency aid, but farmers say more needs to be done to attack the root cause of the problems.

Why is farming in such a state?

There are many reasons. The UK pound is very strong compared to other currencies, which makes it hard for British farmers to compete abroad. It is cheaper for buyers in this country to import produce from abroad than buy home-grown goods.

An even bigger problem is the global decline of food prices. It might sound surprising in a world full of hunger, but there is a glut of agricultural produce on the market – this pushes the price of farm produce down.

British farmers say their goods cost more to produce because of high environmental, employment and animal welfare standards in the UK. For example, the UK Government has recently banned tethers in pig farming and untethered pigs cost more to raise. UK farmers say too much red tape is a big problem - that there are too many rules and regulations, such as meat hygiene restrictions, abattoir costs and the beef on the bone ban – all of which make UK goods more expensive to produce.

BSE (mad cow disease) and the ban on the export of British beef have also taken their toll. The economic crises in Asia and Russia has meant their demand for UK imports has collapsed. Russia was the biggest market for sheep pelts and cattle hides.

The Guardian, 28.9.1999

A little bit more than muck and grannies

THIS YEAR has been full of fear and outrage about food and farming. Conventional farmers are going broke. Consumers are rejecting genetically modified foods and livestock fed on antibiotic growth promoters. And demand for organic food is huge. Gone are the days you could rely on advice from granny and a liberal dose of manure.

The Guardian, 19.10.1999

WHAT'S WRONG WITH OUR FOOD?

Environmental campaigners last night demanded a Europe-wide ban on the world's biggest selling weedkiller – the bulk of which is produced by US biotechnology firm Monsanto – after warnings that it could kill insects and spiders vital to agricultural ecosystems.

The Guardian, 13.10.1999

British pig producers warn of hundreds of jobs at risk as cheap bacon and ham imports threaten to push one in 10 out of business

The Guardian, 6.10.1999

SMALL FARMERS ARE DESTROYED TO BENEFIT BIG AGRO-INDUSTRIALISTS

Price support for farming in Britain has always helped big business at the expense of small. It rewards the biggest farmers with the most machinery and equipment by subsidising their production costs, but wipes out the smaller farmers by raising the price of land and machinery.

The Guardian, 23.9.1999

Fish farming leaves a nasty taste in the mouth

Farmed salmon is now 20p a lb cheaper than cod. The cheap farmed product now battered in fish and chip shops is a poor relation to its wild cousin. Salmon is farmed in cages at higher densities than battery-farmed turkeys, fed a diet of chemicals and artificial colourings, injected with vaccines and growth drugs, then starved for 10 days before being killed. Farmed salmon depends on a diet that is 45% fishmeal and 25% fish oil, and it requires four tonnes of wild fish to produce just one tonne of farmed salmon.

The Guardian, 12.10.1999

Many hundreds of years ago the population of the UK was little more than a million people. Many worked on the land and produced the food their families needed. Any surplus produce was sold in local markets or exchanged for other goods and services, such as clothes and tools.

In the 1700s and 1800s the population of the UK began to expand and people started to move from rural areas into growing towns and cities to work in the new factories. They needed to buy food, and so farmers started to produce more and more foodstuffs for sale. More and more woodland areas were cleared to provide agricultural land. Machines were invented to help harvest crops. Pesticides and other chemicals were introduced to reduce disease and waste. Farming became much more scientific so yields were able to rise without the need for more labour.

After the end of the Second World War in 1945, the UK Government introduced farm subsidies to keep farmers in business and continue to increase their yields by using more and intensive farming methods. The UK could not import many foods during the war and unless farmers were kept in business the population could have starved.

To increase yields, farmers have been given subsidies to use more machinery, more chemical fertilizers and pesticides on crops, growth and antibiotic drugs in animals, and introduce intensive factory farming methods.

Livestock, such as pigs, lambs and cows, are slaughtered by machine in huge abattoirs rather than by hand on the farm. Little is wasted in agriculture today. Even the brains, spinal columns and other parts of animals not sold as choice cuts of meat are pulped into products such as beefburgers and sausages, or *gelatine* used to bind the ingredients of all manner of food products together such as yoghurt, sweets, and cakes.

However, the overproduction of some agricultural products has caused their prices to fall, and farmers' incomes have been reduced. UK farmers also have to compete against cheap food imports from overseas. In addition, many consumers have become worried about the safety of many of the foods supplied from modern agricultural production. For example, in the mid 1990s many thousands of cows had to be slaughtered and their carcasses burnt to stop the spread of BSE, the 'mad cow disease'. It is thought the disease passed to cows from dead sheep and other infected cows 'recycled' back into animal feedstuffs. The disease is carried in the brain tissue and spinal columns of cows, and there are fears that the use of these products in many food products has been spread to humans as a fatal brain disease called CJD.

These and other health fears among consumers have resulted in a growing demand for organic foods. These are produced without chemicals. More people are also buying free range meats or becoming vegetarian because they dislike 'cruel' factory farming methods. Because the UK has to import so much organic food to meet demand the UK government is now trying to encourage farmers to use organic farming methods. These trends in agriculture and consumer demands seems likely to continue.

Factory farming – facing a consumer backlash

Organic foods – on the increase

Fishing

The seas around the UK are fished by many different countries to catch cod, haddock, hake, crabs, shrimps and many other types of fish and shellfish. The UK fishing fleet is made up of around 7,800 boats. Most of these boats are small (less than 10 metres in length) and operated by small family businesses.

Fish populations in the seas around the UK have been declining due to marine pollution and overfishing by many countries. The UK fishing fleet is now much smaller than it was 50 years ago.

Forestry

Many hundreds of years ago the UK was covered in forests and woodland. Many people built their homes and shelters out of timber they cut for themselves. However, as the population and demand for food grew, woodland was cleared for farming and housing.

▲ *The UK fleet faces strong competition from its neighbours*

Forestry involves planting and managing woodlands to produce wood, new trees for sale, or for conservation and leisure purposes. In 1998 the forest area of the UK was 2.5 million hectares, or 10% of the total land mass. Around 30% of the forested area is owned and managed by the Forestry Commission, an executive agency of the Government (see chapter 6).

▼ *Consumer goods*

Manufacturing

What is manufacturing?

Manufacturing activity turns natural resources into finished and semi-finished products. **Semi-finished manufactured goods** include materials, chemicals, and component parts used to make **finished manufactured goods** for consumers to buy.

Finished manufactures include goods produced for individual consumers or business consumers. **Consumer goods** satisfy the needs and wants of individual consumers. Some of these are consumer durable goods because they last a long time – for example, cars, washing machines, CDs, and computers. Non-durable goods are those which are used up quickly, such as food products, drinks, petrol and washing powders.

▼ *Capital goods*

Capital goods are machines and tools used by other firms in the production of other goods and services. A firm that buys capital goods to use in productive activity is said to be investing. **Investment** involves the purchase of productive assets – machines, tools, factories, shops and offices.

Below is a list of the various types of manufacturing activity carried out by many firms in the UK today.

UK classification of manufacturing activity

Food products, drinks and tobacco
Made-up textiles and wearing apparel, dressing and fur dyeing
Leather, leather goods and footwear
Wood and wood products
Pulp paper and paper products
Publishing and printing
Reproduction of recorded media
Coke refined petroleum products and nuclear fuel
Chemicals, chemical products and man-made fibres
Rubber and plastics
Other non-metallic mineral products
Basic metals and fabricated metal products
Machinery and equipment
Electrical, medical and optical equipment
Transport equipment
Furniture

Portfolio Activity 5.8

Look at the photographs and charts on pages 231–235.

1. What goods are being manufactured in each photograph? Which of the manufacturing activities shown in the photographs do you think were more important in the UK in the past, and which ones do you think are important today?

2. What long-term and more recent trends in UK manufacturing activity can you identify from the graphs? Which activities were expanding in the 1990s and which ones were shrinking. What do you think may have caused these trends?

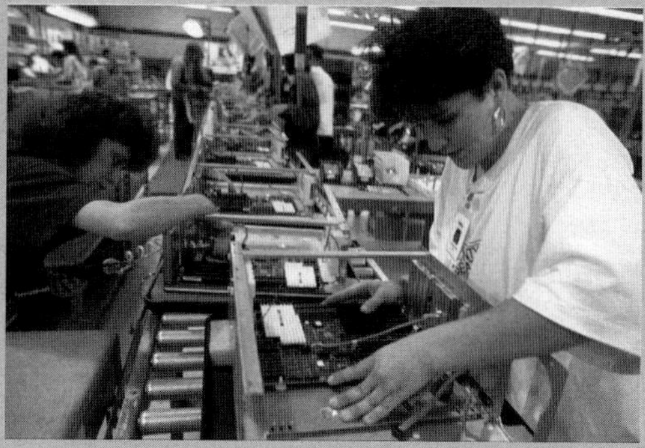

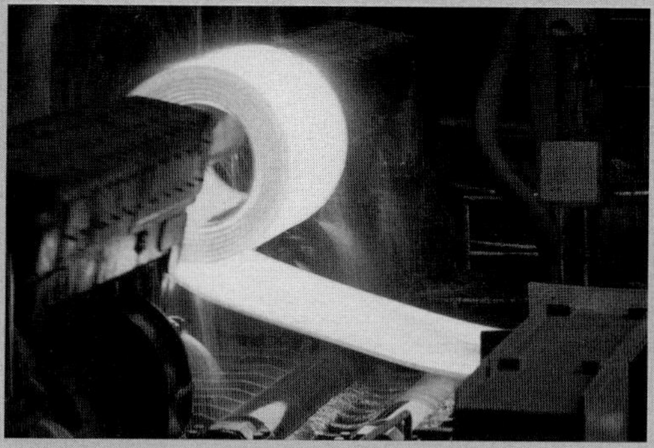

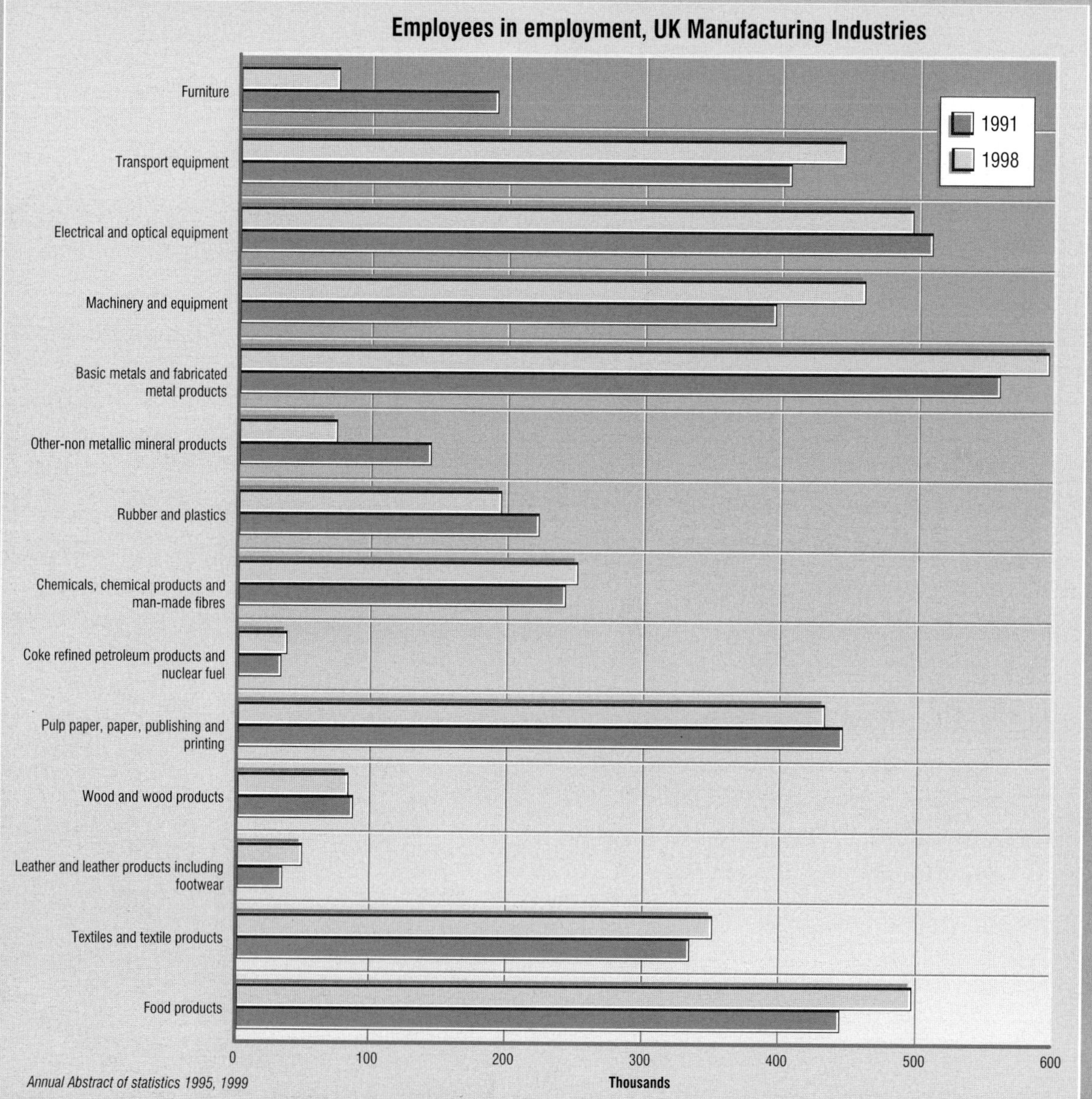
Employees in employment, UK Manufacturing Industries
1991
1998
Furniture
Transport equipment
Electrical and optical equipment
Machinery and equipment
Basic metals and fabricated metal products
Other-non metallic mineral products
Rubber and plastics
Chemicals, chemical products and man-made fibres
Coke refined petroleum products and nuclear fuel
Pulp paper, paper, publishing and printing
Wood and wood products
Leather and leather products including footwear
Textiles and textile products
Food products
0
100
200
300
400
500
600
Thousands
Annual Abstract of statistics 1995, 1999

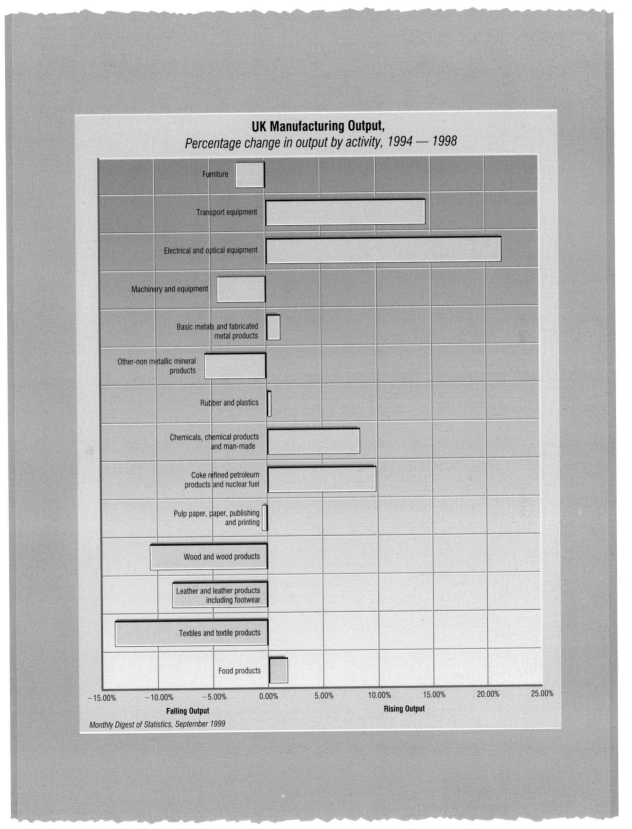

UK Manufacturing Output,
Percentage change in output by activity, 1994 — 1998

Furniture

Transport equipment

Electrical and optical equipment

Machinery and equipment

Basic metals and fabricated metal products

Other-non metallic mineral products

Rubber and plastics

Chemicals, chemical products and man-made

Coke refined petroleum products and nuclear fuel

Pulp paper, paper, publishing and printing

Wood and wood products

Leather and leather products including footwear

Textiles and textile products

Food products

-15.00%   -10.00%   -5.00%   0.00%   5.00%   10.00%   15.00%   20.00%   25.00%

Falling Output   **Rising Output**

Monthly Digest of Statistics, September 1999

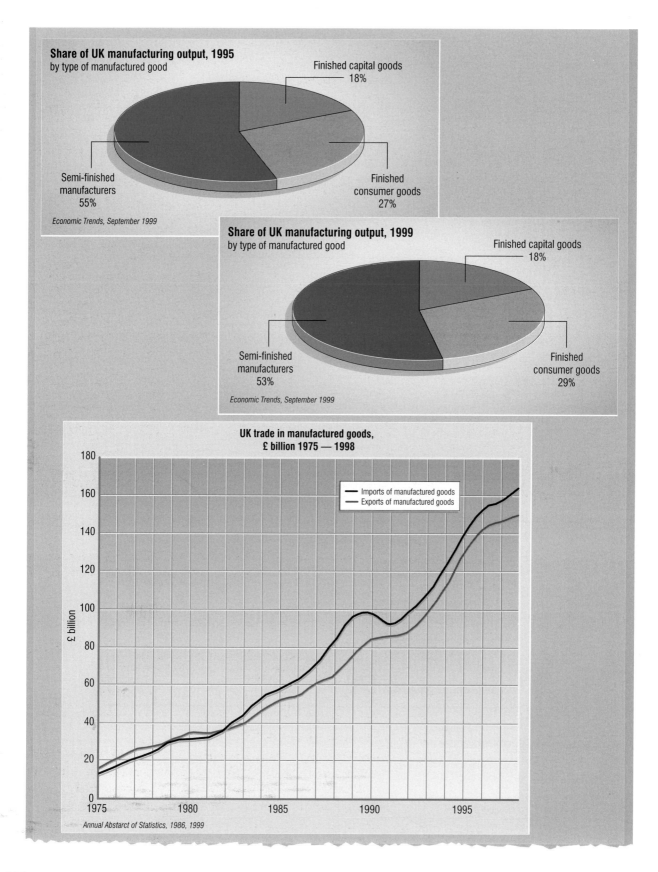

Share of UK manufacturing output, 1995
by type of manufactured good

Finished capital goods
18%

Semi-finished
manufacturers
55%

Finished
consumer goods
27%

Economic Trends, September 1999

Share of UK manufacturing output, 1999
by type of manufactured good

Finished capital goods
18%

Semi-finished
manufacturers
53%

Finished
consumer goods
29%

Economic Trends, September 1999

**UK trade in manufactured goods,
£ billion 1975 — 1998**

— Imports of manufactured goods
— Exports of manufactured goods

£ billion

Annual Abstarct of Statistics, 1986, 1999

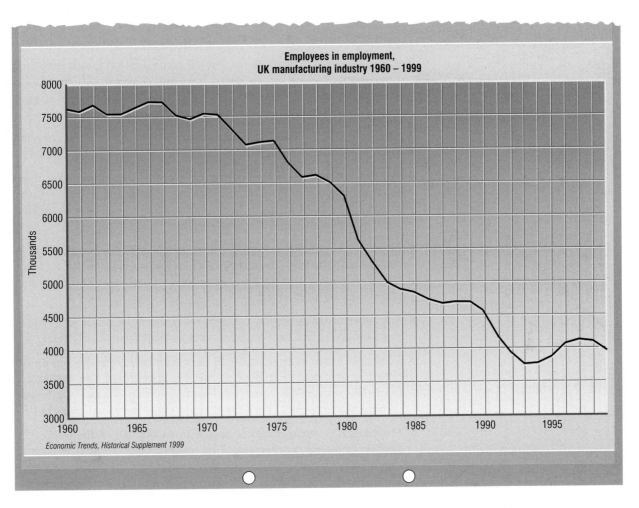

Employees in employment, UK manufacturing industry 1960 – 1999

Economic Trends, Historical Supplement 1999

Deindustrialization

There has been a long term decline in manufacturing industries in the UK and many other developed countries. This has been called deindustrialization.

Primary	Secondary	Tertiary
Declining;	Declining;	Growing;
Agriculture	Iron and steel	Financial and business services
Mining	Shipbuilding	Leisure
Fishing	Motor vehicles	Medical services
Water supply	Machine tools	Communications
Quarrying	Textiles	Digital technologies
	Construction	E-commerce

Deindustrialization in the UK has meant:

● The number of jobs in manufacturing has fallen steadily through time. UK manufacturing employed over 7.6 million people in 1960. By 1999, manufacturing employment had fallen to just over 4 million, with most of these jobs having been lost since the early 1970s.

● The output of manufactured goods has fallen compared to the total output of all goods and services produced in the UK (see figure 5.2).

- The UK share in the output of manufactured goods from all over the world has fallen.

- The UK now spends more on foreign manufactured goods (imports) than it earns from selling its own manufactured goods to foreign countries (exports). Before 1983 the UK had always sold more manufactured goods overseas than it imported each year.

A number of reasons have been suggested for the decline of manufacturing industry in the UK and many other developed countries:

- The biggest decline in manufacturing has been in old industries such as textiles, iron and steel production, shipbuilding and railway locomotives. These have been replaced by new manufacturing industries making new products with new technologies.

- Increasing competition from business organizations overseas, many in newly industrialized countries, such as Japan and, more recently, China, Malaysia and Taiwan, where wages and, therefore, product prices tend to be cheaper.

- A number of UK firms have closed down and moved their operations to newly industrialized countries because wages there are lower.

- As people have become wealthier they have been spending more on personal services such as banking, property and car insurance, financial and legal advice, leisure activities and improved communications. As a result the service sector has grown rapidly.

- More recently, manufacturers have blamed the high value of the UK pound against other currencies. This means overseas countries have to spend more pounds on UK exports of manufactured. UK exports have become more expensive to buy and so demand for them has fallen.

However, some manufacturing activities in the UK have been growing: hi-tech electronics equipment, chemicals, petroleum products, and aerospace. Output, jobs and exports have been increasing for many business organizations in these industries. These are relatively new manufacturing industries, all using the latest technologies, lots of hi-tech equipment and requiring highly skilled manufacturing workers. They have taken over from old labour-intensive engineering industries as the pace of technological innovation and change has increased, sweeping away products and manufacturing processes of the past and introducing new products and new ways of making them.

▲ Hi-tech manufacturing

▼ *Every so often there have been major innovations in production processes, power supplies, materials and products which have significantly changed manufacturing industries, business organizations and jobs*

The time line		Major innovations
1785		Water power
		Textiles
	60 years	Iron
1845		Steam power
		Railways
	55 years	Steel
1900		Electricity
		Chemicals
	50 years	Internal combustion engines
1950		Petrochemicals
		Electronics
	40 years	Aviation
1990		Digital networks
		Computer software
Into the millennium		Biotechnology

Wings of success

As it celebrates the recent delivery of the 2000th set of wings it has designed and manufactured for the successful family of airliners produced by the European consortium Airbus Industrie, British Aerospace can rightly claim to be one of the world's leading experts in this highly demanding highly skilled sector of aerospace.

World Airnews, August 1999

Technology in the factory

In many industries robots are now used to perform dangerous, repetitive, or very intricate jobs faster and more accurately than human labour. This has improved the working conditions of many workers no longer required to do these tasks, but it has also meant that many manufacturing jobs have simply disappeared.

Most robots are simply 'intelligent arms' which can be programmed and controlled by computers to carry out assembly work, paint spraying, packing, welding and other tasks. This is known as **computer-aided manufacture (CAM)**.

Computer-aided design (CAD) is capable of generating, storing, and using geometric graphics. CAD is used by design engineers in many industries to solve design problems, from modelling new products and packaging to designing a new office layout.

The newspaper and magazine printing and publishing industry has also been revolutionized by the introduction of personal computers and desktop publishing software. Journalists are now able to write and design the layout of their articles on computers directly linked to the printing presses. The craft skills of typesetters are now no longer wanted.

Retailing

What is retailing?

Retailing is often thought of as the final link in a chain of production that starts with natural resources and ends with the selling of goods and services to the people and other businesses that want them (see chapter 1). **Retailing** is a service provided by many businesses which involves selling goods and services to consumers. Business organizations that specialize in selling goods and services are called **retailers**.

What do retailers do?

Retailers will offer a number of services in order to attract consumers and make sure they return time and time again to buy their goods and services. These will include

- stocking a supply of different goods and services

- buying in bulk and selling smaller quantities to consumers

- ensuring their products are of good quality and priced competitively

- providing customers with product information

- advertising their products and retailing services

- an after-sales service, for refunds, exchanges or repairs

- listening and responding to customer needs and any complaints

- arranging hire purchase for customers buying expensive items

- a home delivery service

- accepting credit and debit cards (see chapter 9)

- looking after customers with special needs, for example, providing wheelchair ramps and allowing guide dogs into stores with their owners (see chapter 1)

Any retailer who fails to provide a good service risks losing customers to rivals.

Who are the retailers?

There are many different types of retailer in the UK today, offering a wide variety of ways to consumers to buy goods and services.

- **retailers without shops** such as street and market traders

- **independent small traders,** such as local shops owned by sole traders and partnerships (see chapter 6)

- **retailers with shops,** such as large multi-product chain stores (e.g. WH Smith and Boots), supermarkets and hypermarkets (like Asda, Tesco and Sainsburys), department stores (e.g. Harrods and Selfridges), and co-operative retail societies (see chapter 6)

- **mail order companies,** such as Great Universal Stores (distributors of the Kays and Choice catalogues), supply goods to consumers from their warehouses and take orders for goods over the phone, by fax, post and even e-mail. These companies advertise the goods they sell in glossy catalogues or adverts placed in newspapers and other publications. There are also mail order cable and satellite TV channels such as 'Shop!'

- **e-tailers** sell goods direct to consumers over the internet

- **wholesalers** store, sell and distribute goods to retailers

SUMMARY OF MULTI-SECTOR RETAIL GROUPS

The arrangement by number of outlets does not imply ranking by turnover

		Approx. No. of Outlets
Whitbread	1,500 off-licences[1]; 1,317 restaurants; 100 tea and coffee	2,917
Kingfisher	282 DIY; 255 electrical; 705 drug stores, 783 variety stores; 47 music/entertainment	2,072
Boots	1,331 chemists; 413 car accessories; 291 opticians; 4 photocentres	
Arcadia	714 men's clothing (incl. 127 shops-in-shops); 1,300 women's clothing (incl. 307 shops-in-shops); 12 camping/leisurewear	2,026
Allied-Domecq	1,488 off-licences[1], 373 restaurants/cafés	1,861
Lloyds Chemists/AAH	1,211 chemists, 97 drugstores; 39 health & beauty	1,347
Minit UK	360 shoe repairs; 60 accessories; 623 photo-processing/cleaners	1,043
Sears	601 women's clothing; 363 children's clothing	964
Dixons	724 electrical; 132 telecommunications; 56 computers	912
WHSmith	641 newsagents & bookstalls; retail travel 98	739
J. Sainsbury	404 supermarkets/Savacentres; ca. 300 DIY	ca. 704
Thorn	550 TV rental; 94 household equipment	644
Storehouse	343 children's clothing, 155 variety stores	498
Coats Viyella	59 menswear; 304 ladieswear, 17 factory/clearance shops (incl. concessions and joint outlets)	
Next	Departments within mainline stores: 278 menswear; 292 ladieswear, 245 childrenswear; 78 homewares; 1 café	
HMV Media Group	185 bookshops; 105 music/entertainment	290
Three Cooks	178 bakers; 104 restaurants	282
Peacocks Stores	218 furnishers; 59 camping/leisurewear	277
Tulchan	77 hosiery; 166 knitwear	243
John Lewis Partnership	117 supermarkets; 23 department stores	140

Note: [1]Now included in Allied Domecq/Whitbread joint venture   *Marketing Pocket Book 1999*

Recent trends in retailing

Growth in consumer spending has led to an expansion in retailing. In 1988 UK consumers spent £300 billion on goods and services and just over 3 million people were employed in retail trades. Ten years later, total consumer spending had risen to £540 billion and the number employed in retailing was over 4 million. There have also been many changes within the retailing industry and the way people shop over the last few years.

Portfolio Activity 5.9

The following newspaper articles and charts are all about recent changes in retailing. What are the changes and what impact have they or are they having on retail organizations?

ASDA SCRAPS LOYALTY CARD IN PRICE WAR

SUPERMARKET giant Asda became the first of the big supermarkets to scrap its loyalty card scheme yesterday.

Although shoppers hold millions of the cards, offered by Asda and rivals Tesco, Sainsbury and Safeway, they have failed to keep customers loyal to the stores issuing them.

Asda said it was scrapping its cards in favour of the old-fashioned supermarket attraction of lower prices.

Asda's latest move in the supermarket price war was met with derision by Tesco.

Spokesman David Sawday said: 'We have made nine major price cuts in the last eight years. Whatever others claim to do, we will better.' *Metro, 13.8.1999*

RETURN OF THE CORNER SHOP

STORE wars have returned to the high street with the news that Sainsbury's is planning to open 200 corner shops in the next three years.

The move to in-town stores is not solely down to customer demand. Government planning changes over recent years have forced retailers to use central locations where possible rather than the sprawling out-of-town sites with their increased car usage.

Evening Standard, 22.7.1999

The Bluewater effect

IT HAS BEEN the South East's most feared and seismic event since the advent of the supermarket, but the aftershocks which have followed the opening of the £350 million Bluewater shopping centre outside of Dartford last month, are now beginning to ripple.

Across the Thames at the Lakeside centre, the evidence of Bluewater is clear, with empty car parks and shopping malls empty of shoppers. The north Kent town centres of Bromley, Gravesend, Chatham and Maidstone have all gone into decline which began on 16 March when the 320 stores which occupy Europe's newest and biggest out-of-town shopping complex opened their doors.

Evening Standard 21.4.1999

Retail Grocery Sales,
Own label share of total revenue

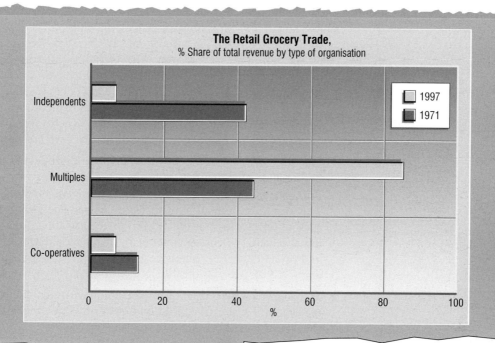

The Retail Grocery Trade,
% Share of total revenue by type of organisation

Legend: 1997, 1971

(Categories: Independents, Multiples, Co-operatives; x-axis: % from 0 to 100)

Sainsbury and Asda plan big boost in home hopping

The battle for the lucrative home shopping market in London is heating up with plans from two of Britain's leading food retailers to build multi-million pound depots dedicated to the service

Financial Times, 17.5.1999

Death of the corner shop

FOR 61 years, it has stood firm against the retailing revolution.

The corner shop of W English & Son survived by offering personal service, home deliveries, free credit, and fine foodstuffs from around the world.

Next week, however, this bastion of tradition will bow to so-called progress.

Bryan English will pull down the shutters at Chatsworth Stores for the last time after conceding defeat to the new supermarket 200 yards down the road.

He said yesterday: 'Shutting up the shop will be a sad day but it's inevitable, I'm afraid. We're catering to a dwindling generation of customers, and I am too old and set in my ways to adapt.'

Daily Mail 12.10.1995

Car prices tumble in Internet trading war

UP to £4,700 could be slashed from the cost of a car in an Internet motoring price war.

Two Internet sales sites are offering cut-price deals for UK buyers, it was announced yesterday.

A Vauxhall site can deliver cars to customers up to £1,000 cheaper than dealers' prices.

But the Internet service provider Totalise has gone even further, launching a Carsave site offering savings of up to £4,700.

Metro, 15.10.1999

SPEND SPEND TESCO TAKES OVER THE WORLD

SUPERMARKET giant Tesco will create 20,000 jobs by opening 39 new stores this year – 13 of them abroad.

And last night a City analyst said: 'It seems as if there is no stopping them now they are on such a roll. "Today Britain, tomorrow the world. That seems to be their mission."

Yesterday's announcement came just two days after bitter rival Sainsbury said it was axing 1,100 managers after a £20 million slump in profits.

Daily Mirror, 5.6.1999

Some major changes have taken place in retailing over the last 20 years:

- Retailing has become dominated by large multiple retail organizations, such as Tesco, B&Q and Boots. In 1997, 92% of total retail spending by UK consumers was in only 20% of the organizations. Many small independent shops have been unable to compete on price and product range and have gone out of business. Others have joined together to form small voluntary chain groups such as Spar, Londis and Happy Shopper, so that the shop owners can benefit from bulk buying discounts from wholesalers and produce their own label brands for sale

- There is increasing competition on prices and product ranges between large retailers as they try to attract shoppers away from each other. Price wars have broken out among many large supermarket groups. They have also offered bonus schemes to customers who remain loyal, such as cheap flights and bigger price discounts, and made many improvements to customer services, such as free buses for the elderly and home deliveries. Shops that do not offer good value for money and good service will quickly lose customers

- Many large retailers offer their own credit cards for their customers to use and will often give additional rewards, like money off points, if they use the cards to buy things in their shops

LARGE GROCERY STORES AND GROCERY SUPERSTORES

Estimated number in Great Britain

	Large Stores[1]	Super-stores[2]		Large Stores[1]	Super-stores[2]
Aldi	23	. .	Safeway	219	160
ASDA	8	199	Sainsbury	130	251
Budgens	12	. .	Savacentre	. .	13
Co-op	232	70	Solo	3	. .
Dales	1	6	Somerfield	188	13
Food Giant	12	15	Tesco	210	277
Gateway	4	1	Waitrose	110	7
Kwik Save	9	. .	Independents	17	6
Morrison	6	74			
Presto	18	. .	**Total**	**1,202**	**1,092**

Notes: [1] Stores with between 10,000–24,999 sq. ft. selling area, as at January 1998. [2] Stores with over 25,000 sq. ft. selling area, as at March 1998.

Source: Institute of Grocery Distribution Research Services.

MULTIPLE GROCERS: SALES

	Sales, £m[1]		Sales, £m[1]
Tesco	13,763	Aldi	548
Sainsbury	10,894	R.O.G. (S.C.W.S.)	385
ASDA	6,955	Netto	375
Safeway	6,364	South Wales & Worcester CRS	347
Somerfield	3,545	United Norwest Co-op	347
Kwik Save	3,490	Budgens	340
Wm. Morrison	2,176	South Western CRS	335
Waitrose	1,600	South East Retail CWS	321
Iceland	1,399	Central Midlands Co-op	292
Savacentre	898	Northern CRS	281

Note: [1] Year to end of January 1997.
Source: ACNielsen.

▲ *Tesco currently has the biggest market share of all the supermarket chains in the UK*

- Huge shopping complexes have been developed in large towns and out-of-town areas. These offer many shopping and leisure facilities 'under one roof' for many thousands of people to use. This has caused decline in many older and smaller shopping centres. Government planning controls now restrict the development of new out of town complexes because they encourage people to use their cars more causing congestion and pollution

- Many large retailers now sell many different goods and services. For example, Tesco is a food supermarket chain but now has large superstores that also offer computers, clothes, hi-fi and audio equipment, petrol, books, CDs and videos, and even banking and insurance services

- Supermarkets and other retail chains are selling more and more of their own label products. Own label products are often cheaper than manufacturer's own brands, such as Coca-Cola and Heinz Baked Beans

- Late night and Sunday shopping have been introduced giving consumers more flexibility when to shop

- There has been a growth in the number of convenience stores, especially on petrol and railway station forecourts. These shops pick up 'passing trade' from commuters and motorists

- Increasing shopping via the internet (e-commerce)

The growth of e-commerce

One of the biggest developments in retailing in recent years is shopping using the internet. This is called **e-commerce**, and it is expected to lead to a revolution in the way people and firms buy and sell goods and services.

Spending in the UK using e-commerce is expected to rise from £3 billion in 1999 to £9.5 billion in 2001. In contrast, American consumers spent $8 billion on internet shopping in 1999 with Business to Business e-trade of $43 billion.

Specialist computer programmes called 'search engines' and 'intelligent shoppers' are now available on the internet for people to search for suppliers offering the best prices for the goods they want from anywhere in the world. To make purchases, customers will have to enter their address and credit card details and send them over the internet to their preferred supplier. These details can be protected by password to stop other people misusing their credit card numbers.

Look at the excerpts from newspaper articles below and suggest how e-commerce may affect many UK retailers, and the likely advantages and disadvantages of growth in e-commerce.

Tesco sets its sights on global power

Britain's biggest supermarket group yesterday brushed off the threat of a food price war and outlined bold new plans for international expansion and for selling books on the internet.

The company – which already has 75,000 online grocery shoppers – is due to double the number of stores servicing them. It says business is already profitable and has gone into partnership with a mail order company, Grattan, to sell household goods on the Internet.

The Guardian, 22.9.1999

THINK SMALL AND GROW

The Internet is closing the gap between big business and smaller companies. It is giving smaller businesses the opportunity to find better value deals and become better informed.

The Guardian, 30.9.1999

Credit fraudsters stalk the net

The boom in Internet shopping is fuelling a massive rise in credit card fraud. Consumers who pay for goods over the Net are 20 times more likely to fall victim to fraud than if they pay at a till or over the telephone.

The Guardian, 12.9.1999

Blair puts finger on the e-problem

Prime Minister Tony Blair delivered British businesses a stark warning yesterday to become internet literate or run the risk of going bankrupt.

He said there were 'worrying signs' that Britain was lagging behind America, Canada and Scandinavia with Germany and France closing. 'The challenge is here and now and if we fail it, we will be poorer in the future', he said.

The Guardian, 14.9.1999

GOODBYE MR TAXMAN

The Institute of Directors is right to warn that the government could lose £10 bn a year in VAT revenues as a result of the expected swing towards trading on the internet. But, the loss of tax is not a reason for trying to slow down the pace of e-commerce because, as Bill Gates reminded us last week, anyone who does not do business on the net will face ruin in five years time.

It is not just VAT that is at risk because it will also be difficult to tax the incomes of people who are (say) working in the UK on a software product and sending the finished product electronically to the US or Australia. Who even knows who they are?

The Guardian, 2.9.1999

Price of entry to brave new world

The 1999 World Competitiveness Report places the UK 13th in the number of computers per capita and 11th in the extent of internet connections. A panel of experts judged us as 21st in the extent to which electronic-commerce was developed for business use. In all of these areas we are out-performed by five or six other European countries, plus the USA, Canada, Singapore, Japan, Australia, and New Zealand.

Two of the reasons for this dismal performance are self-imposed. We have inadequate telecommunications provision. Telephone costs here are far higher than in Germany, Japan, Italy, the US and Canada. Another reason is "bandwidth" - the capacity of a communications channel to transfer data. Relatively few UK users have anything other than two copper wires through which to connect to the world, so the potential for multi-media use, rapid file transfer or video conferencing is very limited. In addition, we rank only 14th in the world, and 10th in Europe in the number of telephone lines per 1000 of population.

The Guardian, 25.9.1999

E-commerce will cause big changes in the way we shop in the 21st century. It will also mean great change for many retailers. The UK Government wants to encourage e-commerce in the UK. Firms that fail to provide Internet shopping services may lose out to those who do. This could mean increasing spending on goods and services from overseas and rising unemployment in the UK.

The advantages of e-commerce

- Consumers can shop for a much wider variety of products from a greater variety of suppliers from all over the world. Increased competition to supply goods and services will help to lower prices and improve customer services

- People will not have to travel to shops so often. This will help reduce traffic congestion and pollution in many major shopping centres

- An increase in consumer demand for many goods and services provided over the Internet. This will benefit many firms and help boost wealth and job creation

Possible problems with e-commerce

- Retailers will be forced to offer internet shopping services to compete with other suppliers

- Fierce e-competition may result in some shops having to close down

- Increasing imports and more money flowing out of the UK if consumers increase purchases from overseas suppliers

- Falling government tax revenues as UK consumers switch spending from UK suppliers to overseas suppliers, and download some products directly into their homes (e.g. software, music)

- Increased risk of credit card fraud

Transport and communications

Some of the biggest leaps in technology in the last century have taken place in the transport and communications industries. Similarly, spending by UK households on travel services and communications leapt from £11 billion in 1985 to £31 billion in 1998. These industries employ around 1.4 million people in the UK.

Portfolio Activity 5.11

Look at the photographs, news articles and graphs below. What do they reveal about recent developments in transport and communications? Why do you think these developments have taken place and what impact have they had on business?

London's Piccadilly Circus then and now.

INTERNET MELTDOWN

THE race is on to prevent Internet meltdown as the industry becomes more popular, according to a company which runs the UK service.

The London Internet Exchange – or Linx, which handles about 80 per cent of Britain's Internet traffic – says the number of people using the web doubles every four months.

Metro, 11.11.1999

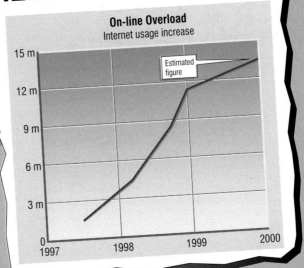

On-line Overload
Internet usage increase

Estimated figure

TELLYCOM 2000

ORANGE is set to launch the world's first mobile video phone within weeks. Users will be able to see each other while they talk, thanks to a four-inch screen.

The superphone – just seven inches long – will also allow owners to store and replay favourite TV clips, or access weather and traffic maps.

The revolutionary £500 device, also connected to the internet, is expected to be in the shops before Christmas, as the first of a string of new high-tech gadgets for the millennium.

The Mirror, 23.10.1999

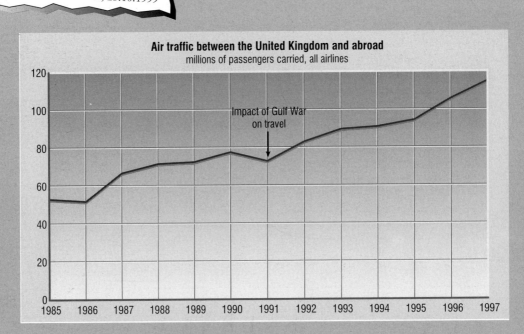

Air traffic between the United Kingdom and abroad
millions of passengers carried, all airlines

Impact of Gulf War on travel

SMALL TALKING

THE number of children using mobile phones has soared.

Industry experts estimate an astonishing 250,000 under-16s now have them.

Only two year ago fewer than 3,000 children aged under 16 owned their own mobile. Now almost that number are getting one every week.

The playground boom comes despite a string of worrying reports linking the devices to possible brain tumours and genetic damage.

New figures revealed for the first time today have shocked experts probing the health implications of the £300 billion-a-year global industry.

Figures up to the end of April this year show there were 14,179,000 mobile phone subscribers in Britain. That was an increase of 1,178,000 since the Christmas boom – 90,000 new users a week. Market analysts say three per cent of them are of school age.

Sunday Mirror, 13.6.1999

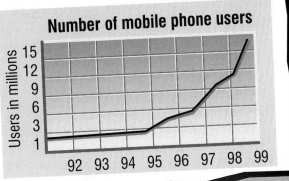

Number of mobile phone users

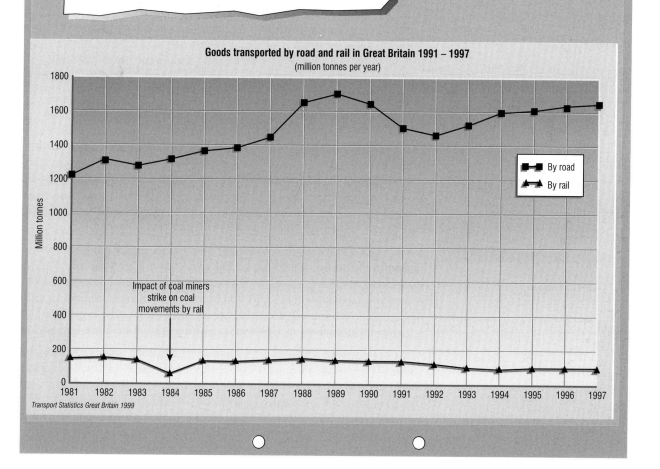

Goods transported by road and rail in Great Britain 1991 – 1997
(million tonnes per year)

Impact of coal miners strike on coal movements by rail

By road
By rail

Transport Statistics Great Britain 1999

A time of great change

The number of ways, times, distances and speed we travel has changed significantly in a relatively short space of time. Business relies on transporting materials from suppliers and finished goods to customers quickly and cheaply. Business owners and managers also need to travel to and from business meetings quickly. Transport networks and services in the UK and all over the world have expanded and changed to meet the needs of people and businesses to travel. For example, the motorway network connects all the major cities. Flights by airline operators, like British Airways, connect the world's major cities. Specialist transport companies have developed to deliver parcels and freight, such as DHL and FedEx, and manufacturers have developed special transport vehicles and equipment to help them do so, such as juggernaughts, refrigerated lorries, freight planes, oil tankers, drive-on ferries and hovercrafts, ambulances, and even the humble van.

Telecommunications allow people to keep in touch and can reduce the need to travel. For many years people and business could only keep in contact by posting letters. The introduction of the telephone in the early 1900s was a big leap forward. But the biggest revolution in communications is only now taking place due to computer and digital technology. New technologies can transmit sound, video and written messages to anywhere in the world a matter of seconds (see chapter 4). Technology is changing the way organizations conduct business.

Improvements in transport and communications have reduced the need for business to locate so near to customers, suppliers or employees. They have also allowed businesses to expand and locate their operations in many different places, even overseas, without losing touch with their head offices.

Railways

Until steam railways were built in the early 1800s most travel was made by horse-drawn carriage or by boat on inland waterways. Most people didn't have to travel far very often. People lived and worked in the same towns. Others lived and worked on their small farms. However, as the railway network developed people were able to live away from their places of work. And as the railways network grew so did the towns and cities.

In the late 1800s, tracks were laid in tunnels under London to run underground trains. The network of underground stations and lines is little changed today, except the new underground trains carry many more thousands of people each day. The new Jubilee Line extension was opened in 1999 and connects the city of London with the big office and housing developments in Docklands, and the new Millennium Dome.

The railways were run by private companies for profit until, following the second world war, they were nationalized and taken into Government ownership (see chapter 6). The rail network was run by British Rail and the London underground network by London Underground. Bus companies were also nationalized. This was to make sure loss making bus and rail services were kept going to provide a public service to those who needed to travel and had no other means of doing so (see chapter 1).

▲ *Railways brought growth and prosperity*

Many businesses also relied on the railways to transport bulky materials and finished goods. However, over time rail freight has fallen significantly as old industries like coal and iron and steel making have declined. Many business organizations now use their own lorries to transport goods. This allows greater flexibility in delivery times and destinations, and reduces the need to load and unload at railway stations.

In 1996 British Rail was broken up in many different businesses, including the rail freight businesses, and privatized (see chapter 6). The network of tracks and stations is now owned and run for profit by Railtrack, and passenger services are run by franchises operated by companies such as Virgin Trains and Stagecoach. On some routes, competition between different train operators has lowered fares and increased on-board services. However, the UK Government pays subsidies to many of these train companies to keep loss making lines open.

London Underground and London buses were still owned by the Government in 1999 but elsewhere bus services are run by private companies for profit. The company Stagecoach owns many of these and many other bus companies all over the world. The original owners of Stagecoach started their business with just one old bus in Scotland in the late 1970s.

Bus and rail companies transport many millions of people each day to and from their places of work, shopping centres and for leisure purposes. They have to anticipate changes in demand as people change their times of travel and their origins and destinations over time, and run more or less services as required. Businesses rely on their workers being able to travel easily to work. If employees cannot travel to their places of work easily, businesses may face a shortage of labour and may have to pay much higher wages to encourage people to travel longer distances to work. Businesses may even have to relocate to other areas to find workers (see chapter 7).

Car usage and the road network

The motor car arrived in the early 1900s but remained the privilege of the few until mass production in the 1950s made cars cheaper and rising incomes made cars affordable. Car ownership and usage has grown significantly since to over 27 million cars in 1999 (see figure 5.2). At the same time successive UK governments spent a lot of money building more and more roads. The first motorway, the M1, was opened in 1959. By 1999 there was over 3,000 km of motorway network in Great Britain and a total road network of 370,000 km.

The freedom of the car has allowed people in the UK to visit places of interest and has, therefore, benefited tourism in hotels, tourist attractions and shops. But today, cars clog many roads in towns and cities as people drive to work and shopping centres. The growing volume of cars is causing congestion and air pollution. Congestion causes delay – to people trying to get to and from work, and for businesses trying take and make deliveries of goods and services. Because vehicles can get caught up in traffic, businesses have to buy more lorries and vans, and employ more drivers to transport their goods and provide services.

The UK Government has increased taxes on petrol dramatically in an attempt to reduce car use and in 1999 gave local authorities powers to introduce additional road or 'congestion' charges for vehicles in busy areas. Parking charges in city and towns centres have also been increased to encourage people to leave their cars at home and use bus and rail services instead. All these things could raise business costs and some businesses may reconsider their locations in major towns and cities.

Air travel

Limited passenger services on aircraft became available in the 1930s but were very rare and very expensive. The number of destinations were few and the propeller aeroplanes used were slow, noisy and needed to refuel frequently. However, they were much quicker than journeys by ship, which were the only means of travel overseas until air passenger services became available.

The jet engine was developed during the Second World War for military planes. Small passenger jet aircraft were introduced in the 1950s but further technological developments have since made planes bigger, faster, quieter, more comfortable and able to fly very long distances. The Boeing 747 family of 'jumbo jets' was first introduced in 1969 and can fly between 420 and 566 people, including luggage and freight, up to 8,500 km non-stop at speeds of over 500 mph. It was originally developed by the US company Boeing as a military cargo plane, but the company cleverly anticipated the growing demand for long haul air travel and turned it into a passenger carrier. The 747 series has been the most successful airliner range ever, and in 1999 there were over 1,000 in service.

The Airbus Integrated Company of Europe is Boeing's main rival in the market to build and supply passenger aircraft. It plans to introduce a double-decked plane in 2005 that can fly 650 or more people up to 8,500 km non-stop. Airbus will spend $12 billion developing the new aircraft.

▼ *Business rivals: Boeing and Airbus*

In 1980 there were 506,000 flights carrying just over 42.5 million passengers to and from the UK. In 1997 there were over 1 million flights carrying over 114 million UK passengers. Holiday-makers and business travellers can travel easily all over the world in comfort on passenger airlines. Competition between rival airline operators is very aggressive and has reduced fares significantly. It is now cheaper to fly than ever before.

▼ *The world's busiest airport: London Heathrow*

In the late 1940s, Heathrow was just a small military airfield in the South East of England. It is now the world's busiest airport with more passengers and more flights to more destinations around the world than any other in the world. Because of this, many firms have located premises around the airport and the motorways that serve it. Many are hi-tech , knowledge based businesses in computers, electronics, pharmaceuticals and financial services, who need to deliver their high value/low weight goods quickly to their customers all over the world.

Air travel has been a huge boost to tourism in the UK. The tourist industry is probably the biggest and faster growing industry in the UK today, covering the spending of UK and foreign visitors on UK airlines, at airports and tourist attractions, in shops, hotels and restaurants, and on buses, trains and hire cars.

Communications

New digital communications technology has increased the ways people and business can communicate, the speed at which they can communicate, and the quality of their communications. For example, airline operators and ships can now obtain up to the minute information and images on world weather patterns from earth observation equipment fitted to satellites.

New technology and fierce competition between providers of communications services and equipment have cut the cost of communications. Even the smallest of organizations can now afford new information communications equipment. Electronic mail, the internet, mobile and video phones, are becoming commonplace (see chapter 4). They have reduced the need for senior managers to travel to meetings in large businesses which have multiple locations. Because senior managers can be kept more in touch with what is happening in their businesses it has allowed organizational structures to become flatter by reducing layers of management (see chapter 2).

The new technologies have also reduced the need to produce, record and store information on written letters and documents. Information can now be held on computer reducing the need for storage space and paper use (see chapter 9). E-mail saves on postage costs and response times have also increased. Businesses can now respond to customer enquiries and orders much quicker than before. They can also communicate with their suppliers quickly. As a result, customers and suppliers now expect speedy responses. Any business that fails to respond quickly will not maintain good relationships with them, and will lose business. It is vital, therefore, that modern businesses invest in the new communications technologies in order to remain competitive.

Some other services

Rising incomes and changing consumer wants has created a demand for many different services. The markets for financial services, health care, and leisure services have expanded significantly in recent years. Growing consumer demand has encouraged many business organizations to provide these services.

Portfolio Activity 5.12

You are a member of a group of business entrepreneurs who have recognized the trend growth in many services.

1. The group has collected the information below and has asked you to prepare a written report for the next business meeting. Your report will examine trends in consumer spending in a number of different service sectors. Produce a graph of spending on different services over time and identify those sectors which have been growing the fastest. Pick the top two and suggest reasons why these sectors have been growing so fast.

2. You must also prepare a short talk for the business meeting on the key findings in your report, with overhead projection slides listing the main points. Now make your presentation to your business group (i.e. your class and teacher).

3. At the business meeting your group decides to build and operate a new leisure and sports complex. Your group hopes to earn a healthy profit from their new business and must design the new facilities and services to meet consumer wants. Providing the wrong facilities will not attract customers nor generate revenue. Using the information suggest what facilities the proposed complex should provide, including those that are sports and fitness related, and why.

Trends in participation in sport, games and physical activities: 1986, 1990, 1993 and 1996

Persons aged 16 and over	Great Britain			
Active sports, games and physical activities	Percentage participating in the 4 weeks before interview			
	1987	1990	1993	1996
Walking	38	41	41	45
Swimming	13	15	15	15
Keep fit/yoga	9	12	12	12
Snooker/billiards	15	14	12	11
Cycling	8	9	10	11
Weight training				6
Weight lifting	5	5	5	1
Soccer	5	5	4	5
Golf	4	5	5	5
Running (jogging, etc)	5	5	5	5
Tenpin bowls/skittles	2	4	4	3
Badminton	3	3	3	2
Tennis	2	2	2	2
Lawn/carpet bowls	2	2	2	2
Fishing	2	2	2	2
Table tennis	2	2	2	2
Squash	3	3	2	1
Horse riding	1	1	1	1
At least one activity (exc. walking)	45	48	47	46
At least one activity	61	65	64	64
Base = 100% *Sample size*	19529	17574	17552	15696

'Living in Britain: Results from the 1996 General Household Survey', (1999)

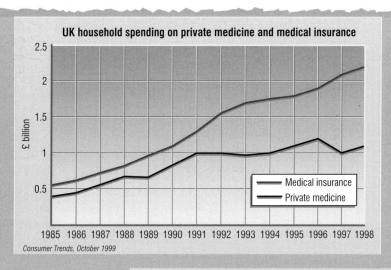

UK household spending on private medicine and medical insurance

£ billion

Medical insurance
Private medicine

Consumer Trends, October 1999

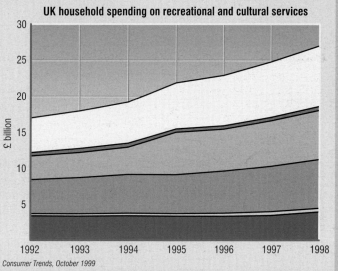

UK household spending on recreational and cultural services

☐ Educational services (incl. night schools)
■ Social subscriptions
■ Betting and Gaming
■ Other admissions
☐ Cinema admissions
■ Television and video charges

£ billion

Consumer Trends, October 1999

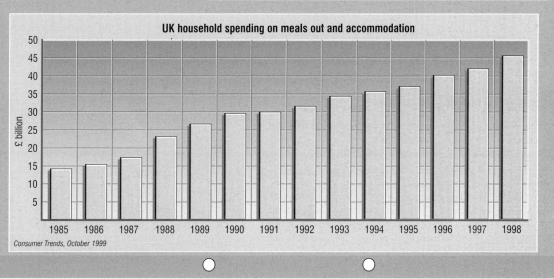

UK household spending on meals out and accommodation

£ billion

Consumer Trends, October 1999

Some of the most significant trends in services in recent years have occurred in the sectors below.

- Around £45 billion was spent on having meals out and accommodation in 1998 compared to £14.5 billion in 1985. Employment in hotels and restuarants also increased, from just over 1 million employees in 1985 to 1.32 million in 1998.

- Spending on recreational and cultural services increased from £9 billion in 1985 to over £20 billion in 1998. Employment in businesses providing these services grew from 490,000 employees to 535,000 over the same period.

- Although the National Health Service provides free and subsidized health care, spending on private health care and insurance has increased significantly in recent years. In 1998 spending on private health care and insurance was £3.3 billion, up by 350% on 1985. Around 1.5 million people are employed in health services in the UK. This includes many nurses and doctors as well as people employed in the administration of health services and providers of health insurance.

- UK household expenditure on financial services was £30 billion in 1998 compared to £14 billion in 1985. The financial services sector of the UK includes banks, credit card companies, building societies and insurance companies. Together, these sectors employed just under 1.1 million people in 1998, up from 750,000 employees in 1985.

Rising incomes mean more people want to save more, and also want to borrow more to buy houses, cars, luxury holidays and other goods. In 1998 loans made by UK banks summed to over £2,000 billion, compared to £589 billion in 1985 and just £167 billion twenty years earlier. Increased wealth has also increased demand for insurance, and increasing foreign travel has boosted the demand for foreign exchange services. Credit and debit card use has also risen significantly. Over 3.7 billion individual purchases were made with a credit or debit card in 1997 compared to just over 400 million in 1985 (see chapter 9).

Today, many banks are offering 'home banking' services for customers over the Internet. As home banking increases, banks will be able to shut some high street branches and save on costs of staff and premises.

From building society to bank

Unlike commercial banks, building societies are non-profit making organizations. Any surplus of revenue over costs is spent on improving services and offering their savers higher rates of interest.

Building societies are mutual societies owned by their savers but in recent years many of these organizations have become banks. As banks they are owned by shareholders who may or may not save with the organization, and will aim to make profits for their shareholders. Former building societies who have become banks include the Abbey National, Alliance and Leicester, Northern Rock, the Woolwich, and the Cheltenham & Gloucester.

▼ Many building societies have converted to banks so that they can earn profits for their owners and offer a wider range of financial services

Choose a business organization to investigate. Write a report about how trends in the business sector to which it belongs are affecting the business.

Your report should

- briefly describe your chosen business (name, location, products, annual sales and profit, main rivals)

- describe the business sector or industry in which the business operates

- examine long term and more recent trends affecting the business sector (for example, growth or decline in employment, sales, consumer demand) and reasons for them

- display graphs showing the key trends in the business sector

- explain how your chosen business has been affected by these trends (in terms of employment, organizational structure, sales, profits, products and services, prices, location, etc.)

Your chosen business could be a local one, a national organization or a multinational company. Large companies will provide annual reports and other information if you ask them to. You can also contact many large businesses via the Internet.

Section **5.4**

The diversification and growth of business

What is diversification?

Because of increasing competition for customers and profits between business rivals, many organizations are expanding their business activities in the UK and by moving overseas. Competition between many firms is now on a global scale.

Business organizations can expand their activities by producing many more different types of goods and services. This is called **diversification**. Businesses diversify because it reduces risk. If consumer demand for a particular good or service falls, those organizations that supply the good or service will suffer and may eventually have to close down. If those same businesses also produced many other goods and services, a fall in demand for one may be offset by a rise in demand for their other products.

Firms can diversify by combining with rival firms. They can also combine with their suppliers and even their major business customers. In this way, a firm is able to produce more and better products for consumers, faster and cheaper than rival firms. A firm that is able to do this may have a much better chance of achieving business aims of more sales revenue, a bigger market share and more profit (see chapter 1).

How can business organizations get bigger?

Internal growth

There are two methods by which business organizations can grow in scale. The first is by **internal growth** where the firm increases its own size by investing and producing more and without a change of management structure. Internal growth can be financed from business profits, borrowing money from banks, or by forming a limited company and selling shares (see chapters 6 and 8).

External growth

Most businesses grow by **amalgamation** (or **integration**). This occurs where one or more firms join together to form a larger organization. Firms can amalgamate or integrate in a number of ways.

1 **Take-over:** A **take-over** or **acquisition** occurs when one company buys 50% or more (sometimes all), of the shares in the ownership of another company. In this way, the firm being taken over by another company often loses its own identity and becomes part of the other company. In a hostile take-over one company makes a bid to take-over another without the agreement of that company. It does this by buying up shares in the other company until it has the majority shareholding.

   Alternatively an entirely new company may be formed for the sole purpose of buying up shares in the ownership of a number of other companies. This is known as a **holding company**. The companies acquired in this way may keep their own names and management but their business strategies and objectives are decided by their holding company. For example, HSBC Holdings Plc is one of the biggest UK companies and owns many other companies around the world in financial services.

2 **Merger:** A merger occurs when two or more firms agree to join to form a new business. This is usually done by shareholders of the two or more companies exchanging their shares for new shares in the new company.

3 **Joint ventures:** These are formed when two or more business organizations agree to work together on a joint project. The businesses remain separate but they have the advantage of sharing their knowledge and resources.

There are three main forms of integration or amalgamation between firms.

1 **Horizontal integration**: This occurs when firms involved in the same business activity combine. For example, British Petroleum and the US company Amoco joined forces in 1999. Both companies are active in oil and gas extraction and the manufacture of petroleum products.

   This type of integration may allow firms to spread overseas and provide significant cost savings from large scale production. These are called **economies of scale**. For example, the employment of more specialized machines and labour, the spreading of administration costs and bulk buying, and loans on more favourable terms from banks because large firms are less risky and more likely to repay their loans.

   A major criticism of firms linking horizontally is that very large firms are formed which are able to dominate markets for particular goods and services. They are able to raise prices and see off smaller competing firms. This is one reason why the UK government uses Competition Policy to investigate and stop, if necessary, proposed mergers and take-overs (see chapter 7).

2 **Vertical integration:** A business organization that is vertically integrated is active in different stages of production. For example, BP Amoco is a vertically integrated organization because it drills for oil, refines oil into petroleum products and then retails petrol at petrol stations.

Organizations which integrate vertically do so to make sure they have a ready source of supply of the natural resources or components they need, and/or to ensure they have retailers willing to sell their products to consumers.

3 **Lateral integration:** This involves combining organizations producing different goods and services. This will form **conglomerates**. These are large firms who produce a wide range of products. For example, Unilever is a firm famous for its detergents but with diversified interests in food, chemicals, paper, plastics, animal feeds, transport and tropical plantations.

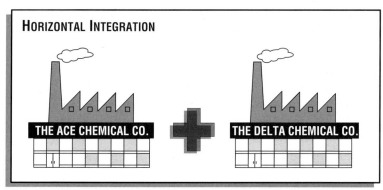

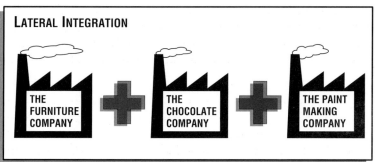

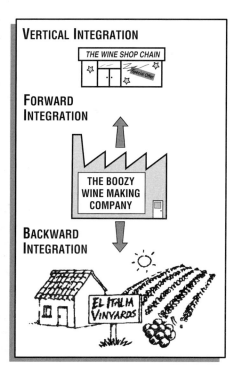

Portfolio Activity 5.14

1. Which of the following business amalgamations are horizontal, which vertical, and which lateral?

  a A firm producing cars takes over an electronics manufacturer

  b A bank merges with a travel agent

  c A menswear retail chain merges with a women's fashion store chain

  d A bus manufacturer and a car-maker form a joint venture.

  e A sand quarry merges with a gravel quarry company

  f A brewery takes over a chain of pubs

  g A chain of clothes shops takes over a clothing manufacturer

  h A shoe-maker is taken over by a cigarette manufacturer

2. Now read the article below about a hostile take-over bid. Which company has launched the take-over bid and why? What type of integration is proposed? Try to find out if the take-over was successful or not, and why.

THE MIRROR, *Saturday, November 20, 1999*

£80bn.. THE WORLD'S BIGGEST TAKEOVER BID

Vodafone move for German rivals

By CLINTON MANNING, Business Editor

MOBILES giant Vodafone AirTouch launched the world's biggest takeover bid yesterday. It offered an astonishing £80 BILLION for German phones and engineering group Mannesmann.

Vodafone chief executive Chris Gent pounced after Mannesmann rebuffed friendly approaches.

He said the deal would benefit shareholders, customers and workers. Mr Gent, 51, added that the group could slash £1 billion off costs by 2004 and pledged there would be "no redundancies."

City experts believe the savings could lead to lower charges for consumers. But they warned that the takeover would create a "monster company" with a powerful stranglehold on the market.

"It would put them in a very dominant position," said one expert.

"And that could mean they can dictate to customers, who will have less choice."

The deal would make Vodafone, which recorded a £1.2 billion profit in the six months to October, the world's biggest mobile phone company. It has seven million Brits among its 42 million customers.

BID: Chris Gent

Key wordsearch

Hidden in the jumble of letters are key words and terms from this chapter. Use the descriptions below to help find them.

```
B F S D V A N I P R I M E T A R G S I C X
U C L E C O M M E R C E I L I N Y R N M I
N U A I F L U F R E T A I L I N G U E S N
O W D N O Q F R S E T E R K I Y V S D E D
P H E D R D F E O C E M O R N L M H I C Y
R O A U N O D T N V A E G A G F A M N O U
I L C S I C I M A I L O R D E R N O D N S
M E D T A U V A L K S V E P C N U N U D R
H S C R S M A T S L E A R H I O F T T A T
T A B I T E S E E R H S O T R H A A R R W
E L O A E N P R R O T X P U C T C I E Y Q
R I N L G T L P V P F I G O U Y T N K I A
Z N J I N S I E I N G L A S S P U B L N N
X G O S O L C T C K I E B R X Y R F S D C
I I V A D I K Y E L N Y N P Y T I G W U L
N N I T F P R O S D G H L O P N N L P S E
C A P I T A L G O O D S O T U O G U L T G
R I P O W S O E Q Y P X P B N M K X O R R
Y A W N A P R I M A R Y I N D U S T R Y O
```

- The name used to describe all business activities that provide services
- An industry involved in selling goods and services to the general public
- Industries that extract and provide natural resources
- Products, like machinery and tools, produced for business organizations to use in the production of other goods and services
- A term used to describe the decline of manufacturing industry
- The process of turning natural resources in semi-finished and finished consumer and capital goods

- Shopping on the Internet
- Shopping from a catalogue or direct mail advert via the post or over the telephone
- A collective term for manufacturing and construction industries
- Organizations who store, sell and distribute goods to other retailers
- These tertiary activities provide a personal touch
- Short for the official classification of UK industries used to collect and group financial, production and employment data on different business activities

Test your knowledge

1 Which of the following is most likely to cause an increase in the demand for motorcars?
A a rise in interest rates
B a rise in the price of petrol
C a rise in incomes
D a rise in car tax

2 If consumer confidence falls due to news reports about rising job loses, which of the following is most likely to happen?
A consumers will borrow more money
B people will buy more foreign holidays
C savings will rise and spending will fall
D savings will fall and spending will rise

3 Which of the following is an example of a secondary industry?
A farming
B mining
C car manufacture
D oil drilling

4 Which of the following is an example of a tertiary industry?
A house building
B fishing
C banking
D farming

5 National Westminster Plc is an example of
A a partnership
B a tertiary organization
C a primary sector industry
D a nationalized industry?

6 Which organization is in the secondary sector of the economy?
A Lloyds TSB
B Virgin Atlantic
C The Samaritans
D BAE Systems

7 A primary industry
A is the most important
B produces natural resources
C maximizes profit
D uses raw materials to manufacture?

8 Which occupation is most likely to be in the tertiary sector?
A A coal miner
B A farm labourer
C An accountant
D A chemical engineer

Questions 9 – 11 share the following answer options;
A the increase in demand for chocolates before Easter
B the fall in demand for gas during summer months
C the rise in air travel
D the fall in demand for cigarettes

Which of the above is an example of

9 a long-term upward trend in consumer demand?

10 a short-term increase in consumer demand?

11 a short-term fall in consumer demand?

12 a Explain how consumers create demand for goods and services and affect the activities and decisions of business organizations.
b Suggest three reasons why the demand for personal computers by business consumers has increased in recent years.
c Describe some of the main changes that have affected businesses in the following industries in recent years.
● retailing
● manufacturing
● farming
● transport

13 a Explain what the following industries produce and give two examples of each:
● primary industries
● secondary industries
● tertiary industries
b Tertiary sector employment and output in most developed countries has expanded significantly over time while manufacturing industry has been in decline. Suggest and explain two possible reasons for these developments.

chapter 6 *Types of business organization*

WHO WANTS A PIECE ?

THE BIG COMPANY PLC

What you need to learn

There are several different types of business ownership.

Private sector organizations are owned by private individuals. These include **sole traders, partnerships, private limited companies, public limited companies, co-operatives** and **franchises**.

Public sector organizations are owned and controlled by **local authorities** and **central government**. They include **government departments, executive agencies** and **public corporations**.

Business owners will have different roles and responsibilities in business depending on the type of ownership. Owners of sole traders and partnerships have **unlimited liability**. This means they are responsible for all the debts of their business. **Shareholders** in limited companies have limited liability and can only lose the amount of money they invested in their firm if it goes bankrupt.

You will need to find out the main features of these different types of business ownership.

You will also need to understand why different business organizations have different types of ownership.

Section **6.1** **Starting a business**

The role of the entrepeneur

People who start up and run business organizations are known as **entrepreneurs**. They are the people who take the risks and decisions necessary to organize production and make a firm run successfully.

▼ *Figure 6.1: Types of private sector business organization*

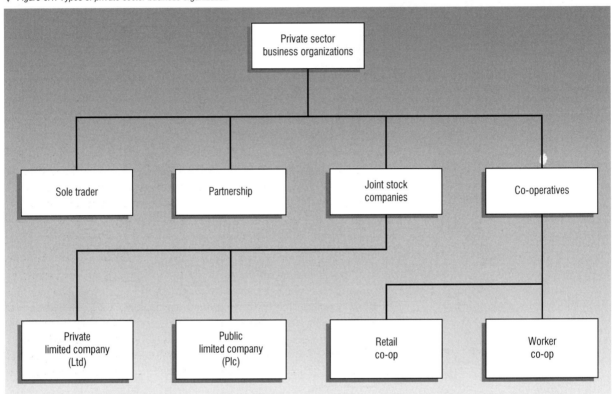

Within each industrial sector in the UK there are a wide range of different types of business organization that can be started by private individuals, from small one-person businesses to huge multinational firms. Walk down your local high street or browse through a local business phone directory and you will see many examples of each type of business.

Each type of business organization can be distinguished from other types by considering:

● Who owns it

● Whether owners will have to repay any business debts

● Who controls the organization from day to day

● How the business is financed

● Who gets the profits

▼ *Paula Smith wants to start her own business*

Some key considerations

To find out about different types of business organization and ownership, we shall follow the fortunes of a young entrepreneur called Paula Smith.

Paula is an unemployed school leaver. She is good at cooking and so she decides to set up her own catering business providing sandwiches and snacks to nearby office workers. However, before she starts up her business venture, Paula, like all entrepreneurs, must ask herself three vital questions. The answers to these questions will help her to decide which type of business is best for her.

Question 1: Will I have enough money?

To start a business an entrepreneur will need **capital**. This is the money used to finance a business. Money used to pay for premises, machinery, and other equipment is known as **fixed capital**. Money used to pay for bills, such as electricity, purchases of materials, wages, the telephone, etc., is known as **working capital**.

Some businesses will need more capital than others. If Paula cannot raise enough money herself to equip her business she may need to find other people, or **partners**, who would like to help finance her business and share in its ownership. This type of business is known as a **partnership**. If yet more money is needed, Paula might consider forming a **limited company** and selling shares in the ownership of her business to other people.

Once the business is established, it could become self-financing if Paula is able to earn enough revenue from the sale of her catering services to more than cover the cost of providing them. Paula can draw on her profits to give herself a weekly or monthly wage to live on. Any profit left over can be used to invest in her business, for example, to buy new equipment or move into larger premises. So-called **retained profits** provide a major source of finance for established firms of all types and sizes, reducing their need to take on expensive bank loans to pay for business expansion.

Small firms are the business!

A survey by Lloyds Bank reveals that 55% of small business owners put in more than 50 hours a week, while almost all – 95% – worked more than the national employee average of 38 hours a week. Some 7% worked more than 70 hours each week, while over a third worked every weekend. Only one in ten never worked on Saturdays.

The findings come from the Lloyds Bank/Small Business Management report. It shows that 39% of their time is spent producing goods or serving customers, 21% on paperwork, 15% on the phone, 11% at meetings, 8% travelling, and 6% dealing with the taxman.

Daily Mirror 9.6.1993

Question 2: Can I manage the business alone?

All budding entrepreneurs, including Paula, must decide whether or not they can manage alone before choosing the type of business organization they wish to form. Running a business on your own will often require working long hours and being a 'jack of all trades'. Paula must not only be a skilled caterer, but will also need to manage the business, do the accounts, advertise, employ staff if necessary, be familiar with employment laws, pay the bills, negotiate with suppliers – and much more. Setting up in business with other people can spread the load and allow more work to be done.

Question 3: Will I risk everything I own?

As the owner of her own business, Paula is entitled to any profits she makes. However, she also has the responsibility of finding money to pay for the firm's debts if the business should fail. This financial responsibility is called the **owner's liability**.

Before starting up her business, Paula must decide if she is willing to risk all her savings and possessions if the business were to fail. The answer to this question will influence the type of business organization she chooses, because some businesses are more risky than others.

Some business owners have **unlimited liability**. This means that they are liable to pay all business debts and may have to sell their personal possessions – house, car, furniture, jewellery – to do so. Business owners will be taken to court and declared bankrupt if debts are not repaid.

However, some business owners enjoy **limited liability**. This means that they will only lose the amount of money they invested in the business if it fails. They will not have to sell personal possessions to raise money to clear business debts. This reduces the risks involved.

Section **6.2**

Types of private sector business ownership

The sole trader

A **sole trader** is a business owned and controlled by one person. It is the oldest and most popular type of business in the UK, because it is easy to set up. Many of the largest and most successful businesses in the world started life many years ago as sole traders.

Most sole traders are small organizations in the tertiary sector selling personal services such as hairdressing, carpet cleaning, aromatherapy, painting and decorating, plumbing, and running small local shops.

Sole traders will usually dip into their own savings to start their business, or will borrow from family, friends, or a high street bank. Some may grow to employ several people or have a number of branches, but so long as there is only one owner, the business will remain a sole trader. Most sole traders employ few if any staff, and many work from home in order to save the expense of paying for premises.

▼ *A sole trader*

Sole traders can trade under their own name or a suitable trading name. The name of the business does not have to be registered, but care must be taken not to use the name of another business or one that would imply a connection with royalty or government. For example, if you were to set up a small record shop, you could not call it 'HMV' or 'Royal Records'.

Portfolio Activity 6.1

Read the article and list the advantages and disadvantages of being a sole trader:

THE LOCAL INFORMER

Serving Up SNAX!

Paula Smith is now the proud owner of 'SNAX' sandwich and coffee shop in the High Street. Paula was busy serving home-made takeaway rolls, pasta dishes and salad snacks to hungry office and shop workers from nearby when we popped in to sample her lunchtime menu. We asked her why she decided to open her own shop.

'I was unemployed for a long time,' explained Paula.'By running my own business I am ensured a job and I get any profits – not that I've made any yet. I have to work every hour I can and run the business on my own; buying food, making sandwiches, cooking, serving, cleaning, doing the accounts. You name it, I do it.'

Starting your own business is expensive, as Paula soon discovered. 'I used most of my savings to get the business off the ground, and my bank manager supplied me with a small loan. What with the rent of the shop space, hire of machinery, insurance payments, heating and lighting bills, I have to make at least

£600 a month from the shop before I can break even. And of course if I can't, I am out of work again and left holding the debts!'

Customers can look forward to a personal and friendly atmosphere in the shop and, with a prime location near to offices in the town centre, Paula may be able to look forward to better times ahead. 'I certainly hope so,' she agreed. 'I might even be able to give other people jobs, but I will still be the boss. My own boss! I don't have to answer to anyone. Not bad, is it?'

SNAX also provides sandwiches and snacks for business functions and parties.

The advantages of a sole trader

- **The sole trader business is a very personal one.** The owner of the business will have personal contact with customers and staff. S/he will be able to find out quickly what people want and then change what the business produces to suit what customers wish to buy. Furthermore, because anybody dealing with the firm deals with the owner personally, this can encourage customers to be loyal to the business.

- **The sole trader is his/her own boss.** Because s/he is the only owner of the business, the sole trader does not have to consult anyone else before making a decision. This means that they can make decisions quickly. They can decide whether or not to expand the business, what jobs to do and when, who to employ, etc.

- **The sole trader receives all the profit.** Being your own boss means not having to share profits with anyone. This is an important advantage to most people and it explains in part why the sole trader type of business is so popular.

- **It is easy to set up a sole trader business.** Sole traders need very little capital to start up with, so it is fairly easy for one person to set up a business alone. There are also very few legal formalities to complete before starting to trade.

Disadvantages of the sole trader

- **The sole trader has unlimited liability.** Unlimited liability means that the sole trader could lose his or her possessions to pay off debts in the event of bankruptcy. Unlimited liability exists because, in the eyes of the law, the sole trader business and its owner are one and the same. So if the business owes money, its owner must pay up.

- **The sole trader has full responsibility for the business.** As the sole owner of a business, the sole trader must take all of the decisions. Most people are not good at everything, but sole traders still need to be able to manage the business, do the bookkeeping, advertising, buying and selling, and many other things. This means that the sole trader may have to work long hours and if they are ill, or go on holiday, there is no one to take over the running of the business.

- **Sole traders lack capital.** Sole traders like Paula often have to rely on using their own savings or loans from family and friends to start up their businesses. Banks are often unwilling to lend money to new small businesses, especially if the owner has little experience of business and there is a risk of failure. Banks loans are also expensive to repay once interest is added.

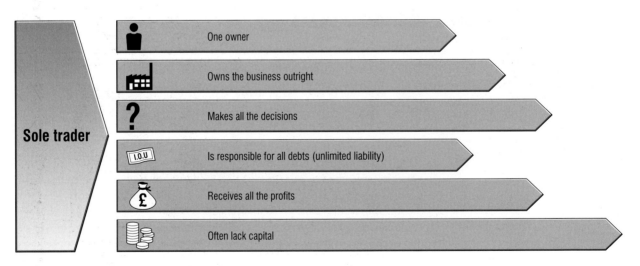

Partnerships

A sole trader may find it difficult to manage a business alone or raise enough money to expand. A partnership can help overcome this problem, and can be set up quite easily.

A **partnership** is a business agreement, normally between 2 to 20 people, to finance and work together in a business with the aim of making a profit. Partnerships are common in professions such as doctors, insurance brokers, and vets, although they can also be found in other occupations such as builders, garages, and in small factories. Firms of accountants, solicitors, and members of the Stock Exchange are allowed to have more than 20 partners.

Most partnerships will draw up a **deed of partnership**. This will usually contain the following information:

- How much capital each partner invested in the business
- How profits (and losses) are shared among the partners
- Rules for accepting new partners and expelling existing ones
- Rules for ending the partnership

Terms and conditions like these help partners to avoid disagreements.

Let us assume Paula Smith's business is doing well and she decides to expand SNAX. She takes on two partners, Tom and Sarah. They now own the business with Paula, help to manage it, and share in any profits. The reasons why Paula has decided to share her business are explained by the advantages of forming a partnership.

Portfolio Activity 6.2

Read the article below and identify the advantages and disadvantages of forming a partnership.

THE LOCAL INFORMER

SNAX Bites Newtown!

Today Paula Smith, owner of SNAX, celebrates over one year's successful trading with the opening of another new shop, this time in Newtown. So what is the secret of Paula's success?

'There is clearly a market for high-quality competitively priced sandwiches and snacks for business functions and for people to take away to eat for breakfast or lunch. People seem to come back again and again. They like the variety we offer.'

Using her own money, Paula Smith acquired the premises and equipped her shop. Banks were unwilling to lend her money to expand because of the obvious risks such an outlet faces from increasing competition from fast food chains. With giants such as McDonalds, Pizzaland and Burger King in nearly every high street, the threat of competition has become stronger. 'Luckily I have made contacts in my business dealings and have two partners now to help run and finance the business.' Paula

explained. 'Not only have they put up a large amount of money, but they will also be able to relieve me of some of the responsibilities I've carried for over a year now. For example, Tom is a qualified Chef and Sarah is an accountant by profession.'

Tom Blunt and Sarah Foster are the two new partners in the SNAX enterprise. Running a business poses many risks and the collapse of the firm could mean all those personally involved losing their possessions to repay debts. So why did Sarah take the risk? 'It's a challenge,' she said. 'I was an accountant, but now I'm a full-time housewife and I wanted something else to keep me occupied.'

What problems, if any, do the partners think may occur? They told us that finding

the money to decorate and refit the shops is their biggest problem. 'And we all had disagreements about how to layout the two stores. But we're all friends, really,' they laughed.

Advantages of a partnership

- **Partners bring new skills and ideas to the business.** Paula has taken on Sarah and Tom as partners because they have skills which her business needs. This means that the partners can carry out a wider range of jobs than a sole trader could alone, and they can provide cover when one partner is ill or on holiday.

- **More partners means more money for the business.** If other people want to share in the ownership and control of a business then they must pay money to do so. This money can then be used to expand the business.

- **Partners can help in decision-making.** A sole trader has full responsibility for making decisions in a business, whereas in a partnership all decisions are shared.

- **Setting up a partnership is easy.** There are few legal requirements involved in setting up a partnership, although it is advisable to use a solicitor to draw up a partnership agreement.

Disadvantages of a partnership

- **Partners can disagree.** The more partners there are, the more likely are disagreements. If Paula, Sarah, and Tom find they cannot agree on important decisions affecting the company, the business will suffer.

- **Partnerships have unlimited liability.** Just like a sole trader, in an ordinary partnership, partners stand to lose everything they have if the business goes bankrupt. Furthermore, each partner is held responsible for the actions of the other partners.

  It is, however, possible to have a **limited partnership** where some partners have limited liability. They are called **limited partners** or sleeping partners. Like ordinary partners, they pay money into the business in return for a share in the ownership and profits. However, they do not play a part in the day-to-day running of the business.

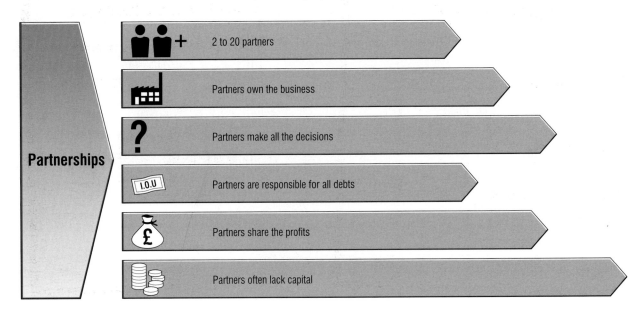

Partnerships

- 2 to 20 partners
- Partners own the business
- Partners make all the decisions
- Partners are responsible for all debts
- Partners share the profits
- Partners often lack capital

- **Partnerships lack capital.** Because there are more people in a partnership, the business will have more money than a sole trader, but it is still difficult for a partnership to have more than 20 partners (except for firms of solicitors, accountants and stockbrokers). This puts a limit on the amount of money that may be brought into the business.

None of the very large businesses in the UK, or indeed in the world, are partnerships. This is simply because no partnership could raise enough money to expand into a large enterprise. Other types of business are needed to do this. These other forms of business enterprise are known as **joint stock companies.**

Joint stock companies

Joint stock companies are also known as **limited companies.** These are companies that sell shares to investors in order to raise money.

There are two main types of limited company:

- The **private limited company** (Ltd)

- The **public limited company** (Plc)

Most of the smaller joint stock companies are private limited companies, and there are about half a million in existence in the UK at present. Public limited companies tend to be much larger in size, but fewer in number.

In order to set up a limited company the law requires that two legal documents are drawn up. These are;

- A **memorandum of association**

- The **articles of association**

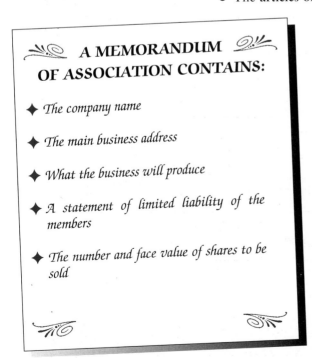

A MEMORANDUM OF ASSOCIATION CONTAINS:

✦ The company name

✦ The main business address

✦ What the business will produce

✦ A statement of limited liability of the members

✦ The number and face value of shares to be sold

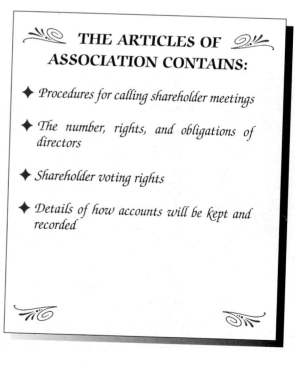

THE ARTICLES OF ASSOCIATION CONTAINS:

✦ Procedures for calling shareholder meetings

✦ The number, rights, and obligations of directors

✦ Shareholder voting rights

✦ Details of how accounts will be kept and recorded

Once these two documents have been agreed they are sent to **Companies House** – a government body that watches over limited companies. If everything is in order, the Registrar of Companies issues a **Certificate of Incorporation** which allows the company to start trading.

The private limited company

After several years of trading, the SNAX Partnership has become very successful. To build upon this success, the partnership now wants to open up a chain of shops around the country, but to do this they need a lot more money.

To raise the capital they need to expand the business, they can form a private limited company. These companies can be recognized by the letters 'Ltd' after their names, i.e. SNAX Ltd. However, forming a limited company means changing the form of ownership and control of the business, and how profits are used.

Portfolio Activity 6.3

Read the article below;

1. How do private limited companies like SNAX raise the money they need to expand?

2. What does the word 'limited' stand for in 'private limited company'?

3. What is the name given to the people who are elected to run a private limited company?

4. Paula Smith suggests in the article that she would like to remain 'at the head of the company' and run the business from day to day. Who will decide if Paula can remain in this position, and how is this done?

5. Draw up a list of advantages and disadvantages of forming a private limited company.

THE LOCAL INFORMER

SNAX to become a Limited Company

SNAX, the chain of catering shops, has just announced plans to become a private limited company by selling shares in the ownership of the organization. This will raise capital to finance their new expansion programme. Miss Paula Smith, Managing Director and founder member of SNAX, explained how allowing the business to be owned by more people can provide the money she needs to open more SNAX shops around the country.

'We simply invite people to buy share certificates in the company,' she said, 'and this allows them to become owners of the business and share in its profits.' Shares will normally be sold to family, friends and workers in the company.

As a shareholder of SNAX, a person will also be allowed to have a say in how the company should be run. 'Of course,' Paula continued, 'I would like to remain as a director of SNAX but if all the other shareholders decide they don't want me at the head of the company, they can vote me out and elect other directors to run the business.' Each year shareholders can vote for directors at a special shareholders' meeting.

We asked Paula Smith why people would want to buy shares in her company. 'We are a growing and profitable company,' she replied. 'The more profit we make, the more shareholders receive in dividends. Also, as we are a private limited company, all shareholders will benefit from having limited liability, and so in the very unlikely event of SNAX closing down due to bad debts, shareholders would only lose, at most, the money they paid for their shares.'

▼ *An ordinary share certificate*

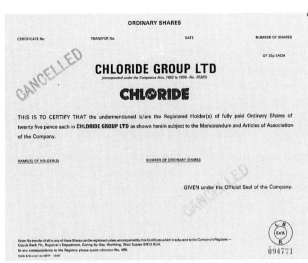

ORDINARY SHARES

CERTIFICATE No.   TRANSFER No.   DATE   NUMBER OF SHARES

OF 25p EACH

CANCELLED

CHLORIDE GROUP LTD
(Incorporated under the Companies Acts, 1862 to 1890 - No. 35385)

CHLORIDE

THIS IS TO CERTIFY THAT the undermentioned is/are the Registered Holder(s) of fully paid Ordinary Shares of twenty five pence each in **CHLORIDE GROUP LTD** as shown herein subject to the Memorandum and Articles of Association of the Company.

NAME(S) OF HOLDER(S)   NUMBER OF ORDINARY SHARES

CANCELLED

GIVEN under the Official Seal of the Company.

Note: No transfer of all or any of these Shares can be registered unless accompanied by this Certificate which is to be sent to the Company's Registrar:— Lloyds Bank Plc, Registrar's Department, Goring-by-Sea, Worthing, West Sussex BN12 6DA. In any correspondence to the Registrar please quote reference No. 489.

094771

How a private limited company raises money

Private limited companies can raise money for expansion by selling shares to people. A **share** is simply a piece of paper which states that the person who holds it has paid for part of the company and now has a share in its ownership. The value printed on a share, or its **face value**, is the price at which the company first sold the share.

If SNAX Ltd sells 10,000 shares at £1 each, then the company will receive £10,000. The people who buy these shares are called **shareholders**. The more shares a person holds, the more of the company they own, and the bigger their share of profits. The profit paid out on a share is known as a **dividend**. For example, SNAX Ltd may pay out 10 pence of their profits for every share held. Therefore, a person who owns 1,000 shares will receive total dividends worth £100 (1,000 × 10 pence).

Ownership and control

Most shareholders do not wish to become involved as owners in the daily running of their company. Instead they appoint a board of directors to run the company on a daily basis (see chapter 2). This is done by voting at the shareholders' meeting.

Every company must hold an **annual general meeting (AGM)** every year. At this meeting the board of directors report on company performance during the year and the shareholders then vote on whether they wish the existing board to continue to run the business. Each shareholder gets one vote for every share they own. Shareholders with a large number of shares can vote for themselves to be a company director if they wish.

In the case of SNAX, Paula, Tom, and Sarah will only stay in charge if the other shareholders remain happy with their performance, or if they together hold 51% or more of the shares. Any person, or group of persons acting together, holding over 51% of the shares in a company is said to have the **controlling interest**. That is, they can outvote all of the other shareholders if they wish.

Advantages of a private limited company

- **Shareholders have limited liability**. A person who owns part of a limited company is only responsible for the repayment of any debts up to the value of the shares they hold. Without limited liability, people would be unwilling to buy shares, because if the company went bankrupt they would end up losing a lot of money – and even their personal possessions – to repay debts.

- **Shareholders have no management worries.** If shareholders in a company had to run the business, they would have to take on all the worries and responsibilities themselves. However, they can choose to pass on this responsibility to company directors to manage the business on their behalf.

- **The company is a separate legal entity.** In the eyes of the law, a limited company is not the same as its owners. As a result, if the company owes money, the company can be sued and taken to court, but the owners cannot. The company can be forced to pay its debts or pay compensation out of company funds because it has a separate legal entity. Owners' funds are entirely separate.

Disadvantages of private limited companies

- **Limited companies must disclose information about themselves to the general public.** All limited companies are required by law to keep detailed records of their trading activities and to publish this information in a set of **annual accounts** so that their shareholders can read about what their company is doing (see chapter 9).

- **Limited companies must hold an annual general meeting (AGM) of shareholders each year.** This is to allow the company owners to vote on how the company should be run and who should run it. This is an advantage to the shareholders as it gives them a say in the running of the company, but it also means that the original owners of the company could lose control.

- **Private limited companies cannot sell their shares to the general public.** Private limited companies have to sell their shares privately to people they know, like family, friends, and employees. This is a big disadvantage because it is possible to sell many more shares, and raise far more money by advertising shares for sale to anyone who wants to buy them. This means that private limited companies are confined to being small to medium-sized firms, unable to raise vast amounts of money to expand.

Private Limited Company
- 1 or more shareholders
- Shareholders own the business
- Shareholders have limited liability
- Shareholders share the profits
- Shares are sold privately
- Companies must publish accounts and hold AGMs
- Directors are elected to run the company

The public limited company

Imagine now that SNAX has become so successful that it develops plans to expand overseas into major cities around the world. To do this, Paula Smith and the other shareholders decide to form a **public limited company**. This will allow them to raise capital from the sale of shares to the general public and other business organizations in the UK and abroad.

Public limited companies are among the largest and most successful firms in the UK. Examples include such well known names as British Airways Plc, Marks and Spencers Plc, British Telecom Plc, HSBC Holdings Plc, and BP Amoco Plc.

1. How do public limited companies like SNAX Plc raise finance for expansion?

2. How much money will the SNAX share issue raise?

3. Why is it easier for a Plc to raise capital than a private limited company?

4. Why are the original owners of the Plc more likely to lose their control of the company than if they were in a smaller company?

5. Draw up a list of advantages and disadvantages of forming a public limited company.

THE CITY TIMES

SNAX Attacks the Stock Market

SNAX, one of the country's leading private catering firms, has announced plans to sell shares through the Stock Exchange. The Council of the Stock Exchange revealed yesterday that the company has received a full listing which will allow it to float shares on the full stock market and become a public limited company (Plc).

'Our plans are to open a number of SNAX outlets overseas in major business capitals such as Paris, Brussels, Madrid, Frankfurt, Tokyo, and New York,' explained Tom Blunt, one of the original partners in the SNAX organization. 'This of course requires a substantial injection of cash into the company, but we feel confident that sales and profits will be extremely good.'

SNAX was formed nine years ago by Miss Paula Smith, an unemployed cook from London. The company first sold shares privately to friends and workers four years ago and has gone from strength to strength, with a sales turnover for last year topping £10 million and profits after tax of £940,000.

The new issue of two million shares at 120 pence each will be available from next month and, with dividend forecasts looking good, it is likely that the shares will be snapped up quickly by many thousands of investors.

Going public by selling shares to the general public can be expensive, but the financial rewards can be great. A major advertising campaign in national newspapers will prepare prospective shareholders for the launch of the company onto the full stock market.

The issue of who controls the company will be discussed and subject to vote at the next AGM, where existing shareholders will be joined by many of the new shareholders. Ms Paula Smith, Ms Sarah Foster, and Mr Tom Blunt – the three original partners – are confident, however, that with their controlling interest in share ownership they can retain their positions as company directors.

'My only fear is that the management may find it difficult to cope if the company grows too quickly or gets too big,' explained Miss Smith. 'Good managers who can run the various outlets in the company and who can work as part of a team are hard to find.'

The application list for the purchase of the shares will open on Thursday June 21st. Dealings in shares are expected to start a week later.

▼ *An advertisement for the sale of shares in McBride Plc.*

McBride plc

Share Offer

McBride is the largest manufacturer of private label household and personal care products in Europe. Private label household and personal care products are sold by retailers as an alternative to branded products. The Group's principal customers comprise many of the major European grocery retailers which sell its products under their own labels or as minor brands, including Asda, Safeway, J Sainsbury and Tesco in the U.K. and Intermarché, Leclerc and Promodes in France. Typical household products include textile washing powders, dishwash products, fabric conditioners and other cleaning products. Personal care products include shampoos, foam baths, deodorants, toothpastes and mouthwashes.

For further information on how to apply for shares in the McBride Share Offer, please call your stockbroker or one of the Share Shops listed below:

City Deal Services Limited
01708 738887

Skipton Building Society
0113 245 2888

Hargreaves Lansdown
0117 988 9977

The Share Centre Ltd
0800 800008

ShareLink Limited
0345 665665

YorkSHARE/Yorkshire Building Society
0800 736736

Sponsored by S.G. Warburg & Co. Ltd

Advantages of a public limited company

- **Public limited companies can sell shares on the Stock Exchange.** The UK Stock Exchange is one of the largest markets in the world for the purchase and sale of shares. A Plc is able to raise money from the sale of its shares on the stock market to people all over the world.

- **A Plc can advertise the sale of shares.** The Plc can attract shareholders by placing advertisements in newspapers and on television. Private limited companies are not allowed to do this.

Disadvantages of a public limited company

- **Forming and launching a Plc is an expensive business.** Many legal documents are required. Advertisements in newspapers are needed, and a prospectus needs to be published as a pamphlet or as a spread in a newspaper.

- **The original owners of the company may lose control.** This is especially a risk where there are many shareholders. They have the right to attend annual general meetings (AGMs), to vote on company policy, and on who should be a director to manage the company from day to day.

Many Plcs have thousands of shareholders, many of whom do not have the time to attend such meetings. This is especially true of the small shareholder who has only a limited number of shares, and therefore limited voting power. Only a handful of shareholders actually use their vote, and so directors, once elected, act very much on their own. In this way, the majority of owners may lose control over their business. This is known as the **divorce of ownership from control.**

Another problem for small shareholders is the tendency for large financial institutions like pension funds and insurance companies to buy up large quantities of shares (most shares in the UK are owned by these institutions). As there is only one vote per share, small shareholders can be regularly outvoted by the large financial institutions.

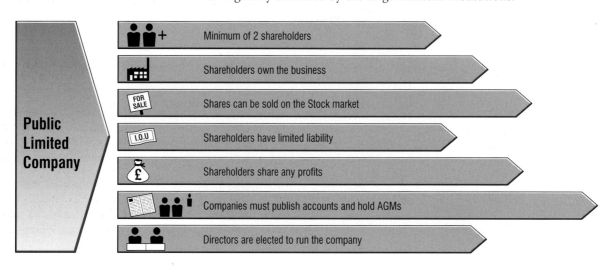

Public Limited Company

- Minimum of 2 shareholders
- Shareholders own the business
- Shares can be sold on the Stock market
- Shareholders have limited liability
- Shareholders share any profits
- Companies must publish accounts and hold AGMs
- Directors are elected to run the company

- **Some Plcs may have management problems.** Some companies may grow so large that it becomes difficult for the senior managers to control all aspects of the business effectively. The more people there are in a business, the more people there are to consult when decisions are taken. This can make decision-making slow and disagreements can occur.

Co-operatives

A **co-operative** is an organization formed by people joining together to organize production, make decisions, and share profits. All members have an equal say in running the business and share equally in the profits.

There are two main types of co-operative enterprise:

- **Worker co-operatives** are organizations which are owned by their workers, as in a farming co-operative. They pool their money to buy equipment and share equally in decision-making and any business profits. The number of worker co-operatives grew rapidly during the 1970s when many firms were closing down and making their workers unemployed. The UK government set up the **Co-operative Development Agency (CDA)** to provide advice and financial assistance to help employees to buy the firms they worked for.

There are very few worker co-operatives in the UK compared to countries like France, Spain, and Italy, where this type of business ownership is very popular.

▼ *Retail Co-operatives*

- **Retail co-operatives** are shops run for the benefit of their customers. The first retail co-operative society was formed in 1844 when a group of workers who could not afford to pay high food prices joined together to buy food direct from wholesalers. Because they were able to buy food in bulk, suppliers would often give them discounts.

The principles of modern retail co-operatives are much the same:

- Modern co-operatives are owned by their members
- Any person can become a member by buying a share – often for as little as £1
- Members elect a board of directors to run the co-operative
- Each member is allowed one vote regardless of the number of shares they hold
- Profits are shared between members and customers

Today many of the smaller retail co-operative shops have closed because of competition with large supermarkets. To compete, a number of co-operatives have formed into larger superstores selling a wide variety of goods and services, normally located on large out-of-town sites.

The co-operative movement has also successfully expanded into other activities such as banking, insurance, travel agents, funeral services, and bakeries. The largest single retailing co-operative is the Co-operative Wholesale Society based in Manchester.

Worker co-operatives	Retail co-operatives
Workers own all the shares	Owned by its members
Managed by its workers	Managers run the organization
Workers have limited liability	Owners have limited liability
Workers share the profits	Members receive profits

Little big hit

Franchising has almost been a licence to print money for husband and wife team Bob and Christine Little. They are one of the star businesses in KallKwik's nationwide network of 200 printing centres. The couple now in their fifties set up in 1984 with a £20,000 bank loan.

Turnover has escalated to more than £600,000 a year and now they employ more than 14 people at their Peterborough shop. Bob Little said, 'The beauty of franchising was that we were buying into a successful business. It has been hard work, but very rewarding.'

Daily Mirror 7.3.1995

Franchises

This form of business ownership was first introduced in the USA but is now very popular in the UK. A franchise is an agreement between two parties:

- The **franchiser** – an existing, usually well known company with an established market for its product

- The **franchisee** – a person, or group of people, who buy the right to use the business name of the franchiser and make or sell its product in a particular location. Well known examples of franchise operations include McDonalds, Sock Shop, Wimpy, Prontaprint and Pizza Hut. It is also increasingly common for smaller organizations to franchise parts of their operations. For example, your local milkman may have franchised his round from the dairy. Department stores will also franchise space within their stores to other retailers.

To buy a franchise a person, or group of entrepreneurs, will have to pay an up-front fee plus a percentage of their sales revenue to the parent company. In return, the parent company will often provide training, equipment, materials, advertising, and help finding premises.

Advantages of buying a franchise
- Product likely to be well known

- Franchiser will often advertise and promote the product

- Banks may be more willing to lend money to a well known franchise

- Risk of business failure is lower than starting a new business

▼ *Prontaprint is a well known franchise operation.*

Disadvantages of buying a franchise
- Cost of buying franchise could be high

- A proportion of business profits are paid to the franchiser

- Franchise agreement can be withdrawn

- Role of business owners reduced to 'branch managers'. Most aspects of business will be decided by the parent company

Portfolio Activity 6.5

A friend has asked for your advice on buying into the franchise advertised opposite.

Write a short report using a word processor offering the following advice to your friend:

- What is a franchise?

- How a franchise works

- The advantages of buying a franchise rather than setting up a sole trader organization or partnership

- The disadvantages of buying a franchise

You can find out more about this fast growing business sector from the British Franchise Association and from *Business Franchise* magazine.

Interested in running a business with a difference, something with a massive industry and demand?

Well, Auto Aid has the answer.

We have developed and helped design a major breakthrough in repair technology and have turned a good idea into a massive money making business for the nineties, with **earnings that you would not believe.**

Our repair and renovation service is being demanded by vehicle owners, operators and insurers as well as hotels, restaurants, pubs, clubs, airlines, car hire, car leasing, in fact anyone who has any plastic or fabric — We need repair distributors to join our fast growing business in the UK.

We offer the most comprehensive Mobile Repair Service available, and can supply repair systems that will repair things that you would never believe possible, they include car carpets, car dashboards, car door lining, car bumpers, car seats, three piece suites, chesterfields, leather top desks, bar counters, chairs, settees and any kind of carpet. Priced at £2,350 + VAT

Call for more information 01908 217818

Portfolio Activity 6.6

1. Below is a table listing how different types of business are owned, controlled, pay debts, raise finance, and use their profits. Copy out and complete the table by filling in the blank spaces.

2. Look around your local area and try to identify businesses that are:
   a sole traders
   b partnerships

c private limited companies
d public limited companies
e co-operatives
f franchises

For each business try to explain why you think the type of business, and what it produces, is suited to that particular form of organization. A local phone directory would be a useful source of information.

Business Feature	Sole trader	Partnership	Private Limited Company	Public Limited Company	Worker co-operative	Retail co-operative	Franchise
Ownership				Shareholders			
Control	Run by owner						
Main source(s) of finance	Own savings/ bank loans		Selling shares to family and friends				
Liability							
Who gets profits?				Shareholders		Given to customers as stamps or lower prices	

Section **6.3**

Public sector organizations

Central and local government

The **public sector** in the UK is made up of organizations which are funded by, and responsible to, local and central government. These organizations affect our daily lives by the way in which they raise money and through the services they provide and the rules they make.

Some examples of central government services	Some examples of local government services
Major road building and maintenance	Street lighting
Tax assessment and collection	Parking enforcement
National Health Service	Refuse collection
Armed services	Libraries
Social security payments	Parks
Collection of economic and social statistics	Schools
Consumer protection	Cutting grass verges
Immigration services	Local road building and maintenance
Industry sponsorship	Council housing
Law and order	Housing benefits
Post Office	Fire service

▼ *Town Halls are the offices of Local government*

Local government

Local government includes:

- District councils
- County councils (regional councils in Scotland)
- London borough councils

Local voters elect council representatives to make decisions that affect their communities. Each representative is known as a **councillor** and usually represents one of the main political parties. If voters are unhappy, they will choose another set of councillors to represent them at council elections which are held every four years.

The decisions of local councils and the day-to-day running of their offices are carried out by paid employees known as **local government officers**.

Expenditure and finance

Local authorities provide public services to local businesses and communities such as education, leisure facilities, refuse collection, housing, the maintenance of local roads, and parking enforcement.

Councils raise money in a number of ways:

- Most of their money is provided by grants from central government
- Council Tax
- Charges for services, such as the use of swimming pools or leisure centres
- Rents from council houses
- Proceeds from the sale of council houses and council land
- Loans

The Council Tax

The **Council Tax** was introduced on 1 April 1993 to replace the Community Charge (or 'Poll Tax'). The Council Tax is a local tax set by individual councils.

Each household receives a tax bill each year based on the value of their property. Each house or flat will have been placed in one of eight Council Tax valuation bands. Charges for each band are set each year by local councils and may differ between different areas.

In general, the higher the value of the property, the more Council Tax the household will pay. People living on their own qualify for a 25%

discount. Those on low incomes and the disabled can also claim reductions. It is usual for people to pay the tax in ten monthly instalments.

Business rates

Businesses do not pay Council Tax. Instead, they pay a tax called the **Business Rate** based on the value of business property. Business rates are collected by local authorities but paid to the central government. The central government then shares out the revenue among councils, based on local need.

Central government

Voters elect members of parliament to form the **central government** to be responsible for mainly national issues. The political party with the most MP's forms the government. The Conservative Party formed three central governments in the UK between 1979 and 1997. If voters are unhappy with their member of parliament, or the government as a whole, they can vote for another representative every four to five years. The Labour Party was elected to form the central government in 1996.

The main decision making body in the central government is the *Cabinet* which normally consists of 22 ministers headed by the Prime Minister. Each minister is appointed by the Prime Minister to be responsible for the activities of a **government department**. There are around 20 central government departments including the Department for Education and Employment (DfEE), the Department of Trade and Industry (DTI), Her Majesty's Treasury and the Ministry of Defence (MoD). Each department has its own budget to spend on the provision of a range of services and has to submit these spending plans to the Treasury each year for approval.

Civil servants are employed by the central government in departments to develop and control economic, social, environmental, and foreign policies.

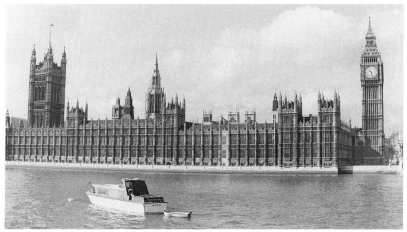

▼ *Central government in the UK is based at the Houses of Parliament*

Expenditure and finance

Central government raises money mainly from taxes. There are two main types of tax:

- **Direct taxes** on incomes and business profits
- **Indirect taxes** on goods and services, such as Value Added Tax (VAT) and customs and excise duties

Central government also raises some money from interest charged on loans, dividends on shares it owns in some public limited companies, and charges for some public services, such as post office deliveries.

The Government uses the money it raises to pay for the provision of public services such as the NHS, social security, and major road-building schemes. If government spending in one year is greater than the amount raised in taxes and other revenues, the government will borrow the difference.

In 1999–2000 UK government and local authorities spent around £350 billion paid for from taxes and other public sector revenues.

▼ Figure 6.2: Public sector expenditure and receipts, 1999–2000

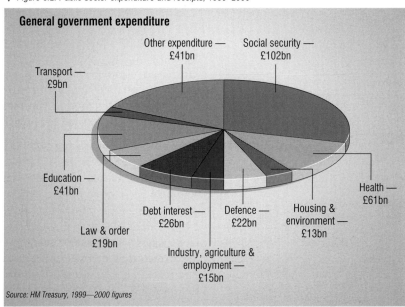

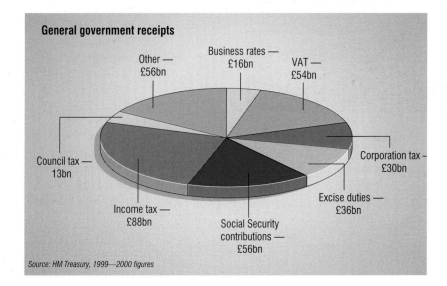

1. Look at Figure 6.2. How much did the government need to borrow in 1999–2000?

2. From Figure 6.2 make a list of the sources of government revenue in order of size. Which is the most important source of revenue to the government?

3. Every year in March the Government announces its plans for spending and raising revenue. This is known as the **Budget**. Make sure you watch or listen to the next Budget to find out about the government's plans and the reasons for them. National newspapers carry full reports of the Budget announcements the following day. Use these to write a short report explaining what taxes have gone up/down and why, how spending plans have changed, and why. Produce pie charts like those in Figure 6.2, using a computer spreadsheet for the new revenue and spending plans.

▼ *The Meteorological Office and Forestry Commission are both run by executive agencies.*

A number of organizations are under central government control. These are:

● Executive agencies

● QUANGOs

● Public corporations

Executive agencies

A number of public services, such as the Royal Mint, prisons, the provision of statistics, passports, and benefit payments are run by **executive agencies**. These organizations are run in a business-like way with independent control over how they spend the money allocated to them each year from central government. However, agencies remain accountable to government ministers.

QUANGOS ('quasi-autonomous non-government organizations')

These are unelected government bodies run by boards of directors to manage a particular government initiative. They include regional health authorities, research councils and employment tribunals. The number of QUANGOs has increased in recent years. Being 'quasi-autonomous' means they can be run from day to day rather like a private sector business without the direct control of government officials.

Public corporations

Most public corporations are responsible for the day to day running of industries owned and controlled by central government which sell goods or services directly to consumers. These are called nationalised industries. For example, the Post Office is run by a public corporation. However, few industries remain nationalised in the UK today because most, like British Rail and British Telecom, are now run by private sector organizations.

Public corporations also run The Bank of England, which is not a 'trading activity', and the British Broadcasting Authority (BBC) which is neither owned by the government nor the private sector.

▼ *The Post Office and the Civil Aviation Authority are run by public corporations.*

Public corporations have a number of features in common:

- Each is controlled by a government minister. For example, the BBC is accountable to the Home Office minister, the Post Office to the Secretary of State for Trade and Industry, and the Bank of England to the Chancellor of the Exchequer at the Treasury.

- Each has a board of directors who are responsible for the organization. These are appointed by the government minister responsible for the industry.

- Each has a separate legal identity from the government. This means that legal action can only be taken against a corporation and not the government.

- Each must publish an annual report and financial accounts.

- Each is financed by revenues from the sale of its services to consumers and by central government grant. (The BBC is financed by the TV licence fee set by the Government each year and by revenues from the sale of programmes).

- Public corporations do not have to make an overall profit, although they are expected to earn at least an 8% profit on the value of any new investments (this is known as the **required rate of return**). For example, if the Post Office invested £100,000 in a new post office shop, it would be required to earn at least £108,000 in revenue from it.

- Public corporations may be allowed by central government to retain all or some of any profits made to plough back into improving their services. However, the government may instead decide to use these profits to finance other public services and help reduce taxes.

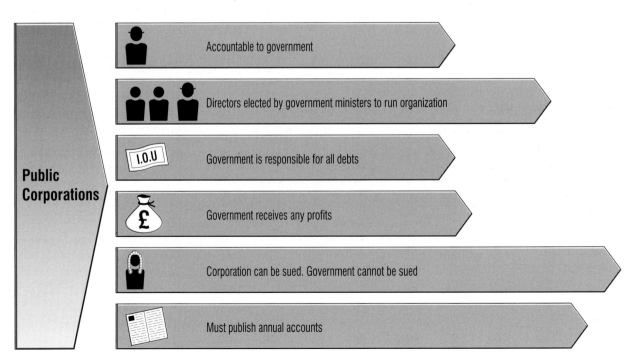

Public Corporations

- Accountable to government
- Directors elected by government ministers to run organization
- Government is responsible for all debts
- Government receives any profits
- Corporation can be sued. Government cannot be sued
- Must publish annual accounts

Nationalization or privatization?

Nationalization refers to the transfer of an industry from private to public ownership by the passing of an act of parliament forcing private owners to sell their shares to the government. Between the end of second world war and the late 1970s successive UK Governments took over the ownership of all the firms in industries such as coal, electricity, gas, telecommunications and the railways. Each nationalized industry was run by a public corporation.

Key nationalized industries 1982

British Coal	National Girobank
Electricity (England and Wales)	British Airways
N of Scotland Hydro Electric	British Airports Authority
S of Scotland Electricity	British Rail
British Gas	British Waterways
British Steel	National Bus Company
British Telecom	Scottish Transport Group
Post Office	British Shipbuilders
London Transport	

Why were industries nationalized?

UK governments have in the past taken into public sector ownership entire industries for the following reasons:

- **To control natural monopolies** – In some industries firms need to grow very large in order to take full advantage of the cost savings large scale production can bring (see chapter 8). However, this can result in one very large firm becoming the only supplier of a product to a market and, if unchecked, it could take advantage of this market power to charge high prices to consumers. To prevent this, natural monopoly providers of the gas, water, electricity and railway supply networks, were controlled by the government.

- **For safety** – Some industries, such as nuclear energy, are thought to be too dangerous to be controlled by private entrepreneurs.

- **To protect employment** – Some firms were nationalized because they faced closure as private sector loss making organizations. For example, in 1975 the Central Government rescued British Leyland to protect the jobs of car workers.

- **To maintain a public service** – Nationalized industries can provide services even if they make a loss, such as postal deliveries and rail services in rural areas. Private firms seeking to make profit would not operate these services.

Privatisation

Since 1979 most nationalised industries have been returned to private sector ownership. **Privatization** refers to the sale of shares in government-owned nationalized industries to the general public and private sector firms. The first most significant sale was in 1984 when British Telecom was sold. In 1999 only the Post Office and British Nuclear Fuels (BNFL) remained nationalised organizations. There are plans to sell BNFL and to privatize some parts of the Post Office.

The UK Government also has plans to privatise many executive agencies.

Those in support of privatization argue that:

- If these industries are forced to compete for profit they will become more competitive, improve their product quality and lower prices.

- Whereas there used to be only one nationalised supplier, consumers will be able to choose from a wide variety of goods and services from different producers. For example, there are now many rival suppliers of communication services to British Telecom.

- The sale of shares in these industries raises revenue for the government which can be used to lower taxes. For example, the sale of British Gas raised over £6 billion.

- Private individuals can own shares in these organizations and vote on how they should be run.

Those against privatization argue that:

- Many privatized industries still dominate the markets they supply and have been able to raise their prices and cut services. For example, rail and water companies are local monopoly suppliers.

- Private sector organizations will not protect public services. Many fear private sector firms providing railway services will cut services and raise fares in the long run. Complaints about rail services are rising all the time.

- Most of the shares in privatised organizations have been bought by large financial organizations such as banks and insurance companies who are interested only in making big profits.

Privatization also involves allowing private sector firms to compete with public sector organizations to supply a product or even take over the activity completely. For example, local councils now pay private sector organizations to collect rubbish rather than employing their own refuse collectors to do so.

'Air traffic sell-off will make passport fiasco look like peanuts'

Air travellers face a chaotic build up of delays "that will make the Passport Office queues fiasco look like peanuts" unless the government drops its planned privatisation of the National Air Traffic Service.

This warning comes from leaders of 4,800 air traffic control staff comes on the eve of publication of the Government's draft Bill for a £1 billion sell-off.

A campaign of protest against privatisation is to be launched on Thursday by an emergency delegate conference called by the air traffic controllers' union, IPMS.

However, Sir Roy McNulty, the new chairman of the National Air Traffic Service (Nats) argues that privatisation is the only way forward and warns that the European high holiday season will be an air traffic control disaster. "There is going to be one hell of an inquest after this summer," he said.

The Government has already shelved plans to sell off the Royal Mint following widespread objections; but it is set on privatising air traffic control.

IPMS general secretary Paul Noon said "Privatisation is a bigger threat to air safety over the United Kingdom than the soaring number of flights.

"Key investment decisions are being held up by uncertainty over the Government's intentions while staff struggle to keep up with record levels of growth at airports and air traffic control centres.

The service is responsible for the safety of 1.9 million flights a year over Britain and the number of passengers will rise to 103 million by the year 2000.

Mr Noon added that controllers are having to handle an eight per cent growth in air traffic this year alone with "ageing and often outdated equipment".

The air traffic controllers have logged a record number of overload reports but the Civil Aviation Authority claims that British air space is still among the safest in the world.

Evening Standard 20.7.1999

1. How does a nationalized industry differ from a public limited company in terms of ownership, control, finance, use of profits (if any), and owner's liability?

2. Explain what privatization is

3. What are the economic arguments for and against privatising the National Air Traffic Service in the UK?

4. What other concerns are raised by the privatization? What impact could they have on a. airlines, and b. the travel industry?

1. Identify seven business organizations, each one representing a different form of business ownership. Your chosen organizations should include at least:
   - one public sector organization
   - one private sector organization
   - one small or medium-sized private sector organization
   - one large private sector organization

2. For each business organization you have chosen, write a brief summary covering the following information:
   - the name of the organization
   - where it is located
   - public or private sector
   - main purposes of the organization
   - main types of activity, goods or services
   - type of ownership and number or owners
   - who controls the organization
   - usual sources of finance
   - use of profits, if any

Key crossword

Use the clues below to complete the key words and terms in the crossword

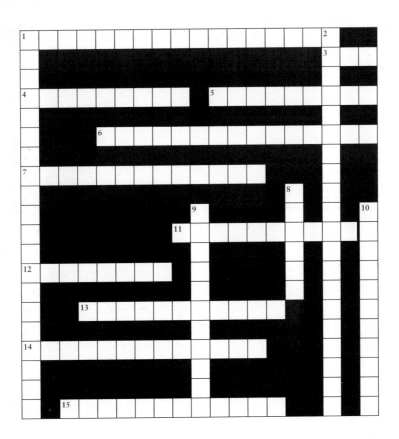

Clues across

1. A government organization responsible for the day to day running of a nationalised industry. One also runs the BBC (6, 11)
3. Short for a yearly event at which shareholders vote on important company issues (1,1,1)
4. Business owners responsible for debts have this. It can be limited or unlimited (9)
5. You can buy the right to use the name and sell the products of this type of company in return for a fee and a share of your profits (8)
6. Do not disturb this business associate who owns part of a business alliance but plays no active part in running it (8,7)
7. These are levied on the price of goods and services to raise money for the central government (8,5)
11. One person owns this business (4,6)
12. A payment to shareholders from company profits (8)

13. This type of business ownership is popular among professions and most are owned by between 2 and 20 people (11)
14. This process involves private sector organizations taking over the provision of goods and services from public sector organizations (13)
15. A person who takes the risk to start up and run a business organization (12)

Clues down

1. A state owned industry (12,8)
8. A public sector non-government organization in which managers are able to make their own day to day business decisions (1,1,1,1,1)
9. A business organization owned by its members, who could be its workers or customers (11)
10. A person who owns part of a limited company (11)

1 What is the main role of the managing director of a company?
   A managing a particular department
   B marketing products and winning sales
   C long-term planning
   D controlling budgets for all departments

2 What is the most likely main purpose of a sole trader grocery?
   A get well known among customers
   B sell the best quality groceries
   C make a profit for owner
   D sell as many groceries as possible

3 What is the main purpose of a government-owned organization?
   A to provide a service to the public
   B to grow as quickly as possible
   C to provide competition for private firms
   D to make as much profit as possible

4 In which type of organization does the owner or owners have unlimited liability?
   A sole trader
   B private limited company
   C public limited company
   D franchise

5 A limited company is owned by:
   A directors
   B a public corporation
   C the Government
   D shareholders?

6 The maximum number of partners there can be in an ordinary partnership is
   A 2
   B 11
   C unlimited
   D 20?

7 A business where a member of the public can buy the right to use another firms name and products is known as a
   A charity
   B co-operative
   C sole trader
   D franchise?

8 Services like the fire service, police and ambulances are provided for everyone. These services are paid for by
   A sales revenues
   B sponsorship by industry
   C charitable donations
   D Government?

9 Which of the following organizations is **not** likely to be in the public sector?
   A a sixth-form college
   B a hospital
   C a supermarket
   D an employment service centre

10 In 1996 Ken Webster opened a shop 'Games, Games, Games' selling computer games and machines. By 1997 business was so good that he decided to open another shop. He asked his sister if she would invest her savings in his business and run the new shop as his partner.

   a What is a sole trader?

   b What were the advantages of forming the partnership for Ken?

   In 1998 Ken and his sister decided to expand further by opening a chain of new shops in different towns. To raise the money they needed they formed a private limited company and sold shares in their business to family and friends. By 1999 Games, Games, Games Ltd had 15 shops.

   c What does the word 'limited' refer to in the company name?

   d What percentage of shares should Ken and his sister hold if they want to keep overall control of the company?

   In 2000 Ken decided to franchise their business idea rather than forming a plc in order to expand.

   e What is a Plc?

   f What is a franchise?

   g Suggest and explain two possible reasons why Ken chose to franchise rather than to from a plc.

chapter 7 The business environment

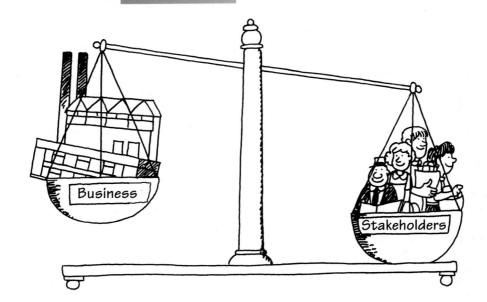

The decisions and actions of **businesses are influenced by many different factors**. In order to be to be successful businesses must respond to these influences. Sometimes this means weighing up different interests – for example, whether to locate business premises near to major customers or near to major suppliers.

All businesses have **stakeholders** – people who have an interest in, or influence on, the business. Stakeholders include:

- customers
- employees (including managers)
- shareholders
- the local community
- the Government

You will need to identify the main interests of the stakeholders in businesses you are investigating and find out about any recent changes in their interests and expectations. You will also need to understand how each type of stakeholder has an influence on businesses you are investigating, and how these businesses are responding to their stakeholders.

For example, stakeholders can influence business location decisions. Businesses **locate** where they believe they will be successful. The reasons for this can include:

- the need to be near suppliers and raw materials
- the need to be near customers
- transport links for supplies and distribution
- the number of people available to work in a particular area and their skills
- the cost of premises
- the need to compete with other businesses in the same activity
- financial help from the Government
- history and tradition

287

Section **7.1**   What is the business environment?

1. Read the articles below then write a few brief sentences to explain how the activities and decisions of each business are being influenced by forces beyond their control.

Plans for 400 out-of town stores beat Government plan

Last month the Environment Secretary announced a virtual end to the building of out-of-town shopping, business parks and housing, which could only be reached by car, in order to protect shops in towns. While in response some grocery chains have cut their building programme, Sainsbury still aims to open 20 new stores a year for the next four years. Safeway has cut its target from 25 new stores but is still aiming for 21 to 23 new superstores a year.

Mr Richard Hyman, Chairman of Verdict, an independent retail consultancy, doubted whether limits on out-of-town shopping by government would be acceptable. The fact is that a very large slice of British retailing has grown up because of the convenience of people being able to use their cars when shopping.

The Daily Telegraph 4.4.1994

2. Collect further evidence of influences on business activities from newspapers, magazines, and TV programmes.

3. Using the articles and others you have collected, sort the different types of influences into the following categories:

- Actions of rival firms
- Actions of consumers
- Actions of employees
- Changes in laws
- Changes in nature

Assemble the articles and your comments into a folder.

Sunday working rights for shop staff

NEW RIGHTS for shop workers to protect them from being compelled to work on Sundays are contained in the new Sunday Trading Act. It gives shop workers the right not be dismissed, made redundant, or subjected to any other detriment for refusing to work on Sundays.

Employment Gazette May 1994

Ferry firm's live aid

The P&O ferry firm threatened yesterday to stop carrying live animals across the Channel for slaughter. Chairman Lord Sterling said the warning followed a review of the opinions of passengers, members of the public and members of staff.

They were all clearly worried about conditions for animals while they were being moved long distances on the continent after leaving the ferries. Under current rules, live animals can be carried for up to 24 hours without a break including for water and this limit is often broken on the continent according to the RSPCA.

The RSPCA and other animal welfare groups have been waging campaigns to highlight alleged cruelty in the live animals export trade. Britain exported 2 million last year.

Daily Mail 30.7.1994

Coca-Cola market share falls below 50%

Coca-Cola's share of the £670 million UK cola market has fallen below 50% for the first time, say figures from Taylor Nelson AGB, the market research group. This was shortly after the arrival of new colas from Mr Richard Branson's Virgin group and supermarket chain Safeway, and six months after Classic Cola was launched by J Sainsbury, the UK's biggest food retailer. These figures highlight the threat posed to Coca-Cola, which has dominated the market since its UK launch in 1921, by this year's new products.

Financial Times 19.12.1994

Brussels finally goes bananas

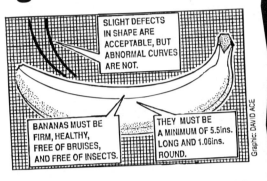

SLIGHT DEFECTS IN SHAPE ARE ACCEPTABLE, BUT ABNORMAL CURVES ARE NOT.

BANANAS MUST BE FIRM, HEALTHY, FREE OF BRUISES, AND FREE OF INSECTS.

THEY MUST BE A MINIMUM OF 5.5ins. LONG AND 1.06ins. ROUND.

Graphic: DAVID ACE

THE ruling from Brussels was straight to the point – bananas should not bend. Or to be precise, they must not bend 'abnormally'. If they do they will be banned from sale from next year.

The latest decree of the European Union (EU) also insists that they must be a minimum of 5.5 inches long and 1.06 inches round. They have to be firm, healthy, practically free of bruises, and as free from insects as possible, they say.

EU-wide standards were needed, it has been argued, to improve the quality of bananas on sale in the shops, and to help traders who order their fruit by telephone.

Daily Mail 21.9.1994

Storms and quakes hurt RSA

Royal and SunAlliance the accident prone insurer, yesterday admitted that earthquakes and hurricanes may have cost it £42 million in the third quarter of this year. The three months to September 30 had brought damage claims from earthquakes in Turkey and Taiwan, Hurricane Floyd in the US and Bahamas, and Typhoon York in Hong Kong.

The Times, 12.10.1999

Organic food is 'healthy option'

Organic food is more popular than ever with one third of Britons buying natural products in the past three months. New research by the Soil Association found that most consumers had turned to organic products because they believed they were the safest and healthiest option. The rise in popularity of natural produce was especially evident in the baby food sector, where one fifth of products sold were organic. A third of babies now eat some organic food in their first year of life. The association said retailers had responded well to growing demands by expanding their ranges of organic foods.

Metro 12.10.1999

FORD PLANT HIT BY PAY AND DISCIPLINE DISPUTES

More than 400 tool-makers at Ford's main Dagenham plant in Essex went on strike yesterday in a dispute over pay parity. At the same time a group of paint-shop workers staged an unofficial walkout after a colleague was disciplined.

The tool-makers are trying to resolve a long-standing dispute over a weekly allowance of up to £75, which is paid to their counterparts at other Ford plants but not to them.

Union negotiators are also seeking a reduction in weekly working hours from 39 to 37, to bring them more in line with Ford's other European plants.

The toolmakers' action is unlikely to have much impact on production at Dagenham, which has already been reduced to operating four days a week to match demand.

The Guardian, 10.11.1999

It has been said that 'business is war'. This means that being in business involves competing with other firms to win a share of their sales and profits, while at the same time trying to stop other firms taking away your own customers and profits. As in a real war, the battlefield is always changing, as armies advance or retreat and new tactics and offensives are planned and carried out. The side that is best able to plan for and cope with all these changes will win.

In business, the enemies are rival firms, and the battlefield is the environment in which businesses operate. The decisions and activities carried out within a business will be influenced by changes taking place in this 'business environment'. A business that ignores these changes will not be successful and in some cases could be breaking the law and be forced to close down.

▼ *The business environment*

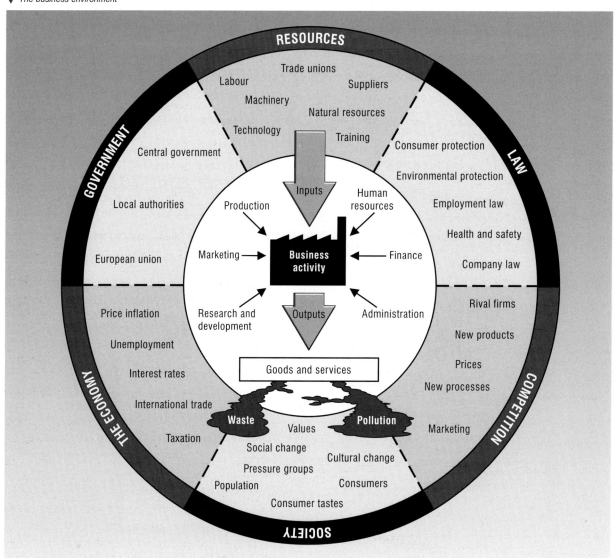

The business environment is influenced by:

● changes in the weather and the **natural environment**

● the actions of rival firms introducing new products, prices and advertising campaigns in the **competitive environment**

● changes in the attitudes, expectations and purchasing decisions of consumers determine the **social environment** in which businesses operate

● changes in laws and other controls by central and local government determine the **economic, regulatory and legal environment** that affects business

● the skills, actions and expectations of employees, shareholders and financiers in the **internal environment** of a business

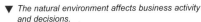

▼ *The natural environment affects business activity and decisions.*

COKE MACHINES WILL CHARGE MORE IF IT'S HOT

Coca-Cola has admitted it is planning to create a vending machine which will automatically increase the price of cold drinks during hot weather. The scheme is being designed to reconcile supply with consumer demand by raising prices when demand increases during hot periods.

"Coca-Cola is a product whose utility varies from moment to moment' said Doug Ivester, chairman of the US soft drinks giant. 'In a summer sports championships, when people meet in a stadium to enjoy themselves, the satisfaction a person gets from a chilled Coca-Cola is very high. So it is fair it should be more expensive. The machine will simply make this process automatic".

Whether the public think it is fair remains to be seen.

Evening Standard, 29.10.1999

The natural environment

The physical or natural environment will always have a great impact on the way in which businesses operate. Changes in the weather can affect crops, which will affect the price of the raw materials for a great many food manufacturers. For example, a drought can result in a poor harvest which will force up the price of wheat. The weather can also have an affect on consumers' buying habits, for example, with spending on clothes and holidays following changes in the seasons.

Fierce storms, flooding, and earthquakes can cause a lot of damage, and firms must ensure they have adequate insurance cover. The natural environment will also affect where some businesses locate.

In recent years people have also become aware that business activity can affect the natural environment. Atmospheric pollution from burning oil, coal, and petrol has caused acid rain which has destroyed forests and killed fish. Chemicals and other sewage dumped at sea has caused disease in marine animals.

The competitive environment

It would be easy to create a successful firm if being in business simply involved supplying a product that people want and are willing to pay for. But running a business is much harder than this, because other firms are always trying to take sales away from you by introducing their own new and improved products and marketing strategies.

Successful firms not only have to provide what the customer wants and will pay for, they also have to do it better than the competition. This means firms need to undertake regular market research in order to keep up to date with the wants of their customers and the actions of their rival firms, and be prepared to continuously change and update their products (see chapter 9).

Portfolio Activity 7.2

Pools firm Vernons prepares to write off £100m

THE NATIONAL Lottery has given football pools firms a £100-million kicking.

Ladbroke boss Peter George now accepts that the once-prized Vernons name could now be worthless and is writing off its £100 million value.

Ladbroke reckons Vernons' takings could be down by as much as £30 million from last year's £174 million. It is already saving cash by cutting 95 jobs at the firm's Liverpool HQ. And it hopes that bigger prizes and TV ads will help pull in more punters.

Daily Mirror 9.3.1995

1. What does the article suggest has happened to the market share of football pools companies in the market for betting and gambling, and why this has happened?

2. Suggest how the owners of Vernons pools plan to compete with the National Lottery. What other marketing communication methods and product developments could they use? Give reasons for your recommendations.

3. Investigate competition in a market for a good or service of your choice. Write a report which describes:

- The major firms in the market

- How they compete on prices

- How they compete by other means, for example, on packaging, brand image, quality, etc.

- How effective their means of competing are

- Other strategies firms might use to try to expand their market shares and the total size of the market

Include in your report any examples of marketing materials used by the firms to promote their products.

▼ *Price competition*

▼ *Non-price competition*

Competition between rival firms for the purchases of consumers can take many forms. **Price competition** involves competing to offer the consumer the best price for a product. This can include cutting prices, holding sales, offering discounts, and other special offers such as 'two for the price of one' promotions.

Firms can also compete on aspects other than price, for example, by trying to outdo each other on product quality and special product features, and also through advertising and other promotional strategies (see chapter 4). These are all forms of **non-price competition**.

The social environment

The social environment is people. People are consumers, and through their spending decisions they will determine the success or failure of many business organizations. Apart from their level of income, the spending decisions of individuals will be determined by their values, beliefs, and attitudes (see chapter 5).

By making choices on which products to buy, people have a major influence on what firms produce. In the end, firms must listen to what their customers want, or they will be replaced by other firms who do.

In recent years consumers have become more health-conscious, and more concerned about the environment and animal rights. For example, many people now prefer to buy from firms that promote a more caring image towards the environment and animals rights, like The Body Shop and the Co-operative Bank.

Consumers' views can be influenced by pressure groups who are themselves just groups of concerned consumers. These can be groups fighting local issues such as the building of a new road through woodland, or international groups such as Greenpeace fighting global issues such as cruelty to animals and pollution.

The economic, regulatory and legal environment

The actions, policies and laws of local and central government in the UK and the government of the European Union can have a major impact on businesses.

EU and UK governments have passed a number of laws and regulations which aim to protect consumers, workers and the environment from the possibility of being mislead or mistreated by businesses. The owners of firms found to be breaking these laws could be fined heavily or even imprisoned. Conforming with laws and regulations can raise business costs.

Government economic policy aims to create economic conditions in which businesses can prosper by keeping price inflation low and stable, stimulating consumer demand and encouraging employment. However, the actions governments take to achieve these conditions can impact significantly on business. For example, to control inflation in the UK the Government may raise taxes and interest rates. Raising taxes on business profits will reduce after tax profits. Raising taxes on peoples incomes will reduce the amount of money they have to spend on goods and services . Raising interest rates will raise costs for businesses repaying bank and mortgage loans (see chapter 8).

The Government collects taxes to pay for many of the goods and services it provides, many of which are of direct benefit to business. For example, the Government has used tax revenues to build roads, schools and hospitals (see chapter 6). Businesses rely on having an educated and healthy workforce, and good transport links (see chapter 5).

The internal business environment

The ability of a business to survive changes in its external environment, prosper and achieve its business aims will depend very much on its workers, managers and the people and other firms who provide the business with finance. The skills and attitudes of employees, including the quality of management and the confidence investors have in the business will affect the performance of the business. For example, if employees think they are being treated unfairly by the business, they may take disruptive actions which can raise costs and lose the business custom. If the people who finance the business lose confidence in the ability of managers to take decisions that will improve sales and profits, then they may replace the managers or withdraw their financial help.

In the following section we will study in more detail all the different aspects of the business environment and how they can affect businesses.

Section **7.2** **Business stakeholders**

What is a stakeholder?

All businesses have **stakeholders** – that is, people or other organizations who have an interest in or influence on the actions and performance of business. Stakeholders in business include:

- **consumers**
- **employees (including managers)**
- **shareholders (and other providers of business finance)**
- **local communities**
- **government**

The wants of consumers dictate to businesses what to produce and at what price. Rising consumer demand can benefit business. Falling consumer demand can result in falling sales, profits and possibly closure of many businesses.

Employees provide their labour and skills to produce the goods and services consumer want and therefore help a business achieve its aims (see chapter 1). However, finding and recruiting the right workers can be expensive (see chapter 3). Workers also demand good working conditions and wages. Employee demands for higher wages increase business costs and reduce profits for the business owners. Workers may even go on strike if they cannot obtain the working conditions and wages they want.

Stakeholders also include people and organizations who provide businesses with the finance they need to start-up and pay for day-to-day business costs, such as rents and business rates, wages and the cost of materials (see chapter 8). A business may borrow money from a bank or building society. These financial organizations will want to make sure the businesses they lend to will be successful and run well by their managers so that they will be able to afford to repay their loans. If a business cannot repay a loan it may have to sell off its stocks of finished goods and materials, machinery and premises to do so. This could mean the business is unable to continue. Shareholders are the owners of limited companies (see chapter 6). They will want to make sure business managers are making profits so that they will earn a return on the money they have invested in their shares. Shareholders will often vote on who they want to manage the businesses they own and how they should be managed.

People who live in local communities and the national community also have an interest in the activity of firms, because they expect businesses to produce their goods and services without damaging the environment and the health and well-being of people nearby.

Finally, the Government is an important stakeholder in business because it relies on the activities of businesses to create jobs, incomes and economic prosperity for the country. The Government also has an interest in business because it relies on them to produce the tax revenue with which it pays for the schools, hospitals and other provisions of the public sector. The Government also affects business through the policies it uses to control price inflation and employment in the UK economy.

In order to be successful, businesses need to identify who their main stakeholders are and then act in ways which balance the needs of the various stakeholders involved. For example, a local community may want local firms to produce as quietly and with as little pollution as possible, whilst shareholders may wish the firm to spend as little money as possible on pollution control in order to maximise profits. Sometimes business organizations are forced by law to account for the needs of particular stakeholders. For example, the government has passed a range of anti-pollution laws in order to prevent businesses from damaging local and global environments, and employment laws to protect the rights of workers.

Consumers as stakeholders

Who are consumers?

People who want and use goods and services are called **consumers** (see chapter 1). Consumers of products can be individuals, other firms, or even governments.

For example, individuals are likely to want bread, houses, cars, DVD players, clothes, haircuts and other personal goods and services. Firms will want machinery and materials to be able to produce other goods and services. Local and central government will also want machinery and equipment such as computers, fire engines, tanks and street lamps to provide their public services (see chapter 1). Many goods and services produced in the UK are also sold to households, firms and governments overseas as exports.

How consumers influence business

Quick-shop drivers fuel garage boom

BRITISH shoppers now spend £31 billion a year in 'convenience shopping' in what is seen as a dramatic change in shopping habits.

The corner shop still attracts the majority of the business, 38 per cent, while high street grocers have 32 per cent, supermarkets 19 per cent, and specialist chains 11 per cent. Petrol station forecourts now have 6 per cent. The forecourt business – now worth £2 billion a year – has doubled in the last two years.

Shell is investing £350 million in convenience shopping on its forecourts, with facilities in a quarter of its sites by the end of 1994.

Daily Mail 15.11.1994

Best-dressed salads put cream in peril

The nation's best-selling salad cream could be scrapped, with foreign holidays being blamed for a drop in demand.

Heinz is reviewing the future of its product, which it introduced in 1914. Mayonnaise, olive oil and vinaigrette have all become more popular on salads and cold meat over the past 20 years as British tastebuds have adjusted to a wider range of dressings.

A spokesman said: "Heinz is considering whether it will become extinct or whether to invest in the product. It's looking at the long-term future. One option would be raising the price. There is a committed and loyal following.'

The British spent $143 million on salad dressing last year. About £24 million of this was on Heinz salad cream at 57p for a 285g bottle.

The Times 11.10.1999

The articles above show just how important consumers are to the success of a business. Consumer demand is able to influence the following business decisions:

- The type of goods and services produced
- The quantities produced
- The price at which goods and services are sold
- How goods and services are produced

Consumers create demand

Consumers create demand for goods and services. **Consumer demand** refers to the willingness of consumers to buy goods and services. However, firms must be sure that consumers have the money to pay for their products. That is, consumers must have **purchasing power**.

Consumers with enough money to buy the goods and services they want have **effective consumer demand**. This means that firms are likely to meet their demands for goods and services. Without effective consumer demand, firms would be unable to sell goods and services to make a profit. Workers would not be required to make goods and services, and many people would be unemployed.

Strong or weak demand?

If sales for a particular good or service are rising and remain high, this indicates that consumer demand is strong. When demand is strong, consumers may be willing to pay a higher price to obtain the goods and services they want. Firms will also want to expand production to meet the demand, because they are likely to earn more sales revenue and profit. Because of the potential for profit, new firms may start up to produce the goods and services that are in strong demand.

If, however, consumer demand for a good or service is weak, sales will be low and probably falling. Prices may have to fall to tempt consumers to buy up stocks of finished goods and to use services. When demand for a good or service is low, there is only room for a few firms to produce all that consumers want. Some firms may be forced to cut production. Others may close down or switch to the production of goods and services for which demand is rising or strong.

Strong demand

Weak demand

Consumers stimulate the supply of goods and services

Effective demand encourages firms to produce goods and services in the hope of earning a profit. Video recorders are only produced by firms because consumers want them and are willing to pay a price that yields a profit for the manufacturers. Similarly, chickens are farmed to produce eggs because people want to eat them and are willing and able to pay for them at a price that gives farmers a profit.

The Government is the largest single consumer in the UK, spending over £350 billion in 1999 alone on everything from supplies of paper to the building of new hospitals and motorways. Private sector firms are willing to supply anything from supplies of paper to major construction services because the UK government is willing and able to pay for them.

Changes in consumer demand

Because consumers stimulate a supply of goods and services through their spending decisions, it follows that changes in demand can affect the production decisions of firms.

- An **increase in demand** for a particular good will provide firms with an incentive to increase their production. If more people want a product, firms can sell more and earn more profit. For example, there has recently been an increase in demand for herbal drinks. Consider the impact this has on business:

  - Firms that produce herbal drinks experience an increase in their sales revenues

  - Stocks of herbal drinks fall as demand increases

  - Producers of herbal drinks expand their output. To do this, they need more herbs and other ingredients, plus more cans, bottles, and paper for labels. They may also need to buy more machinery and hire more workers

  - Firms that supply the herbs and other materials experience an increase in orders. At first they supply these orders from stock, but as stocks run out, they too must expand their output to meet the increased demand.

- A **fall in demand** means consumers buy less goods and services. As firms' sales revenues fall, stocks build up and production has to be cut. For example, many smaller video rental shops have closed down in recent years because more people are now going to the cinema, buying films on video, or paying for film channels on satellite and cable TV. The video rental market is now dominated by Blockbuster, which has had to expand into video sales and computer game rentals in order to keep attracting consumers.

Changes in demand for goods and services occur for many reasons (see chapter 5). The main reasons are changes in the amount of money consumers have available to spend over time, and changes in consumer attitudes, tastes and wants. As incomes rise, people have more money to spend on all goods and services. However, consumers may only increase their spending on some goods and services as their tastes and attitudes change. For example, people in the UK are now buying more wine than beer each year, the reverse was true in the past. Attendances at the opera and theatre are up, while attendances at football matches are down.

Changes in demand for some goods and services may also occur because of concerns over the way they are produced. For example, demand for organic food products has increased because of health fears over the use of chemicals and drugs in the production of crops and meats. Farmers may have to change the way they produce food products in order to survive. Similarly, there has been an increase in demand for 'cruelty-free' products such as cosmetics that have not been tested on animals. Firms that continue to test their products on animals may suffer falling sales. The spending decisions of consumers can, therefore, affect the way goods and services are produced.

From consumers to customers

Business is about turning consumers into customers. Private sector organizations will only provide the goods and services consumers want if they are willing and able to pay for them. Paying customers provide firms with revenue to pay for their costs of production. Any sales revenue over and above costs is profit (see chapter 8).

More and more business organizations today are adopting a 'customer focus'. This means that they concentrate their activities on attracting and keeping customers, by finding out what consumers want and providing these products, in the amounts they want, when they want them, and at prices they are willing to pay. Customers expect accurate product information, high standards of service and quality and reasonable prices. However, some firms may be tempted to mislead customers or cut corners in order to make a bigger profit and more quickly.

BUSINESS ORGANIZATIONS NEED CUSTOMERS BECAUSE THEY:
1 PROVIDE INCOME
2 PROVIDE REPEAT BUSINESS
3 CONTRIBUTE TO PROFIT
4 ARE AN IMPORTANT SOURCE OF INFORMATION
5 ENSURE THE SURVIVAL OF THE BUSINESS

So why are customers so important to business?

1. Customers provide income

Every firm needs a flow of income in order to buy machinery and materials, pay wages, rent, rates, and other business expenses, so that it can continue in production.

Customers provide firms with income, or revenue, by purchasing their goods and services. The amount of income a firm is able to earn will depend on the number of customers it has, and how much they spend. If enough customers buy enough of the product, there may be a surplus of income, or profit, left over after the firm has paid out all its costs (see chapter 8).

2. Firms need the repeat business of customers

Many organizations are only able to earn regular income because of repeat business from their customers. For example, it would be of little use to a manufacturer of breakfast cereal if customers bought their product only once and then went off it. Unless there are repeat sales, the cereal manufacturer will not earn enough income to survive in business.

If customers are happy with the good or service they have purchased, they are more likely to buy the same product again, whether it is a packet of breakfast cereal or a make of car or television set. A happy customer is also likely to recommend products and organizations to family and friends to use. In this way, existing customers can help attract new ones.

The loyalty of the regular customer is, therefore, very important in business. Some firms even offer regular customers special privileges in order not to lose them, such as bonus offers, special discount cards, or exclusive shopping evenings.

3. Customers contribute to profit

Most private sector organizations and some public sector organizations, such as the Post Office, are run to make a profit. Profit is calculated as the difference between the total revenues and total costs of a business.

If customers are willing to pay more for a particular good or service than it cost to make, they will be providing the firm with a contribution to total profit. Thus, usually the more customers a business has, and the more it sells, the more profit it will make.

Profit is important in business because, as well as providing a return for the business owners, it provides funds for business expansion, or for investing in new, more efficient, machinery (see chapter 8).

4. Customers provide a source of market research information

Firms can only survive by making what their customers want – and they will only know what customers want by asking them and by being in regular contact with them.

Finding out about consumer wants is called **market research** (see chapter 2). Market research involves gathering information on customer wants from surveys and sales figures. Careful analysis of the results of surveys and sales figures can help a firm to develop products and promotions which will satisfy their wants, attract more customers, and increase the number of possible sales.

5. Customers ensure the survival of the business

Without customers an organization cannot survive in business. Customers provide income and profit for a business. Without this, there is no financial reason or incentive to be in business.

Different businesses can survive with different numbers of customers. A sole-trader decorating business may survive with steady work from, say, around 50-100 people per year. Others would be forced to close down long before customer numbers became so low.

▼ The Sainsbury's Saver Card offers discounts for regular customers.

Simply by looking at sales figures over time, a firm can discover important information about its customers. For example:

● What they want to buy

● What they do not want to buy

● Where they prefer to buy

● The product features they like

● The prices they are willing to pay

● The frequency of their purchases

● Their likes and dislikes

● How they respond to advertising and special promotions

Clubs tackled over cost of kit

Football fans and their parents can today look forward to cheaper replica kits after manufacturers and top clubs were criticised by the principal consumer watchdog for inflating prices. They could face significant fines if they continue to do so.

After a two and a half year enquiry, Mr Bridgeman – the Director General of the Office of Fair Trading – found that manufacturers illegally threatened to withhold supplies if retailers sold cut price kits. Although he declined to name them, he said that there was 'conclusive' evidence that some premiership sides have encouraged manufacturers to block discount pricing.

At present, adult fans pay an average of £40 for an adult replica shirt, and £55 for a full kit of shirt, shorts and socks. Children's outfits tend to be only £5 and £10 cheaper. Shop prices could be up to five or six times the cost of manufacture.

Mr Bridgeman announced that the Football Association and English premier League clubs had prevented manufacturers from stopping suppliers from offering discounts in the £210 million a year replica kit market.

The announcement was welcomed by football supporters after years of complaints that clubs were taking advantage of the loyalty of fans. Parents have long complained about the "updating" of strips which instantly renders last season's kit unfashionable and redundant.

Mr Bridgeman said that "Retailers are now free to cut their prices and I hope that we will soon see a variety of discounts!"

The Times 7.8.1999

1. What evidence is there from the article that manufacturers of football kits are making decisions which may conflict with the interests of their customers? Why do you think they have acted in this way?

2. In what ways do consumers have a 'stake' or interest in how the football kit manufacturers and football clubs act?

3. What action has the UK Government taken to prevent football clubs and kit manufacturers acting against the interests of consumers. Why do you think the government in the UK has done this?

Government protection for consumers

Because most private sector firms are in business to make profits, some may be tempted to mislead their customers, for example, by making exaggerated claims about their products to increase sales or by overcharging them. To prevent firms behaving in ways that are against the best interests of their customers, the UK government has created **consumer protection laws,** and organizations to enforce them, such as local **Trading Standards Offices** and the **Office of Fair Trading.**

Consumer protection laws make it an offence to:

● supply a good or service which is not satisfactory condition or of poor quality

● give false written or spoken descriptions of goods and services

- mislead consumers about the true price they will pay for a good or service, by excluding any hidden charges, interest charges or value added tax

- make false statements about price reductions, for example, by suggesting the sale price of a product is 50% off the recommended price when it is not

- to sell or possess goods for sale which are unsafe

- to give customers short weights or measures

- to demand payment for goods delivered to customers who did not want them

- prepare and sell food in unhygienic conditions, or with harmful ingredients

- not to offer customer refunds, even if they cannot produce a receipt

- to restrict competition, for example, if a group of firms agree to all charge the same high price or to work together to force new rivals out of business

In addition, some industries have developed their own codes of good practice for their member firms to follow. Examples include, the Federation of Master Builders and the Association of British Travel Agents (ABTA). Similarly, the Advertising Standards Authority helps regulate advertising and promotions. Consumers can appeal to these organisations if they feel they have been mistreated or misinformed by particular organizations.

Employees as stakeholders

Employees are key stakeholders in business. They depend for their livelihoods on the incomes they earn from work and also upon the prospects available to them for career progression. The majority of successful firms recognise the importance of their staff, and these firms spend a great deal of time and effort in training and developing their workforce and improving their working conditions so that their employees are happy and motivated at work (see chapter 3).

Wages vs profit?

However, firms are also responsible to their owners for making profits. In order to make profits, businesses must keep their costs low and, on average, wages account for around 70% of total business costs. Cutting wage costs can increase profits significantly. This can mean some firms may resist pay rises and may reduce the size of their workforces, by replacing workers with new technology or by expecting their remaining workers to work harder and for longer. Alternatively some businesses could shut down and move to another part of the world where workers are cheaper to employ. This will result in workers being made unemployed in the UK.

Sometimes firms show a different level of loyalty and care towards employees located in different parts of the world. The articles below illustrate the choices some firms have made when balancing the needs of their employees against the interests of their owners.

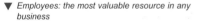
▼ *Employees: the most valuable resource in any business*

Shell's Shock for London

The World economic crisis dealt London a savage blow today with a shock announcement that Shell is to close its headquarters with the possible loss of up to 2,000 jobs.

Most of those likely to be affected work in information technology, marketing, planning and accounting. Some were expected to be found jobs elsewhere in Shell but a number of redundancies were thought inevitable.

Shells' oil exploration arm is also transferring jobs out of London to Aberdeen where its operational headquarters are located. Shell Expo's managing director Malcolm Brinded said moving out of the capital would achieve 'significant cost savings' though he acknowledged that the announcement would be unsettling for staff.

The news came hard on the heels of a spate of major closures and redundancies, including those at the Fujitsu factory in the Prime Minister's Sedgefield constituency and the loss of more than 1,000 defence jobs at Vickers.

Evening Standard 18.9.1998

Top Shops use Europe's 'gulag labour'

British high street retailers are using factories in eastern Europe where female workers are humiliated with strip searches and others where employees are paid so little that they have to scavenge for food.

Marks and Spencer, C & A, Debenhams and Laura Ashley are among companies using factories where workers are fainting at their machines or developing chronic health conditions that they cannot afford to treat.

In an extensive four week investigation, undercover reporters located and visited eight textile factories which produce goods for British Stores in Latvia, Bulgaria and Romania —countries which Western buyers privately refer to as "gulag Europe". Wages of 20p an hour are so low in some of the decrepit former communist textile plants that labourers are forced to live in slums without running water or modern sanitation.

The Sunday Times 26.9.1999

Recruiting and keeping good workers can be expensive, but good workers can mean higher output, more sales and more profits in the long run. So often the additional costs of higher wages, longer holidays, better pension schemes and staff facilities to attract and retain good workers is worthwhile.

Raising the productivity of employees

Modern organisations are always looking for ways they can improve **productivity** (see chapter 2). Increasing productivity is about raising output and product quality without increasing costs by the same amount. If more can be produced with the same or fewer numbers of employees, machinery and materials, then productivity will have increased and the cost of each unit produced will be lower.

Businesses will wish to have the most productive workforce they can. A firm can raise the level of skill and productivity of its workforce through a combination of the following:

- training workers to improve their existing skills and learn new skills

- rewarding increased productivity with performance related pay and other bonus payments

- encouraging employees to buy shares in their organisation. Improved productivity will help to raise profits and pay higher dividends on their shares (see chapter 8). In this way workers will directly benefit from their own efforts

- improving job satisfaction, for example, by improving working conditions (see chapter 3), making jobs more interesting, involving workers in business decisions and giving regular feedback on their performance

- introducing new production processes and working arrangements designed to reduce waste, improve quality and increase output, such as computer aided design and manufacturing (see chapter 5)

- replacing old machinery and equipment with new, more efficient machines and tools

All these things will tend to raise the cost of employing workers in the short run. However, if productivity improves, production costs will fall and profits will tend to rise. Lower costs can be passed onto consumers as lower prices in an attempt to boost sales. If consumer demand rises then demand for employees may also rise.

Empowerment and **team working** became popular terms in business in the 1990s. Empowerment refers to the motivation of staff in lower grades by allowing them to contribute to decision making in organizations. This can be as simple as sales staff in McDonald's being allowed to greet and thank customers in their own way rather than having to use standard phrases recommended by the senior managers. In other firms, teams have been empowered with the responsibility to organize their own work. Worker representatives may even be allowed to attend board meetings to discuss company plans and policies with all the other directors.

COMPANIES FIND IT'S GOOD TO TALK

If you tell people what is going on you are more likely to retain staff. This is without doubt according to companies like AA Insurance.

AA's communications system won the Cranfield School of Management and Human Resources award for excellence. Trieve Nicholas, sales channel development manager says "In the past couple of years productivity, customer satisfaction and employee satisfaction improved greatly. Independent surveys show that morale has increased significantly and our staff retention is very good'.

Colin Kent, chief executive of Key Communications, helps companies to use new communications technology effectively. He says "Failure to communicate change and to build a teamworking environment is costing companies small fortunes in lost business as staff take less interest and pride in their work. In one company where we carried out a detailed audit, £800,000 was being spent on recruitment and less than £500,000 on listening to and understanding the needs of staff – though more than £10 m was being spent on external communications'.

The Sunday Times 13.9.1998

Grouping employees in teams and giving them responsibility for organizing their work can improve their sense of pride in the goods and services they produce. Team members will work together to improve their work and may often compete against other teams to be the best. Teams can also form **quality circles** which meet regularly to discuss how to improve their work and solve work-related problems.

Team working has also allowed many organizations to implement **total quality management (TQM)**. The aim of TQM is to focus the attention of all staff on the quality of what they do at every stage in the production process. This is achieved by encouraging staff to believe that they are all working for the customer, even those staff who provide other employees with services. So for example, an office engineer would treat a worker with a faulty computer as a valued customer rather than as a nuisance, even though both work for the same firm.

Working arrangements

Working arrangements of different employees in different organizations and jobs will vary. Many organizations have introduced more flexible working arrangements which allow them to match staffing levels more easily to changes in consumer demand for their products, and to reduce their business costs. For example, a growing number of firms are:

- employing more people on a part-time, temporary and casual basis instead of on permanent full-time contracts. If all employees were on permanent contracts, cutting the number of staff employed during periods of low or falling consumer demand would lead to high redundancy payments for a firm. Staff who are employed on short term contracts for less than two years are not entitled to any redundancy payments from their employers

- replacing fixed hours of work by shift-work and flexitime so that organizations can remain in production longer or stay open later to serve customers

- introducing new communications technology. This allows more people to work from home and keep in touch with their offices via electronic mail and video phones (see chapter 4). This is called **teleworking.** It also allows organisations to become flatter with less layers of management because employees are now able to keep in regular contact with senior managers using new telecommunications equipment

- introducing teamworking and giving teams the responsibility of taking their own decisions on how their work should be organized.

▼ *Seasonal workers*

▼ *Temps*

▼ *Casual workers*

conflict of interest: one-day strikes by underground train ...vers in 1998 lost revenue for London Underground and ...rupted the journeys of many thousands of commuters as ...y struggled to find alternative routes to work.

A business that fails to increase productivity, improve product quality and introduce modern technology is unlikely to stay competitive against rival firms and products. However, some employees will dislike changes in their working arrangements and the introduction of new technology. If workers feel their jobs are threatened by new machinery and changes in working arrangements they may take actions to disrupt their businesses. This can mean lost output, lost sales and higher costs for the businesses affected. For example, workers may vote to go on strike so that the business has to close down until the dispute is settled (see chapter 3). In this way the interests of employees conflict with those of the business owners and also customers. To avoid industrial actions employers will often discuss any changes they want to make with their employees so that they can agree reforms which are acceptable to both sides. For example, a cut in the size of the workforce may be agreed only if redundancies are voluntary and redundancy payments are increased. Again, this will have the impact of increasing business costs but will be cheaper than a long strike by employees.

Government protection for employees

Some businesses may be tempted to exploit their workers in order to keep their costs down and make bigger profits. For example, a business may sack women who are intending to leave to have babies instead of letting them have maternity leave, or may force employees to work overtime or in unsafe conditions. For these reasons, UK and European Union governments have introduced **employment laws** to protect the rights of workers to fair treatment, and health and safety regulations for workplaces. These laws and regulations give employees legal rights to:

- a healthy and safe working environment
- compensation for industrial injury or redundancy
- equal treatment regardless of sex, race, religion, or disability
- maternity pay and leave for women
- equal pay for work of equal value for men and women
- equal treatment for full-time and part-time workers
- a maximum working week of 48 hours
- itemized pay statements
- rest periods and a minimum of four weeks paid holiday each year
- freedom to join trade unions and take strike action
- written terms and conditions of employment
- return to work after sickness or pregnancy
- a national minimum wage in 1999–2000 of £3.00 per hour for any employee over 18 years of age, and £3.60 for any employee over 21 years of age

These rights and others are discussed in detail in chapter 3. Some employers argue that too many laws and regulations on employment raise business costs and, therefore, reduces the demand for labour. As a result fewer people are employed. Higher business costs may also be passed on to consumers in higher product prices.

In addition, the Government is also a stakeholder in business because it has an interest in the total level of employment in the UK. Lower unemployment means more people in work and more output, and less government spending on benefits for the unemployed. For these reasons, the UK Government provides financial help and assistance to many firms to help create new job opportunities and to provide training for workers in new skills (see chapter 7).

Portfolio Activity 7.4

Read the articles below. From them explain the various impacts employees and employment laws can have on businesses, and suggest how the interests of employees may conflict with those of business owners.

Sparks pay joy

Electricians yesterday won a pay rise of up to 30% over the next two years. The deal between the Amalgamated Electrical and Engineering Union and the Electrical Contracting Association, will boost basic pay by up to £70 a week. Unions hope the deal incorporating travel allowances into pay, will increase productivity and halt wildcat strikes which plague projects such as London's Jubilee Line extension and the Millennium Done. Some workers there already earn £1,200 a week.

The Sun 3.10.1999

Row over 13-week parental leave plan

Proposals to give working parents the right to 13 weeks unpaid leave so that they can care for their children have sparked a furious row. Business leaders warned the move would be hugely disruptive, especially to smaller firms, while unions warmly welcomed the proposals. Trade and Industry Secretary Steven Byers said a million parents would benefit from a new 'family friendly' package of measures being introduced later this year under a European Directive.

Metro 5.8.1999

TUC welcomes expansion of employee rights

Five new employee rights came into force today designed to improve protection for individual employees. Their arrival was welcomed by John Monks, general secretary of the Trades Union Congress, who said they would have no effect on the majority of employers but only those who bullied or exploited their workforce.

However, solicitors warned they could lead to a large increase in litigation and increased pressure on employers over cases of unfair dismissal compensation, with the maximum award entitlement before an employment tribunal rising from £12,000 to £50,000. Many law firms believe that the changes will lead to higher settlements for many employees who will be able to use the new limit as a bargaining counter in negotiations over severance.

Financial Times 11.6.1999

Shareholders as stakeholders

Shareholders are the owners of limited companies (see chapter 6). Shareholders can be individuals or other organizations, such as pension fund companies and banks. By buying shares in a company they provide that company with finance.

The main concern of shareholders is that their companies are successful and make more profits. Shareholders will benefit in two ways from higher profits. Firstly, they will earn dividends each year on their shareholdings. The more shares a person or organization holds and the more profits their company makes, the more dividends they will receive. Secondly, the more successful their company, the more their shares will be worth, and they will be able to sell their shares for more than they paid for them (see chapter 8).

The divorce of ownership from control in large companies

The owners of large limited companies will not necessarily be the managers of those companies. Instead the owners employ managers, or directors, to run their companies from day to day. This is known as the divorce of ownership from control' (see chapters 2 and 6).

In large companies, owners may only be consulted on big business issues. However, if the owners do not like the way their directors are running their businesses, or because company sales and profits are falling, they may replace their management teams. Where there are many hundreds or thousands of shareholders in a public limited company, that company will hold annual general meetings at which its shareholders can vote on the management team. Shareholders with voting rights can either attend an AGM or vote by post.

Conflicts between managers and owners of companies can often occur. For example, managers may want to spend more on expanding the businesses they control. Shareholders will want the return on their shares from profits to be as big as possible. Spending more on new premises and machinery reduces profits and can land the company in trouble if it expands too much and cannot sell enough to pay its extra costs.

Similarly, the managers of one company may resist being taken over by another because they do not want to lose their jobs. Shareholders in that company may, however, welcome a takeover by another company if it means they can sell their shares at a higher price or will earn more profit.

However, company managers depend on shareholders for their jobs and incomes. In the long run they must make their companies successful and profitable, or they risk losing their jobs. Furthermore, an unsuccessful company will not be able to attract more shareholders to raise more finance.

Worker shareholders

The UK Government and a growing number of businesses are encouraging more workers to buy shares in the companies they work for. Some companies even give their workers shares instead of higher wages. Workers who are also shareholders in the company they work in will be directly concerned that their company makes more profit and so are likely to work harder and keep costs down in order to do so. In this way, conflict between the interests of workers who will push for more wages and holidays and the interests of shareholders who will want more profit, will be reduced.

Portfolio Activity 7.5

NatWest staff pay the price of bid warfare

NatWest Bank yesterday promised to axe a further 1,650 jobs and sell businesses such as its investment arm, Greenwich NatWest, to fund a multi-million pound windfall for shareholders in an attempt to win their backing against Bank of Scotland's £21billion hostile takeover bid. The Bank of Scotland has made a generous offer to NatWest shareholders in a bid to take ownership of their bank.

NatWest also intends to sell Ulster Bank, its fund management business Gartmore, and NatWest Equity Partners. The money raised will add to NatWests existing £1.5 billion cash pile and all of it will be given to its shareholders.

NatWest said it was not as efficient as some of its rivals and its costs were too high. But NatWest claimed that the Bank of Scotland was making unrealistic claims about the costs that could be cut if it took over.

It said it had already started to reduce costs and reshape its business before the Bank of Scotland came along and any savings from the restructuring should benefit NatWest investors. Peter Burt, Chief Executive of Bank of Scotland said NatWest's claims were undermined by "its history of poor performance under the same management team".

Adapted from The Guardian 28.10.1999

1. What is a 'hostile take-over bid' ? (See chapter 5 for help.)

2. What primary business aim do you think the Bank of Scotland has in wanting to take-over NatWest?

3. If the Bank of Scotland were able to take-over NatWest, what would this mean for the directors and senior managers of NatWest Bank?

4. What is NatWest proposing to do in order to stop the Bank of Scotland from taking it over and why?

5. How is NatWest proposing to balance the interests of its workers and its shareholders as stakeholders?

The local community as a stakeholder

Why do we care what businesses do?

Do you live near or visit areas close by to factories, offices, shops, farms, mines and quarries, or an airport? If so, you will have an interest in the actions of the businesses that own or use these facilities. You may be concerned because you, your family or your friends use and enjoy these facilities, are employed at them, or work in other businesses that supply them with goods and services and therefore depend on them for employment and incomes. You may also be concerned about the impact these firms have on the environment.

For example, people who live near large airports are concerned about the increasing number of flights, especially at night, pollution from aviation fuel, and increasing traffic congestion on roads leading to the airports. A decision to expand an airport could also mean knocking down nearby houses and woodland to build new runways and terminals. However, many local people may work at their nearby airport and a decision to expand could create more employment, not just at the airport but in nearby shops and hotels, and on rail and coach services which take people to and from the airport.

But even if you do not live near to business activity, the actions of firms can still affect you. For example, when the oil tanker Exxon Valdez ran aground in Alaska, spilling its cargo of oil into the sea and along the coast, it caused widespread pollution and many fish, birds and marine animals died as a result. Although few people lived along the coast affected, many people all over the world were upset about the level of pollution caused. Similarly, the burning of fossil fuels such as coal, oil and gas in many production processes can cause widespread air pollution and is thought to have contributed to global warming. That is, the activities of firms can be of interest not just to local communities, but also to national and international communities if they have a large impact on the environment.

▼ *The actions of some firms can have widespread impacts of concern to people in many countries*

Green victory over oil explorers

Whales, dolphins and coral reefs in the North Atlantic will benefit from a victory by environmentalists over the Government and the oil industry yesterday.

A High Court Judge ruled that the Government had failed to apply the European Commission's habitat and species directive in awarding licences for oil exploration in the Atlantic frontier.

Lord Melchett, an executive director of Greenpeace, said that the ruling by Judge Maurice Kay meant that Tony Blair had been forced to put conservation before oil exploration.

Green campaigners said that the victory would limit oil exploration and force the Government to survey marine life between 12 and 200 nautical miles from the coast to identify any vulnerable species and designate sites as special conservation areas.

"The decision is a huge victory for whales, dolphins and coral reefs. The Government should learn form this and review whether it can afford to continue to license new oil exploration given the damage that it will cause to marine life and the global climate" he said.

The Times 6.11.1999

Protesters take wind out of clean air claim

Clean air campaigners today challenged a claim by Deputy Prime Minister John Prescott that air pollution in Britain is beginning to decline. They hit out after the Government revealed plans to relax its air quality target for deadly particles which are suspected of causing 8000 deaths a year. The National Society for Clean Air and Environmental Protection accused Mr Prescott of backsliding over plans to clean up air, particularly in London.

Roger Higman of Friends of the Earth said "Mr Prescott is choosing to relax the target for particles rather than take action to get people out of their cars. Thousands of people could die early as a result".

Evening Standard 2.11.1999

Making your concerns known

People can make their concerns about business activities known to firms by writing to them or by refusing to buy their products. For example, in 1991 the Italian fashion giant Benetton was forced to abandon the testing of chemicals on animals after a 10-day boycott of their products by many people all over the world. This was a well-organized international campaign, but many campaigns are local and small. For example, local rail users may group together to protest to their local rail operator about changes to their services. They may also write to their local councils or members of parliament, organize marches and take out adverts in newspapers.

Lobby groups are groups of people with an interest in influencing the actions and decisions of firms and governments. For example, Greenpeace and Friends of the Earth are well-known international lobby groups which aim to protect the environment from pollution, while the World Society for the Protection of Animals campaigns against cruel practices involving animals.

Lobby groups can be very powerful because they can create a great deal of bad publicity and persuade consumers not to buy goods and services. Bad publicity and the threat of falling sales is often enough to persuade some firms to change their decisions and actions.

▼ *The League Against Cruel Sports urged people to lobby the Prime Minister to ban hunting with dogs*

Dear **Mr Blair,**

Thank you for promising to ban hunting. Please do not wait for any more animals to die in the name of sport. Ban hunting as soon as possible.

Yours sincerely,

NAME_____

ADDRESS_____

_____

_____

_____

PLEASE AFFIX STAMP HERE

Rt Hon Tony Blair MP

10 Downing Street

London

SW1A 2AA

League Against Cruel Sports Limited, Sparling House, 83-87 Union Street, London SE1 1SG. Tel: 0171 407 0979, 403 6155.

Public relations

Many firms try to establish and maintain good relationships with the local communities in which they are based because many will depend on local people to work in their firms and as customers. Large firms may get actively involved in their local communities because it is good publicity, for example, by donating money and equipment to local schools and hospitals, or by paying for trees to be planted in local parks. Some will also meet with local community groups and councils regularly to discuss local concerns. Good public relations helps a business win new customers and keep existing ones.

▼ *A good relationship with the local community is good publicity for a business*

Government as a stakeholder

Portfolio Activity 7.6

Read the news articles and headlines below. Use them to suggest why and how the UK Government tries to influence business activity.

Interest rate rise to slow inflation

The Bank of England's monetary policy committee considered raising interest rates more sharply this month in an attempt to keep the lid on price inflation.

Financial Times 18.11.1999

Chancellor on course to beat forecasts

Chancellor Gordon Brown is on course to beat comfortably his latest forecasts for the public finances after receipts of corporation taxes on profits surged to a monthly record. Official figures revealed yesterday fanned speculation that Mr Brown was building a war chest of "surplus cash" that could be used to increase spending and cut taxes.

Financial Times 19.11.1999

Britain has 4m children who live in poverty

More than four million children – one third of all those aged under 18 are living below the poverty line, new research shows. The findings highlight the widening gap between the richest and poorest households in Britain and indicate the scale of the challenge facing the government which has promised to eradicate child poverty within 20 years.

PRESCOTT TO AIR £80BN 10-YEAR TRANSPORT PLAN

John Prescott, the Deputy Prime Minister, will today announce plans to draw up an £80bn 10-year programme of investment in transport. He will signal increased spending on roads, the building of new light rail systems, the renewal of rolling stock and the installation of satellite tracking systems to deliver real time information to bus passengers.

The £80bn planning total includes direct public spending, money from passengers and investment by the private sector. The Deputy Prime Minister also expects to generate funds from congestion charges on motorists on busy roads and future increases in petrol taxes.

New work rules to 'aid family life'

New employment rules based on European Union directives came into force today. Under he new laws maternity leave is to be extended by four weeks to 18. This will benefit an estimated 85,000 women in employment.

Financial Times 13.12.1999

VIDEO GAMES PROBE

Major stores were yesterday accused of operating a cartel to fix the price of video games. Richard Branson's Virgin Megastore chain, HMV and Britain's biggest electronics retailer Dixons are among the giants facing claims of collusion over the cost of PlayStation titles. Yesterday all these stores increased the price of the most popular games such as Driver and Tomb Raider 3. Woolworths will today add £15 to the shelf price of chart titles such as V and Rally 2.

The Office of Fair Trading said the fact that a number of stores had increased the cost of certain games by identical margins on the same day indicated that they were colluding with each other. If an enquiry uncovers evidence of anti-competitive behaviour then the firms will be referred to the High Court where they will have to give assurances that they will not repeat the offence.

Daily Mail 7.7.1999

£15 cut off our electricity bills

ELECTRICITY bills are to be cut by around £15 a year under proposals announced yesterday. About 5 per cent will be shaved off the average bill after industry regulator Ofgem ordered companies to change the way distribution costs are calculated.

Metro, 13.9.1999

Tax on cigarettes up by 20pence

Toyota invest £32m in Rotherham factory

Toyota, the Japanese car group, yesterday announced further inward investment creating 400 jobs at a new components factory in northern England. Toyota, which will get a £1.7m government grant and up to £800,000 from the local authority, will make rubber seals for car doors.

Financial Times, 15.6.1999

MPs warn energy tax is threat to business and the economy

Watchdog in threat to ice cream dominance

The Competition Commission will today lay the ground for an assault on Unilever's dominance of the British ice cream market. The commission will publish a list of measures to open the market to competitors by forcing Wall's, Unilever's ice cream business, to sell off its retail distribution operation.

Financial Times 20.7.1999

Why do governments try to influence business decisions and activities?

The UK Government and the Government of the European Union (EU), have a great deal of influence over business practices. The reasons why governments use their powers to influence business are:

- to reduce price inflation

- to increase national output, employment and wealth

- to make firms more competitive and sell more goods overseas

- to raise taxes to pay for goods and services provided by government, such as law and order, health care, defence, roads, and education

- to control the prices set by some powerful firms, who may be the only suppliers of a particular good or service that people need. For example, the UK Government controls, or regulates, the prices electricity, water and gas companies can charge their consumers, and what passenger train operators can charge on some routes

- to increase competition between firms over product prices and quality

- to stop powerful firms being anti-competitive, for example, if they agree between them to fix prices at high levels or to force new rivals out of business

- to protect consumers from misleading advertising, faulty and unsafe products, and dishonest businesses

- to persuade people to buy more of some products by keeping their prices low, or to discourage the purchase of some products by keeping their prices high. For example, taxes on the price of cigarettes have been raised in an attempt to stop people smoking and damaging their health. In turn, this may reduce the demands on the National Health Service

- to raise the incomes of some producers to encourage them to continue to supply their products. For example, farmers incomes have often been protected because if they go out of business a valuable domestic source of food supply will be lost (see chapter 5)

- to encourage firms to invest in new technologies and employee skills, so that they can compete better against overseas suppliers

- to reduce poverty and inequalities in incomes and wealth

- to protect employee rights

- to protect the environment

- to encourage new home and overseas businesses to locate in areas of high unemployment

Government can influence business decisions and activities in a number of ways.

Macro-economic policy

'Macro' means 'big' and macroeconomic policy refers to measures used by the Government to influence general price inflation, total employment, growth in the national output and overseas trade. The UK Government can influence these things through changes in the overall level of taxation, public expenditure and interest rates.

The UK Government, like most governments, has a number of macroeconomic objectives. These are:

- To keep price inflation low
- To reduce unemployment
- To encourage growth in the national output
- To improve the competitiveness of UK firms against overseas rivals

If these objectives can be achieved, the Government will create an economic climate which is good for business. For example, rapidly rising prices or **inflation** can reduce consumer demand for many goods and services and increase business costs. When the prices of many UK goods and services rise quickly, consumers at home and overseas will be unable to afford to buy so many of them with their incomes and so demand for them will fall. Goods and services produced by overseas firms may be cheaper and demand for them will rise instead. If UK firms suffer falling sales, they may cut back on production and shed workers causing unemployment to rise. Workers may also push for higher wages to keep pace with rising prices. Increased wage costs may reduce firms demand for employees. Therefore, if the Government can prevent prices rising so fast in the first place, it can prevent falling consumer demand, reduce pressure on business costs and stop unemployment from rising.

If prices are rising rapidly because consumer demand is too high relative to the supply of goods and services, the Government can raise taxes to reduce the amount of money people have to spend or cut back its own demand by spending less on public sector activities. Changing taxes and public spending to influence the level of demand for goods and services is known as **fiscal policy**. In addition, the government could raise interest rates to make it more expensive to borrow money to spend. Altering interest rates to influence the demand for goods and services is known as **monetary policy**.

Fiscal and monetary policy can be used to achieve other Government macroeconomic objectives as the table below demonstrates.

Government objective	What can the government do?	
	Fiscal Policy	**Monetary Policy**
Reduce price inflation	Raise taxes on peoples incomes and reduce government spending to reduce demand for goods and services	Raise interest rates to reduce borrowing and therefore, reduce the amount people have to spend
Ruduce unemployment	Lower taxes and increase public spending, to create more demand for goods and services. Firms may need to employ more people to help expand production to meet demand	Reduce interest rates to make borrowing money to spend on goods and services more attractive
Increase national output	Lower taxes on incomes to motivate employees to work harder, and reduce taxes on profits to make business more attractive	Reduce interest rates so that it becomes cheaper for firms to borrow money to invest in new equipment and machinery to raise output
Increase UK exports overseas and reduce demand for imported goods and services in the UK	Raise taxes on incomes and reduce public spending to reduce demand for imported goods	Lower interest rates. This will help to reduce the value of the UK currency 'sterling' against overseas currencies. As the value of the UK pound falls exports become cheaper to buy overseas and imports to the UK become more expensive

An increase in interest rates relative to those offered in other countries will increase the demand for UK saving deposits. People overseas will wish to increase the amount of money they keep in UK banks and other financial institutions to earn higher interest. However, to do this they must buy UK pounds sterling with their own currencies. Like any other product, as the demand for pounds increase so does their price in terms of other currencies. As the value of the pound rises exports of UK goods and services sold overseas become more expensive and demand for them is likely to fall. However, the price of many imports the UK buys from overseas will tend to fall thereby reducing inflation. UK imports of raw materials for use in UK industry is significant. Falling import prices can reduce production costs which can be passed on to UK consumers in lower prices.

It follows that lowering interest rates and lowering the valueof the pound, can help UK firms sell more exports overseas and can reduce demand for goods and services imported to the UK from overseas. Instead, UK consumers may increase their demand for goods and services produced by UK firms.

▼ How a fall in interest rates can help UK firms sell more goods and services overseas

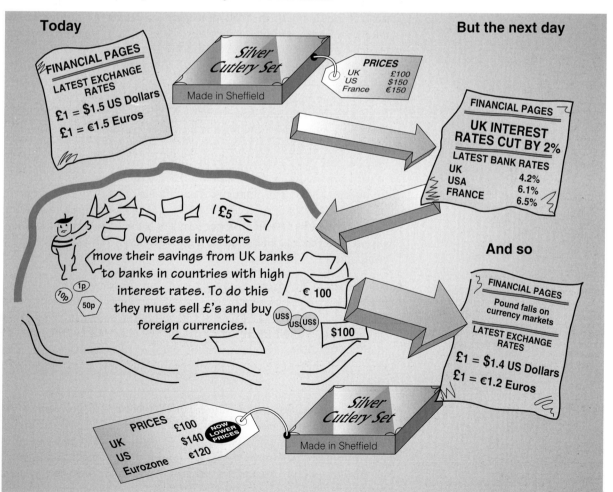

Micro-economic policy

'Micro' means 'small', so microeconomic policy refers to measures used by the government to influence the actions and decisions of groups of firms and individuals. Many microeconomic policies are designed to promote jobs, low inflation and growth in output by removing barriers to increasing productivity and competition between firms. These include:

- **Competition Policy** is a set of laws and regulations, including consumer protection laws, designed to stop firms from restricting competition and forcing product prices to rise and quality to suffer. For example, it is illegal for firms to act together to fix their prices at high levels or use their power to charge prices below costs to force smaller rivals out of business. Anti-competitive behaviour by powerful firms can be investigated by the competition authorities in the UK. They have the power to fine firms by up to 10% of their revenue if they are found guilty. Increasing competition gives firms an incentive to produce better quality products at lower costs and prices than rivals. Better quality and lower prices will increase consumer demand for UK products and help boost employment.

- **Privatization:** In the past one way to regulate powerful firms or to protect employment in firms that were in danger of closing was to take them into public ownership. This is called **nationalization**. Under Government control, the prices and quality of many goods and services, and employment levels, could be controlled. Entire industries such as gas, water and electricity supply, telecommunications, the railways, coal, and large firms, namely British Petroleum and Rover, were nationalized for these reasons. However, most have now been returned to private sector ownership following privatization (see chapter 6). As private companies they may become more efficient because their shareholders will want them to earn profits and because they will have to compete with each other to attract customers. Industry 'watchdogs' now set standards of service and regulate price increases in a number of these industries. For example, the Office of Water Services (Ofwat) regulates the water supply companies, and Ofgem regulates electricity and gas supply companies.

- **Deregulation** involves removing old and unnecessary rules and regulations on business. For example, the Deregulation and Contracting Out Act (1994) removed some 450 statutory regulations on business, including restrictions on opening hours, the sale of methylated spirits, the licensing of employment agencies, etc. The removal of these restrictions should reduce business costs and help to increase output and lower prices.

- **Improving education and training:** For UK firms to be successful when competing in international markets it is essential they have highly trained and skilled workers. Because of this, the UK Government is investing more in education and training facilities, encouraging more people to attend universities and colleges, and introducing new courses to teach modern skills.

- **Encouraging new research and development (R&D):** The Government provides funds to help firms invest in new research and development of better products and production methods. It can also encourage firms to invest in R&D by giving them tax relief on the money they spend on it.

- **Environmental protection:** The Government has passed laws which make it illegal to pollute the environment. For example, the Clean Air Act and Environmental Protection Act set limits on the type and amount of pollutants firms can discharge into the atmosphere, rivers and seas. Together, these laws control many thousands of different production processes. The Government has also raised taxes on landfill waste to encourage businesses to reduce waste, and raised taxes on petrol to reduce car use.

- **Employment laws:** These laws protect the rights of workers and their employers. For example, laws have been introduced in the UK which limit the power of trade unions to call strikes and take other disruptive actions. Some powerful unions were able to use these actions to force firms to pay their members higher wages which were not matched by increases in worker productivity.

- **Reducing the tax burden:** The UK Government recognizes that cutting taxes on incomes and profits can have a direct effect on the efforts of workers and firms to produce more output and be more competitive. As such, rates of tax on incomes and profits in the UK have been reduced over time.

▼ *Environmental protection laws are supposed to stop this happening but some businesses continue to break or oppose such laws because of the costs they can impose on business*

Your green tax will cost us jobs, steel bosses tell Brown

Steel bosses are trying to convince the Government to re-think a planned anti-pollution law before it is introduced. The new charge is aimed at encouraging factories to use less fuel, thus cutting the amount of 'greenhouse' gases such as carbon dioxide that are released into the atmosphere and help cause global warming.

Britain's steel producers say such a move will add £238 million a year to their costs, allowing cheaper foreign rivals to grab trade. They warn that steel plants will be bound to close, with experts estimating that at least 5,000 of the UK is 60,000 steel employees would lose their jobs.

Labour committed Britain to a 12.5 per cent reduction in greenhouse gas emissions by 2010 at the 1997 World environment conference in Japan.

Daily Mail 20.7.1999

Look at the table below. In the first column is a list of possible government policies. In the second column is a jumbled list of their possible impacts on business. Your task is to match government policies with their likely impacts on business. Each policy may have more than one impact on business. Use a table like the one at the end of this activity to complete your task and in the third column explain why each policy is likely to have these impacts

Some possible government policies	Possible impacts on business
An increase in the minimum wage	Consumer demand for goods and services falls
A reduction in income tax	The demand for workers increases
A cut in VAT on electricity	Labour productivity rises
An increase in interest rates	Wage costs increase
An increase in public spending on new training schemes	Profits fall
A reduction in corporation tax on the profits of small and medium sized businesses	Profits rise
A tough new law requiring all firms to recycle at least 50% of all their waste paper	Consumer demand for goods and services rises
	Fewer workers are employed
An increase in business rates in South East England	An increase in business costs
All vehicles wishing to use motorways being made to pay an additional £150 each year for a licence	Business costs fall
	Businesses relocate premises
An increase in corporation tax on profits over £1 million per year	Less investment in new products and production processes
A cut in interest rates	

Government policy	Possible impacts on business	Reasons for the impact
Increase in taxes on petrol	● Increase in business costs ● Profits fall ● Consumer demand falls	Transport and delivery costs increase. If firms do not pass on their higher costs to consumers their profits will be reduced. People will have to pay more for petrol for their cars and this will leave less income to spend on other goods and services.

Section **7.3**

Business location

Choosing the right location for a business can mean the difference between success or failure. There is no such thing as a perfect site for a factory, office, or shop, but some locations are clearly better than others, and the choice of location can often depend on the influence of business stakeholders.

Sometimes firms have only a limited amount of choice about where to locate. For example, establishing a shipbuilders inland and many miles from the sea is not a good idea. A coal mine can only locate where there are coal deposits. An international airport will need a lot of land and should be away from residential areas, although not so far away that people are unwilling to travel to it.

However, for most business organizations the major concern is cost. The cost of establishing a new business, either by moving into existing premises or building new ones, can be very high. In general, any firm will attempt to choose a location that offers the least disadvantages and the most advantages at the lowest possible cost.

Portfolio Activity 7.8

In groups, consider the following plans for four new firms. Make a list of the factors that each firm should take into account before deciding upon a final location.

The supermarket

A new supermarket requires a 20-acre site with ample parking space. A wide variety of goods and services will be sold by a staff of 150 people. Restaurants and customer facilities will also be offered.

The steel plant

A large plant will occupy over 75 acres and many of the new materials will be imported from overseas. For every ton of steel produced, 4 tonnes of coal, limestone, and iron ore are required. A workforce of 300 people is required.

The motor car company

A 250-acre site of flat land is needed to accommodate a new automated car assembly plant with a proposed workforce of 450 people. Car parts will be received from other plants around the country and brought to this plant for assembly.

Cable TV station

A new cable TV company wants to find an existing office block to house its equipment and a workforce of some 150 technicians. It will need space outside the building to place satellite dishes to receive satellite TV stations, and parking space for 50 cars. The company aims to have at least 1 million households connected to the cable TV system within 3 years.

▼ *Some businesses have to be located in particular places.*

There are a large number of factors which affect the location decision of a firm. These include:

● **Taking advantage of natural factors.** Some firms may want to take advantage of natural factors such as the weather or soil conditions. For example, many fruit and vegetable producers have located in the Scilly Isles because of the early Spring. Similarly, a major port was located at Southampton on the south coast of Britain because of the size of the natural harbour and because there are four high tides each day.

- **Being near to suppliers and raw materials.** Many years ago, whole industries grew up around deposits of the raw materials they used for power and to produce other goods. For example, Sheffield become an important centre in the UK for steel production because of nearby deposits of coal, iron ore, and limestone. Old heavy industries, such as ship and locomotive engine building, also located near to coal deposits and producers of iron and steel, primarily in northern England. These materials were bulky and expensive to transport over long distances.

   Today, many raw materials such as coal, iron ore, and wood are bought from overseas, and so a large number of firms are located near to major ports. The biggest port is at Rotterdam in the Netherlands. The port has giant terminals in which it stores iron ore, oil, grain, and many other commodities which are then distributed to the vast mainland European market.

- **Being near to the consumers.** Any firm that makes and sells goods or services will want to be within easy reach of its customers. A shop may wish to locate in or near to the shopping centre of a town. A factory

▼ Advertising to attract business

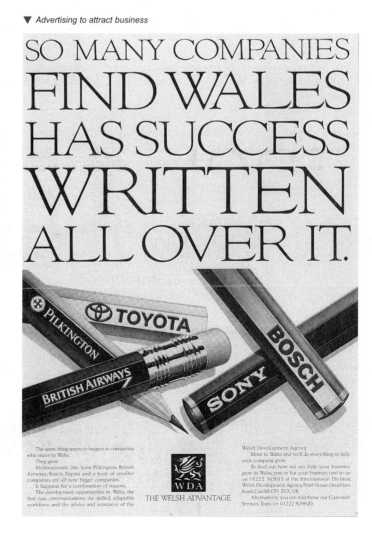

may also wish to be near its point of sale because the goods made may be heavy and expensive to deliver. For example, many firms producing electrical and other parts for cars are located near the large car producers in the Midlands area of the UK.

● **Being near to transport facilities.** Transport is an important consideration for any firm. Raw materials and finished goods need to be transported cheaply and easily to wholesalers and retailers. Customers also need to be able to reach shops easily and workers need to get to their place of work. Good road and rail links can reduce the costs and time it takes to travel and to transport goods.

Market or materials?

Wherever a firm locates, it will have to pay transport costs for bringing materials and component parts to it or for delivering the finished products to customers. All firms must take these costs into account when choosing a location.

A firm that is **bulk reducing** may find it cheaper to locate near to suppliers of raw materials or components. This is because the raw materials or components used by a firm are bulkier and/or weigh more than the finished products. A good example of bulk-reducing production is the making of steel from iron ore. Four tonnes of iron ore, coal, and limestone rock are used to produce just one ton of steel in a blast furnace.

A firm that is **bulk increasing** may find it cheaper to locate nearer to its customers than to a source of supply. Bulk-increasing production involves either using smaller components to assemble larger

products – for example, making cars, video recorders, or furniture – or adding weight to raw materials used. For example, beer making involves adding a lot of water to hops and barley. The beer then has to be transported in bottles or barrels.

For some industries, however, transport costs are not a significant factor in their choice of location. These are called **footloose industries**. The production of new communications and computer equipment tends to be footloose because materials, components, and finished products tend to be light and easy to transport. However, many of these footloose firms have tended to locate together near to major motorways and airports, especially in the South East of England. This gives them easy access to London and international markets, and proximity to a large supply of skilled workers.

▼ *Bulk reducing*

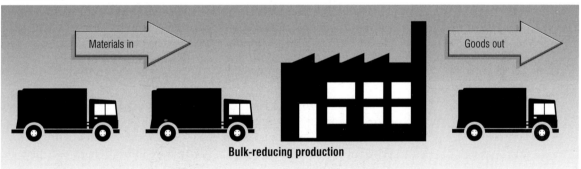

Materials in   Goods out

Bulk-reducing production

▼ *Bulk increasing*

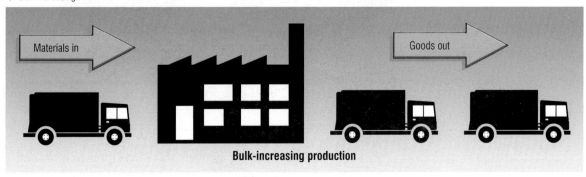

Materials in   Goods out

Bulk-increasing production

- **Being near to a supply of labour with the right skills.** Many firms require a large and skilled workforce. They will need to locate near to densely populated areas. Workers may not be keen to travel long distances to and from work, especially if public transport or road links are poor. Some firms requiring large amounts of labour may choose to locate in areas where unemployment is high because workers may be willing to work for lower wages rather than remain unemployed.

  Many firms will require employees with specific skills. Workers in some regions of the country already have particular skills and so will need less training. For example, there are a large number of computer and electronics companies based in and around an area of the UK called 'Silicon Valley' in Cambridge. This means that there are many potential employees located nearby with specialist skills in computing and electronics. A new firm locating in Cambridge would have the advantage of being able to select employees from a group workers who have already been trained by other firms. Similarly, many employees who live in and around London have skills in many aspects of financial services, such as banking and insurance, because of the number of banks and other financial companies that have located in London for many years.

▼ *'Teleworking' from home is becoming increasingly popular*

- **Locating on cheap land or in cheap premises.** A large factory will need to locate on cheap land. Not only must this land be available, it is helpful if it is also cheap to rent or buy. Fords at Dagenham, Essex, occupies 500 acres of land, chosen among other reasons because it was so cheap.

  A growing number of people are operating small businesses from home, often because it is the cheapest and most convenient option. Most home-based businesses will either manufacture products that do not require a large amount of machinery and other equipment, such as stuffed toys or dried flower arrangements, or will provide personal services such as child-minding or consultancy.

- **Being near to rival firms.** Sometimes it is an advantage for a business to locate near competing firms. This is because there are likely to be a range of suppliers, or **ancillary firms** nearby which will be able to supply the business with the parts it requires. There will also be a good supply of workers with the right skills.

  Groups of rival firms that locate together with major business customers and suppliers form **business clusters**. For example, 'Silicon Valley' is an example of a cluster in the computing and hi-tech electronics business sector (see above).

- **Financial help from government.** Firms may be offered financial and other incentives, both by local and central government, to locate in areas of high unemployment in order to create jobs and incomes for local people. For example, local authorities may provide rent-free premises or reduce the business rates a firm would have to pay for a period of time. Central government also offers a range of incentives, from special grants to pay for new machinery and to help pay for worker training, to contracts to carry out government work.

Regional policy

Both the UK and European Union Governments operate a **regional policy** to encourage firms to locate and expand in areas which suffer from high unemployment and industrial decline. These areas are called **Assisted Areas** and firms in, or thinking of moving to, these areas can apply for financial help called **Regional Selective Assistance (RSA)**. This is a grant awarded to firms who can show that their projects will safeguard or create jobs, particularly skilled jobs.

Assisted areas are reviewed from time to time by the UK Government because of changes in regional employment, investment, population, migration and income patterns. In 1999 assisted areas were redrawn into three different groups as the map below shows.

▼ Figure 7.1 : Assisted Areas in the UK in 1999

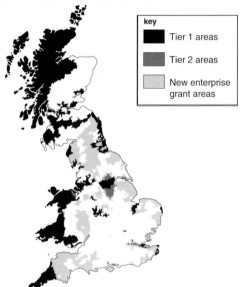

key

■ Tier 1 areas

▨ Tier 2 areas

▢ New enterprise grant areas

There are two main types of assisted area in the UK;

● Tier 1 areas include Cornwall, Merseyside, South Yorkshire and West Wales and the Valleys. Northern Ireland is included as an area of exceptional concern. Firms in tier one regions can apply for grants of up to 40% towards the cost of buying machinery and premises for a new business project that will safeguard or generate jobs.

● Tier 2 areas include the Highlands and Islands area of Scotland, and parts of the East and West Midlands, the North East and West, Yorkshire and the Humber, East Anglia and London. Firms in these areas can apply for grants of up to 20% of the cost of their new projects.

A third tier of **Enterprise Grant Areas** was introduced to provide assistance to small and medium enterprises employing less than 250 people. These areas include local authority districts with high unemployment, old coalfield areas, and rural development areas.

Regional Selective Assistance is provided through the Scottish Executive, the National Assembly for Wales, the Northern Ireland Office, and eight **Regional Development Agencies (RDAs)** in England.

In 1999–2000 RDAs had a total budget of over £1 billion to spend in their regions on

● encouraging economic regeneration
● promoting business efficiency, investment and competitiveness
● promoting employment
● developing and improving workforce skills
● improving the environment

Other UK Government help for regions

The assisted areas policy is linked with other Government schemes which aim to bring improvements to different areas of the UK. In 2000 these included:

● **The Single Regeneration Budget (SRB)** provides money to help 'regenerate' communities suffering from multiple problems including low levels of employment and skills, poor transport links, poor health and housing, and high levels of crime and drug misuse. SRB schemes range from employment and training programmes, to community safety and drug abuse projects.

● **Employment Zones** target help at improving the chances of employment for people who have been unemployed for a long time.

● **Education Action Zones** aim to raise educational standards in areas where attainment and skills levels are low.

● **Excellence in Cities** is a programme aimed at raising standards in run down city areas, by providing new opportunities for learning and developing skills in schools.

● **The Coalfields Enterprise Fund** targets financial help at small firms with high growth potential in areas blighted by the closer of coal mines in the 1980s and 1990s.

European Structural Fund Areas

Many of the assisted areas in the UK also qualify for additional help from the European Union, especially Tier 1 areas in which the average incomes of people are below many other areas. These are called 'objective one' areas under the terms of the European Structural Fund.

EU Objective	Types of area
1	Helping areas suffering general decline, deprivation and poor infrastructure (transport, schools, hospitals, etc.)
2	Assisting areas of industrial decline
3	Combating long term unemployment
4	Helping workers adapt to industrial change
5a	Helping agriculture adjust to new conditions
5b	Rural development

Other objective one areas in Europe include eastern Germany, all of Greece, north-west Ireland, central and southern Spain, southern Italy and parts of Austria. Financial help is available in these areas to create jobs, invest in new skills and technologies, build new roads and schools, and improve the environment.

Portfolio Activity 7.9

1. Choose an area of the UK that receives UK and/or EU government assistance.

2. Try to find out more about the forms of assistance offered to firms in the area.

3. What other advantages does your chosen area have that would make it an attractive place for new firms to locate?

4. Design a poster to advertise your chosen area as a good place for new firms to locate.

A useful source of information on regional policy is the Department of Trade and Industry (DTI).

Tesco puts 69p wine at the end of the Chunnel

WINE was selling for almost a quarter of its British supermarket price yesterday when Tesco opened its massive cut-price liquor store in Calais, France.

The food giant, which says it lost £46 million to the cross-Channel drinks trade last year, has joined the retail exodus to France with its own range of 1,500 wines, spirits and beers.

'Customers have been coming to us to buy food and going across the Channel to buy drink since European trade barriers came down in 1993. We needed to open a store where they were going to buy the drink,' explained Tesco spokesman Steve Clarke.

Daily Mail 23.3.1995

A dangerous world for business

According to a survey of international security risks, Algeria is the most dangerous place in the world in which to do business, while Syria, Botswana, Malaysia, Singapore, and Switzerland are among the safest.

Algeria, where extremists are carrying out a campaign of sabotage against foreign businesses, particularly oil and gas installations, is rated as 'high risk.' Colombia, where drug trafficking and guerrilla violence is commonplace, also ranks among the high risk countries.

The UK, where bombs have exploded in the City of London, is rated as 'medium risk' – on a level with Bangladesh, North Korea, and the Philippines. France, Germany, Poland and Hungary are considered low risk.

The Times 25.8.1994

The government of the European Union (EU) operates a similar **regional policy** to encourage firms to locate and expand in deprived areas of Europe, including in the UK.

- **Planning controls.** For environmental and social reasons, firms are not allowed to locate anywhere they want. For example, it would not be particularly pleasant if a huge power station was built on a local beauty spot, or in the middle of a residential area. The government has introduced a number of controls on new development to protect environmental, social, and other business interests.

- **Other factors.** There are a great many other factors a firm will take into account when choosing a suitable location. For example, a business owner may simply choose to locate his or her business in an area they like. An existing business may choose to stay where it is simply because it has always been there, despite the fact that the original reason for locating there no longer applies – for example, to be near a source of coal for power. Staying put rather than re-locating despite a need to expand or move nearer the market, is known as **industrial inertia.**

A firm considering moving overseas will also need to take account of a host of other factors:

- Rules and regulations in foreign countries
- Language and cultural barriers
- Different currencies
- The economic climate. For example, is business booming or in a slump?
- Political stability

Many Japanese and US firms have set up plants in the UK in order to be inside the European Union (EU) area. The EU adds a large tax (known as a **tariff**) onto the price of goods imported from non-EU member countries. This makes imported goods expensive, so that European consumers do not buy so many of them. By producing and selling goods inside the EU, foreign firms can avoid this tariff.

Businesses that have operations located in more than one country are known as **multinationals**. These will often employ many thousands of employees and raise many billions of pounds in revenue from the sale of their goods and services. For example, Imperial Chemicals Industries Plc (ICI) is a British-owned multinational company with business operations in more than 50 countries.

Portfolio Activity 7.10

You and a partner want to open a small restaurant in your local area serving different dishes from around the world.

Obtain a detailed ordnance survey map and street map of your local area. On the map identify as far as possible the location of your possible suppliers, rival restaurants, and the area from which you are likely to attract customers.

Use the maps and your local knowledge to pick **three** possible sites for your new business venture. Make a list of the advantages and disadvantages of each site, and then select the 'winning' site. Write down the reasons for your final choice of location.

Inward investment

Inward investment refers to the location of foreign-owned business organizations setting up operations in the UK. There are now over 4,000 US and 210 Japanese manufacturing companies in the UK. Together they employ nearly 20% of UK manufacturing employees. There are also many foreign-owned organizations providing services in the UK.

▼ *The UK is more successful at attracting US and Japanese firms than any other European country.*

Many foreign-owned firms have been attracted to the UK because they are able to gain access to the large European market, the availability of skilled workers, and because grants are available to them to set up in areas of high unemployment.

Key wordsearch

Hidden in the jumble of letters are key words and terms from this chapter. Use the descriptions below to help find them.

```
S T E A K H O L E M P O W E R M E N T E N K T Q M
A T M A N U F A C T U R I N E P R O E D U C T I N
M W A L S O D I T Q W H J O G K N I A G P O G F X
I S T K E N T E L E W O R K I N G Y M Y C I K L P
C L A Q E K A T E A H R T Y O U C T W A N T Y U R
R A N U X H E T H E R L O C N U T J O A S I M S O
O D K A P I O F E R T I T P A R S L R S A Q O T D
E E G L N T G L F V Z C I N L I K E K C B P N A U
C M I I O O M E D O T K B T P O L E I H K I E F C
O E R T N E G I E F I S Y O C A T N U I D T T T I
N T L Y S M S W Q Z R E L O L A M P G I O V A E I
O A I C O N S U M E R S X U I S C H I A X S R R V
M L C I B D U S T A N F I S C A L P O L I C Y C I
I L K R S U B O N E S Q W R Y A P U P P Y U P U T
C I C C O M P E T I T I O N P O L I C Y I L O Y Y
P C U L X P U P P E T M A S T E R X C R E T L I R
O A P E U T O U C H M A J L O E D O H R T O I E U
L A S S I S T E D A R E A S R O G E R A N D C S S
I B E A T I T I C K L E M Y P U M A S L I P Y O O
C O C O N U T E M P L O Y M E N T L A W H J K P F
Y N X U P Y O S R E N T A Q U I C K Y M A R T B U
F J F O O T L O O S E I N D U S T R I E S L U K G
H O L I S T I C V E N T Y O U R A N G R Y U N L C
M V C A R T M A N S T A N K Y L E K E N N Y H A R
O I N W A R D I N V E S T M E N T L A U R E L D Y
```

- People and organizations who have an interest in or influence on business activities and decisions
- The name given to all government policies that attempt to control aspects of particular business sectors or activities
- Government policy that is targeted at deprived areas
- Groups of employees with complementary skills working together in the workplace
- Business activities that are not tied to locations near good transport links, customers or suppliers
- Short for the focus in business on all aspects of quality at every stage of production
- Government macroeconomic policy to control price inflation using interest rates
- Firms will improve this, and lower their costs, if the amount of output produced per period by labour using other resources is increased
- Working from home or away from the usual workplace and keeping in-touch with the office or other employees using modern communications technology

- Short for the type of financial assistance given to firms that create employment opportunities in deprived areas
- Motivating staff by allowing them to contribute to decision making in organizations
- Government macroeconomic policy designed to affect the level of demand for goods and services in the economy using taxes and public spending
- The body of laws used to protect the rights of employees
- Problem solving teams in business
- People and organizations who want goods and services, and are willing and able to buy them
- Not a cereal, but the name given to areas where groups of firms in the same line of business locate together
- The location of foreign owned businesses in the UK
- Regions of the UK which are designated in need to government financial help to create new jobs and incomes

Test your knowledge

1 Brush Arts Ltd sells paintings and art materials. Which of the following would be the most suitable place to locate?
   A near a small village
   B in a seaside town
   C in the countryside
   D near a densely populated city

2 Which one of the following businesses is best located near to natural resources?
   A a cinema
   B a bank
   C a coal fired power station
   D a take away restaurant

3 A supermarket chain wants to build a new superstore. Which of the following information would be most useful when choosing between two areas?
   A size of local population
   B numbers of males and females
   C cost of living
   D road and rail links

Questions 4 - 6 share the following answer options;
   A near a large residential area
   B near a supply of skilled labour
   C near a source of raw materials
   D near good transport links

What is likely to be the best location for the following businesses?

4 A supermarket

5 An international business management consultancy

6 A television parts manufacturer

7 All of the following are external influences on business **except** which?
   A government economic policy
   B new laws regulating advertising
   C better management of sales staff
   D more competitors entering the market

8 All of the following are stakeholders in a large computer manufacturing company **except** which?
   A the Government
   B the workforce
   C the local community
   D a supplier of car parts

Questions 9–11 share the following answer options.
   A a change in the natural business environment
   B a change in the competitive business environment
   C a change in the social business environment
   D a change in the economic, regulatory and legal environment

Which of the above is described by the each of following situations?

9 A rival business introduces a new improved product

10 The Government introduces additional charges on cars and lorries for motorway use

11 A business changes the way it organizes its departments to reduce layers of management and to improve communications

12 Government macroeconomic policy involves:
   A new measures to protect consumers
   B regulating competition between firms
   C the control of inflation and unemployment
   D measures to protect workers rights and working conditions

13 You are the managing director of a large international cosmetics company.
   a List who the main stakeholders in your company are.
   b Which group of stakeholders are likely to be the most important to your company in the long run and why?
   c Explain three ways the UK Government can affect your company.
   d Your company wants to open a new factory somewhere in Europe. List and explain four factors that are likely to influence your choice of location.

Business Finance

About this unit

This unit provides an introduction to business finance. Business organizations use information on costs and revenues to make decisions about producing new products. This unit discusses the main types of costs and revenues for particular products, how to estimate cash flows and the profit or loss of the business, and how to calculate the break-even level of sales at a given price needed to cover production costs.

It also discusses the different documents used in business to record financial transactions when goods or services are bought or sold.

unit

3

| **chapter 8** | *Business costs and revenue* |
| **chapter 9** | *Business transactions and documents* |

chapter **8** # Business costs and revenues

When businesses are planning to produce a new good or service, they must carefully work out the costs involved and the revenue they are likely to make from selling their goods and services. Businesses need to consider the following costs:

- **Start-up costs**, which need to be met before a business can start selling the new product. These include paying for market research, and buying premises, machinery and fixtures and fittings
- **Running costs**, which need to be met so that business can go through the day to day process of producing and selling their products. These include advertising costs, paying rent on premises, paying for power to run the machinery and paying for raw materials and the wages of employees

You will need to recognize typical costs and revenues involved in a range of businesses, and identify which costs are start-up costs and which are running costs.

Businesses need to work out how much money they will have coming in and how much they have to pay out. If they do not do this, they may run out of money and be unable to continue in business. You will need to understand how preparing a **cash-flow forecast** can help businesses manage their cash-flows, and identify which are:

- **cash inflows** – sales revenues, bank loans, government grants
- **cash outflows** – payments for raw materials, wages, rents, telephone bills, machinery hire

You will need to complete a simple cash-flow forecast that shows the cash inflows, outflows, and cash balance.

A business activity only makes a profit when the revenue from sales is greater than the costs of supplying the product or service. **Break-even** is the point at which revenue from the sale of output just covers business costs.

To work out the break-even level of output of a business, you will need to know:

- **variable costs,** which vary directly with how much a business produces. These include the wages of production workers and raw materials costs
- **fixed costs,** which must be paid however much a business makes and sells. These costs include machinery hire charges, rents, rates and administration
- **sales revenues**

You will need to calculate the break-even point for a business using a plot of costs and revenues or using the following formula:

$$\text{Break-even level of output} = \frac{\text{Fixed costs}}{\text{Price per unit} - \text{variable costs per unit}}$$

The level of profit or loss can also be found from a break even chart, as well as from a **profit and loss statement**. This records sales, costs of sales, gross profit, overheads, and net profit. You will need to understand the format of a profit and loss statement, and how calculations of profit or loss are made for a business activity.

Section **8.1**

Raising finance for a new business project

The cost of a bright idea

Gordon Watt is about to launch a new business venture, making and selling long-lasting, low-voltage light bulbs. He has spent £2,000 of his own savings on market research to find out what consumers want in light bulbs and the prices they are likely to pay. He decides to call his business Northern Lights.

Gordon has a good business case and his bank manager agrees to lend him £5,000 to buy fixtures and fittings to equip his business premises. Gordon has bought a factory unit on a new industrial estate with a commercial mortgage for £150,000 from a building society. His mortgage and bank loan repayments will total £870 each month. On top of these he will also have to pay business rates of £220 each month.

A local supplier has leased Gordon the machinery and other equipment he needs to make light bulbs. The lease charges are £260 per month. Gordon has also used another £2,100 of his own savings and a grant of £1,500 from the government to buy office equipment and other things he need to start up his business. He knows the equipment he has bought will wear out over time so he has allowed £100 each month to cover the cost of replacing them in 3 years time. By then he will have saved up another £3,600.

Gordon will also need to pay telephone bills, insurance, electricity and other costs each month to run his business. To keep track of all the things Gordon needs to pay for he decides to list how much he has spent starting up his business and how much it will cost to run each month, regardless of how many light bulbs he makes and sells.

Using his list, Gordon estimates business costs of £1,800 each month whether he makes and sells 1,100 or even 10,000 light bulbs every month. These costs must be paid for from the sales revenue of the business or Northern Lights will go out very soon!

Gordon will employ three workers to help him make light bulbs. The cost of employing them will be £6,000 each month. Most of this is the cost of paying wages, but he will also have to pay employer's National Insurance contributions for each worker to the Government. The cost of employing labour is the biggest cost faced by most businesses. Around 70% of total business costs are due to wages and other employment-related costs.

Gordon has set Northern Lights a target to produce 6,000 light bulbs each month. To make this number of light bulbs he estimates he will have to buy £3,000 worth of materials and other components from suppliers, and pay £1,500 for the making and printing of packaging by another company. The cost of electricity to

Northern Lights

Cash in (from bank loan)	+£5,000
(from government grant)	+£1,500
Cash out (from savings)	−£2,000
	−£2,100
Cash balance at bank	+£2,400

Monthly outgoings (estimate)

Bank loan repayments (including interest of £10 per month)	£70
Mortgage repayments	£800
Business rates	£220
Water meter charges	£15
Electricity (for heating and lighting)	£90
Machinery lease charges	£260
Insurance	£100
Telephone	£50
Cleaning service	£75
Equipment maintenance	£20
Equipment wear and tear	£100
Total costs per month	**£1,800**

Northern Lights

Production cost estimates

Target – 6,000 light bulbs per month

	Total	Cost per bulb
Labour	£6,000	£1
Materials	£3,000	50 pence
Packaging	£1,500	25 pence
Power	£300	5 pence
Total	**£10,800**	**£1.80**

power the machinery and other production equipment to produce 6,000 light bulbs each month he estimates as £300. So the total cost of labour, materials, packaging and power to produce 6,000 light bulbs is £10,800, or £1.80 per light bulb.

So does this mean all Gordon needs to do is charge a price of £3 for each bulb to make a profit of £1.20 per bulb? No, because Gordon also needs to make enough revenue from the sale of light bulbs to cover all the other costs he needs to pay to run his business, such as mortgage and lease charges, business rates, and telephone bills. Only if Gordon makes and sells enough light bulbs to cover all his business costs will he make a profit.

Controlling business costs

Northern Lights illustrates two very important things about business. The costs of running business and the need for business finance. Whether a business is new or an existing one, large or small, it will incur costs and will need to pay for them. We will consider these two aspects of business before we return to the problem Gordon Watts is trying to solve, namely how many light bulbs to produce to cover his business costs.

Costs and profits

Running a business is all about making decisions on how best to use resources – premises, machinery, materials, and labour. Most business organizations do this because they aim to make a profit, where

Profit = revenues from sales – business costs

Businesses will use information on their business costs and revenues to calculate their profit. Every business decision – whether to start-up, make a new product, increase advertising, re-locate premises or expand – has an impact on the costs of running a business and, therefore, on profit. Because the primary aim for most private sector businesses is to make a profit, it is therefore essential that businesses are able to keep their costs down and generate as much revenue as possible. Controlling costs is equally important to public sector organizations and charities, who do not aim to make a profit but will try to keep their business costs as low as possible.

In order to control costs, it is first necessary to be able to identify what the costs are, calculate how much they are and then set targets for future cost levels. There are a number of different ways in which costs can be classified and calculated.

What are business costs?

Business costs can be classified and calculated in order to assist managers in planning and controlling the operation of their businesses. These are:

Fixed costs: Before a business can start production and make goods and services for sale it will need to pay for many costs. It will need to obtain premises, machinery and tools, office equipment, pay wages to office staff, and undertake market research. These are **start-up costs.** Starting up a business or developing a new product can be expensive and there will be no revenue to cover these start-up costs until the products are on sale and consumers are buying them.

Even when a business is up and running it will still need to pay many costs whether it is making and selling many or very few goods and services. **Fixed costs**, such as mortgage payments or rents on premises, interest charges on bank loans, lease charges for machinery and telephone bills, tend not to vary with the amount of goods or services produced.

Fixed business costs will include:

- buying or renting premises
- buying or hiring machinery
- business rates
- lighting and heating
- fixtures and fittings
- equipment maintenance
- insurance
- cleaning
- sales and distribution costs, such as advertising and transport
- loan repayments and interest charges
- the wages and salaries of office staff and managers
- wear and tear of office equipment (called the **depreciation** allowance)

Many of these costs are also known as **overheads**.

Variable costs: Unlike fixed costs, variable costs are directly related to the amount of goods and services. That is, **variable costs** vary with the level of output of a business. The main variable costs in business are the costs of:

- materials and component parts used to make the product
- employees directly involved in making the product
- power used in production

The sum of fixed costs and variable costs gives the total cost of the activities of a business organization. It is important to know total cost in order to be able to work out total profit.

Portfolio Activity 8.1

1. The Comfy Coffee Bar ran up the following costs last year. Which costs would you classify as fixed costs and which items are variable costs?

The Comfy Coffee Bar

Purchases of coffees, teas and sugar	£8,500
Supplies of soft drinks	£4,300
Telephone bill	£1,200
Consumables (Paper cups, washing up liquid, serviettes)	£1,700
Wages of serving staff	£22,000
Electric bill	£1,070
Wages of office clerk	£11,500
Business rates	£1,300
Deliveries of pastries and cakes from local bakery	£5,300
Insurance for employees	£650
Insurance for the public	£700
Lease charges for coffee making equipment	£500
Cost of advertising in local newspapers	£200
Office stationary orders	£2,500
Computer maintenance contractor	£300

2. Investigate costs in two businesses. One should be in retailing, and the other a manufacturing business. Try to arrange interviews with the owners, if they are small businesses, or with managers in their finance departments. Ask them what are their main business costs, and then sort them into fixed and variable costs. How do the types of costs incurred by the two businesses, and the things they need to buy, differ?

Raising business finance

What is capital?

Capital is the money a business uses to buy **assets**, such as land, buildings, machinery and office equipment, and to pay for running costs such as telephone bills, insurance and loans repayments.

Businesses need capital: to finance business start up, to pay for business expansion, for the research and development of new products, and to finance the introduction of new technology. You will recall that Gordon Watt financed his capital requirements from his own savings, a bank loan and a mortgage from a building society. These are just some of the ways a business can raise money or capital to finance its activities. It is the job of the Finance Department in large organizations to find the best and cheapest sources of finance for their businesses (see chapter 2).

The money raised by a business can be used in different ways:

- **venture capital** is often used to describe money used to pay for starting up new businesses, usually new limited companies

- **investment capital** is money used to buy assets, such as premises and machinery, and

- **working capital** is money used to pay the day to day running expenses of a business, such as the cost of raw materials, electricity, telephone bills, insurance, loan repayments etc.

Money for these purposes may be found from inside a business, for example, from the personal savings of the business owner and from profits, or from external sources, such as banks and building societies.

▼ *Capital is the money businesses need to start-up, buy assets and pay running costs*

▼ *Businesses can raise finance from a variety of sources*

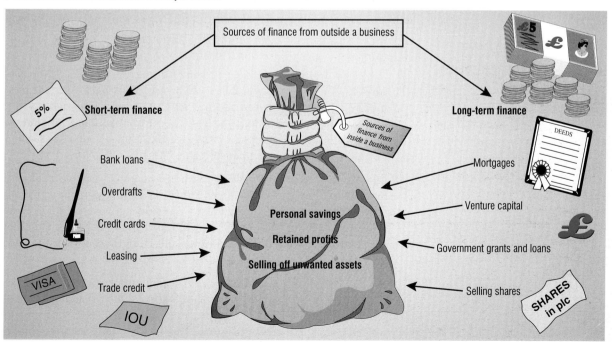

Internal sources of business finance

A business organization may already have some capital of its own to use. The main sources of **internal finance** are:

- **Personal savings** of business owners are an important source of finance for many small firms, especially sole traders and partnerships (see Chapter 6). For example, in a partnership, people can be asked to become a partner by 'buying in' to the business with money.

- **Retained profits** are profits not paid out to the business owners but used by the business to buy more assets. Using profits is a cheap way of financing new purchases. Because the funds are not borrowed, no interest need be paid for the use of retained profits. Many large organizations plough back profits into their businesses. However, most new and smaller businesses are unlikely to be making enough, (if any), profit to be able to do the same.

- **Selling off unwanted assets** can help raise money for an established business. For example, a business may raise cash by selling old computers it no longer needs or an area of land that is surplus to requirements.

External sources of business finance

Most firms will be unable to finance all their capital requirements from internal sources. Most business organizations, therefore, raise the money they need from **external sources** such as banks and other lenders.

Because business assets, such as buildings and machinery, can last for a long time, it is usual to spread payments for them over many years. To do so requires **long-term finance** from lenders. In contrast, **short-term loans** are often used by businesses to pay for assets that will not last as long, such as computer equipment, and day to day running costs, such as orders for stationary, wages, insurance, etc. As a rule of thumb, short-term finance is normally paid back within three years while medium- to long-term finance is repaid over many more years.

Short-term loans

- **Bank overdrafts** are often used to pay for unexpected bills. If the bank agrees, a business will be able to draw out of its bank account more money than it has in the account so that it goes into debit. Banks normally insist that overdrafts are paid off relatively quickly. Interest is charged on the amount of the overdraft on a daily basis and is normally slightly lower than the rate charged on loans.

- **Bank loans** are a good way of raising money for a new business to buy equipment and other small items. Loans have to be repaid in regular fixed monthly installments over an agreed period of time, typically anything from six months to ten years. Interest is charged on the total amount of the loan and is fixed from the time the money is borrowed.

Loans and overdrafts can be an expensive way of borrowing but they are one of the most popular forms of short-term finance available to small businesses such as sole traders and partnerships (see chapter 6). However, small and new businesses can be risky and may go out of business. As a result banks are often reluctant to lend to these organizations, or may charge high rates of interest to cover the risk of non-repayment.

- **Credit cards:** Businesses can make small purchases and pay for expenses such as business travel using credit cards (see chapter 9). Visa, Mastercard, American Express and Diners Club are examples of credit card companies. Depending on the credit card, users can pay bills or make purchases and will not have to pay for them until up to eight weeks later. Each month they will receive a statement of their transactions. The card user can then decide whether to pay the balance in full or in part. If payment is made in full, no interest is charged. Interest charges can be quite high.

- **Hire Purchase:** This is a popular method of finance used by smaller firms to buy equipment, tools and machinery. A hire purchase agreement with a bank or finance house will normally require a firm to pay a deposit on the items purchased, and then to pay off the balance, with interest, in regular installments over a few months or several years. If a business the unable to pay the agreed installments, the hire purchase provider is legally entitled to repossess the items.

- **Leasing:** Leasing is like paying rent for the loan of equipment or machinery over a fixed period of time. At the end of the loan period the equipment is returned to its owner. The advantage is that businesses can get expensive equipment without spending a lot of money in one go. During the period of the lease, maintenance and servicing of loaned equipment and machinery is the responsibility of the owner of the equipment.

- **Trade credit:** Many suppliers allow their business customers to but now, pay later. Payment can be up to one and three months later. This is equivalent to an interest free loan of up to 90 days.

Long-term business finance
- **Mortgages:** Most businesses will use a commercial mortgage to buy business premises – shops, offices, factories, farm buildings, etc. A mortgage is a long-term loan, typically over 25 years, of up to around 80% of the purchase price of a business property. The premises are used as security against the loan; and if the business fails to repay regular installments, the mortgage lender can take possession of the property. Mortgages are available from building societies and banks.

- **Venture capital:** Money used to start up new limited companies can be made available from specialist venture capital companies. These are business organizations who specialize in loans to new and risky businesses who might otherwise find it difficult to raise finance. Investors in Industry (3i) Plc, Paribus, Pi Capital, and banks such as HSBC and NatWest are some of the biggest and best-known venture capital firms. They usually lend money to a new company in return for shares in the ownership and running of that company. If the company does well, it can sell its shares at some future date for a much higher price.

- **Government assistance:** The UK Government offers a considerable amount of free advice and financial assistance in the form of grants, loans and training to new and existing firms, especially in areas of high unemployment and industrial decline (see chapter 7).

- **Selling shares:** A private limited company can raise money by selling shares in the ownership of the company to friends, relatives, employees and other people known to the business owners. Public limited companies can sell their shares to members of the general public. A **share** is simply a document that entitles its holder to a part of a company. The price paid for a share when it is issued, or its face value, is printed on the front of a share certificate.

▼ *A share certificate for British Telecommuications Plc*

The people and organizations that buy shares in companies are called **investors**. In return for buying shares in a company, investors or **shareholders** share in any profits made by that company. Profits paid out to shareholders are called **dividends**. In general, the more shares a shareholder owns, the more dividends that shareholder is entitled to.

The big advantage to a company of raising money from the sale of shares is that it never has to repay them. If shareholders want their money back, they must sell their shares to somebody else. If they are able to sell their shares for more than their face value, they will make a **capital gain**. The Stock Exchange in London provides a market where people and firms can buy and sell shares in public limited companies.

Most shares issued in the UK are bought by financial organizations known as **investment trusts, unit trusts, pension fund** and **insurance companies**. These companies accept people's savings and use this money to buy the shares of other companies. Dividends and any capital gain in the value of shares are passed on, in part, to savers as interest.

▼ Retained profits, bank and mortgage loans, share sales, and government grants, are just some of the useful sources of capital that can be used to finance business assets, such as machinery and premises, and to pay running costs.

Section **8.2**

Forecasting cash-flows

Controlling cash in and cash out of a business

Gordon Watts knows he must make sure Northern Lights has enough cash each month to pay his business costs. If he is unable to pay his bills, suppliers of raw materials will stop supplying him, the telephone company may cut off his phone, the electricity company may stop supplies of power, and the building society may repossess his business premises. To stop this happening to Northern Lights, Gordon must try to forecast how much cash he needs each month to pay his business costs and make sure he has enough cash in the bank or even in his pocket to pay them. That is, he must forecast how much cash is likely to come in to Northern Lights each month from the sale of light bulbs, and how much cash the business will need to pay out each month. This is known as **cash-flow forecasting**. Gordon starts by listing his estimated cash inflows and cash outflows, and when they are likely to occur.

Northern Lights: cash-flow estimates

Cash inflows	Amount £	When?	Cash outflows	Amount £	When?
Bank loan	£5,000	at start-up only	Wages	£6,000	Monthly
			Materials	£3,000	Monthly
Government grant	£1,500	at start-up only	Mortgage repayments	£800	Monthly
			Bank loan repayments	£70	Monthly
Drawing from savings	£4,100	at start-up only	Business rates	£220	Monthly
			Water meter charges	£45	Every 3 months
Sales revenue	£9,000	month 2 only	Electricity	£1,170	Every 3 months
			Machinery lease charges	£780	Every 3 months
Sales revenues	£18,000	end of each month from month 3	Insurance	£1,200	Once a year
			Telephone	£150	Every 3 months
			Cleaning service	£225	Every 3 months
			Equipment maintenance	£480	Once a year
			Depreciation allownace	£100	Monthly

Most of the cash outflows from Northern Lights will occur every month, but some only happen every 3 months or once a year. That means, every 3 months Gordon's business will face large bills for electricity, the telephone, leases for machinery and cleaning services, and extra large bills at the start of each year from his maintenance contractor and insurance company. Gordon must make sure Northern Lights has enough cash to pay these bills when they occur. This means keeping a cash reserve in his business account at the bank, and adding to the reserve when cash is plentiful. Gordon can then draw on his cash reserve when monthly outflows of cash are greater than inflows.

What is a cash-flow forecast?

Northern Lights shows just how important cash-flow forecasting is in business. Once a business has raised enough finance to start-up, launch a new product or expand production it must make sure it has enough money to keep the business or new project running. This requires forecasting how much cash the business needs to pay for business costs and how much cash the business will earn from sales. **Cash-flow forecasting** allows a firm to plan for and manage the payment of business costs.

A **cash-flow forecast statement** is simply a budget for cash (see also chapter 1). It lists all expected monthly receipts and payments over a given period of time, usually six or twelve months, so that a business can identify when cash will be short supply or in surplus. Using this information the business could arrange a loan to cover a **cash deficit**, when cash outflows exceed cash inflows. Alternatively, the business can save a **cash surplus** for use later in the year when cash reserves are low. When the net cash-flow is in surplus, cash inflows have been greater than outflows. Using cash-flow forecasting to even-out cash surpluses and deficits over time is called **cash-flow smoothing**.

How much cash does a business need?

Cash simply refers to notes and coins held on the business premises or in bank or building society current accounts which can be withdrawn at short notice, usually by using a cheque to make payment.

Knowing exactly how much cash to hold and being able to forecast future cash requirements is one of the most important and difficult jobs facing finance managers in business. A business can be very profitable, but if it invests all of its cash into new machinery and plant it may not have enough money left over to meet day to day bills. When this happens, a firm is said to be **insolvent**.

If a business is insolvent, it may be forced to borrow money from banks and other lenders at high rates of interest. If interest rates rise quickly, an otherwise profitable firm may find itself unable to meet its debts. At this point **creditors** – the people or other firms to whom the business owes money – may decide to demand repayment of their loans. The firm will then have to stop trading and shut down in order to sell off key assets like premises and machinery to raise cash to pay its debts. This is known as **liquidation**.

At first it may seem odd that a profitable business could end up in this situation. However, cash flow problems may occur because of the time difference between receiving revenues from sales and making payments.

For example, wages and salaries have to be paid out in cash each month, and raw materials must also be paid for, usually before finished products can be sold to customers.

What does a cash-flow forecast look like?

The format of a cash-flow forecast will vary between firms. However, within any forecast there will be three main sections. These are:

- **Receipts:** details of cash inflows from various sources – for example, revenues from cash sales, and injections of new capital from loans or share sales. Interest payments on any surplus cash invested in a bank deposit account or other interest bearing accounts can also produce cash for a business.

- **Payments:** details of cash outflows to pay for various items such as wages and salaries, purchases of raw materials and business assets, and overheads, such as telephone and electricity bills, office supplies, rent and rates, which do not vary with the level of output. Mortgage and bank loan repayments, including any interest, will also be included within this section.

- **Summary balance:** This is at the bottom of a cash-flow forecast. It adds up total inflows and total outflows each month and shows the **net cash-flow**. If the net cash-flow is in surplus, the surplus is added to the balance of cash in reserve held in a bank account. If the net cash-flow is in deficit, the deficit is drawn out from the cash reserve to pay for the additional bills. The **opening balance** is the amount of cash held in reserve on the first day of each month, and the **closing balance** is the amount of cash in reserve at the end of each month. The closing balance for one month is, therefore, the opening balance for the next month.

▼ Figure 8.1: Cash flows in and out of a typical private sector business

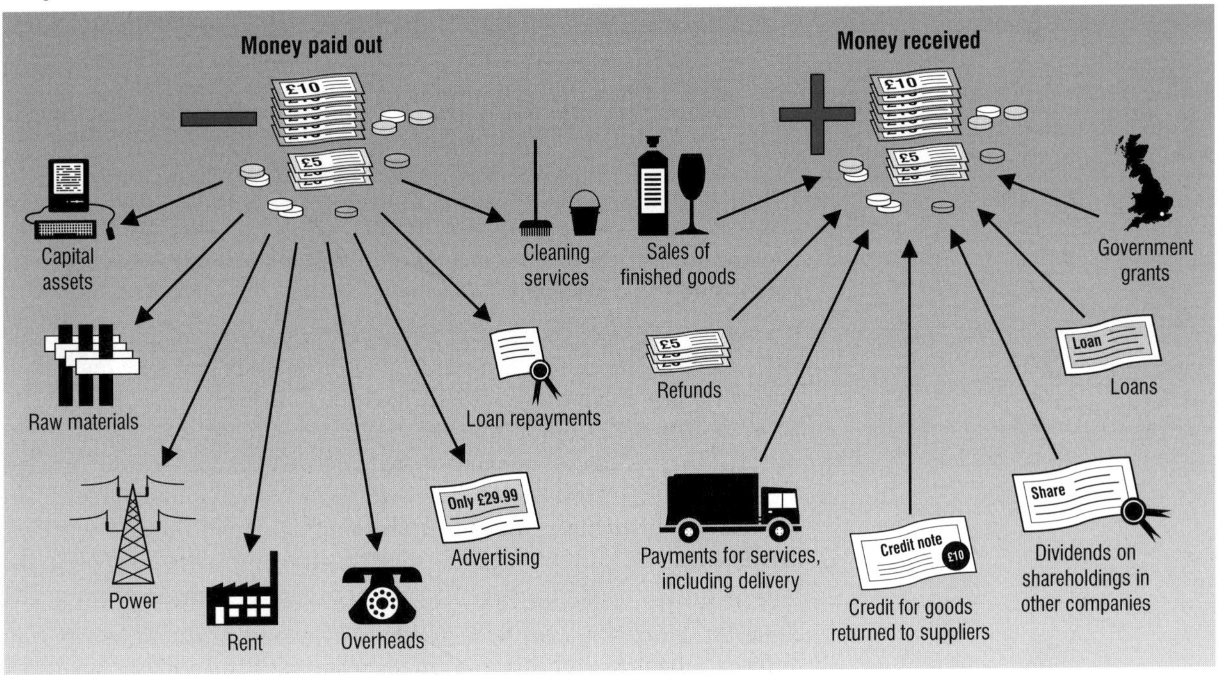

Figure 8.2 shows the cash-flow forecast Gordon Watts has prepared for Northern Lights.

▼ Figure 8.2 : A cash-flow forecast for Northern Lights

		£					
Cash inflows		January	February	March	April	May	June
Cash sales					18,000	18,000	18,000
Credit sales				9,000			
New capital:	Bank loan	5,000					
	Grant	1,500					
	Savings	4,100					
Total cash inflows (A)		**10,600**	**0**	**9,000**	**18,000**	**18,000**	**18,000**
Cash outflows							
Cash purchases:	Market research	2,000					
	Equipment etc.	3,600					
	Material		3,000	3,000	3,000	3,000	3,000
Wages and salaries			6,000	6,000	6,000	6,000	6,000
Overheads:	Mortgage repayments		800	800	800	800	800
	Loan repayments		70	70	70	70	70
	Business rates		220	220	220	220	220
	Water meter			45			45
	Electricity			1,170			1,170
	Lease charges	780			780		
	Insurance	1,200					
	Telephone			150			150
	Cleaning			225			225
	Maintenace	480					
	Depreciation allowance	100	100	100	100	100	100
	Other?						
Total cash outflows (B)		**8,160**	**10,190**	**11,780**	**10,970**	**10,190**	**11,780**
Net cash-flow (A–B)		**2,440**	**−10,190**	**−2,780**	**7,030**	**7,810**	**6,220**
+ Opening bank balance		**0**	**2,440**	**−7,750**	**−10,350**	**−3,500**	**4,310**
= Closing bank balance		**2,440**	**−7,750**	**−10,350**	**−3,500**	**4,310**	**10,530**

The cash flow forecast for Northern Lights is for the first six months in business. It shows in the first month the amount of money Gordon Watts received from his bank loan and the Government grant and the savings he put into the business to pay for market research and some equipment.

Only at the end of the second month in business will Northern Lights be ready to start selling light bulbs, but it is only likely to produce 3,000 light bulbs for sale in March. These first 3,000 light bulbs are sold on credit to the retail chain that wants to stock Northern Lights bulbs. The retail chain can wait 3 months before making payment of £9,000 for them. From April production will be on target for 6,000 light bulbs per month at £3 each. Cash inflows from March onwards are the expected sales revenues.

The cash-flow forecast predicts Northern Lights will have a net cash deficit in February and March. This means drawing down reserves in the bank account to pay for the costs not covered by sales revenues. The balance at the bank is used up and goes negative. This could mean bad news for Gordon. He will not have enough money to pay his business costs. However, his bank manager has allowed Gordon to have a bank overdraft of up to £12,000. This will help Gordon cover his costs.

From April the net cash flow of Northern Lights is forecast to be in surplus because sales revenues exceed monthly costs. These net cash surpluses are used to pay off the overdraft and by May the balance at the bank will be back into credit.

The net cash-flow forecast for Northern Lights can be plotted on a graph (see figure 8.3).

▼ Figure 8.3 : A graph of the cash-flow forecast for Northern Lights from figure 8.2

Portfolio Activity 8.2

Completing cash-flow forecasts by hand can be time-consuming. Incorrect entries may also be overlooked and carried forward from one month to the next. To overcome these problems and improve accuracy, Gordon Watts has asked you to set up a spreadsheet on a computer to help him calculate cash-flows and closing balances for Northern Lights. Using a spreadsheet will automatically re-calculate total inflows and outflows, and opening and closing cash balances each month, every time a figure is changed.

1. Load a spreadsheet package, for example EXCEL or LOTUS 123, on to your computer and copy the cash-flow forecast for Northern Lights from figure 8.1.

2. Enter formulae to sum the spreadsheet column totals for receipts and payments each month.

3. Also enter formulae to calculate the net cash-flow each month by subtracting the cell containing total payments from the cell containing total receipts.

4. Enter formulae to calculate the opening balance and closing balance and to carry forward the closing balance each month to the next.

5. Check that your spreadsheet works before proceeding.

6. Use your spreadsheet to adjust the cash-flow forecast for Northern Lights to allow for the following additional flows:

   ● Northern Lights sells an additional £500 of light bulbs on credit in April

   ● the bill for electricity is £400 more than expected in June

   ● sales are £300 less than expected in May

7. Gordon has forgotten that value added tax of 17.5% is added to the price of each lightbulb. Any VAT receipts must be paid over to the Customs and Excise department of the government every six months. What impact does a payment of £11,500 in value added tax receipts in June have on the cash-flow forecast for Northern Lights?

8. Why is cash-flow forecasting so important in business?

What causes cash-flow problems?

A business that fails to forecast their cash-flows with some accuracy could run out of cash and be unable to pay its business costs. It may be forced to raise cash quickly by selling off some assets which are important for the business. This will damage the future profitability of the business. Alternatively the business may have to borrow money at very high rates of interest and this will eat into profits. In the worst case, the business may have to close down.

Businesses can run short of cash because of the following problems:

- expanding too quickly (**overtrading**)
- buying too many fixed assets
- holding too many materials and finished goods in stock
- giving too much credit
- borrowing too much
- unexpected price inflation
- seasonal variations in sales and costs

Overtrading: A business that tries to expand production too quickly and runs out of cash doing so is said to be overtrading. Increased production creates a need for more cash to pay for extra raw materials and possibly overtime payments for workers. However, it may be some time before the business is ready to sell the extra output to raise more revenue.

Buying too many fixed assets: Spending too much money buying fixed assets, such as new machinery, can be a significant drain on business cash reserves. It may be better spread the cost of new machinery by leasing them or buying them on hire purchase.

Overstocking: A business may run of cash because it has spent too much building up stocks of materials and finished goods. Stocks may also become unwanted if fashions or technology change or if there is fall in demand for the product.

Borrowing too much: A firm may borrow too much money. This means loan payments each month will be high. If interest rates rise loan payments will get even bigger. These payments are likely to be a severe drain on cash-flow and profit.

Poor credit control: A business must make sure that credit is only given to customers who are reliable and have enough financial resources to pay their bills on time. A business may run short of cash if customers take too long to pay for the goods and services they ordered. Some business customers may purposefully delay paying their own bills because they have cash-flow problems of their own.

Price inflation: If, for example, wages and raw material costs rise suddenly and unexpectedly, cash reserves will be used up quicker and leave too little cash for other unforeseen costs. Firms often underestimate the impact of rising prices on their costs in their cash-flow forecasts.

Seasonal fluctuations: Some businesses are seasonal with cash in-flows and outflows varying by time of year. For example, firework manufacturers may spend money throughout the year producing fireworks but find that their main source of cash inflow is in the weeks leading up to early November. The business will therefore have to manage its cash-flows carefully so that revenues in the period leading up to November are sufficient to pay for costs throughout the following year.

THE PROBLEM WITH CASH-FLOW

The future never holds to plan. There is likely to be a difference from forecasts almost from the moment they are made. Rob Johnson, lecturer in Entrepreneurship at the London Business School says that the most common problems are that sales fall below expectations, costs are higher and the pricing of the product or service is too low. The last problem is very difficult to put right because customers will not like prices being raised.

As a result "most new business ventures run into cash-flow problems", Johnson says,

requiring refinancing or worse. Companies that are "profitable" on paper frequently go bust because they have run out of cash. Atlantech, a computer software firm were so obsessed by cash for the first three years of life – by which time sales annual were heading for £5 million – it ran its business mainly on a cash basis. Whilst many start-ups are driven by entrepreneurs with a marketing bent, business advisors argue that there is a strong case for a finance expert to be part of the team from day one

The Financial Times 25.4.1995

Portfolio Activity 8.3

Deft Designs is a small business run by Denise Thorn from a small rented art studio. She designs and makes handmade greetings cards to sell in craft shops. In most months she produces and sells 1000 greeting cards at £2 each.

Denise would like help producing a cash-flow forecast so that she can manage her business finances better and plan for unforeseen events which may impact on her business costs and revenues. She was sick a few months ago and was unable to meet some orders. As a result her revenue was down and she had to use a bank overdraft to cover a large electricity bill. The overdraft has now been paid off but Denise does not want to run out of cash again.

Set up a cash-flow forecast for Denise on a computer spreadsheet showing total cash in and out of her business each month, and her cash balances. She currently has £1,500 in her business account at a bank and has made you the following list of regular outgoings.

The cash-flow forecast will be from June to December. Quarterly bills for electricity, the telephone, and insurance premiums are payable in June, September and December.

Denise always manages to sell more cards at Christmas so she has asked you to double her purchase of materials and paints in November and double her sales revenue in December.

Deft Designs

Cash outflow	Amount	How often
Rent for studio	£75	Each month
Materials	£50	Each month
Paints	£25	Each month
Loan repayments	£35	Each month
Telephone	£60	Every 3 months
Bus fares	£18	Each month
Cleaner	£20	Each month
Electricity	£150	Every 3 months
Insurance	£80	Every 3 months
My wage	£800	Each month

Denise has applied for a bank loan of £1,000. The bank has agreed and will advance this amount in July. She will use the money to help her buy a computer for £2,500 in August. Denise will use the computer to make and save new designs and keep financial records.

Section **8.3** **Using information on costs to make business decisions**

Eurostar looks desperately for the arrival of breakeven point

Football is proving to be an attractive game for Eurostar. Last July, the number of fans travelling to France for the World Cup helped the cross-Channel train operator to record it smallest monthly loss to date. The £4 million deficit was a victory in the company's eyes – the closest it has come to breaking even. And next Summer, another football tournament could see it break through the zero profit and loss barrier.

Should England and the other home nations somehow struggle through to the finals. Nearly five years after the start of services, break-even has assumed monumental importance to Eurostar: breaking even will help prove that it is more than just an expensive train set. It is desperate to woo new customers to fill trains that are still running to Brussels and Paris less than a third full in off-peak hours.

The obvious target as with airlines is the business traveller, a loyal and lucrative market for Eurostar, accounting for only 37 per cent of revenues. But the trick to increase revenues is to fill the empty seats in economy and it is the leisure traveller that is the focus of marketing efforts.

For now losses continue. Eurostar UK lost £180 million in 1996, £135 million in 1997 and £95 million last year. Trains to Paris are still running half full. Those to Brussels are even emptier, with only 35% of seats sold

The Times 7.7.1999

1. Eurostar must pay charges to run trains on the tracks owned by Railtrack Plc in the UK. Part of the charge is a fixed amount, and the rest is made up of a variable charge which depends on the number of trains run. What other costs do you think Eurostar has to pay to provide a train service? Make a list, sorting the cost items into those you think are fixed costs and those costs which are variable.

2. Passenger fares are the major source of revenue for Eurostar. But in what other ways can Eurostar make revenue? (hint: are passengers the only things the trains can carry? What services may be available for passengers to use on board?).

3. In the article, Eurostar has had problems making enough revenue to cover its business costs. What does breaking-even mean and why is it an important step for Eurostar to make?

4. Eurostar trains are not attracting enough passengers. What pricing and service level strategies could Eurostar adopt in an attempt to attract more passengers?

The cost of different levels of output

Plotting total costs

A business can use information on business costs to help it decide how much it needs to produce and the selling price it needs to charge to make a profit.

You will recall from section 8.1 that businesses have fixed costs which do not vary as a result of changes in the level of output of goods or services. Examples include rent and rates, loan repayments, lease charges for machinery, and office overheads. The fixed costs for Northern Lights are £1,800 each month whether Gordon Watt produces 1, 100 or 10,000 light bulbs. If we plot fixed costs against output, the fixed cost line will be flat (see figure 8.4).

▼ Figure 8.4 : A plot of fixed costs against output of light bulbs at Northern Lights

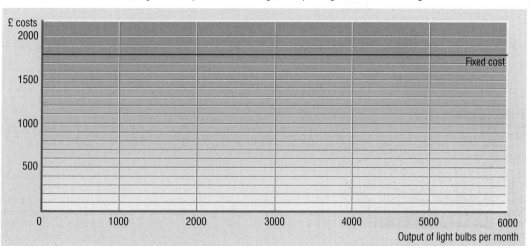

Remember also that business costs which do vary directly with the level of output are called variable costs. Example will include the costs of raw materials, power, packaging costs and the wages of production workers. Gordon Watt has estimated the variable cost of producing each light bulb is £1.80. If we plot variable costs against output the variable cost line will slope upwards, showing that total variable costs increase as more is produced (see figure 8.5).

▼ Figure 8.5 : A plot of variable costs against output of light bulbs at Northern Lights

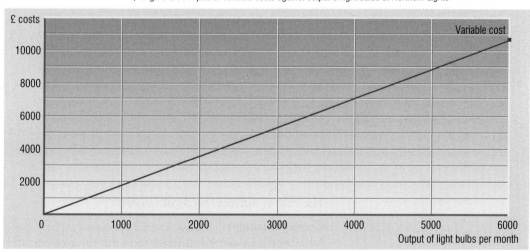

Adding fixed and variable costs together gives the total cost of production in a business.

Total cost (TC) = total fixed costs (FC) + total variable costs (VC)

The total cost of production is the cost of producing any given level of output. As output rises total cost will increase because total variable costs will increase. So, for example, if Northern Lights produces 6,000 light bulbs each month, its total costs will be £1,800 of fixed costs and £10,800 of total variable costs: £12,600 of total costs.

We can plot the relationship between total costs and output of light bulbs at Northern Lights in a graph. When output is zero total cost is exactly equal to fixed costs. When output is 6,000 light bulbs per month, total cost is £12,600. The total cost line is upward sloping because variable costs increase with output (see figure 8.6).

▼ Figure 8.6 : A plot of totals costs against output of light bulbs at Northern Lights

Northern Lights

Monthly cost schedule

Output	Fixed costs	Variable cost (£1.80 per unit)	Total cost
0	1,800	0	1,800
1000	1,800	1,800	3,600
2000	1,800	3,600	5,400
3000	1,800	5,400	7,200
4000	1,800	7,200	9,000
5000	1,800	9,000	10,800
6000	1,800	10,800	12,600

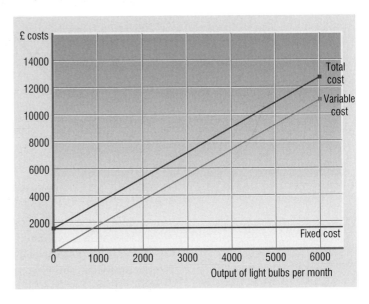

Calculating an average cost

It is useful to calculate the average cost of producing each unit of output using the following equation:

$$\text{Average cost per unit} = \frac{\text{total cost}}{\text{total output}}$$

Northern Lights produces 6,000 light bulbs each month at a total cost of £12,600. This is made up of £1,800 of fixed costs and £10,800 of variable costs (or 6,000 x £1.80). Therefore, the average cost of producing each light bulb is

$$\text{Average cost per light bulb} = \frac{£12,600}{6,000} = £2.10$$

Gordon Watt must, therefore, charge a price higher than £2.10 per light bulb to make enough revenue to pay the variable cost of producing each light bulb and to pay off some fixed costs. But he must be careful not to charge too high a price, otherwise consumers will not buy his light bulbs and he will not make any revenue. Gordon has chosen a price of £3 per light bulb based on his market research.

Once a business has been able to calculate the average cost of producing each unit of its output it can add a 'mark-up' for profit to give an appropriate selling price per unit. Gordon Watt has added a mark-up of 90 pence per light bulb to his average cost of £2.10 per light bulb to give a selling price of £3 each.

In the same way a business can calculate the average cost per unit of a service. For example, the average cost of one hour of labour from a car mechanic or one train mile. All a business needs to know are the fixed and variable costs associated with these activities. So, if a mechanic spends three hours working on a car at a total cost of £270 in wages, materials, power, administration and other overheads, then the average cost of each labour hour is £90 (i.e. £270 ÷ 3 hours).

Similarly, if it costs a total of £6,000 for a train to travel 200 miles then the average cost per train mile is £30 (i.e. £6,000 ÷ 200 miles).

What is break-even analysis?

The break-even level of output
Gordon Watt wants to know if his production and sales target for Northern Lights of 6,000 light bulbs each month will make enough revenue to cover production costs and make his business a healthy profit. He would also like to know what is the minimum number of light bulbs he will need to produce if things go wrong to make sure he can just cover his costs and stay in business. To do this he must use break-even analysis.

Break-even analysis is used by many business organizations to predict the level of sales they will need to achieve to cover their costs and to see how changes in output, costs and prices affect profits.

The **break-even level of output** is that level of output where total sales revenue is exactly equal to total costs. At this point, the firm neither makes a profit nor a loss. That is, the break-even point occurs where:

Total revenue (£) = total cost = (total fixed costs + total variable costs)

Calculating break-even point
A firm can calculate its break-even level of output if it knows its costs and the price it can charge for each unit of output. There is a simple formula. Gordon Watt can use the formula to calculate the break-even point for Northern Lights. He knows that Northern Lights has fixed costs each month of £1,800 and variable costs of £1.80 per light bulb, and that his light bulbs sell for £3 per unit. He puts these figures into the formula below:

$$\text{Break-even level of output} = \frac{\text{total cost}}{\text{price per unit} - \text{variable cost per unit}}$$

So the break-even point for Northern Lights is

$$1{,}500 \text{ light bulbs per month} = \frac{\pounds1{,}800}{\pounds3 - \pounds1.80} = \frac{\pounds1{,}800}{\pounds1.20}$$

That is, Northern Lights must produce and sell 1,500 light bulbs each month at a price of £3 each just to break-even. If more than 1,500 light bulbs are sold each month, Northern Lights will make a profit. If less than 1,500 are sold each month the business will make a loss.

DangerDVD.com is a company that supplies DVD video and audio discs to customers over the internet from a rented warehouse in Cardiff. The company is owned and managed by Christopher Mush.

The rent for the warehouse is £150 per week. Chris also pays out £20 a week on heating and lighting and £80 on the repayment of a bank loan. He has also hired some computer equipment and fork lift trucks at a cost of £50 per week and employs two friends to help him meet customer orders. At present they pay themselves 50 pence for each DVD disc they send out. Postage and packaging costs for each disc are £2.50. Each disc costs £10 for Danger DVD to buy and is sold on for £18.

1. Calculate the total fixed costs of Danger DVD. What is the variable cost per disc delivered?.

2. Calculate total cost, total revenue and profit or loss for the following number of discs delivered each week:

   a 20   b 60   c 200

3. What is the average cost per disc delivered when (a) when 60 discs are delivered each week, and (b) when 200 are delivered each week

4. Calculate how many discs Chris Mush needs to sell each week to break-even.

5. What would happen to his break-even level of output if:
   • the company that supplied him with DVDs offered a bulk discount reducing the cost of each disc to £9
   • because of fierce competition from business rivals, Chris had to lower the price he sold each disc for to £16

6. Suggest how break-even analysis can help Chris plan future output and prices.

Break-even charts

The break-even point can be also be found by plotting total costs and total revenues on a break-even chart.

The first step involved in producing a break-even chart is to calculate total cost and total revenue for a number of different levels of output (from zero upwards). Table 8.1 is a schedule of outputs in Northern Lights from 0 to 6,000 light bulbs per month and their corresponding costs and revenues. These figures can then be used to plot lines for total cost and total revenue in the break-even chart in figure 8.7.

▼ Table 8.1 : Schedule of monthly outputs, costs and revenues for Northern Lights

Output per month	Fixed costs	Variable cost (£1.80 per unit)	Total cost	Total revenue (at £3 per unit)	Profit or loss
0	£1,800	£0	£1,800	£0	−£1,800
1,500	£1,800	£2,700	£4,500	£4,500	0
3,000	£1,800	£5,400	£7,200	£9,000	£1,800
4,500	£1,800	£8,100	£9,900	£13,500	£3,600
6,000	£1,800	£10,800	£12,600	£18,000	£5,400

Figure 8.7 : A break-even chart for Northern Lights

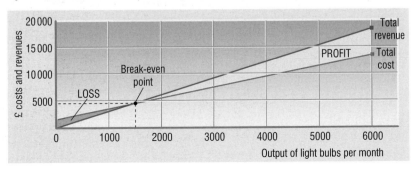

In the break-even chart the minimum level of output Northern Lights must produce and sell each month is found at the point at which the total revenue line crosses the total cost line. Break-even is at 1,500 light bulbs per month.

When the total cost line is above the total revenue line Northern Lights will make a loss because it is not producing and selling enough light bulbs to cover its costs. When the total cost line is below the total revenue line Northern Lights will be making a profit. Gordon Watt must make sure he produces and sells enough lights bulbs each month to make sure Northern Lights stays above break-even point and in the area of profit in the break-even chart.

Break-even analysis and business planning

Break-even charts are a useful business planning tool. This is because managers can use these charts to forecast what might happen to the break-even level of output and profits if their business costs or prices change. For example, if prices fall then the break-even level of output will rise because more units will need to be sold to cover production costs.

Figure 8.8 shows the impact on Northern Lights of a price reduction from £3 to £2.70 per light bulb. Now Northern Lights must produce and sell 2,000 light bulbs each month to break even rather than 1,500.

Figure 8.9 shows the impact of a rise in materials costs on the light bulb business. Variable costs per light bulb are now £2.10 instead of £1.80. In order to break even Northern Lights must now sell 1,800 light bulbs at £3 each month to break even. An increase in the fixed costs of the business would have a similar impact.

▼ *Figure 8.8: The impact of a price reduction on break even*

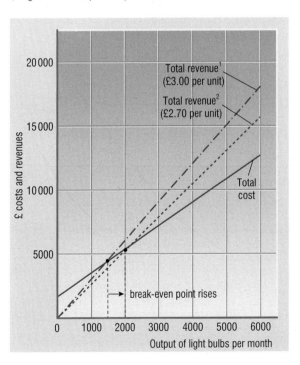

▼ *Figure 8.9 : The impact of an increase in variable costs (VC) on break even*

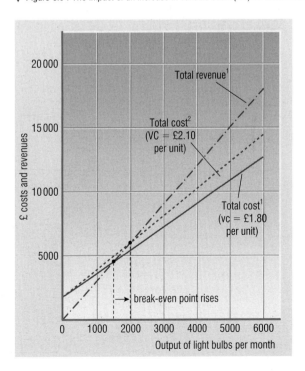

The margin of safety

Once a business has forecast the level of output and sales that it must achieve at a given price to break even, it will attempt to exceed this level in order to make a profit. In the case of Northern Lights, Gordon Watt plans to make and sell 6,000 light bulbs each month – 4,500 more than he requires to break even. The firm will be operating above break even output and will be in the area of profit. This difference between his target level of sales and his break-even output is known as the margin of safety. In other words, Gordon Watt has allowed his business a **margin of safety** of 4,500 units. Sales of light bulbs can therefore fall by up to 4,500 below his target of monthly sales before Northern Lights will start to make losses. This is clearly shown in figure 8.10.

▼ Figure 8.10 : The margin of safety for Northern Lights

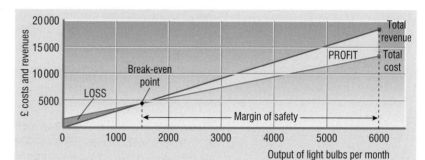

Portfolio Activity 8.6

Dream Chocs Ltd is a small business that sells hand-made chocolates to up-market sweet shops and department stores. It has fixed costs of £50,000 per year and variable costs of £2.50 per box of chocolates. Each box of chocolates sells for £5.

1. Use a computer spreadsheet to complete the following schedule of costs and revenues for different levels of yearly output from Dream Chocs Ltd.

Boxes of chocolates per year	Fixed costs	Total variable	Total costs	Total revenue	Profit/loss
0	£50,000				
10,000					−£25,000
20,000			£100,000		
30,000					
40,000		£100,000			
50,000					
60,000				£300,000	

2. What is the break-even level of output per year at Dream Chocs?

3. Use the information from your spreadsheet to plot total costs and total revenue against output in a break-even chart .

4. For each one of the following events, recalculate each column in your table and then replot your break-even chart. What is the impact on break-even of:
   ● an fall in product price to £4.50 per box
   ● an increase in the variable cost per unit to £3 per box
   ● an increase in fixed costs by £10,000 per year.

Section **8.4**

Calculating profit or loss

The profit and loss statement

What is profit?

Profit is a reward for risk taking in business. When Gordon Watt started Northern Lights he took a risk. If the business failed, he would have lost the money he spent from his own savings on market research and equipment. He would also have to sell off his business to raise cash to pay off pay his bank loan and mortgage. If he were unable to raise enough money to clear his business debts he might have to draw out more of his own savings to pay them, or sell off his personal possessions to raise cash. However, if Northern Lights did well, Gordon Watt would be rewarded with profit.

With the exception of charities, the main objective of most private sector organizations is to make a profit (see chapter 1). A profit is made when total revenue exceeds total expenditures or costs. A loss occurs when costs are greater than revenues. A business can either make a profit, loss, or break even when revenues are exactly equal to costs.

At the end of his first year in business Gordon Watt wants to calculate how much profit he has made. Northern Lights has performed better than expected and a significant cash reserve has built up in his bank, but he still has some bills to pay from this. Gordon can use a profit and loss statement to calculate how much profit he has made over the last year.

▼ Profit

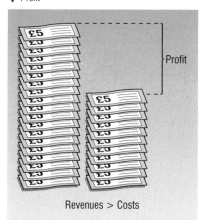

Revenues > Costs

▼ Breaking even

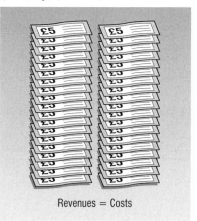

Revenues = Costs

▼ Loss

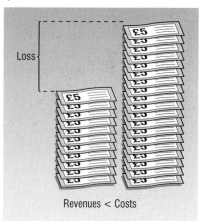

Revenues < Costs

A **profit and loss statement** shows how much profit or loss an organization has made over a 12-month period. It shows:

● **Turnover** = total sales revenue

● **Gross profit** = the difference between turnover and the cost of producing all the goods or services sold (known as the **cost of sales**)

● **Net (or operating) profit** = gross profit less all other overhead expenses, such as rent, rates, administration, advertising, telephone, etc.

▼ *What happens to profit?*

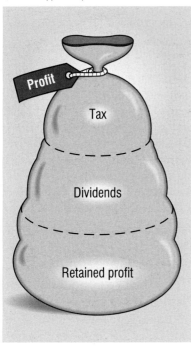

- **Profit before tax** = net profit plus any other income, less any interest paid on loans

- **Profit after tax** = profit less corporation tax

If a profit is made after tax at the end of a 12-month period, some is likely to be paid out to the business owners either in the form of drawings, or, in the case of limited companies, as dividends on shares. The remainder of the profit after tax may be retained by the business as savings or used to buy more assets, such as bigger premises or machinery.

So, will Northern Lights go out this year?
Northern Lights sold a total of £200,000 light bulbs in the first 12 months of trading. Gordon Watt has added up the cost of all the materials and wages paid out to make these light bulbs. These are the costs of sales and they add up to £120,000. He has also added up all his overhead expenses for the year – business rates, telephone and cleaning bills, etc. – and this sum comes to £33,000. Total interest charges for the year on his bank loan and mortgage were £9,700.

Using this information Gordon Watt produces a profit and loss statement for Northern Lights and calculates the amount of profit made over the last year. His profit and loss statement is shown in figure 8.11.

▼ *Figure 8.11 : A profit and loss statement for Northern Lights.*

Northern Lights

Profit and loss statement for the year ending 31.12.0X

Turnover	**£200,000**
less costs of sales	£120,000
Gross profit	**£80,000**
less overheads	£33,000
Net profit	**£47,000**
Less interest	£9,700
Profit before tax	**£37,300**
Less corporation tax	£7,460
Profit after tax	**£29,840**
Of which:	
profit paid to owner	£20,000
profit retained by business	£9,840

The gross profit made by Northern Lights last year was £80,000 – the difference between sales revenues and the total variable costs of producing the light bulbs sold. But Gordon should not celebrate his good fortune just yet. He still has to deduct all the business overheads from gross profit to get a net profit of £47,000 for the year. After deducting interest payments on his loans and his mortgage, Gordon arrives at a profit before tax of £37,000 for his business. The Inland Revenue has informed Gordon that he must pay corporation tax of £7,460 from the profit his business has made. This will cut his after tax profit to £29,840. Not bad for his first year in business, thinks Gordon. He decides to celebrate by using £20,000 of his profit after tax to buy a new car, pay off some credit card debts and have a luxury holiday. This leaves £9,840 of profit in the business which he can use to expand Northern Lights.

Portfolio Activity 8.7

1. Copy the profit and loss statement for Northern Lights in figure 8.10 into a computer spreadsheet. Set up your spreadsheet so that it calculates gross profit, net profit and profit before and after tax automatically.

2. Input an equation to calculate corporation tax as 20% of profit before tax.

3. Calculate and record the impact on profit after tax at Northern Lights if each of the following had occurred instead:

- sales were £240,000
- costs of sales were £140,000
- overheads were £50,000
- interest charges were only £5,000
- corporation tax was cut to 10%

Key words

In your own words, write down explanations and definitions for the following key words and terms in this chapter:

Profit	Long-term finance	Dividends	Overtrading
Fixed costs	Short-term finance	Capital gain	Break-even point
Start-up costs	Retained profit	Cashflows	Average cost
Overheads	Overdraft	Cash-flow forecast	Margin of safety
Variable costs	Bank loan	Cash-flow smoothing	Profit and loss statement
Capital	Leasing	Creditors	Gross profit
Assets	Mortgage	Insolvent	Net profit
Venture capital	Investors	Liquidation	Profit before tax
Working capital	Shareholders	Opening and closing balances at bank	Profit after tax

Test your knowledge

1 Which of the following business costs is normally thought of as a variable cost?
A mortgage repayments on business premises
B supplies of materials and components
C wages of office workers
D business rates

2 Which of the following would increase fixed costs in a business?
A a rise in sales revenues
B a rise in interest charges on loans
C a rise in raw material prices
D a rise in packaging and printing costs

3 The break-even level of output in a firm can be found at the point at which?
A total sales revenue = business start-up costs
B total sales revenue = total variable costs
C total sales revenue = total costs
D total sales revenue = fixed costs

4 If a business plans for a 'margin of safety', it has planned to?
A increase its cash holdings in a bank account
B produce at the break-even level of output
C produce an output greater than break-even
D produce any output where sales revenue covers variable costs

5 A business producing protective cases for mobile phones has fixed costs of £240,000 per year. The variable cost per case is £2. If each case is sold for £10 how many cases must the firm produce and sell to break even?
A 24,000
B 120,000
C 30,000
D 10,000

6 What is the difference between gross profit and net profit?
A overheads
B interest payments on loans
C corporation tax on profits
D the costs of sales

Questions 7 to 9 share the following answers:
A £52,000
B £80,000
C £215,000
D £65,000

A small business has recorded the following financial information over the last year.

Sales turnover	£320,000
Costs of sales	£105,000
Overheads	£135,000
Interest charges	£15,000
Corporation tax payable	£13,000

7 What is the gross profit of the business?

8 What is the net profit of the business?

9 What is profit after tax for the business?

Questions 10 and 11 share the following answers
A −£3,500
B £6,700
C £3,600
D −£9,100

A small business has the following regular cashflows each month.

Wages	£36,000
Electricity	£1,940
Sales revenue	£78,000
Telephone	£340
Cleaning	£120
Insurance	£130
Materials	£23,500
Transport	£970

10 Last month the business had an overdraft of £8,300 at the bank. What will be the closing balance of cash held in the business bank account this month?

11 Next month the business has to pay a VAT bill for £18,100. What will be the closing balance of cash held in the business bank account next month?

12 a Explain, using examples, the difference between fixed and variable costs in business.

b A small manufacturing firm producing penknives has fixed costs of £150,000 per year and variable costs of £3 per unit. Each penknife is sold for £15. How many penknives must the firm produce and sell each year to break even?

c How much profit would the firm earn if it produced and sold 25,000 penknives each year?

d Use the information from b and c above to draw a break-even chart for levels of output between 0 and 25,000 penknives. Show the break-even point and the areas of profit and loss on your chart.

13 a Explain, using examples, why cash-flow forecasting is so important in business.

b Give three examples of likely cash-outflows from a new business.

c Give two examples of likely cash inflows to a new business.

d Suggest two ways a new business could finance start-up.

e Explain three things that could cause cash-flow problems in a new business.

chapter 9 Business transactions and documents

What you need to learn

When a business buys or sells goods and services, a variety of **financial documents** are completed in sequence. A business must be aware of these documents and how, when and why they should be completed.

Why it is important for all firms to keep records of all their financial transactions: **to monitor incomes and expenditures, to record purchases and sales, to keep accounts with customers up to date, to produce financial accounts** for business owners and for the tax authorities, **to monitor business performance, to obtain finance,** and **to reduce the risk of mistakes, theft and fraud.**

The purpose of each financial document and the part it plays in the sequence of ordering, checking, recording and paying for goods and services.

How to complete examples of financial documents accurately, and understand why accuracy is so important in business. Mistakes can be expensive. Businesses can reduce mistakes and the risk of fraud and theft by introducing a range of security checks including

authorisation of orders, checking invoices against orders and goods received notes and **authorised cheque signatories.**

Purchase documents record goods and services bought in to a business and the money paid out for them. They include **order forms, good received notes** and (paid up) **invoices.**

Sales documents record goods and services sent out to customers and the money paid in for them. They include **order forms, delivery notes, invoices, credit and debit notes, remittance advice notes** and **statements of accounts.**

Receipts documents record how much money has been paid for goods and services supplied. They include **receipts, cheques, paying in slips** and bank **statements.**

Some businesses fill-in documents by hand; others use computer programs. You will need to find out about a **computerised finance system** and the advantages or disadvantages of using a computer spreadsheet.

Section **9.1**

What are financial transactions?

Trade takes place when producers supply their goods and services to consumers in return for money or other goods and services. A **financial transaction** takes place whenever a person or organization pays money to another person or organization for goods and services ordered or received.

Many millions of financial transactions take place every day all over the world. Whenever you buy an ice cream or a can of drink in a shop, you are making a financial transaction. You pay money to the shopkeeper to receive the ice cream or drink. When you travel on a bus or train, you pay money for a ticket which allows you to use the service.

Inward and outward transactions

Because most firms are not just producers, but also consumers of goods and services, they not only receive payments but also make payments to other people and organizations. That is, most firms will receive money and also pay money out. This means there are two types of financial transaction in business:

- **Inward transactions**
- **Outward transactions**

Inward and outward transactions

▼ *Inward transactions*   ▼ *Outward transactions*

Inward transactions are payments of money received by a firm. For most business organizations inward transactions will include:

- Payments for goods and services sold to members of the public
- Payments for goods and services sold to other businesses
- Loans of money from banks and other lenders

Other organizations can receive inward transactions in other forms. For example, limited companies can receive money from the sale of shares; charities will receive donations; and the government receives money in the form of taxes (see chapter 6).

Outward transactions are payments made by a firm to other firms or people. A firm will usually make payments for:

- Wages for the hire of workers
- Raw materials and component parts from suppliers
- Services, such as cleaning, maintenance, insurance, and advertising
- Fixed assets such as premises, machinery, vehicles, and other equipment
- Overheads such as telephone charges, stamps, stationary, rent and rates
- Loan repayments and interest charges
- Any Value Added Tax (VAT) collected on goods and services sold will also have to be returned to the Government's Customs and Excise Department

▼ *Some consumer goods and services*

Every purchase made by a business or individual customer is a sale to the firm that receives money in payment. An outward transaction is a payment for goods and services. An inward transaction is a sale.

Payment is made once an **invoice** is issued following an order for goods and services. An invoice will contain details of goods and services supplied, how much is owed by the customer, and when payment is due (see 9.2).

Business to consumer sales

Organizations that sell goods and services to private individuals are suppliers in **consumer markets**. They will sell finished products which are for the immediate use, or consumption, of those who buy them. These include:

● Durable goods, e.g. video recorders, cars, jewellery, clothes

● Non-durable goods, e.g. washing powders, food and drink, paper

● Personal services, e.g. hairdressing, window cleaning, insurance

Business to business sales

However, not all organizations supply consumer goods and services. Many supply **industrial markets** in which the consumers are other business organizations. The goods and services supplied to business consumers are wanted because they will be used in the production of other goods and services. Raw materials, component parts, machinery, computer equipment, vehicles, stationary are just a few examples of unfinished and finished goods used by firms in producing, selling, and distributing their own goods and services. Specialist services such as advertising agencies, management training, maintenance, haulage, commercial insurance and banking, and many more, are also available to business customers.

Selling goods and services

In general, firms sell consumer and industrial goods and services in one of two main ways:

● **Cash sales** mean that goods and services are paid for immediately they are received, either by cash or by cheque. Most shops sell goods and services on this basis. When you buy a bar of chocolate or a CD, you will normally pay for it there and then.

● **Sales on credit** involve the customer 'buying now and paying later'. Sales on credit can take a number of forms.

Trade credit is often given by suppliers to their regular business customers. They are allowed up to 30, 60, or even 90 days to pay in full for goods and services they have received.

Credit sales are a popular method used by mail order firms. The customer is allowed to spread their payments for goods received over a number of weeks. A relatively low-price item, such as a pair of jeans, can usually be paid for in regular weekly amounts over 12-24 weeks, while a high-price item, such as a three-piece suite, can be paid for over 52 weeks, or sometimes even more. The customer owns the goods received after the first instalment has been paid.

Hire purchase (HP) also allows the customer to pay for the goods or services they have received in regular (monthly) instalments, often including an interest charge, with the repayments spread over anything from 6 months to a number of years. Unlike credit sales, an HP agreement will normally require the customer to pay a deposit of 10% or 20% of the total price immediately the goods or services are ordered or received. The goods do not become the property of the customer until the final payment has been made.

HP is a popular method of payment used by smaller firms to buy the machinery and other equipment they need. Many suppliers now offer interest-free HP to encourage customers to buy their goods and services.

▼ An example of a hire purchase payment for a television

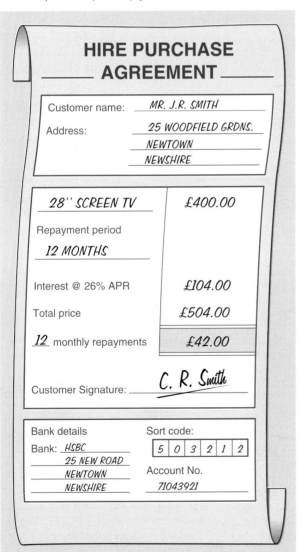

HIRE PURCHASE AGREEMENT

Customer name: MR. J.R. SMITH

Address: 25 WOODFIELD GRDNS.
NEWTOWN
NEWSHIRE

28" SCREEN TV	£400.00

Repayment period
12 MONTHS

Interest @ 26% APR	£104.00
Total price	£504.00
12 monthly repayments	£42.00

Customer Signature: C. R. Smith

Bank details
Bank: HSBC
25 NEW ROAD
NEWTOWN
NEWSHIRE

Sort code: 5 0 3 2 1 2

Account No. 71043921

People and organizations to whom goods or services have been sold on credit are known as **debtors**. The business organization that allows customers to pay on credit is known as their **creditor** until they pay for the goods and services they have received.

Allowing customers to pay on credit can encourage sales because they are able to spread their payments. This is an especially important advantage for individual and business customers who have limited incomes and/or savings. However, for the supplier there is always a risk that the customer may default - that is, not pay up. This will involve spending time and money chasing the debt in writing, and even legal action through a court if they still fail to pay.

Methods of payment

There are a number of ways an individual or business customer can choose to settle cash sales or payments for trade credit, credit sales, or hire purchase:

- **Cash:** Cash is generally thought of as notes and coins, and is the most popular method of payment. However, only smaller purchases tend to be made with cash. Around 90% of the total value of all payments today are made by other means. This is because cash can be awkward to handle, especially in large amounts, and is easily lost or stolen.

  Many small businesses like to be paid in cash because there is little chance of it being traced if they do not declare it as income to the Inland Revenue for tax purposes. This is illegal. However, most large firms are unlikely to pay using notes and coins and prefer to receive payments by more secure methods.

● **Cheques:** Most people and businesses have bank or building society accounts into which they can deposit money and from which they can make payments. Cheques are simply a way of transferring 'cash' from one account to another. Cheques avoid the inconvenience of cash and are more secure, provided they have been filled out properly and signed by the account holder. The name of the account holder will usually be printed on the cheque. We will look at cheques in more detail in section 9.2.

▼ *Most financial transactions today are made using cheques. In 1997 £1,196 billion worth of cheques were cleared by UK banks.*

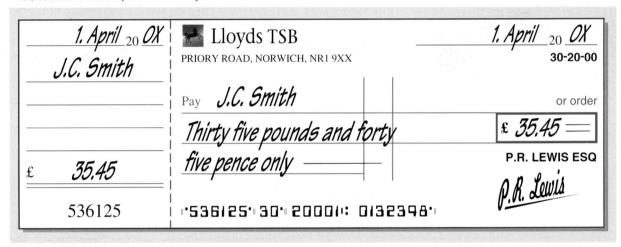

▼ *Figure 9.1: An example of how a cheque makes payment*

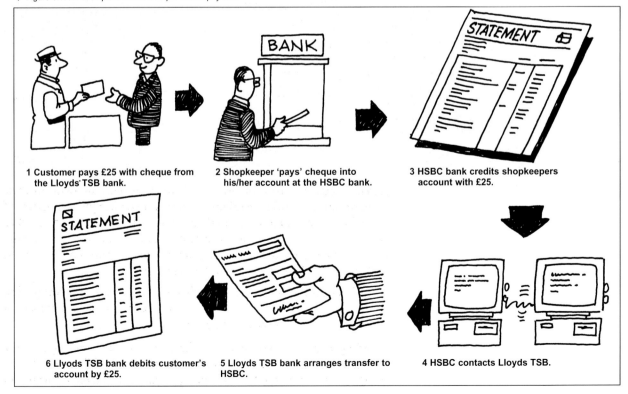

1 Customer pays £25 with cheque from the Lloyds TSB bank.

2 Shopkeeper 'pays' cheque into his/her account at the HSBC bank.

3 HSBC bank credits shopkeepers account with £25.

6 Llyods TSB bank debits customer's account by £25.

5 Lloyds TSB bank arranges transfer to HSBC.

4 HSBC contacts Lloyds TSB.

▼ There are two debit cards available from UK banks: the CONNECT card and the SWITCH card.

● **Debit card:** Debit cards are a relatively new and easy method of paying for goods and services issued by banks to their account holders. Over half the adult population in the UK now hold a debit card.

The debit card saves the customer the time and trouble of writing out a cheque. The advantage of debit card payment for the business making the sale is that the payment is transferred into their bank account immediately. Cheques have to be taken to their bank and may take several days before they are 'cleared' for payment by the customer's bank.

To use a debit card, the shop or other supplier must have an electronic cash register linked to the **EFTPOS** system **(Electronic Funds Transfer at Point Of Sale).** When the card is swiped through the electronic register, details of the purchase are relayed to the card user's bank, and the amount to be paid is deducted automatically from their account and credited to the account of the business that has sold them goods or services.

The cash register will issue a voucher as a record of the payment. The debit card user must then sign the voucher to show they have agreed to the transaction.

▼ The holding of plastic cards has increased over time

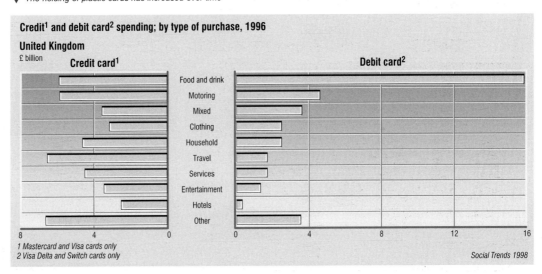

Credit[1] and debit card[2] spending; by type of purchase, 1996

United Kingdom
£ billion

1 Mastercard and Visa cards only
2 Visa Delta and Switch cards only

Social Trends 1998

● **Direct debit:** A person or firm can issue a written authority to their bank or building society to allow regular, or even irregular, transfers of agreed amounts of money from their account to the account of another person or firm to whom they owe money. The person or firm owed the money will arrange the necessary computer instructions on the amount and timing of the transfer from their customer's bank account.

The direct debit system is particularly useful for credit card companies, and gas and electricity suppliers, who receive a large number of variable payments every month or quarter from their customers.

● **Standing order:** If payments for the same amount are regular, for example, monthly mortgage repayments to a building society, or payments for credit sales and hire purchase, a person or firm can instruct their bank or building society to make regular transfers to the account of the person or firm to whom they owe the money. This is known as a **standing order**.

- **Banking Automated Clearing Services (BACS):** Paying by cheque and taking cash and cheques and other payments to and from banks can be time-consuming. In order to speed up standing order payments to regular suppliers, the major high street banks and building societies use a system known as **BACS (Banking Automated Clearing Service)**, which they jointly own. The system allows funds to be transferred between accounts electronically using computers.

  A bank account holder wishing to make a regular payment completes a standing order form to tell their bank who they are to pay money to, how much should be paid, and how often. The bank will then input these instructions to a computer and the payments will be made automatically. Irregular payments by direct debit can also be made using BACS.

▼ Figure 9.2: How the Banking Automated Clearing Service works

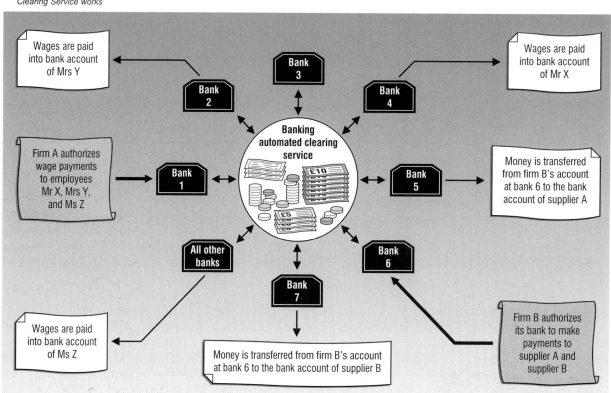

Today, most workers, especially those in medium-to-large organizations, are paid their wages directly into their bank or building society accounts through BACS.

- **Electronic Data Interchange (EDI):** This system allows all the documents and payments involved in a sales transaction to be transmitted electronically using computers, rather than using fax or post. To do this, both the business customer and supplier must have computers connected to the telephone network by a modem.

▼ *Electronic Data Interchange reduces the need to record details of transactions by hand. Supermarket giant Tesco uses EDI to transmit almost all its orders and invoices.*

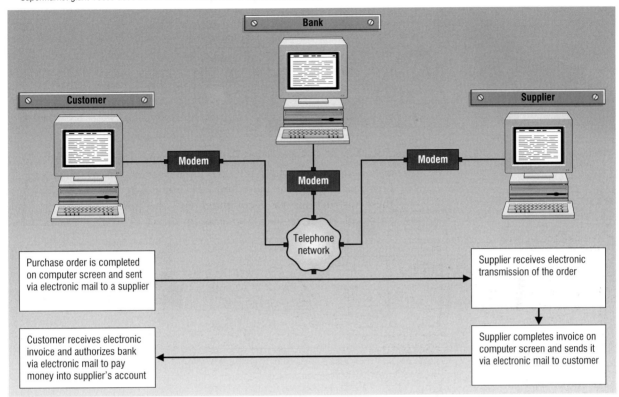

▼ *An increasing number of companies are offering credit cards to customers. In 1998 around 13 pence in every pound spent by consumers was by credit card.*

At present EDI is used mainly by larger retailing organizations which need to place regular orders for new stock with their suppliers. Barcode readers monitor sales at store checkouts and maintain an up-to-date record of stocks. When stock reaches a certain pre-set minimum level, the store's computer automatically generates and sends an order for more stock to the computer of the supplier.

EDI can also send invoices requesting payment, and instructions to a bank to make payments to suppliers

● **Credit card:** Instead of the supplier offering direct credit terms to their customers, a number of specialist organizations now issue cards that can be used to 'buy now, pay later.' Visa, Mastercard, American Express, and Diners Club are examples of credit card companies who provide cards for general use. Many large retail organizations also offer their customers credit cards which can be used only in their stores. For example, Marks & Spencer and Tesco operate credit card services.

With a credit card transaction, firms supply goods and services to the card holder but then have to wait for the credit card company to settle their bill. Suppliers need to send proof of the sale to the credit card company before they pay. The credit card company will then expect the card holder to pay them (by cheque or BACS), usually between 4-6 weeks after the sale was made (see Figure 9.3).

▼ *Figure 9.3: An example of how a credit card can be used to make a purchase*

1 **Customer pays £50 for goods with credit card.**

2 **Shopkeeper issues credit card invoice for £50.**

3 **Shopkeeper deposits invoice copy in his/her bank account.**

4 **Shopkeeper's bank arranges for invoices to be sent to credit card company.**

7 **Customer sends a cheque to his credit card company to settle his account balance.**

6 **Credit card company sends account statement to the customer listing all his purchases with his credit card.**

5 **Credit card company pays £50 to shopkeeper's bank.**

How credit card purchases are authorized

If a business is offered payment by credit card, they must check that the card is acceptable and gain necessary authorization. Most organizations today are able to do this electronically, but a number of smaller businesses still rely on manual methods.

Electronic methods

New technology means that businesses can get authorization from credit card companies much more easily than before:

- A sales assistant will swipe the card through a special terminal which then transmits the card details through to computers in the appropriate credit card company.

- The computers check that the card is not listed as stolen and checks that the card holder has not spent over his or her limit.

- A sales voucher with purchase and card details is then issued by the terminal. The card holder signs this and keeps the top copy as a proof of purchase

▼ *Printed electronically*

```
12:27                    13/08/0X
COMPLETED

B & Q PLC

NEW MALDEN
Till 8

02357423.6767  608658

VISA
No: 2033005731376667
Expiry date: 08/04


THANK YOU
£25.95              Sign below

.................................
```

How credit card purchases are authorized

Manual authorization

- First of all the business checks that the card is not a stolen one. This can be done by looking at up-to-date lists of stolen card numbers issued by the major credit card companies or by telephoning the appropriate credit card company. Using the telephone can be slow if the credit card company is busy.

- The business can also phone the credit card company to check that the customer has enough money left to spend on their card to pay for the goods or services. If they have, the credit card company will issue an authorization code to write on the sales

voucher. This code guarantees that the business will be paid by the credit card company.

- If the checks prove OK, then the business fills out a carbonated sales voucher. Card details are printed onto the voucher using a special hand-operated imprinting device. Purchase details are then written in before the customer signs it and receives the top copy as proof of purchase. The second copy is sent to the credit card company for payment, while the third and fourth copies are kept by the supplier.

▼ *Completed by hand*

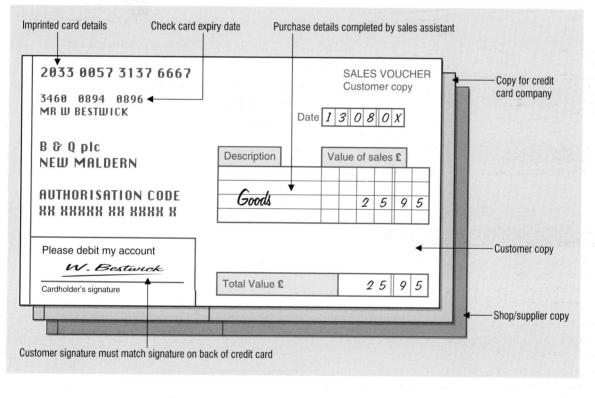

Imprinted card details · Check card expiry date · Purchase details completed by sales assistant

2033 0057 3137 6667

3460 0894 0896
MR W BESTWICK

B & Q plc
NEW MALDERN

AUTHORISATION CODE
XX XXXXX XX XXXX X

Please debit my account

W. Bestwick

Cardholder's signature

SALES VOUCHER
Customer copy

Date | 1 | 3 | 0 | 8 | 0 | X |

Description	Value of sales £			
Goods		2	5	9	5

| Total Value £ | | 2 | 5 | 9 | 5 |

Copy for credit card company

Customer copy

Shop/supplier copy

Customer signature must match signature on back of credit card

Portfolio Activity 9.1

1. Try to find out how people can apply for a credit card. What information do they need to supply and how does the credit card company check whether they are telling the truth and are trustworthy?

2. Watch how credit card payments are accepted in a shop. Draw up a flowchart to show each task in the process of making and accepting payment. Suggest why all these tasks are necessary from the point of view of the customer and the supplier.

Why is it important to record financial transactions?

Whenever a firm exchanges goods and services for money, it is important that it keeps detailed and accurate records. The types of information it will need to record include:

For inward transactions...

- Customer details, including name and address

- Type and amount of goods and services ordered or supplied

- Price of individual items and total price, including delivery, discounts, and VAT

- Payment details, including date, amount, and method

For outward transactions...

- Who money is being paid to, including name and account

- Type and amount of goods and services ordered or received

- Price of individual items and total price, including any delivery charges, discounts, and VAT

- Payment details, including date, amount, and method

Portfolio Activity 9.2

Investigate the recording of transactions in a business organization with which you are familiar.

Write a short report using a word processor to explain:

- The transactions that occur in the business

- Why the organization keeps records (or if it doesn't, why it should keep detailed records!)

- The types of information about transactions the organization records

- How the organization uses the information it records

- How the organization records information (i.e. on paper or in a computer file?)

Alternatively, imagine that some friends of yours are about to start up their own business. Prepare a report for them on the importance of recording transactions, the information they will need to record, and how best they might keep and access records.

It is essential for all business organizations to keep accurate and detailed records of their financial transactions. There a number of reasons why this is so important.

- **To monitor incomes and expenditures:** A firm will need to know exactly how much it is spending and how much it is earning from day to day. This is so it knows how much money it has to spend on wages, materials, and all other items it needs to carry on making and selling its products. If spending is greater than income and the firm has no savings to draw on it will run into financial difficulties and may not be able to continue in production.

- **To record all purchases and sales:** A business needs to know what it has bought and sold and how much money it has spent or received, or how much money it owes or is owed.

1. Look at the illustrations below. What do they suggest about the need for business organizations to keep accurate records of their incomes and expenditures. Are there any other reasons you can think of?

2. Investigate why a business organization of your choice keeps records of financial transactions.

Imagine you are a manager of a factory making computers. You will need to know how many computers to produce to meet demand from customers and how many memory chips to buy to make the computers. If you do not record your purchases of memory chips, you may order too many or too few. Buying more memory chips than you need will waste money. Ordering too few may delay production and customers may buy computers from rival firms. If orders for new computers are not recorded accurately, you may decide to make too few or too many computers. Producing too many computers to meet customer demands will mean stocks will build up and may have to be sold off cheaply. Making too few will mean some customers will go elsewhere and your business will lose sales. Keeping a record of the movement of goods in and out of the factory will help to keep stocks of memory chips to the minimum necessary to make the right amount of computers to meet customer demands, and will avoid wasting money.

It is also especially important for a business to know how much money it owes to suppliers and how much is owed to it by customers. Unless a business keeps accurate and up-to-date records it may forget to pay a bill and find that one of its suppliers will refuse to supply goods or services in the future and may even take legal action to get the money they are owed. Imagine, for example, the problems a business will face if its telephone and electricity are cut off, or materials it needs are no longer supplied, because it forgot to pay its bills. And how will a business check that a customer has paid it for goods supplied, or investigate a claim by a customer that he or she has been overcharged if it doesn't have accurate records on sales?

- **To keep customer accounts up to date:** Allowing business customers to pay for goods or services up to 90 days later is a way of attracting their custom. However, it also means that the business that has supplied the goods or services on credit must keep an accurate record of who owes them money and when payment is due. Without these records, it will not be able to identify customers who fail to pay.

  Regular customers will receive regular statements of the goods and services they have bought on credit from a supplier. An account statement will show all the purchases made by the customer including any returns and the total amount, or balance, that needs to be paid to clear the account. (see 9.2).

  If accurate records are not kept, customer accounts will not be up to date and will show the wrong amount. If it shows too much, the customer may get angry and take their business elsewhere. If the account balance is too low, then the revenues of the supplier will be lower than they should be.

- **To monitor business performance:** The final accounts of a business provide a record of how well a business has performed over the last accounting period in terms of sales, costs, and profits. These figures can be compared to those from earlier periods to see if business performance has improved, stayed about the same, or deteriorated.

The performance of a business can also be compared to that of competing firms in order to judge whether or not it is doing better than its rivals. For example, Figure 9.4 shows how pre-tax profits have changed over time in some well known supermarket chains. From the chart it is clear that Tesco Plc out-performed its main rivals in 1997, but by 1998 Sainsbury's had almost caught up with the market leader.

▼ Figure 9.4: Pre-tax profits of selected supermarket chains

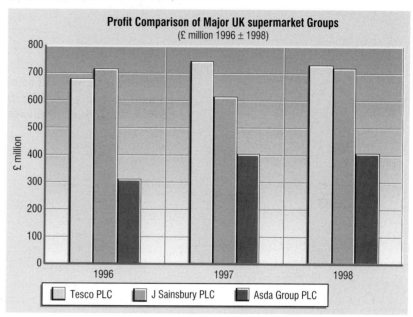

Dun and Bradstreet, Key British Enterprises, 1999

● **To produce accounts:** To help monitor business performance, organizations need to keep-up-to date accounts showing how much the business is spending, what it is spending money on, and how much it is earning from sales and any other sources of income. These records will also be needed by shareholders and government authorities such as the Inland Revenue (see below).

Business accounts produced regularly for the use of business owners and managers are known as **internal accounts**. For example, separate accounts can be kept to provide up-to-date information on:

– purchases, and how much is owed to individual suppliers
– sales for cash and on credit, and how much is owed by individual customers
– VAT paid on purchases and VAT received from sales
– inflows and outflows of cash
– cash held on the premises
– deposits and withdrawals from the organization's bank account
– wages and salaries paid
– expenses, such as electricity, telephone, advertising, stationary, travel, etc.
– all incomes and expenditures

▼ Business organizations produce financial accounts for their own internal use and because the law requires them for tax purposes.

At the end of each 12-month period, these accounts can be used to calculate the total value of assets, such as premises, machinery, and other equipment owned by a business. This is known as a **balance sheet**. Records can also be used to provide a summary of the total costs, revenues, and profit or loss for the year. This is known as a **profit and loss statement**. Business owners and managers will use these end-of-year accounts to judge business performance and make decisions on how it might be improved over the next 12 months (see chapter 8).

● **To meet legal requirements:** The law requires that all business organizations produce annual accounts every 12 months so that the government's tax authorities can calculate how much tax each one must pay, if any.

Sole traders and partnerships may be liable for income tax on their earnings, while limited companies may have to pay corporation tax on their profits to the Inland Revenue. Any VAT collected on goods and services sold will have to be paid to the Customs and Excise department.

Private and public limited companies are also required to provide copies of their final year accounts to any person who wants them. These are called **external accounts** (see chapter 6).

● **To ensure security:** Records provide evidence that transactions have taken place. A firm will always be able to check payment demands from suppliers against records of goods and services received and payments made in the past. They will then be able to see whether they have overlooked settling their bill or if the supplier has made a mistake.

A firm may also be vulnerable to theft or fraud if it does not keep accurate records. For example, if a firm did not keep records of how much cash was entering or leaving a till, a dishonest sales assistant might be tempted to take money without permission.

Fraud is a sophisticated type of theft. Examples include people paying for goods using stolen credit cards, or employees paying out money to the bank account of a 'supplier' that does not exist, but to which they have access.

▼ With more ways for customers to pay for goods and services, opportunities for theft and fraud have increased.

- **To secure and maintain finance:** All businesses need money to buy or hire assets, such as premises and machinery, and to pay everyday bills. Many businesses borrow money from banks and building societies. However, these organizations will not lend money to a business that does not display sound financial management. They will want evidence from business accounts that the firm earns enough money to be able to repay a loan.

Section **9.2** **Using documents to record transactions**

Portfolio Activity 9.4

This is the story of Billy Bestwick. He owns and runs a small car repair business. His office staff have run out of paper for the photocopier and printer on the computer. Read the story and then answer the questions.

1. Suggest reasons why business organizations like Billy's garage and Office Supplies Ltd should keep records of their financial transactions.

2. What information should Office Supplies Ltd record to make the process of selling their products easier, less wasteful, and more secure?

3. Suggest possible documents Office Supplies Ltd could use and issue to Billy to record the information they need.

Billy looks at the Office Supplies Ltd catalogue and calculates that it will cost him £70.50 to have 17 packets of white A4 size paper delivered. He phones Office Supplies Ltd to place his order for 17 packets of paper.

The sales assistant ot Office Supplies Ltd makes a written note of Billy's order but writes down 70 packets of paper by mistake.

The next day 70 packets of paper are loaded onto a van at Office Supplies Ltd and sent off to Billy's garage. The van driver has the piece of paper the assistant scribbled down Billy's order on but he cannot read the address properly. After several wrong turns the van driver manages to locate Billy's business and delivers the paper.

'But I only ordered 17 packets!' said Billy as the van driver unloads 70 packets of paper. The van driver apologises for the mistake and agrees to return the unwanted 53 packets to Office Supplies Ltd.

The next day Billy sends off his cheque for £70.50 to Office Supplies Ltd to pay for his 17 packets of paper.

When the cheque arrives at Office Supplies Ltd they can only find the scribbled note for an order for 70 packets of paper and write to Billy demanding payment of £250.

Billy receives the demand and phones up Office Supplies Ltd. He explains that he had only ordered 17 packets of paper and that the van driver had agreed to return the other 53 packets to Office Supplies Ltd.

Unfortunately, the storeman at Office Supplies Ltd had kept no record of stock going out or coming in. As neither Billy nor Office Supplies has any proof of delivery the company asks the van driver to confirm Billy's story. He does and so Office Supplies withdraws their demand.

But the crafty van driver had lied. He did not return the other 53 packets that Billy didn't want to Office Supplies Ltd. Instead he stole them and sold them for £50 to a friend.

'Phew! What a messy business' sighs Billy upon receiving an apology from Office Supplies Ltd. 'In future I think I'll buy my stationery from elsewhere.'

Types of documents

Recording information about transactions often requires a great deal of paperwork. To make the process less time-consuming, businesses have devised special documents to use. Invoices, order forms, purchase documents, bank paying-in slips, and receipts are just a few of the kinds of documents used to record transactions. Although the design of these documents may differ from business to business, the information each must contain will be the same.

The types of documents Billy Bestwick and Office Supplies should have used to make sure their transaction in Activity 9.4 went smoothly, and the order they should have used them in, are shown in Figure 9.5. The types and sequence of documents used are typical of any business transaction.

▼ Figure 9.5: Documents involved in a business transaction

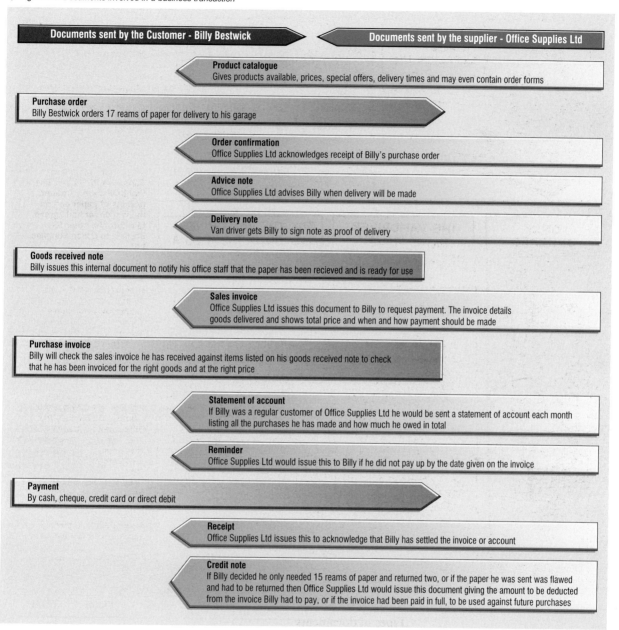

Documents sent by the Customer - Billy Bestwick | **Documents sent by the supplier - Office Supplies Ltd**

Product catalogue
Gives products available, prices, special offers, delivery times and may even contain order forms

Purchase order
Billy Bestwick orders 17 reams of paper for delivery to his garage

Order confirmation
Office Supplies Ltd acknowledges receipt of Billy's purchase order

Advice note
Office Supplies Ltd advises Billy when delivery will be made

Delivery note
Van driver gets Billy to sign note as proof of delivery

Goods received note
Billy issues this internal document to notify his office staff that the paper has been recieved and is ready for use

Sales invoice
Office Supplies Ltd issues this document to Billy to request payment. The invoice details goods delivered and shows total price and when and how payment should be made

Purchase invoice
Billy will check the sales invoice he has received against items listed on his goods received note to check that he has been invoiced for the right goods and at the right price

Statement of account
If Billy was a regular customer of Office Supplies Ltd he would be sent a statement of account each month listing all the purchases he has made and how much he owed in total

Reminder
Office Supplies Ltd would issue this to Billy if he did not pay up by the date given on the invoice

Payment
By cash, cheque, credit card or direct debit

Receipt
Office Supplies Ltd issues this to acknowledge that Billy has settled the invoice or account

Credit note
If Billy decided he only needed 15 reams of paper and returned two, or if the paper he was sent was flawed and had to be returned then Office Supplies Ltd would issue this document giving the amount to be deducted from the invoice Billy had to pay, or if the invoice had been paid in full, to be used against future purchases

Purchase documents

The job of the purchasing department in any business is to buy in services or materials of the right quality, in the right quantities, when the firm needs them, and at the lowest cost possible (see chapter 2). Every pound saved by purchasing is an extra pound made in profits. Each of the different stages in the purchasing process requires different kinds of documentation.

1. The first stage in purchasing usually involves making enquiries with different suppliers to get a range of estimates or quotations, and choosing the best deal available.

2. Once the best supplier is identified, an **order form** is completed and placed with that supplier.

3. When the goods have been delivered, the person receiving them completes a **goods received note (GRN)** and passes it to the accounts department.

4. Finally an **invoice** is received from the supplier. The accounts department will check that information on the invoice matches details of goods delivered on the GRN before making payment.

The order form

The **order form in** Figure 9.6 shows the order for paper by Billy Bestwick.

Billy Bestwick will need to check that his order form contains the following information:

- His business name, the address where the goods are to be delivered, and the address to which the supplier should send the invoice (if different)

- Precise details of the goods or services being purchased, including make, model number, and unit price

- The delivery date required (if delivery by a certain date is very important this should be stated clearly on the order)

▼ Figure 9.6: An example of a Purchase order

BESTWICK AUTO REPAIRS

21 Shrawley Street
Worcester WS17 5YY
Tel: 01905-111119
Fax: 01905-111110
VAT Reg No. 4373 2437 18

Purchase Order No. 1853

Date 16.9.0X

To: Office Supplies Ltd

12 Woodland Way

Northwick NH4 3JX

DESCRIPTION	QTY	Ref. No	PRICE	TOTAL
A4 white photocopy paper	17	34/A	£3	£51

Deliver to above address a.s.a.p

Authorized by: *W.Bestwick*

for BESTWICK AUTO REPAIRS

- The signature of someone with the authority to approve the order. This is important, otherwise anyone in the firm could place an order for goods and services which might then be stolen without anyone knowing.

If Billy has a fax machine, he can send his order immediately to Office Supplies Ltd. Billy will also keep a copy of his order for his own records. This is so that he can check, at a later date, that the right goods have been delivered and that he has been invoiced to pay the right amount for the right goods.

Goods received note (GRN)

When Billy receives the goods he ordered from Office Supplies Ltd, he will complete a **goods received note (GRN)** for his records. The GRN records what has actually been delivered. This is important because goods might be damaged or missing, or the wrong goods may have been sent. Any deliveries should always be unpacked, counted, and carefully checked and recorded.

The person taking delivery of goods will not always be the same person who ordered them, and so completion of a GRN is vital in most organizations. The accounts department in any organization will need signed proof that goods have actually been received by their firm, in the form of a GRN, before it will authorize the payment of an invoice for them. The GRN can be checked against the original purchase order to make sure that nothing is being paid for that was not ordered or delivered. The firm will also check that the goods are not damaged or faulty or need to be replaced by the supplier.

▼ Figure 9.7: An example of a goods received note

BESTWICK AUTO REPAIRS

GOODS RECEIVED NOTE

Supplier:

Office Supplies Ltd

12 Woodland Way

Northwick NH4 3JX

GRN NO: 347

Date: 20.9.0X

Re; Delivery Note:

12/90120

ORDER NO.	QTY	DESCRIPTION	REF NO:
1853	17	A4 white copy paper 3 boxes x 5 reams plus 2 reams	34/A

Received by: *W.Bestwick*

for **BESTWICK AUTO REPAIRS**

Purchase invoice

After the paper has been delivered to Billy's garage, Office Supplies Ltd will request payment by sending him an **invoice**.

▼ Figure 9.8: An Example of an Invoice

INVOICE

Office Supplies Ltd

12 Woodland Way
Northwick NH4 3JX
Tel: 01604-65666
Fax: 01604-65660
VAT Reg No. 234 8999 16

To: Bestwick Auto Repairs

21 Shrawley Street

Worcester WS17 5YY

Date	Order No.	Account No.	Invoice No.
22.9.0X	1853	702300	25241

QTY	Description	Cat No.	Unit Price	Total
17	A4 white copy paper	34/A	£3	£51
1	Delivery		£9	£9

Sub-total	£60
Cash discount	–
Total (ex. VAT)	£60
VAT @ 17.5%	+£10.50
Total due	£70.50

Terms:
Cash discount of 2.5% only applies to orders over £100 if payment received within 10 working days

E & OE

Office Supplies Ltd will need to make sure that their invoice contains the following details:

- Their name and address as supplier

- The name and address of their customer

- The customer's account number (if applicable)

- An invoice reference number

- A full description of the goods supplied and their reference numbers

- The unit price of the goods

- A delivery charge, if any.
- Total price, including VAT and any deductions for any cash or trade discounts offered
- The date by which the invoice should be paid

An invoice is a legal document. Firms must keep all of their invoices in order to provide evidence of the amount they have spent on purchases both for VAT inspectors and for the Inland Revenue. VAT-registered businesses can claim back VAT money paid on purchases, and some may be tempted to claim they have purchased more than they really have. Similarly, a firm may be tempted to claim they spent more than they actually did in order to reduce the profit declared in their accounts, and so reduce the tax they have to pay. This is illegal, and business owners can be fined or imprisoned for misleading the tax authorities.

What else should be on an invoice?

- **Cash discounts:** In order to speed up the payment of invoices many suppliers offer a cash discount. This discount is a percentage of the goods total (usually around 2.5%) which the buyer can deduct if he or she pays immediately rather than waiting until the end of the period specified on the invoice. For example, if Billy Bestwick's order was worth £500, he would receive a cash discount of £12.50 (2.5%) if he paid the invoice within 10 days of receipt.

- **Trade discounts:** In addition to a discount for paying cash, some suppliers also give a discount for regular custom, called a **trade discount**. For example, most retailers will receive trade discount from their suppliers. The discount is deducted from the invoice total and will often vary with the quantity purchased. Bigger discounts tend to be given for bigger orders.

- **Invoice errors and omissions:** All invoices have the letters 'E & OE' printed on them. This stands for 'Errors and Omissions Excepted' which means that if the supplier has made any mistakes or left anything off the invoice, they have the right to correct the mistake later on and demand full payment.

Checking the invoice

All invoices received should be checked carefully before they are paid. Like any business, Billy Bestwick should check that:

- The invoice from Office Supplies Ltd has not been sent to him by mistake
- The order number quoted on it is the same as the number of his original purchase order
- The items listed match those listed on his goods received note
- The price given is the same as in the supplier's catalogue
- All calculations are correct
- It contains any discounts previously agreed with the supplier

If Billy is satisfied that the invoice is in order, he will pass it on to his accounts department for payment.

Payment, whether by cash, cheque, plastic card, or bank transfer, will usually require authorization by a designated member of staff. In Billy's small business this is likely to be Billy himself. In a large organization authorization is likely to be given by a senior manager in accounts. If payments could be made without authorization, some devious employees might write out cheques to themselves, or make payments into their own bank accounts without other people knowing.

Stoneshire County Council has ordered some computer equipment from Computech Ltd, a leading supplier of computer equipment and accessories. Carefully check the purchase order and invoice involved in the transaction. Have they been completed correctly? Is any information missing?

1. Ask your tutor if you can make a photocopy of the order and the invoice in this activity.

2. Mark on each copy where mistakes may have been made and information is missing.

3. Wherever possible, write down what the correct information should be on both documents.

STONESHIRE COUNTY COUNCIL

County Hall, Milton Barnet
STONESHIRE

Tel: 020-7123-6789
Fax: 020-7123-6780

VAT Reg 129 8093 14
Purchase Order No. 0001
Date: 15th April 200X

To: Computech Ltd

Unit 19-22

Moleville Industrial Estate

STONESHIRE ST17 5MW

DESCRIPTION	QTY	Ref.No	PRICE	TOTAL
Microsoft Office 2000	2		£230.00	£560.00
Data ex desktop modem	3	76/M	£164.00	£392.00
Panasonic KX-P4440 laser printer	1	49/PT	£339.00	£339.00

Authorized by: *H. B. Simpson*

for STONESHIRE COUNTY COUNCIL.

Computech Ltd

Unit 19 —22, Moleville Industrial Estate
Tel: 01237-4095, Fax: 01237-4096
VAT Reg No. 707 3434 11

To: Bestwick Auto Repairs
21 Shrawley Street
Worcester WS17 5YY

INVOICE

Your Order No.	Invoice No.	Date
	77771	22 April 200X

QTY	Description	Cat No.	Unit Price	Total
2	Microsoft Works	33/S	£213.00	£526.00
4	Data ex modems	76/M	£164.00	£656.00
1	Panasonic KX—P4440 laser printer	49/PT	£339.00	£339.00
			Sub-total	£1521.00
			Discount 10%	£76.05
Terms:			Total (ex. VAT)	£1444.95
			VAT @ 17.5%	
E & OE			**Total due**	£1697.81

Sales documents

The main objective of the sales department in any organization is to encourage sales and to record revenues accurately so that it can judge how well it is meeting its targets (see chapter 1). In making sales, meeting customer orders quickly, and obtaining payments, a sales department will issue a variety of documents. The main ones are:

1. An **acknowledgement** to a customer that their order has been received. The supplier may also send an **advice note** to tell the customer when delivery will be made.

2. A **delivery note** containing a full description of goods delivered to the customer

3. A **sales invoice** requesting payment for goods delivered

4. If the total price on the invoice is wrong and the customer has been overcharged, the supplier may issue a **credit note.** If the customer has not been charged enough, a **debit note** will be issued.

5. If the customer makes regular purchases from the same supplier, they may have an account which they settle up each month. A **statement of account** is sent each month from the supplier to provide a record of purchases made and the total amount owed by the customer.

6. A **remittance advice note** will often be sent with an invoice or statement of account, summarizing how much is owed by the customer and when it should be paid.

Orders received

When a supplier receives an order, the sales department should check all the details to make sure that the information provided by the customer is complete and correct. For example:

● Has the customer given their full address?

● Does the description of goods ordered match the catalogue or reference number?

● Are there any special requirements? For example, morning delivery only?

● Does the customer qualify for any trade discounts?

The supplier should then check that it is able to meet the order and supply the goods in the right quantity, at the right price, and by the date requested in the order. The sales department may then send a written acknowledgement to the customer to confirm receipt of their order and give precise details of the delivery date and time.

If goods are to be in transit for some time, the sales department may also send an advice note to tell the customer that the goods are on their way. This will give details of the date the goods were despatched, and how they have been sent, for example, by parcel post or courier.

Delivery note

When goods are delivered by vehicle, either by the supplier or by an outside carrier such as TNT or DHL, the driver is given a **delivery note.** This gives a full description of the goods and states the number of packages being delivered. On receipt of the goods, the customer is able to check delivered items against those listed on the delivery note in order to identify any errors or damage. The delivery note is usually carbonated with two copies. It is signed by the customer and one copy is kept by the driver as proof that the goods were delivered as required.

▼ Figure 9.9: An Example of a Delivery Note

Office Supplies Ltd

12 Woodland Way
Northwick NH4 3JX
Tel: 01604-65666
Fax: 01604-65660
VAT Reg No. 234 8999 16

Delivery Note No. 12/90120

Delivery address: Bestwick Auto Repairs

21 Shrawley Street

Worcester WS17 5YY

For delivery on: 20.9.0X

DATE	Order No	Account No.	Invoice No
19.9.0X	1853	702300	25241

QTY	Catalogue No.	Description
17	34/A	A4 white copy paper

Delivery by: Office Supplies Distribution Services Ltd

No. of items: 3 boxes + 2 individual reams

Goods received by: __W.Bestwick__ (signature)

__W.Bestwick__ (please PRINT name)

Issued by: _D Martin_

D Martin
Sales Manager
for Office Supplies Ltd

Please retain this copy as proof of receipt

Figure 9.9 shows the delivery note sent with the paper ordered by Billy Bestwick. Billy has signed the delivery note to provide the driver with proof that the goods have been delivered. Luckily he had time to check his order before signing the delivery note. If this was not possible Billy would have written 'goods received but not examined' on the bottom of the note.

Sales invoice

A sales invoice is issued by a supplier every time goods or services have been delivered without immediate payment. When payment is immediate, such as the purchase of food over a shop counter, no invoice will be issued to the customer.

You have already seen the invoice issued by Office Supplies Ltd to Bestwick Auto Repairs in Figure 9.8. The invoice issued by Office Supplies Ltd is a **sales invoice** to the company, containing details of how much Bestwick Auto Repairs owes them, and what for. For Billy Bestwick the very same invoice received from Office Supplies Ltd is a **purchase invoice** which he will have to pay.

Invoices are normally carbonated so that a number of copies of exactly the same invoice can be produced in one go. The customer will receive the top copy, while the other copies will be retained by various parts of the supplier's organization – the distribution department that sends out the order and the accounts department that receives payment.

Credit and debit notes

▼ Figure 9.10: An Example of a Credit Note

Office Supplies Ltd

12 Woodland Way
Northwick NH4 3JX
Tel: 01604-65666
Fax: 01604-65660
VAT Reg No. 234 8999 16

To: Bestwick Auto Repairs

21 Shrawley Street

Worcester WS17 5YY

CREDIT NOTE NO.
CN123

DATE	Reference Invoice No.	Customer Account No.
26.9.0X	25421	702300

QTY	Description	Cat No.	Unit Price	Total
5	A4 copy paper (pink)	34/A	£3	£15

Reason for credit:
Paper returned – wrong colour

Sub-total	£15
Cash discount	£0
Total (ex. VAT)	£15
VAT @ 17.5%	£2.63
Total credit	£17.63

A **credit note**, often printed in red, is issued by a supplier to a customer if the total price on the invoice is too much. This may be because:

- The supplier has made a mistake and overcharged

- Goods were not delivered because they were lost or stolen in transit

- The customer has returned unsatisfactory or faulty goods

Figure 9.10 shows a credit note that might have been issued by Office Supplies Ltd to Bestwick Auto Repairs if Billy had returned one box containing 5 reams of A4 paper because it was pink and not white as ordered.

A **debit note** will be sent to a customer if the amount on their invoice is not enough - for example, if payment is late and is subject to a surcharge, or if equipment used to deliver goods was on loan but has not been returned.

Statement of account

When a business organization regularly uses the same supplier, it is likely to receive a number of invoices each month. In this case, it is easier for the supplier to send out a **statement of account** summarizing all the purchases made by that customer each month, rather than to send out lots of individual invoices.

It is also more convenient for the customer to make one payment each month on the account balance outstanding, rather than have to make numerous payments to settle each separate invoice. Many firms prefer to pay on receipt of the monthly statement rather than on individual invoices. This is to the customer's advantage as it delays payment. An account statement shows the amount owed, or **balance outstanding**, at the beginning of the month, adding on any invoices for orders during that month and deducting any payments received. The balance left at the end of the month is the amount owed. The monthly statement is, therefore, a summary of transactions made during each month and a request for payment.

Before a supplier sends a statement of account to a customer it should check it is accurate and contains all the following information:

- The name and address of the customer

- The customer's account number

- The balance carried forward from their last account statement

- The month of the statement

- A record of all the transactions made with the customer in that month, including invoices, credit notes, and payments received

- The balance on the account after each transaction

- The balance owed by the customer at the end of the month after adjusting for all the transactions entered into the account

Imagine now that Billy Bestwick is a regular customer of Office Supplies Ltd. His account number is 702300. During the month of September 200X he placed several orders for office stationary with the company. At the end of the month, Office Supplies Ltd issued the statement of the account in Figure 9.11 to Billy Bestwick. You will notice that included in the list of orders placed by Billy is the purchase order (No. 1853) for 17 reams of copy paper from Figure 9.6.

▼ Figure 9.11: An Example of a Monthly Statement of Account

STATEMENT OF ACCOUNT

Office Supplies Ltd

12 Woodland Way
Northwick NH4 3JX
Tel: 01604-65666
Fax: 01604-65660
VAT Reg No. 234 8999 16

Account No: 702300

Bestwick Auto Repairs

21 Shrawley Street

Worcester WS 17 5YY

Statement date: 30.9.0X

Date	Details	Debit	Credit	Balance
1.9.0X	Balance brought forward	£500.00		£500.00 Dr
8.9.0X	Goods(order 1854) Invoice No. 25289	£220.00		£720.00 Dr
22.9.0X	Goods(order 1853) Invoice No. 25241	£70.50		£790.50 Dr
25.9.0X	Payment–thank you		£800.00	£9.50 Cr
26.9.0X	Refund CN.123		£17.63	£27.13 Cr
29.9.0X	Goods(order 1856) Invoice No. 27763	£137.93		£110.80 Dr
	Balance now due			£110.80 Dr

Terms: Payment by 14.10.0X required

* Dr = debit / Cr = credit

Portfolio Activity 9.6

1. Produce the following blank documents, some of which are provided at the end of this chapter for photocopying:

- Invoice
- Remittance advice
- Statement of account
- Credit note

  Alternatively produce your own versions on a word processor using the line draw function, or a desktop publishing package.

2. You work in the accounts department of Computech Ltd. TW Plastics Plc has ordered some boxes of computer disks. Make out an invoice in full for:

- 20 boxes of disks at £10 per box (catalogue number 10/DS)
- Less a trade discount of 5%
- Plus a delivery charge of £10
- Plus VAT at 17.5%

  The invoice should be dated 3 April 200X and given the invoice number 37892.

3. Prepare a statement of account for TW Plastics Plc using the following information for April 200X. Their account number is 654/02345 and the statement should be dated for the last working day of April.

Day

1 Balance of £2,300 brought forward from previous month

3 Invoice (number 37892) for 20 boxes of diskettes plus delivery charge – total amount on invoice £235.00

4 Payment received for £2,300

9 Issue credit note (CN/256) for £300 for goods returned

17 Invoice (number 37953) for 3 laptop computers plus delivery – total amount on invoice £4,277

23 Invoice (number 37959) for 2 laserjet computer printers plus delivery – total amount on invoice £1,293

Do not forget to show the outstanding balance at the end of the month.

4. Produce a remittance advice to include with the statement of account you produced in Task 3.

5. On receipt of their account statement TW Plastics Plc telephone you to point out that invoice 37892 contained an error. Only 10 boxes of computer disks were ordered and delivered. You check your own records and confirm this error. You must now issue TW Plastics Plc with a credit note for the following refunds:

- 10 boxes of disks at £10 per box
- Less trade discount of 5%
- Plus VAT at 17.5%

  Number the credit note CN/26

6. Check and file all the documents you have completed.

Remittance advice

When an invoice or statement of account is issued to a customer, it is also usual for the supplier to send a **remittance advice note** at the same time. This is a brief form which summarizes key information on an invoice or statement regarding the amount that needs to be paid, who it should be paid to, and when it should be paid, and including the appropriate reference number.

If payment is to be made by cheque sent through the post, the customer will simply return the remittance advice note with the cheque. This makes it easier for the supplier to match the payment, once it is received, with the right invoice or statement. If customers did not return remittance advice notes with their payments, the suppliers' accounts staff would have to spend a great deal of time and effort trying to match up many different cheques to invoices.

Figure 9.12 shows the remittance advice note sent by Office Supplies Ltd to Bestwick Auto Repairs. It summarizes the information required to settle the statement of account shown in Figure 9.11.

▼ *Figure 9.12: An example of a remittance advice note*

REMITTANCE ADVICE	**Date:** 30.9.200X
Customer name and address:	**Account No.:**
Bestwick Auto Repairs 21 Shrawley Street Worcester WS17 5YY	702300

Statement Date: 30.9.200X

Amount owing: £110.80

Amount enclosed: ....

Cheque no: ....

Please return this slip together with your payment to:

Office Supplies Ltd
12 Woodland Way
Northwick NH4 3JX

All cheques should be made payable to Office Supplies Ltd.

Receipts documents (proof of purchase)

When you buy a good or service in a shop, you will receive a **receipt** as proof of purchase. Similarly, when an organization makes payment it will require proof that payment has been made for its own records and for the purpose of informing the tax authorities about its expenses.

A number of documents are available to act as proof that a transaction has taken place. These are:

● Sales receipts

● Cheques

● Paying-in slips

● Bank statements

Sales receipts

A sales receipt is usually issued when payment for goods or services received is immediate. It can take many forms, but will always include the following information:

● The name and address of the organization that made the sale

● The date the transaction took place

● A description of the goods or services purchased

● The cost of each item

● The total cost of all items

● The method of payment

Receipts can be produced electronically by tills and computers, or be handwritten on pre-printed forms. Each receipt will be numbered for ease of reference.

Figure 9.13 shows the electronic till receipt Billy Bestwick received when he went to buy a newspaper and a new book on classic cars from a WH Smith store during one lunchbreak. Figure 9.14 shows a handwritten receipt he received when he bought some old car parts from a scrap metal dealer.

▼ Figure 9.13: An example of a sales receipt

```
            WELCOME
              TO
           WH SMITH LTD
                              £
Newspaper                   0.40
Book                       22.50

Balance due                22.90

CASH                       30.00
CHANGE                      7.10

   5320  09  5  1314  11:03:05
          28SEPT0X

  THANK YOU FOR SHOPPING AT
          WH SMITH LTD
           WORCESTER
```

▼ Figure 9.14: A handwritten receipt

BROGAN SCRAP MERCHANTS

Receipt   No. 5387

Received from *Mr W. Bestwick*

the sum of £ *forty five pounds and seventy* | £ 45.70p |

pence only

in payment for   *Ford Fiesta headlamp Units*

and rear bumper

Received by: *J.W.Sharman*   Date: *28. Sept 200X*

Sales Department

Portfolio Activity 9.7

You work in the accounts section of Billy Bestwick's car repair business. Your computer usually prints out receipts for customers. However, today the system is not working and you must design your own receipt. Mr S Moss has just paid £150 in cash to have a new exhaust fitted to his car. Produce a handwritten receipt for the customer.

Most payments by customers to their suppliers are by cheque. The person or organization that writes out a cheque is known as the **drawer.** The amount of money written on the cheque will be withdrawn from their bank account. The person or firm named on the cheque to receive payment is known as the **payee.**

All cheques pass through what is known as the **clearing system** which transfers funds between banks and building society. A cheque will only be cleared for payment once the bank is satisfied that it has been completed correctly, that the signature on it has not been forged, and that the drawer has enough money in the account to pay it. This process takes about three working days.

When payment is made by cheque there is no real need for a receipt to be issued by supplier. Confirmation that payment has been made by cheque is shown on the bank statement of the customer who wrote the cheque and bank statement of the supplier who paid it into its account. A bank statement simply records all the payments made to (deposits) and from (withdrawals) an account at a bank and are considered in more detail on the next page.

Figure 9.15 shows the cheque that Billy Bestwick used to pay £800 to Office Supplies Ltd. on 25 September 200X. This is shown in his statement of account with Office Supplies Ltd in figure 9.11.

▼ Figure 9.15: A completed cheque

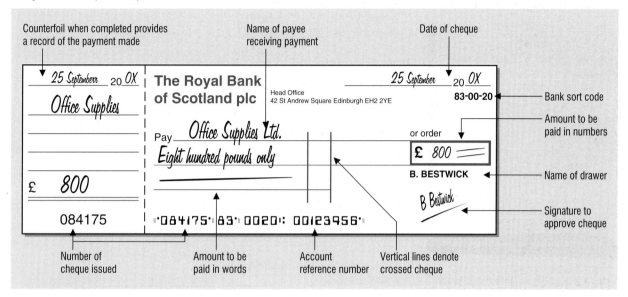

Counterfoil when completed provides a record of the payment made

Name of payee receiving payment

Date of cheque

25 September 20 OX

Office Supplies

£ 800

084175

The Royal Bank of Scotland plc

Head Office
42 St Andrew Square Edinburgh EH2 2YE

25 September 20 OX

83-00-20

Pay Office Supplies Ltd.

Eight hundred pounds only

or order

£ 800

B. BESTWICK

B Bestwick

"084175" 83" 0020": 00123956"

Bank sort code

Amount to be paid in numbers

Name of drawer

Signature to approve cheque

Number of cheque issued

Amount to be paid in words

Account reference number

Vertical lines denote crossed cheque

Completing a cheque

A cheque is simply a pre-printed form that has to be completed accurately and with enough information to allow a bank or building society to transfer money between the drawer's account and the payee's. A cheque book is provided by a bank (or building society) when a current account is opened.

Every cheque has the following information printed on it:

- The name of the account holder

- The name and address of the bank at which the account is held

- A bank sort code (every bank has a unique identification number)

- The number of the account

- An individual serial number

The bank sort code, account number, and cheque number are also usually printed in a format that can be read by a computer.

The person who completes a cheque must, therefore, provide the following information:

- The name of the person or organization to be paid

- How much they are to be paid

- The date the cheque was written

- A signature to authorize the payment

It is usual to write out the sum to be paid in figures as well as in words on a cheque, so as to make sure the precise amount cannot be mistaken. The drawer must also sign each cheque with his or her usual signature.

In most organizations cheques can only be signed by authorized staff, usually in the accounts department. When a cheque is for a lot of money, two signatories may be required, with at least one at a senior managerial level (see 9.3).

Types of cheques

Cheques can be either open or crossed.

- A **crossed** cheque has two parallel lines across it. This tells a bank that it must be paid into the payee's account regardless of who presents the cheque for payment. This makes the cheque of no use to anyone stealing it. For additional security the words 'A/C payee' are often written or printed between the two vertical lines to make sure that the cheque can only be paid into the payee's account.

- An **open** cheque, which does not have the two lines, can be cashed over a bank counter by whoever presents it.

> **A cheque is valid only if:**
>
> - It is written in ink or printed
> - It is signed by the name of the account holder, or, in the case of a business, by an authorized representative
> - The amount in words is the same as the amount in numbers
> - The cheque is made payable to someone or to the bearer (the person holding the cheque)
> - The cheque is dated and is not more than six months old

What is a cheque guarantee card?

Cheque guarantee cards are issued by banks and building societies to their reliable account holders. They can be used to guarantee that the cheque will be honoured (i.e. paid) even if the person who wrote it does not have enough money in their account. However, a cheque will only be guaranteed:

- Up to a maximum of either £50 or £100, depending on the amount printed on the cheque guarantee card

- If the card serial number is copied onto the back of the cheque
- If the name and signature on the cheque match those on the cheque card

Businesses only usually insist on noting the cheque card number on the back of a cheque when a customer pays for goods or services received in person. Clearly this cannot be done if a cheque is sent through the post in payment for goods delivered, which is usually the case.

Portfolio Activity 9.8

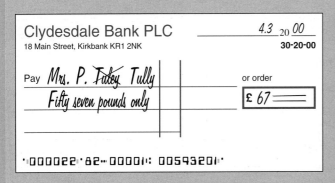

1. You work in the accounts department of Computech Ltd. You have just received the cheque opposite from a customer. Has it been completed correctly? Are you willing to accept it in payment for goods or services Computech has supplied? Explain your answer and mark any errors and omissions on a photocopy of the cheque.

2. Imagine you are the company signatory for cheques up to a value of £5,000. Write out three cheques for the following payments to suppliers from Computech Ltd.

- £575.50 to Opus Technology Ltd
- £2,030 to TDK Electronics Corp.
- £134.37 to British Telecommunications Plc

Obtain some specimen blank cheques from a local bank.

Paying-in slip

To avoid keeping large amounts of money on business premises, takings should be banked regularly. Large organizations with large amounts of money may employ a specialist security company, like Securicor or Group 4, to take the money to the bank in an armoured van.

When a firm pays cash and cheques into a bank it will complete a **paying-in slip** (see Figure 9.16). On the back of the slip is space to list all the people and organizations that have paid by cheque, and the amount of each cheque. The total amount of cheques is then carried over to the front of the paying-in slip and added to the cash total. The amount of each note or coin paid into the bank should be listed separately, for example, '100 x £5 notes' and '300 x £1 coins'.

Figure 9.16 shows a paying in-slip completed by Billy Bestwick on 29 September. Billy has listed his takings in notes, coins, and cheques on the front of the document. Details of individual cheques are also listed on the back of the paying in-slip.

▼ Figure 9.16 A completed paying-in slip

Front

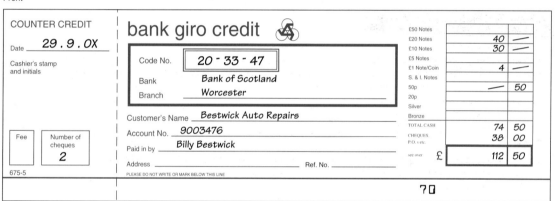

Back

Paying-in slips are used to show the following information:

● The date money was paid into the account

● The bank (or building society) branch at which money was paid in

● The branch sort code (a bank identification number)

- The account holder's name
- The number of the account to be credited
- The amount to be credited
- The name and signature of the person paying in the money

The paying in-slip, along with cash and cheques, is handed to the bank cashier. The bank cashier will then check the totals on the slip against bags of cash and individual cheques. If they match, the cashier will stamp and initial both the slip and the counterfoil. The counterfoil acts as the customer's receipt. The paying-in slip counterfoil provides a means by which the business can check that the entries on its bank statement are correct.

Portfolio Activity 9.9

1. Obtain a blank paying-in slip from a local bank.
2. Billy Bestwick wants to pay some more takings into his bank. Use the paying-in slip to pay the following amounts into the Bestwick Auto Repairs bank account (make up a number for the account).

Cheques	Notes	Coins
£120.00	$15 \times £50 = £750$	$243 \times £1 = £243$
£64.25	$8 \times £20 = £160$	$100 \times 50p = £50$
£400.00	$35 \times £10 = £350$	$600 \times 20p = £120$
£37.50	$6 \times £5 = £30$	$1,000 \times 10p = £100$
£145.47		$600 \times 5p = £30$
£79.98		$800 \times 2p = £16$
		$1,200 \times 1p = £12$

A bank statement

A bank statement provides a monthly summary of receipts and payments made to and from a bank account. Building societies also provide their account holders with regular statements.

A bank statement can be checked by a business for any mistakes against documentary proof that the transactions have been made:

- **Credits** (deposits) can be checked against paying-in slip counterfoils and records of payments from customers
- **Debits** (withdrawals) can be checked against cheque 'stubs', counterfoils issued when debit cards were used, cash dispenser receipts, and direct debit and standing order agreements

The process of checking bank statements is known as **bank reconciliation**. Differences between the bank statement and a firm's records of transactions may arise due to:

- Clerical errors causing figures to be wrongly entered or not entered at all
- Payments being made into the bank which have not been entered in the firm's records
- Cheques being recorded in the firm's books before they have been cleared by the bank.
- Bank charges representing interest on loans or overdrafts and/or charges for other services (some current accounts also pay interest on credit balances).

▼ *Figure 9.17: An example of a bank statement*

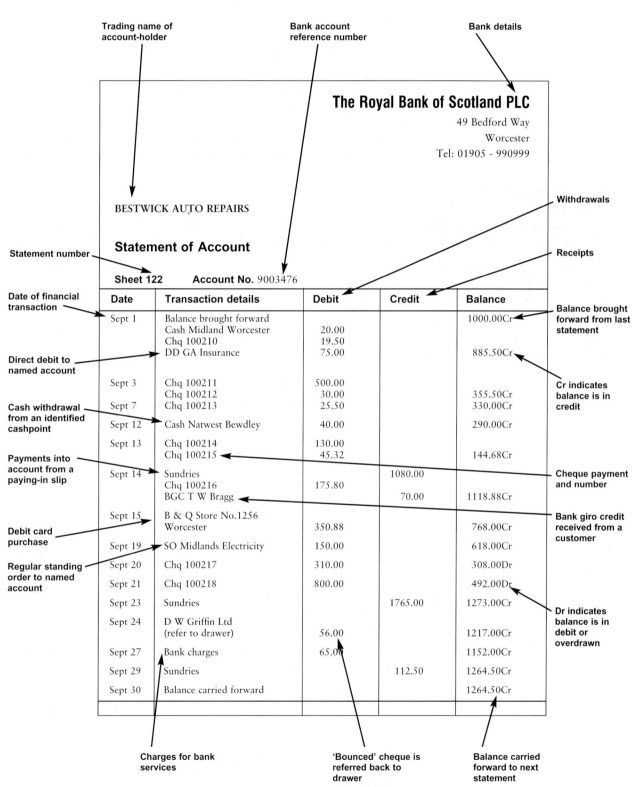

Trading name of account-holder

Bank account reference number

Bank details

Withdrawals

Statement number

Receipts

Date of financial transaction

Balance brought forward from last statement

Direct debit to named account

Cr indicates balance is in credit

Cash withdrawal from an identified cashpoint

Payments into account from a paying-in slip

Cheque payment and number

Debit card purchase

Bank giro credit received from a customer

Regular standing order to named account

Dr indicates balance is in debit or overdrawn

Charges for bank services

'Bounced' cheque is referred back to drawer

Balance carried forward to next statement

The Royal Bank of Scotland PLC

49 Bedford Way
Worcester
Tel: 01905 - 990999

BESTWICK AUTO REPAIRS

Statement of Account

Sheet 122   **Account No.** 9003476

Date	Transaction details	Debit	Credit	Balance
Sept 1	Balance brought forward			1000.00Cr
	Cash Midland Worcester	20.00		
	Chq 100210	19.50		
	DD GA Insurance	75.00		885.50Cr
Sept 3	Chq 100211	500.00		
	Chq 100212	30.00		355.50Cr
Sept 7	Chq 100213	25.50		330.00Cr
Sept 12	Cash Natwest Bewdley	40.00		290.00Cr
Sept 13	Chq 100214	130.00		
	Chq 100215	45.32		144.68Cr
Sept 14	Sundries		1080.00	
	Chq 100216	175.80		
	BGC T W Bragg		70.00	1118.88Cr
Sept 15	B & Q Store No.1256 Worcester	350.88		768.00Cr
Sept 19	SO Midlands Electricity	150.00		618.00Cr
Sept 20	Chq 100217	310.00		308.00Dr
Sept 21	Chq 100218	800.00		492.00Dr
Sept 23	Sundries		1765.00	1273.00Cr
Sept 24	D W Griffin Ltd (refer to drawer)	56.00		1217.00Cr
Sept 27	Bank charges	65.00		1152.00Cr
Sept 29	Sundries		112.50	1264.50Cr
Sept 30	Balance carried forward			1264.50Cr

Figure 9.17 shows the bank statement for the Bestwick Auto Repairs account at the Royal Bank of Scotland in Worcester for the month of September 200X. Note the cheque for £800 paid to Office Supplies Ltd on 25.9.0X as shown in the Bestwick Auto Repairs customer account statement in Figure 9.11. Notes, coins and cheques deposited in the bank by Billy Bestwick using the paying in-slip in Figure 9.16 also appear on the statement on 29 September.

Portfolio Activity 9.10

1. Create a blank bank statement of your own using a computer word processing package.

2. Use the statement to record the following transactions made by a business account holder during one month. Entries should appear in date order.

3. Remember to calculate and show the 'balance carried forward' to the next statement.

Date	Details	Amount
1	Balance brought forward	£200.00
	Drawings:	
3	Cheque No. 10001	£20.50
5	Cheque No. 10002	£68.50
12	Cheque No. 10003	£10.99
14	Cheque No. 10004	£19.00
25	Cheque No. 10005	£30.70
9	Standing order to British Gas	£50.00
10	Cash dispenser withdrawal	£50.00
17	Cash dispenser withdrawal	£20.00
13	Standing order to Britannia Building Society	£100.00
14	SWITCH Tesco Superstore	£36.01
29	SWITCH Houghtons Garage	£15.75
21	Bank Charges	£5.25
	Receipts:	
2	Direct debit received from ABC Ltd	£30.00
9	Cheque No.4256 received	£16.30
17	Cheque No.6060 received	£10.00

Section **9.3** **Using and checking financial documents**

Some useful tips

Financial documents must be completed fully, accurately and neatly if they are to provide a record of flows of money and products in and out of business. Today, many businesses record, check and store their financial information using computers.

1 Check that all the information needed has been provided

A document that has not been filled in with all the information it needs will not do the job it has been designed to do. For example, a cheque without a signature cannot make payment, a purchase order without a delivery address will not be able to order goods, a delivery note that does not list what has been delivered provides no record of delivery, an invoice that does not include the delivery charge will not get paid in full, and so on. In order to complete these documents someone else will need to find out what information they should contain. This means more work.

Most documents are pre-printed with clear spaces and headings where information is needed to reduce the risk of missing out vital information.

2 Make sure that the information provided is accurate

If the information provided on a document is incorrect, the document will be misleading and fail to do the job it has been designed to do. Consider what would happen if someone wrote down the wrong house number on a delivery note, added up an invoice incorrectly or ordered the wrong quantity of goods. Correcting mistakes can waste a lot of time and money.

Often, documents are designed to reduce the risk of making a mistake by asking for the same information twice. For example, a cheque needs to be completed with the amount to be paid in both words and figures. Order forms have spaces to write a description of the goods wanted and their catalogue or reference number.

3 Always write neatly

If you do not write neatly on a document, then other people may not be able to read it. Some people may take a guess but may not get it right. Consider what would happen, for example, if you received a written invoice for building work completed that appeared to read £266.70. You may accept the invoice and happily write out a cheque for this amount. The only problem is that the amount should read £200.10 – you have paid £66.60 too much because the person who filled out the invoice didn't write figures very clearly.

4 If you make a mistake on a document, tear it up and start a new one

Never send out a document which is illegible or which has mistakes scribbled or blotted out. Wherever possible use a word processor to complete documents. These are neater than handwriting but mistakes can still occur. Always double check the information you provide on every document you complete.

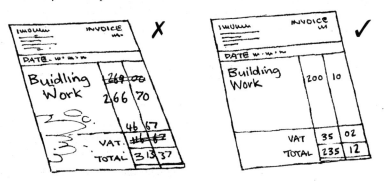

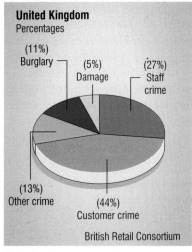

▼ Figure 9.18: Retail crime costs, 1996-97

United Kingdom
Percentages

(11%) Burglary

(5%) Damage

(27%) Staff crime

(13%) Other crime

(44%) Customer crime

British Retail Consortium

Social Trends 1999

Why is security important?

Each year UK business organizations lose billions of pounds due to theft, fraud, and criminal damage. These losses reduce company profits. Maintaining security is, therefore, extremely important in business.

Business organizations can insure themselves against theft and criminal damage. However, insurance premiums can be expensive and will tend to rise as crime increases and insurance companies are forced to pay out more in compensation.

A business may also attempt to protect itself from theft and damage by installing security equipment. However, this too can be expensive and will eat into profits.

In the UK the estimated cost of crime and in shops and other retail outlets alone was £1.4 billion in 1996–97 (see Figure 9.16). External crime (comprising customer theft, burglary, and other crimes such as arson and robbery) accounted for just over half the total cost, with just over a quarter due to staff crime.

Couple's £250,000 BA fraud

A BRITISH Airways computer expert stole £250,000 to finance his champagne lifestyle which included regular first-class trips abroad with a rival airline, a court heard.

Nicholas Mann, 27, masterminded a sophisticated computer fraud enabling him to download payments made to the airline into bank and credit card accounts set up by himself and his wife Andrea, 32.

The couple, of Burpham, Surrey, lived the high life for three years, enjoying expensive meals out, flashy cars and visits to relatives in America – first class on the rival Quantas airline. A routine inquiry last year uncovered the scam, details of which were not released to the court.

Metro 23.11.1999

Fraud

Fraud is the term used to describe deliberate attempts to deceive people and organizations for financial gain. This will often take the form of recording false transactions or altering the accounts so that a firm is unaware that payments have been made. It can often take months to discover that an organization has been defrauded. The use of stolen or counterfeit cheques, credit and debit cards to make payment is also a form of fraud.

How to prevent fraud

To reduce the risk of fraud, most firms carefully record all their financial transactions and check their records thoroughly and regularly. Equipment is also available which can detect stolen plastic payment cards.

Measures used by business organizations to reduce and detect fraud include:

● **Keeping detailed and up-to-date records of all financial transactions.** If an organization keeps no records of goods and services received and money paid out, how will it ever be able to know and check if anything is missing?

- **Checking that all orders are authorized.** Orders for goods and services should be authorized by a member of staff whose job is to check that they are required by the business. Without proper safeguards some employees may be tempted to order items for their personal use or to sell them to other people.

  In a large organization all orders may be made by a central purchasing department after written and authorized requests have been made. Usually, different people within an organization will authorize orders for different items. The more money is involved, the more senior the person must be to authorize the order. For example, an office manager may be able to authorize an order for stationary, but an order for an entirely new computer network costing many thousands of pounds would probably have to be authorized by the board of directors.

- **Checking invoices against purchase orders and goods received notes.** You will remember from Section 9.2 that a purchase order gives details of goods required by a customer. When they are delivered an employee in the customer organization will normally complete a goods received note (GRN) which provides a record of the incoming goods.

  An invoice is sent by the supplier to the customer requesting payment for delivered items. However, the customer should not pay the invoice until the goods ordered have been received and checked to be satisfactory. This means that items charged for on the invoice must match the items ordered and received as recorded on the GRN, and at the prices agreed. Only then should the invoice be authorized and payment made.

  There are a number of reasons why invoices may differ from orders and GRNs. The most common ones are:

  - the invoice contains a mistake
  - the wrong goods were delivered and had to be returned
  - some goods were damaged and returned to the supplier
  - the customer is still awaiting delivery

  Regular customers will normally receive a statement of account listing all their purchases rather than individual invoices (see 9.2). Individual entries in the account must be checked against orders and GRNs before the account total can be accepted and payment authorized.

- **Making sure only authorized personnel approve payments.** Once an invoice or account statement has been authorized, the firm's accounts department will pay the supplier. Whatever the method of payment used (see 9.1), it is usual for a senior member of staff to provide authorization. If any employee was allowed to make payment, some might be tempted to make bogus payments into their own bank accounts or to fictitious companies.

  In some cases, particularly where large amounts of money are involved, two or more members of the same organization may be required to authorize payments and sign cheques. These are known as **company signatories**. The bank that holds the account of the organization will keep sample copies of their signatures so that it can check them against the signatures on cheques and orders to transfer funds out of the company account. Each signatory provides a check on the others and also protects individual signatories against allegations of fraud.

- **Internal audit.** This involves company accountants and independent auditors checking through financial documents and accounts to see that they are in order. If there are errors, omissions, or inconsistencies, these can be checked and the staff interviewed if fraud is suspected.

- **Checking bank notes and payment cards for counterfeits.** This is often done simply by holding notes up to the light, or under ultraviolet lights, to check for watermarks. However, counterfeit notes and plastic cards have become so sophisticated they can be very hard to detect.

Portfolio Activity 9.11

Look at the order, goods received note, and invoice below.

Would you authorize the invoice for payment? If not, suggest why, and what further action you could take to clear up any errors or inconsistencies.

 ISTECH LTD

Unit 4 Silvermead
Industrial Estate
Silvermead SM4 7JW
Tel: 015623-840704
Fax: 015623-840705
VAT Reg No. 5676 0234 60

Purchase Order No. 12345

To: Computer Warehouse

Unit 12 Hampwick Estate

Long Hampwick HP3 9KL

DESCRIPTION	QTY	REF. No	PRICE	TOTAL
Box of 10 3.5" CD recordable computer disks	4	248/c	£10	£40
Cable trap anti-theft security devices	3	936/d	£20	£60

Authorized by: *R. U. Sure*
for VISTECH LTD

COMPUTER WAREHOUSE

INVOICE

Unit 12 Hampwick Estate
Long Hampwick HP3 9KL
Tel: 01312–777666
Fax: 01312–77766
VAT Reg No. 809 3333 12

To: Vistech Ltd.

Unit 4 Silvermead Industrial Estate

Silvermead SM4 7JW

Date	Order No.	Account No.	Invoice No.
4.3.0X	12345	100700	10001

QTY	Description	Cat No.	Unit Price	Total
4	CD-R disks	248/c	£11	£44
3	Cable-traps	936/d	£20	£60
1	Delivery		£30	£30
			Sub-total	£134
			Cash discount	–
			Total (ex. VAT)	£134
			VAT @ 17.5%	£23.45
			Total due	£157.45

Terms:
Cash discount of 5% only applies
to orders over £200 if payment
received within 10 working days

E & OE

GOODS RECEIVED NOTE

VISTECH LTD

Supplier:

Computer Warehouse

Unit 12 Hampwick Estate

Long Hampwick HP3 9KL

GRN NO: 2121

Date: 3.3.0X

Re; Delivery Note:
05/09876

ORDER NO.	QTY	DESCRIPTION	REF NO:
12345	3 boxes 2 boxes	10 x CD-R disks Cable trap anti-theft device kits	248/c 936/d

Received by: *R. U. Sure*

for VISTECH LTD

Section **9.4** **Using computers for financial calculations**

Paper vs computer-based systems

All businesses make financial plans and keep records of their incomes and spending in order to monitor how well or how badly they are doing over time. This is called **financial accounting**.

The methods used to record and store financial information in a business is known as the **accounting system**. An accounting system can be paper-based, computer-based or combine both paper and computer systems. One can act as a back up to the other in case records go missing or are destroyed by accident.

A **paper-based accounting system** involves the recording and storing of financial information on paper documents by hand. However, filling out documents by hand can be very time consuming and errors are easily made. Therefore, to save time and improve accuracy most modern business organizations use computers to help them record financial information, complete documents, and produce accounts.

A **computer-based accounting system** will record and store financial information on computers in computerized images of paper documents, spreadsheets and databases. Information will be typed into computer documents and spreadsheets from the computer keyboard. Computer records may then be printed on to paper to keep in a paper-based accounting and filing system. Computer records must be stored securely on computer disks. Back-up files should be kept in case the original files go missing or are wiped or destroyed accidentally.

▼ *Paper-based accounting*   ▼ *Computer-based accounting*

A good accounting system will make sure financial information:

- can be recorded easily and quickly
- can be understood by users
- is up to date and accurate
- is secure so that records cannot be stolen or tampered with
- is stored easily and safely
- can be retrieved easily

A good accounting system must also:

- be easy to set up and run
- not cost very much to set up and run
- be easy to understand so that staff using the system do not require a lot of expensive training
- use up-to-date methods and practices

▼ *Computer files can be stored on floppy disks*

▼ *and CD–ROMs*

▼ *Computer files can be stored on a hard disk inside a computer*

Computers provide a fast and easy way of storing alot of information. Documents produced using a spreadsheet, word processor or desk top publishing program can be saved as separate files. In most programs the user will be able to type in the file name they want to use.

Records can also be stored on a computer database. For example, a database might be used to store market research survey data, or names, addresses and telephone numbers of business clients and customers. The computer can be used to sort the data into alphabetical order, and/or under different headings. For example, people's names and addresses could be sorted by postcode into different areas. A computer search function can be used to find individual entries in a database.

The advantages and disadvantages of storing information on computer

The great advantages of storing files on computers are:

● there is less risk of making mistakes because a computer will be able to check calculations and will advise the user when information needed to complete a document is missing or wrong

● a firm can save a great deal of floorspace and rent by doing away with filing cabinets and storing business information and documents on computer disks instead.

● information can be retrieved and restored to the computer screen in a matter of seconds. There is no need to go to filing cabinets and spend time looking through lots of papers to find the information you want.

● different people can access and use the same information at the same time if computers are networked or file copies are available on floppy disks. If there is only one paper file, photocopies will have to be made of documents if more than one person wants to use them.

However, relying on computer files to store information can also has disadvantages. These are:

● computer hard disks can be corrupted by viruses or inexperienced users

● computer hackers using computers outside an organization may 'break into' confidential information files stored on computers linked to phone lines

● computers can breakdown and stored information may be lost

● computers cannot be used during power failures

● staff may need to be trained to use computer software

● buying computer hardware and software can be expensive

Computer security

Computer files need to be protected for a number of reasons:

● they can be accidentally overwritten

● they can be accessed by unauthorised users

● computer hardware and disks can be stolen

● they can be destroyed by fire or damaged by water

▼ *Fitting security chains to computer equipment and installing virus guards are sensible precautions to protect computer files.*

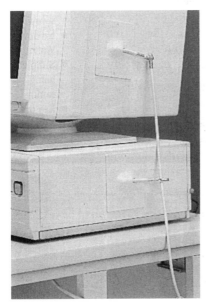

- they can be corrupted by viruses. These are unwanted programs that can wipe out files if copied on to hard disks by mistake from an 'infected' disk or e-mail file

Many of computer security threats can be overcome by taking simple precautions:

- disks can be 'write-protected'. This stops any more files being added to the disk and, therefore, prevents anyone else from accidentally overwriting stored information or deleting it.

- access to computer files can be restricted by using a user identification (user ID) and password system. Authorized users can be given user ID's which the computer is able to recognize. They must also know the correct password which enables the computer to double check that the person logging on is authorized to do so.

- important information in files can be saved on hard disks, floppy disks, zip disks, tapes, and/or CD-Rs, and even in paper based formats. This means you have **back-up files** in case anything goes wrong with one disk or if your computer or disks are stolen.

- security chains or anchoring devices can be fitted to computer equipment to prevent it from being moved easily. Also use electronic security tags or ultra-violet marker pens to mark equipment so that it can be identified easily if it turns up again.

- floppy disks and CDs containing important information can be stored securely at different locations in fire proof boxes or safes.

- a virus guard program can be installed. This detects any unwanted programs and destroys them

Computer software for business finance

Computer software refers to predesigned packages or programs which give instructions to a computer to process text and numbers. Today, a vast array of software is available to businesses to help them record and monitor financial information.

Two of the most useful types of computer program a business can use for financial accounting are:

- **Accounting software**

- **Spreadsheets**

Most programs are 'user-friendly,' meaning that it is relatively easy for a person to learn how to use them in a few days. However, the old saying 'garbage in, garbage out' will always apply to the use of computers. Computers will only use information and follow instructions given to them. If you type in the wrong figures or wrong instructions to a computer, you will get a wrong answer. The computer is useful only because it can perform often complex calculations in a fraction of the time it takes to use a calculator, or to do so by hand. It is therefore important that a person using a spreadsheet or accounting software knows about financial transactions and how to record them accurately.

Accounting software

What can accounting software do? There are many different programs available to businesses to help them record financial transactions and produce their accounts. For example, the advertisement opposite shows an accounting program called 'SAGE Instant Accounting 2000'.

Accounting software for computers is often designed with the small business in mind, because these organizations are unlikely to be able to afford to employ accountants on a full-time basis to produce their accounts.

Good accounting software will enable the user to:

- Record all cash sales and sales on credit
- Set up a database of customer names, addresses, telephone, fax and e-mail numbers, and details of how much discount each one is allowed
- Record how much is owed by different customers and when payment is due
- Produce invoices, remittance advice notes, credit notes, and statements of account to send to customers
- Record all purchases from cash and on credit
- Set up a database of suppliers' names, addresses, telephone numbers, etc.
- Record how much is owed to different suppliers and when payment is due
- Enter details of cash inflows and outflows (see chapter 8)
- Record deposits to, and withdrawals and payments from, a bank account
- Calculate total sales and purchases per period of time
- Prepare an audit showing every transaction made
- Produce ledger accounts (for materials, sales, purchases, VAT, cash, capital, assets, overheads, etc.) and a general ledger
- Produce income and expenditure accounts
- Produce VAT returns showing VAT received on sales and paid out on purchases
- Produce balance sheets
- Produce profit and loss statements (see chapter 8)
- Combine the accounting software with payroll software to calculate wages and print pay slips automatically

● Keep records of incoming and outgoing stocks. Some programs can also link to stock control software to recognize when stocks are running low and automatically complete purchase orders to send via EDI (see 9.1)

● Export accounts to word processors and desktop publishing packages to produce published annual reports and accounts

At the end of each month the software will tell the user to run a function to generate the end-of-month accounts. This will automatically print out a copy of the accounts for the last month, and carry forward the balances on each account (sales, purchases, VAT, overheads, capital, assets, cash, etc.) into the next month.

Spreadsheets

A spreadsheet is a powerful program that can perform complex calculations and present data on a variety of graphs. A spreadsheet is, therefore, a very useful tool for recording, storing, and monitoring financial information.

On the computer screen a spreadsheet looks rather like a large sheet of paper ruled off into rows and columns. Columns are identified by letters: A, B, C..., Y, Z, AA, AB, etc. Rows are identified by numbers: 1, 2, 3, etc. Each box formed by the intersection of rows and columns is called a **cell**. Cells are identified by a column letter and a row number, e.g. A1, D57, X230, etc. Text, numbers, or mathematical formulae can be typed, or entered, into any cell.

Figure 9.19 below shows how a spreadsheet looks on screen. The columns B to F have been given headings in row 1 for each month in a

▼ *Figure 9.19: An example of a spreadsheet in use*

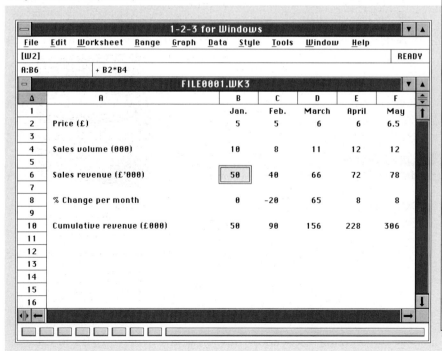

Common spreadsheet functions

A good spreadsheet will allow the user to:

● Insert and delete rows and columns
● Protect specific cells and formulae from erasure
● Expand column widths
● Store and search for data in a database
● Choose the number of decimal places
● Import data from other programs and files
● Copy cells
● Export data to other programs
● Move cells
● Produce and display graphs
● Perform statistical analysis
● Print out specified cell ranges and graphs
● Perform financial analysis
● Perform 'what if' analysis
● Perform mathematical calculations

and much, much more…

sales budget. Row headings for product price, sales volume, and revenues have been typed in cells in column A, which has been expanded in width to accommodate them. Cells in row 6 contain mathematical formulae to calculate sales revenues from figures entered into cells for product price and sales volumes. These cells will show the results of the calculations but will not show the formulae. However, by placing the cursor on one of these cells the formulae will be usually displayed at the top of the screen off the main spreadsheet.

Portfolio Activity 9.12

New accounting software and spreadsheet programs are becoming available all the time. Every new product tries to outperform rival software in terms of number of functions, speed, accuracy, presentation, price, and a host of other factors.

1. Below is a list of some well-known business software that were on sale in 1999. For each program try to find out:

● If it is still available

● If it has been updated

● Whether it is spreadsheet or accounting software

● What it can do

● How much it costs

● Who supplies it

2. From your research try to add at least five programs to the list.

3. Write up your findings in a short report.

4. Find out as much information as you can about one spreadsheet program of your choice. Use the information to create an appealing and informative advert for the product.

Useful sources of information to help you complete all the tasks in this activity will include:

● Computer magazines, such as *Personal Computer World* and *PC Plus*

● Office staff who use computers in business organizations

● Computer shops

● Software suppliers and manufacturers

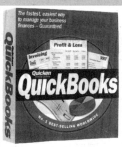

For example, cell B6 contains the formulae B2*B4. This tells the spreadsheet to multiply the figure entered into cell B2 for price by the figure in cell B4 for sales. Similarly formulae entered into cells in row 8 tell the computer to calculate the percentage change in revenue each month and those in row 10 to keep a running total of sales revenues from month 1. The spreadsheet will recalculate these cells automatically every time a new figure is entered into other cells.

'What if' analysis

Spreadsheets are particularly useful for preparing financial plans or budgets (see chapter 1) and testing the impact of possible changes that may occur in the future. This is called **'what if' analysis**. For example, you may want to test the impact of an increase in wages or raw material prices on break-even level of output – or the impact of increasing spending on advertising or lowering product prices on costs, sales revenues, and profits. A spreadsheet can perform these calculations in a matter of seconds. It can also display the results on a variety of different graphs, such as barcharts, pie charts, and line graphs.

Key words

In your own words, write down explanations and definitions for the following key words and terms in this chapter:

Financial transaction	Direct debit	Debit note	Company signatories
Inward transaction	Standing order	Statement of account	Computerized accounting system
Outward transaction	BACS	Remittance advice note	
Industrial markets	EDI	Receipt	Accounting software
Cash sales	Credit card	Cheque	Spreadsheet
Credit	Purchase order	Cheque guarantee card	Back-up files
Hire purchase	Goods received note	Paying-in slip	
Debtors	Invoice	Bank statement	
Creditors	Delivery note	Bank reconciliation	
EFTPOS	Credit note	Fraud	

Test your knowledge

1 What is the main purpose of keeping records of financial transactions for business owners and managers?

  A to provide information for lenders – for example, a bank

  B to provide information for the Government

  C to provide information which will assist in monitoring and controlling the business

  D to provide information to the Registrar of Companies

2 The person who signs a cheque to make payment is:

  A the person who is paying the money

  B the branch bank manager

  C the person to whom the cheque is paid

  D the person who pays the cheque in to the bank account

Questions 3-5 share the following answer options:

  A checking invoices against goods received notes

  B checking invoices against purchase orders

  C requiring authorized personnel to sign orders

  D installing surveillance cameras

Which of the above security measures could reduce the risk of the following situations occurring:

3 The theft of goods from delivery bays

4 Authorizing payment for goods not delivered

5 Employees making fraudulent payments to their own bank account

6 Which of the following would a firm send to a supplier requesting delivery of goods?

  A statement of account

  B purchase order

  C goods received note

  D invoice

Questions 7-9 share the following answer options:

  A a sales invoice

  B a delivery note

  C a statement of account

  D a sales receipt

Which of the above documents would be used to:

7 Provide proof that a purchase has been made?

8 Inform a customer of the value of goods supplied and terms of payment?

9 Request payment for goods delivered?

10 Which of the following is the more usual sequence in which firms will receive and send out documents for transactions?

  A order, invoice, payment, delivery note

  B order, delivery note, invoice, payment

  C order, payment, invoice, delivery note

  D order, payment, delivery note, invoice

11 a. What is a financial transaction?

  b Explain two reasons why businesses need to keep records of all their financial transactions.

  c What is the difference between an inward transaction and an outward transaction? Give two examples of each type of transaction.

12 a. Sports Fashions Ltd has just placed an order for trainers with a major sports shoe manufacturer. Suggest three ways Sports Fashions could pay for their order.

  b What is an invoice and what details should an invoice contain?

  c What is the difference between a delivery note and a goods received note?

  d Explain why it is important for Sports Fashions Ltd to check details on the invoice for their order with their goods received note.

Blank financial documents

The following documents can be photocopied for use in chapter 9:

Purchase order

Computech Ltd

Unit 19 – 22, Moleville Industrial Estate
Stoneshire ST17 5MW
Tel: 01237-4095, Fax: 01237-4096
VAT Reg No. 707 3434 11

To: _____

_____

_____

Purchase Order No.

Date: _____

DESCRIPTION	QTY	Cat No.	PRICE	TOTAL

Authorised by: _____

For Computech Ltd

Sales invoice

Computech Ltd

Unit 19 – 22, Moleville Industrial Estate
Stoneshire ST17 5MW
Tel: 01237-4095, Fax: 01237-4096
VAT Reg No. 707 3434 11

To: _____

_____

INVOICE

Your Order No.	Invoice No.	Date

QTY	Description	Cat No.	Unit Price	Total

Sub-total	
Discount ____ %	
Total (ex. VAT)	
VAT @ 17.5%	
Total due	

Terms:

_____

_____

_____

E & OE

Goods received note

Computech Ltd
GOODS RECEIVED NOTE

Supplier: `'`
_____

GRN No: _____

Date: _____
_____
_____ `·`
_____

Re; Delivery Note:
_____

Order No.	QTY	DESCRIPTION	TOTAL

Received by: _____

For Computech Ltd

Credit note

Computech Ltd
Unit 19 – 22, Moleville Industrial Estate
Stoneshire ST17 5MW
Tel: 01237-4095, Fax: 01237-4096
VAT Reg No. 707 3434 11

To: _____   **CREDIT NOTE NO.**
_____
_____

Your Order No.	Invoice No.	Date

QTY	Description	Cat No.	Unit Price	Total
			Sub-total	
			Discount ____%	
Reason for credit:			Total (ex. VAT)	
_____			VAT	
_____			**Total credit**	
_____				

Statement of account

STATEMENT OF ACCOUNT

Computech Ltd

Unit 19 – 22, Moleville Industrial Estate
Stoneshire ST17 5MW
Tel: 01237-4095, Fax: 01237-4096
VAT Reg No. 707 3434 11

Account No:
Customer name:
Customer address:

Statement Date:

Date	Details	Debit	Credit	Balance
			Balance now due	

Terms: Payment by _____ required

Delivery note

DELIVERY NOTE NO: _____

Computech Ltd

Unit 19 – 22, Moleville Industrial Estate
Stoneshire ST17 5MW
Tel: 01237-4095, Fax: 01237-4096
VAT Reg No. 707 3434 11

Delivery address:

For delivery on:

Your Order No.	Invoice No.	Date

QTY	Catalogue No.	Description

Delivery by: _____
No. of items: _____
Goods received by: _____ (signature)
_____ (please PRINT name)

Issued by: _____
Sales Dept. Computech Ltd

Please retain this copy as proof of receipt

Index

Where more than one page reference is shown for a particular subject, pages containing main text and definitions are in bold if appropriate.

A

Accounting software 400–402
Accounting systems **398–400**
 –computer-based 398–400
 –paper-based 398
 –security 399–400
Administration department 84–85
Advertising 40, 74–75, 112, 140, 166, **177–189**, 215, 238, 313
 –informative 177, 182
 –job 112, 140
 –persuasive 177–179, 181
 –target audience **178**, 189
Advertising media 183–188
 –cinema 185, 186
 –Internet 186
 –newspapers and magazines 184, 186
 –posters 185, 186
 –radio 185, 186
 –TV 185, 186
Advisory, Conciliation and Arbitration Services (ACAS) 143, 144, **148**, 151
Aerospace 250–251
After-sales service 80, 238
Agriculture **227**, 227–229
Ancilliary firms **322**
Annual General Meeting (AGM) 92, **271**, 272
Annualized hours systems 130
Anti-discrimination laws **141**
Apprenticeships 138
Assisted areas **323**

B

Balance sheet 370, 401
Bank loans 334
Bank overdrafts 334
Bank statements **390–392**
Banking Automated Clearing Services (BACS) **362**
Bar charts 7–8
Brand image 181–182, 183
Brand names **179**, 180
Break-even analysis **347–350**
 –margin of safety 350
Break-even charts 348–349
Break-even output **347**
British Standard Industrial Classification (SIC) **217**

Budget **280**
Budgetary control **54**
Budgeting **52**, 52–55
Budgets **52**
Business **18**
Business accounts 369, 370, 402
 –external 370
 –internal 369
Business activities **202–258**
Business aims **28–36**
 –non-profit 34–35
 –profit 28–30
Business communications **158–199**
 –types 160
Business integration **256–257**
 –horizontal 256
 –lateral 257
 –vertical 257
Business location 26, **318–325**
Business meetings 162–164
 –agenda 163
 –cascading 164
 –minutes 163
Business objectives **36–49**
Business operations **25–27**
Business performance **49–55**, 368–369
Business products **20**
Business rates 279

C

Capital **263**, 266, 269, 33, 401
 –fixed 263
 –working 263
Capital gains 336
Capital goods **230**
Career progression 90, 136–137, 301
Cash deficit 338, 340, 401
Cash sales 358
Cash surplus 338, 340, 401
Cash-flow forecasting **337–341**
 –closing balance 339
 –net cash-flow 339, 341, 369
 –opening balance 339
Cash-flow problems 342–343
Cash-flow smoothing **338**
Central government 86, **279**, 279–282, 293, 294, 300–301
Charities 28, 34
Cheque guarantee card 388
Cheques 360, **386–388**
Chief Executive 88
Civil legal action 143, 144, **149**
Collective Bargaining 144
Commercial services 20, **218**
Companies House 270
Company signatories 395
Competition 24, 31, 203, 236, 242, 245, 251, 290, 301, 313, 316, 322
 –non-price **292**
 –price **292**

Competition policy **316**
Competitive environment 291–292
Competitiveness 314
Confederation of British Industry (CBI) 146
Conglomerate **257**
Consumer demand 23, 31, 204–206, 211–215, 245, 296–297
 –causes of change 211–216, 229, 297
 –price factors 211
 –non-price factors 211–216
 –fall 211, 297
 –increase 211, 297
Consumer goods **230**
Consumer goods **20**
 –durables 20
 –non-durables 20
Consumer markets 358
Consumer panels 76
Consumer protection **300–301**, 346
Consumer services 20
Consumer spending 204, 254
Consumer trends **203–216**
Consumers **23**, 293, 294, 295–297, 313, 320–321
 –needs and wants 23
Contract of employment 122–124, 304
 –terms and conditions 124, 153, 305
Co-operative Development Agency (CDA) 275
Co-operative societies 238, 262, **275–276**
 –retail 238, 275
 –worker 238, 275
Cost accountants 83
Cost of sales **351**, 369
Costs 301, **331–332**, 339, 342, 344–347, 352
 –fixed 331–332, 345
 –variable **332**, 345
 –average **346**
 –overhead **332**
 –start-up **331**
 –total 332, 344–348
Council tax 279
Credit cards 238, 242, 245, 335
Credit control 342
Credit note 379, **381–382**
Credit sales 358
Creditors **359**
Customer accounts 368, 376, **382–383**
Customer complaints 238
Customer safety 47
Customer services **41**, 41–47, 79–82, 114, 153
Customer services department 79–82
Customers **23**, 41–47, 50, 81–82, 181, 298–295, 359

D

Data 4
  –analysis 11–13
  –arithmetic mean 11
  –median 12
  –methods of presentation 4–10
  –modal value 12
  –qualitative 4–11
  –quantitative 4
  –range 12
Debit cards 238
Debit note 379, **381–382**
Debtors **359**
Deed of partnership **265**
Delegation 60
Deliveries 45, 78
Delivery note **379–380**
Department stores 238
Departments 60, **67–86**, 90
  –functional interdependence 67
Depreciation **332**
Deregulation 316
Deregulation and Contracting Out Act
  1994 316
Desktop publishing 194
Direct mail **188–189**
Directors 91–92
  –Board of 91
  –executive 91
  –non-executive 92
Disability Discrimination Act 1995 141
Disciplinary procedure 125–126, 151
Discrimination 140
Disposable income 212
Distribution department 78–79
Diversification **255**, 255–257
Divorce of company ownership from
  control **274**, 307

E

E-commerce 186, 216, **243–245**
Economic, regulatory and legal environ-
  ment 291
Economies of scale 256
Electronic communications 175–177
  –e-mail 175–176, 251–252, 304
  –fax 176–177
Electronic Data Interchange (EDI)
  362–363
Electronic Funds Transfer at Point of
  Sale (EFTPOS) 361
E-mail 251–252, 304
Employee grievances 142–143
Employee rights 84, 142, 146,
  151–152, 305–306, 313
Employees 294, 301
Employer Associations 146
Employment 221–222, 226, 306
Employment laws 130, 132, 141, 149,
  305

Employment Rights Act 1996 **149**
Employment tribunal 143, 144, **148**,
  151
Employment Zones 323
Empowerment **303**
Engineering design **69**
Enterprise Grant Areas **323**
Environment 32–33, 291, 313, 317
Environmental protection 317
Equal opportunities at work 140–141
Equal Pay Acts 1970, 1983 132, 141
European Court of Justice 143, 144,
  149, 151
European Structural Fund Areas **323**
European Union (EU) 313, 323, 324
European Union Directives 146
European Working Time Directive **130**
Exchange rates 315
Exchanges and refunds 46
Executive Agency 281
Exports 315
External growth **256**
Extractive industries **218**

F

Finance **334–336**, 371
  –external 334–336
  –long-term 335–336
  –internal 334
  –short-term 334–335
Finance and accounts department 83
Financial accountants 83
Financial analysis 402–404
Financial documents **372–392**
  –purchase 373–378
  –receipts 385–392
  –sales 379–385
Financial organizations 334–336
Financial transactions **357–358**,
  366–371
  –inward 357–366
  –outward 357, 366
Finished manufactured goods **230**
Fiscal policy **314**
Fishing 230
Fixed assets 342
Flexitime 130, 304
Footloose industries **321**
Franchises **276**
Fraud 370, **394**

G

Goods Received Note (GRN) 374,
  375, 395
Government economic policy 293,
  313–318, 323
  –macro **313–314**
  –micro **315–316**
Government training schemes 112
Grievance procedure **142**
Gross profit 351

H

Headhunting 112
Health and safety 84, 134–136, 305
Health and Safety Executive (HSE)
  135, **136**
Health and Safety Laws 136, 151
Hire purchase (HP) 238, 335, **359**
Holding company **256**
Holiday entitlement 129
Hours of work 129–130
Human resource management
  106–154
Human Resources Department 84, 106

I

Imports 315
Income tax 132
Induction training 136
Industrial action 144–145
  –overtime ban 144
  –strikes 145, 305
Industrial design **69**
Industrial goods **20**
Industrial markets **358**
Industrial sectors **216**, 216–224
Inferior goods **213**
Inflation **212**, 293, 314, 315, 342
Information Communications
  Technology (ICT) **175**, 186, 251
Insolvency **338**
Insurance companies 336
Interest rates 213, 313–315, 338
Internal audit **396**
Internal business environment 291,
  293
Internal growth **255**
Internet 176, **186**, 235, 238
Investment capital **333**
Investment trusts 336
Investors in People (IiP) **139**
Invoices 358, 374, **376–377**, 379,
  380–381, 395, 401
Inward investment **325**

J

Job analysis **106**
Job description **108**, 109
Job roles **87–101**
Job rotation 136
Jobseeker's Allowance (JSA) 132
Joint stock companies 262, **269**
Joint stock companies – articles of asso-
  ciation 269
Joint stock companies – memorandum
  of association 269
Joint venture **256**

L

Labour specialization 60
Labour supply 322
Lead times 45

Leasing **335**
Limited liability **264**, 271
Line graphs 9
Line managers 60
Liquidation **338**
Lobby groups **310**
Local government 86, **278**
Logistics **78**

M

Mail order companies **238**
Management 60–63, 293
Management – chain of command 62
Management – span of control 63
Management accountants 83
Managers 92–93
Managing director 88, **92**
Manual labour 114
Manufacturing 114, 218, 221, 223,
224, **230–237**
Market research 74, **76–77**, 299, 331
Market share **24**, 30–31
Marketing department 74–75
Markets **22–23**, 24–25, 30, 38–39
–domestic 23
–international 23
–types 23, 358
Merger **256**
Methods of payment **359–365**
–BACS 362
–cash 359
–cheques 360
–credit cards 363–365
–debit cards 361
–direct debit 361
–electronic data interchange 362–363
–standing order 361–362
Mining 221, **226**
Mixed economy **26**
Monetary policy **314**
Monopoly **38**
Mortgages **335**
Multinationals **27**, **324**

N

National Insurance Contributions
(NICs) **132**
National minimum wage 305
Nationalization **283**
Nationalized industries **283**
Natural environment 291
Natural monopoly 283
Natural resources 217, 225–230, 320
Net cash-flow **339**
Net earnings **131**
Non-manual labour 114

O

Office of Fair Trading (OFT) 300
Oil and gas 221, 226

Operating profit 351
Oral communications 160–163
Organic farming 229
Organization charts **60**
Organizational structure **59–68**
–flat 62–64
–hierarchical 61–62
–matrix **66**
–tall 62–63
Overheads **332**, 352

P

Partnership 27, 262, 263, **266–268**
Pay-As-You-Earn (PAYE) 132
Paying-in slips **389–390**
Pension funds 336
Performance related pay 302
Person specification **110**
Personal services **218**
Pie-charts 5–7
Point of sale promotions 187
Primary sector 26, **217–218**, 220–221,
225–230, 235
Private limited company 27, 262, 269,
270–272
Private sector 262, **264–277**, 297
Privatization 249, **283**
Producers **17**
Product developments 38–40
Production **17**, 17–20
–batch 73
–chain of activity 18–20
–control 73
–costs 298, 345–350
–flow 73
–inputs and outputs 17
–job 73
–just-in-time (JIT) **71**
–monitoring 73
–quality control 74
Production Department 71–74
Production operatives 96–97
Productivity **72**, 302–303
Profit **28**, 28–30, 299, 301, 317, **311**,
342, 368
–after-tax 352
–before-tax 352
–gross 351
–net 351
Profit and loss statement **351–352**,
370, 401
Promotions 75
Public Corporation 281–282
Public limited company 27, 262, 269,
272–275
Public relations 75, 82, 311
Public sector 26, 85–86, **278–283**
Public services **28**, 35
Purchase order **374–375**, 395, 401
Purchasing department 70–71

Q

Quality circles **303**
QUANGO 281

R

Race Relations Act 1976 141
Recruitment agencies 112
Redundancy **126**, 143, 305
Regional Development Agencies (RDAs)
323
Regional policy **323**, 336
Regional Selective Assistance (RSA)
323
Remittance Advice Note 379,
384–385
Research and development (R&D)
69–70, 317
Retail Prices Index (RPI) **212**
Retail surveillance 50
Retailing **237**, 237–245
Retailing trends 240–243
Retained profits 263
Revenue 29, 298, 331, **347–350**, 351

S

Safety committees 135
Safety Signs Regulations 1980 191
Salary **130**
Sales 51, 78, 181, 366, 401, 402
Sales department 78
Sampling 77
Scatter plots 9
Secondary sector **218**, 235
Semi-finished manufactured goods **230**
Sex Discrimination Acts 1975, 1986 141
Shadowing 136
Shareholders 271, 294, 336
Shares **271**, 272, 274, 302, 307, 336
–dividends 271, 336
–face value 271
Shiftwork 130, 304
Single Regeneration Budget (SRB) **323**
Single union agreement 146
Skilled labour 114
Social environment 291, 292–293
Sole trader 27, 262, **264–266**
Spreadsheets 400, 402–404
Staff appointment 123
Staff appraisal 93
Staff appraisal procedures 84
Staff associations 143
Staff motivation 93
Staff recruitment and selection
106–121
–application forms 115–117
–curriculum vitae 117–118
–external recruitment 111–113
–internal recruitment 111
–job interviews 120–121
–letter of application 118–119
–shortlisting 120

Stakeholders **294**
Statement of account 379, **382–383**
Statutory Sick Pay 132
Stock control 73, 78
Stock Exchange 274
Supervisors 94
Suppliers **17**, 368
Support services 67
Support staff 97

T
Tables 5
Take-over **256**
Tariffs **324**
Tax burden 317
Taxation 245, 293, 313–314, 369
Taxation – direct **279**
Taxation – indirect **279**
Teamworking **303**, 304
Technological advance 114, 203, 206,
    209, 223, 236, 245, 251
Telephone communications 164–165
    –mobile 165
    –voice messaging 165
Teleworking **304**
Tertiary sector **218–219**, 222, 235

Test marketing 76
Total Quality Management (TQM) 74,
    303
Trade credit 335
Trade journals 184
Trade Union Congress (TUC) 146
Trade unions **143**, 145–146, 305
    –aims 145
    –types of 146
Trading Standards Offices 300
Training 84, 93, 137–139, 198, 316
    –off-the-job 138
    –on-the-job 138
Transport 245–251
Trends **203**, 204–206, 240–243
Turnover **351**
Types of business organization
    261–286
    –private sector 262, **264–277**
    –public sector **278–283**

U
Unemployment 213, 223
Unit trusts 336
Unlimited liability **264**, 266, 268
Unskilled labour 114

V
Value Added Tax (VAT) 369, 377, 401,
    402
Venture capital 333, **335**
Video conferencing 164
Voluntary sector **34**
Voluntary service 28, 34

W
Wage rate **131**
Wages Act 1986 132
Wages and salaries 130–132, 301, 331,
    345, 369
Wholesaling **238**
Worker shareholders 307
Working arrangements 84, 304–305
Working capital **333**
Working conditions **128**, 127–141,
    302
Written communications 166–174,
    192–198
    –business letters 166–170
    –financial documents 174, 372–392
    –memos 170–171, 193
    –notices 172